The Astrological Judgement and Practice of Physick

Better books make better astrologers.
Here are some of our other titles:

Christian Astrology, books 1 & 2, *by William Lilly*
Christian Astrology, book 3, *by William Lilly*

Degrees of the Zodiac Symbolized, *a set by Charubel, another by Sepharial*

An Encyclopaedia of Psychological Astrology, *by C.E.O. Carter*

Encyclopaedia of Medical Astrology, *by H.L. Cornell, M.D.*

Astrological Judgement of Diseases from the Decumbiture of the Sick, *and,* **Urinalia**, *by Nicholas Culpeper*

Ancient Astrology Theory & Practice: **Matheseos Libri VIII**, *by Firmicus Maternus, translated by Jean Rhys Bram*

Tetrabiblos, *by Ptolemy, translated by J.M. Ashmand*

Electional Astrology, *by Vivian Robson*
Astrology and Sex, *by Vivian Robson*
Fixed Stars & Constellations in Astrology, *by Vivian Robson*

Encyclopedia of Astrology, *by Nicholas de Vore*

Mundane Astrology: The Astrology of Nations & States
   Books by H.S. Green, Raphael & C.E.O. Carter

If not available from your local bookseller, order directly from:

The Astrology Center of America
2124 Nicole Way
Abingdon, MD 21009

on the web at:
http://www.astroamerica.com

The Astrological Judgement and Practice of Physick

Deduced from the positions of the Heavens
at the decumbiture of the sick person

Being the XXX years practice and experience of
Richard Saunders
Student in Astrology and Physick

1677

Astrology Classics

First Published in 1677

On the cover:
Christ Among the Doctors
by Albrecht Dürer, 1506

ISBN: 1 933303 00 X

Published 2003 by:
Astrology Classics
The publication division of

The Astrology Center of America
2124 Nicole Way
Abingdon, MD 21009

on the web at
http://www.astroamerica.com

THE PREFACE

TO THE

READER.

s a Circle is of all other Figures in *Geometry* the most intirely compleat and perfect, because it is a Line equally drawn from the Centre; so likewise those Conclusions are undoubtedly most true, whose Beginnings are drawn from the Centre of Verity; and this is a Maxime, or Fundamental point in this Art, That our Saviour Jesus Christ is *Via, Vita & Veritas*; therefore he that entreth not by him goeth out of the way, he that hath not vegetation from him is dead, and he that swerveth from him, Erreth; in him,. as Holy Writ witnesseth, *In eo omnes Thesauri Sapientiæ & Scientiæ absconditi.* It is he that openeth and no man shutteth, and shutteth and no man openeth; he is the true Light that illuminateth every man that cometh into the world; for as the Sun ascending above the *Horizon* doth not onely penetrate into all places with his sole-heating Raies, but also illuminateth all things; and with his resplendent Beams of Light discovereth those things which before were obscured, and hid with the black Pall of Night's contracted Curtains; so likewise our blessed Saviout Jesus being the true Son of Justice, arising on the Horizon of our hearts, doth not only heat the same with the servency of his Love, but also illuminateth all our Senses, and with the splendour of his Divine light, maketh those things to be in manifesto which before were in occulto; Therefore with all Humility prostrating our selves at the foot of his infinite Mercy, we most earnestly beseech him, of his exceeding Clemency and Bounty, to illuminate the darkness of our Senses, obnubulated with the cloudy black Meteors of Sin and Iniquity, that being assisted by his Divine Aid, we may deliver to all Posterity such infallible grounds of this Art, that this my Book, which by his Direction, and in Honour of his Holy Name, I mean to publish, may worthily deserve the Title it bears; that the true understanding Reader may hereby be resolved of such things as he desireth, concerning the state of any Sick or Diseased Person, in as ample a manner as it shall please the Almighty to decipher unto us by the Theoreme of the Cœlestial Motions and Configurations of the Planets, to the Laud and Praise of his most Holy Name, which is Blessed for ever.

Amen.

Rich. Saunders.

TO THE READER

Upon my worthy Friend (and old Acquaintance)

Mr. RICHARD SAUNDERS

HIS

[Astrological Judgment and Practice of P H Y S I C K.]

Eing now (by the mercy of a most gracious God) arrived to my seventy sixth year current; and of late years having pass'd through much Sickness and affliction of Body (which has too much decayed my sight) it cannot be expected that I should oblige the World with any thing of this Subject, which once I had thought to have attempted, and not only enlarged the Judgments upon the Sixth House in my Introduction, (which as it is, is sufficient for the Instruction of any young Student) But also to have communicated to the grateful Sons of Art divers remarkable Experiments in the Astrological considerations of Diseases from the Decumbiture of the Sick touching Life and Death, &c. I hope therefore this most elaborate Work of my Old Friend, may instead thereof be accepted, in which I find he has (to his great commendation) taken much pains to good purpose, and in every Branch thereof is very copious, and no less perspicuous, both in the Theory and Practick part (which hitherto has been neglected by most Authors that have undertaken this Task

in the English *Tongue) so that I may, without the least partiality, affirm the* Work *to be the most compleat and perfect of any of the Subject I have hitherto seen or read; and do heartily rejoyce (though now in my declining years) to see so Learned a production proceed from an English Pen. In fine, the Work deserves Commendation; and I do really approve thereof, and recommend it to the serious study and perusal of all the Noble Students of this Kingdom, which now I live to see abounds with many hopeful and Ingenious persons that are not only Lovers of,, but Students in the Syderal Science, notwithstanding the Contempt and Opposition it has met withall from some busie Sciolists as Ignorant as Envious; Whence I conclude, this most useful and harmless Art may in few years arrive to great perfection, and consequently, daily meet with Eminent and Noble Favourites to protect it from Calumny and detraction; Though I dare not affirm (as that bold pretender lately did) That Ptolomy is now become as demonstrable (to the Senses) as Euclide. Much more might be said, but the Work speaks its own praise, and I do but hold a Candle to the Sun, I shall therefore conclude with that Old Proverb, Good Wine needs no Bush. Vale.*

From my House in Hersham *Your old Friend and*
  in the Parish of Walton
  upon Thames, 1677.   *faithful Propagator*

                             of Astrology,

                             William Lilly.

TO THE READERS,
Upon this Excellent Work of
ASTROLOGICAL PHYSICK
BY
Mr. *RICHARD SAUNDERS.*

Gentlemen,

aving, at the Booksellers requests, perused this Learned Treatise, and finding therein many excellent Secrets brought to Light; viz. The Natures, Signs, Causes, and Cures of all Diseases *incident to Mankind, as they depend upon the Positions and Aspects of the Planets and Stars; The Doctrine of the* Crisis *explained and applied; and divers experienced Rules and Aphorisms touching the Recovery or Miscarriage of the Patient from the Decumbiture; and a strengthning of the Nature, Signification, and Division of the Twelve Houses, by Physical and Philosophical Reasons, not hitherto performed by any other: together with sundry other matters of excellent Use to all Students in Art. — All which do eminently deserve Commendation; the Author thereof [although he have published many things very much to the advance of Science,] having in this very Work out - done them all: and, like Truth it self in the Miracle, resorted the Best of his Works to the Last. And, because his* **Person** *cannot, (that being* inter mortuos) *his surviving Memory must, receive the Honour due to the Merit of his Pen, for this Exquisite and Elaborate Performance. To which very end, I freely enter my* **Suffrage,** *as approving of it for a Learned, Useful, Plain, and Beneficial Work; and a Secure Guide to Health by the Stars: which whosoever makes use of, shall not need to doubt of Discovering the Disease afflicting, though never so occult and strange, or get of its termination, whether in Life or Death.*

John Gadbury
Student in Astrology and Physick.

Upon the Author, my Worthy Friend

Mr. RICHARD SAUNDERS,

and his Elaborate Work, Entitled,

Astrological Judgment and Practice of Physick.

Antiquity I honour, but I do declare (Chair;
Some things well done, besides from *Plato's*
Hippocrates and *Galen* in their time
Were men of *Fame*, persons of no Design,
And to this day are had in great Repute
Amongst the Learned, who can this refute?
These men well knew the *Stars* had Influence
Upon all Humane Bodies; Then from hence
Withdraw all *Carping Criticks*, that deny
The *Great Art* of *Sublime Astrology*,
Which unto such as have attain'd the *Key*,
Shews the true cause of a *Disease*, and may
Direct the *Doctor* expeditiously
The nearest Course to cure the Malady:
Come all men therefore, and resolve to follow
These *Dictates* of our *English Apollo*,
That for his Art and Ingenuity,
Deserves *Encomiums* Immortally.

HEN. COLEY,

Student in the Mathematicks.

In Approbation
OF THE
*Accurate Work, and deserved Praise
Of the Learned Author, my late
Worthy Friend*

Mr. RICHARD SAUNDERS.

Though I pretend not to *Predicte* Fires,
I'le boldly write what sacred *Truth* inspires,
The Dead are safe, and the *Impartial* Grave
Can tempt no *Flatterers*, what's Good and Brave
Commands Applause; and such this *Piece* I find,
The *Labour'd* Product of a *Learned* Mind;
Whose *Studious* Industry, and active Parts,
Had drawn the *Quintessence* of *deepest* Arts,
A more *Cœlestial Oracle* by far,
Than *Sybills* Leaves, or *Delphian* Answers were:
English Apollo ! who does display
Physick's hid Treasure in the surest way;
For, who without *Astrology* would know
The Art of *Healing*, does but blindfold go,
By dul Conjectures they are wandering led,
Into a Labyrinth without a Thread.
But he removes dark Errours pitchy Shrowds,
Like Sol dispersing Intervening Clouds,
And by affording this Illustrious Ray,
Brings forth bid Science into open day.
    A solid Work! so well compos'd a frame,
    That he, true Artist, shall endear his Name,
    And for Time's date Immortalize his Fame.

Lancelot Coelson.

Upon the Astrological Physick of the late Learned and Judicious
Mr. Richard Saunders.
Go Book, and may'st thou ne're Return until
Thou find thy Equal in the Starry Skill,
None doubts thy *Fortune*, who at first view fees
SAUNDERS Ascending in thy Frontispiece;
But he who farther looks, and sees him strong
In *Dignities Essential* all along;
Especially considering that He
Is found herein the Lord o'th' Sixth to be;
Who weighs these Testimonies, may conclude
To Artists *Light*, and *Health* to th' Multitude.
Guido Bonatus, Haly, Ptolomy,
The World once crack'd on for Astrology,
And well it might, the World was Childish then,
Took up with *Infants*, 'cause it knew not *Men*;
But 'tis grown Wiser in these latter dayes,
Lilly and *Saunders* now share all the Praise:
Lilly on Heav'n's *Twelve Houses* treated well,
Saunders doth *Lilly* on the *Sixth* excell:
Lilly ran Heav'n *all over* for his praise,
Saunders at One dayes Journey won the Bayes.
Lilly for *Introduction* did his part,
Saunders his *Judgment* perfected the *Art*;
Who kindly wrote this *Astrological*
Judgment of Physick, for the good of all;
None e're wrote like him o'th' *Decumbiture*,
None e're prescribed like him for the *Cure*:
And Opportunely *Note*: when others have
Done all they can for to befriend the Grave,
Confirming *old Diseases*, making *New*,
Using *false* Med'cines, 'cause they knew not *true*:
Ev'n Then did *Saunders*, our grand *Counter-Quack*,
Write this, which then the World did chiefly lack.
Avaunt then *Quacks*, *Piss-prophets* disappear,
I can foretell your *Fall* will be this Year;
The *Starrs* and *Saunders* told me so, and Who
Questions the Truth when spoken by those two?

Nathan Nichols.

A Table of the Principal Matters contained in this Treatise.

Of the Legitimate and Laudable Use of this Art. 30
Astrological Judgment, And Practice of Physick...................34
Of Applications and Separations. 37
Of Reception..37
A Table of the Essential dignities of the Planets, ...39
Of Combustion and Subradiation. 40
Of divers Accidents which belong to the Planets. 40
Of the twelve Houses of Heaven, and some Names or.....................40
How to find the Significators of the Sick Person, and the Morbificant Planet. 45
How to find in what part of the Body the Semem Morbificum is, together with the Diseases in the Members. 46
For what Cause the Sickness is, generally observe............................46
The Parts of the Body attributed to the Seven Planets 47
The Parts of the Body attributed to the 12 Signs 48
Diseases attributed to the 12 Signs, and their proper Significations..49
Diseases Attributed to the Seven Planets..51
In the next place we shall briefly (yet fully) Treat of the Crisis in Diseases, as being a principal Subject Relating to this Treatise: And first what Crisis signifies. 54
Next how the true Crisis may be found; or the Hour, Day, Month, or Year, in which the Disease may be perfectly judged. 55
Of Judgment. 63
A Table shewing what Members in Mans Body every Planet signifieth in any of the Twelve Signes..68
Life and Death. 69
Sings Vita. Signs of Recovery. 92
Of the twelve Houses of Heaven, so far as they concern our business of Sickness. 93
Of the Seven Planets, so far as concerns this Subject of Sickness.....94
Of Compound Qualities..96

Experimented Judgments of Life and Death, and of Diseases. 99
Next we are to know and observe, which of the four Virtues or Humours is weaker or stronger than the other, or than it should be, whereby the distemper of the Body doth grow. 106
General Judgments on the House which is the place of the Liver... 117
Figure showing that every House hath 30 degrees, 25 degrees within the Ascendant, and 5 degrees past, or virtually in the next house .. 121
The 4th House. 121
Judgments of the 4 Angles of the Question, and the first House. 122
Now it followeth to speak of the Retentive Faculty. 125
Remedies when the Retentive Virtue is weakened in the Stomach, or that one doth Vomit much or often by reason of too much Moisture. 130
Remedies when the Retentive Faculty is weakened in theLiver by over-much Heat. 130
A Remedy where the Retentive Faculty is weakned in the Belly by cold and moisture, viz. A Clyster to purge and scowr the Belly and Bowels, and purge out Water and Flegm. 131
A very good Clyster in these Causes. 131
A Remedy when the Retentive Virtue is weakened in the Belly, and the Party hath the Flux of a Hot Cause. 131
A Remedy when the Retentive Virtue is too strong in the Matrix, by too much cold and dry Melancholy of ♄, and the Expulsive Virtue too weak, as followeth. 132
Of the Astronomical Judicial of Diseases. 136
The Cure of Diseases caused by Saturn in Aries and in Leo. 137
Preparers and Digesters of yellow Choler are these. 138
These Digest Melancholy. 139
These Syrups do properly digest Melancholy. 139
These prepare Melancholy. 139
These Digest both Melancholy and Choler. 139
You may prepare yellow Choler an Melancholy caused of ♄ in ♈ or ♌ in the first or second degree thus. 139
Or thus: 140
Purgers of yellow Choler. 140
Purgers only of Melancholy. 140
Haustus Melancholicum Humorem concoquens, & ad Evacuationem præparans. 140
Or thus: 140
Of Saturn in Leo. 141

These following do digest Melancholy and yellow Choler of ♄ in ♌ 141
A Digestive against Drowth of ♄ in ♌, the ☽ applying to ☿ in ♉. ...142
Or thus: 142
Digestives of Choler that is thick and yellow, and of Melancholy, with tough Flegm caused of ♄ in ♌, that is hot and dry in the 3d degree. 142
Purgers of yellow Choler and Melancholy caused of ♄ in ♌, hot and dry in the 3d degree. 143
Again, ...143
A Purge against Choler and Melancholy in the third degree, caused of ♄ in ♌. 143
Again, ...144
Of the pain of the Side and Belly caused by Saturn in Leo. 145
Digesters of red Choler and Melancholy, caused of ♄ in ♐, Hot and dry in the extremity of 4 Degrees. 146
Or, ...146
Purgers against red Choler and Melancholy caused of ♄ in ♐, Hot and Dry in the 4th degree. 146
These purge red Choler. 147
Of ♉, ♍, ♑, that are cold and dry, of the nature of the Earth, Melancholick, &c. ♄ 148
♄ in ♑ 149
Of Gemini. 150
Of Libra. 151
Of Saturn in Aquary. 152
Saturn in Cancer. 152
Of the Black Plague caused of Saturn in Cancer. 153
Saturn in Scorpio. 155
Of Pisces. 156
Of Jupiter. 157
Of ♃ in ♊, ♎, and ♒. 159
Jupiter in Gemini. 159
Of Jupiter in Libra. 159
Of Aquarius. 160
Jupiter in Aquarius. 160
Of Jupiter in Leo. 161
Of Jupiter in Sagitary. 161
Of Jupiter in Taurus. 162
Of Jupiter in Virgo. 162

Of Jupiter in Capricorn. 163
Of Jupiter in Cancer. 163
Of Jupiter in Scorpio. 164
Of Jupiter in Pisces. 164
Of Mars in ♈, ♌ and ♐. 165
Of the cholerick Humour subject to Mars. 165
Of Natural Choler. 166
Of Unnatural Choler. 166
Of Urine. 167
Of Mars in Leo. 168
Of Mars in Sagittarium. 169
Of the Cure of Mars in Sagittary. 169
Of Mars in Taurus. 170
Of Mars in Virgo. 170
The Cure. 171
Mars in Capricorn. 171
The Cure. 172
Of Mars in Gemini. 172
The Cure. 172
Of Mars in Libra. 173
The Cure. 173
Of Mars in Aquarius. 174
The Cure. 174
Of Mars in Cancer. 174
The Cure. 175
Of Mars in Scorpio. 175
The Cure. 176
Of Mars in Pisces. 176
The Cure. 177
Of the Sun in Aries, and of his Nature. 177
Of the Sun in Aries. 177
The Cure. 178
Of Sol in Taurus. 178
The Cure. 179
Of Sol in Gemini. 179
The Cure. 179
Of Sol in Cancer. 179
The Cure. 180
Of Sol in Leo. 180
The Cure of ☉ in ♌ of much yellow Choler. 181

Of Sol in Virgo.	181
The Cure.	181
Of Sol in Libra.	182
The Cure.	182
Of Sol in Scorpio.	182
The Cure.	183
Of Sol in Sagittary.	183
The Cure.	184
Of Sol in Capricorn.	184
The Cure.	184
Of Sol in Aquarius.	185
The Cure.	185
Of Sol in Pisces.	185
The Cure.	186
Of Venus in Aries.	186
The Cure.	186
Of Venus in Taurus.	186
The Cure.	187
Of Venus in Gemini.	187
The Cure.	187
Of Venus in Cancer.	187
The Cure.	188
Of Venus in Leo.	188
The Cure.	189
Of Venus in Virgo.	189
The Cure.	189
Of Venus in Libra.	190
The Cure.	190
Of Venus in Scorpio.	191
The Cure.	191
Of Venus in Sagitary.	192
The Cure.	192
Of Venus in Capricorn.	193
The Cure.	193
Of Venus in Aquarius.	193
The Cure.	194
Of Venus in Pisces.	194
The Cure.	195
Of the Properties of Mercury.	195
Of Mercury in Aries.	195

The Cure.	196
Of Mercury in Leo.	196
The Cure.	196
Of Mercury in Sagittary.	197
The Cure.	198
Of Mercury in Taurus.	198
The Cure.	198
Of Mercury in Virgo.	198
Of Mercury in Capricorn.	199
The Cure.	200
Of Mercury in Gemini.	200
The Cure.	201
Of Mercury in Libra.	201
The Cure.	201
Of Mercury in Aquarius.	201
The Cure.	202
Of Mercury in Cancer.	202
The Cure.	202
Of Mercury in Scorpio	202
The Cure.	203
Of Mercury in Pisces.	203
The Cure.	203
Of the Terms being stop't.	204
The Virtue or Faculty Expulsive.	204
A Remedy when the Expulsive Virtue is weakned by too much drowth in any Member,	207
A Remedy where the Expulsive Virtue is weakned by heat and drought,	207
A Remedy where the Expulsive Virtue is weakned, or the Flower stop'd by drowth in the 3rd degr. and by cold in the 2nd degr.	208
To make one Laxative.	208
To cause Women to have easie deliverance.	208
To bring forth a dead Child.	209
Of Luna.	209
Of Flegm.	209
Of Luna in Aries.	211
The Cure.	211
Of the Moon in Leo.	212
The Cure.	212
Of the ☽ in Sagittary.	212

The Cure.	213
Of the Moon in Cancer.	213
The Cure.	213
Of Luna in Scorpio.	214
The Cure.	214
Of the Moon in Pisces.	214
The Cure of Diseases caused of ☽ in ♓, so far forth or they may be cured.	215
Of the Moon in Taurus.	215
The Cure.	215
Of the Moon in Virgo.	216
The Cure.	217
Of the Moon in Capricorn.	217
Of the ☽ in Gemini.	217
The Cure.	217
Of the Moon in Libra.	218
The Cure.	218
Of Luna in Aquarius.	218
The Cure.	218
Of Caput Draconis	219
Of Cauda Draconis.	219
General Judgments, whereby to know the Diseases and Distempers of the Body.	219
To know the Cause of the Disease.	225
Of Application of the ☽ to Planets.	226
♃ Signifieth the Blood and Mirth.	227
Of ♂.	228
Of ☉.	229
Of ♀ in reference to Diseases.	232
Of ☿ in reference to Diseases.	232
The Moon signifieth Travel and Waters, the Menstrues and Whites, Midwives, and great Ladies, and the Mother.	233
To know where the Fault shall be, if theSick be not Cured.	234
Of the 10th House.	239
Of the Seventh House.	242
Of the Fourth House.	247
Of the Sixth House.	248
To know by what means the Party may be Cured, and with what to begin.	252

Of Compounding of Medicines, when and at what time they should properly be compounded and made. 256
As for Example. 258
Of Giving of Medicine. 262
Matrix. 265
Whether you shall Cure him or no? upon the Question of the first Figure. 267
Of Giving the first Medicine to the Sick. 268
Repress Venome by these: 272
Certain Considerations about the Urine, as whether it be his or hers that brings it, or some bodies else. 273
Of Going to the Sick. 274
Judgments of Diseases without the Urine. 282
Whether thou shalt Cure him or no upon the first Figure as followeth. 283
Whether the Disease be in the Body, or Mind or both. 284
Proper Natural Medicines and Cures that belong to every Disease, caused by the Planets passing through all the Signs of the Zodiack. 290
First of ♄ in ♉, the earthly Triplicity, and the Cure. 290
Simples that Digest Melancholy generally. 290
Simples that Purge Melancholy. 290
Compounds that Purge Melancholy. 290
Preparatives against Melancholy, caused of ♄ in ♉ cold and dry in the 2nd Degree. 291
The Cure of (♄ in ♍) Diseases caused by ♄ in ♍. 291
Digesters of strong Melancholy, caused of ♄ in♉, ♍ or ♑ 291
Purges of ♄ in ♉, ♍ and ♑. 291
The Cure of Diseases caused by ♄ in ♊ produced By melancholick Blood having dominion. 292
The Cure of the Diseases of ♄ in ♎. 292
The Cure of ♄ in ♒. 292
Digesters of Melancholy mixed with Blood. 292
Purgers. 292
The Cure of ♄ in ♋. 292
Purgers against these Diseases. 293
The Cure of ♄ in ♏. 293
Digestives. 293
Purgers. 293
The Cure of Diseases of ♄ in ♓. 294

Preparatives. 294
Repressers of Venome. 294
Purgers for the Same. 294
Of the Cure of Diseases caused by ♃ in ♊. 295
These do Prepare Adustive Blood. 295
Diminish the Quantity of Blood. 295
To Purge and Cleanse the Blood. 295
To Purge the Blood of hot and moist superfluous Matter. 296
The Cure of Diseases caused by ♃ in ♎. 296
These are good against Spitting of Blood. 296
Good against hot faculent Blood, stopping the Pipes, obstructing the Breath, causing difficulty in Breathing. 296
These following do nourish good Blood, and Increase the Radical Humidity in Man. 297
These do open the mouths of the Veins. 297
The Cure of Diseases of ♃ in ♒. 297
Against congealed Blood in the Body. 297
Otherwaies. 298
These Mundifie and cleanse the Blood from all Corruption. 298
For Spitting of Blood. 298
For bleeding at the Nose, or bloody Flux. 298
These following open all Obstructions throughOut the Whole Body of man. 298
The Cure of Diseases caused by ♃ in ♈, coming Of blood and yellow Choler, Choler predominating. 299
Digestives of yellow choler mixed with the Blood, choler having domination. 299
Purgers for the same Griefs. 299
The Cure of Diseases caused of ♃ in ♌. 299
Preparatives. 300
Purgers of this yellow Choler. 300
Perparatives. 301
Purges in this case. 301
The Cure of ♃ in ♉. 301
Preparative against Choler caused of ♃ in ♉, Cold and dry. 301
Purgers for the same. 302
The Cure of ♃ in ♍. 302
Preparatives against Diseases caused of ♃ in ♓, proceeding of Melancholy mixed with Blood. 302
Purgers against these Diseases. 303

Preparatives in this case. 303
Purgers against this Disease. 303
A Purge against this Disease. 304
The Cure of Diseases caused of ♃ in ♋ 304
Digesters of Choler caused of ♃ in ♋. 304
Purgers for this Disease. 304
Or, ... 305
The Cure of ♃ in ♏. 305
Preparatives against these Diseases which are cold in the second, and moist in the third degree. 305
Purgers against these Diseases caused of ♃ in ♏. 305
The Cure of Diseases of ♃ in ♓. 305
Digestives against Cholera vitellina, caused of ♃ in ♓, that is cold and moist in the 4th degree. 306
Purgers against Diseases caused of ♃ in ♍, that are cold and moist in the 4th degree. 306
Digestives of Choler of ♂ in ♈. 306
To make thick and gross Choler thin, and easie to be digested. 307
These Allay the Heat of Choler. 307
These following purge Choler well. 307
These purge burnt and Adust Choler. 307
To purge all red and superfluous Choler. 308
Preparatives. 308
Purgers of gross thick yellow Choler, and thin red Choler, caused of ♂ in ♌. 308
Digestives of yellow Choler. 308
These following purge red Choler. 309
Purgers of red Choler and Flegm. 309
These purge red choler and Melancholy. 309
These following purge and clense the Blood mixed with choler, of ♂ or the ☉ in ♊, ♎, or ♒ 309
The cure of Diseases caused of ♂ in ♉, when Melancholy hath the dominion. 309
Digesters of Melancholy are these, of Sirups, and Waters. 310
Digesters of red choler. 310
Purgers against Diseases caused by ♂ in ♉. 310
Or, ... 310
Preparatives of Red Choler and gross Melancholy 311
Purgers of red Choler and Melancholy caused of ♂ in ♍, where Melancholy hath the pre-eminence. 311

Digestives of red Choler and tough Melancholy, caused of ♂ in ♑, Melancholy predominating. 311
These following purge and cleanse the Blood, infected or mixed with red Choler of ♂ in ♊, ♎, or ♒, or of yellow Choler of the Sun in ♊, ♎, or ♒. 312
Purges against Diseases caused of ♂ in ♊ of red Choler mixed with Blood. 312
Preparatives against Diseases caused of ♂ in ♎, of red Choler mixed with Blood, which is more faculent, hotter and dryer than in ♊, viz. in 3 degrees. 312
Purgers against red Choler of ♂ in ♎ 313
Purgers against these Diseases of ♂ in ♎ of red choler mixed with Blood, Blood predominating. 313
To cleanse the Blood thickened by red Choler, ...313
Preparatives against the Diseases of ♂ in ♒, hot and dry in the 4th degree, caused of red choler mixed with thick, gross and faeculent Blood, Blood being the most predominent. 313
To cleanse the Blood being thickened with red choler of ♂ in ♒, A Drink. 314
A Purge against this Distemper. 314
Preparatives against Diseases caused of ♂ in ♋, of flegm, water and red choler. 314
Purgers against these Diseases. 314
Against salt Flegm proceeding of Choler and Flegm. 315
The Cure of cold Humours and red Choler, caused of ♂ in ♓, cold and moist in the 3rd degree. 315
Purges against this Disease. 315
The Cure of Diseases caused by ☉ in ♈, ...315
Digestives of yellow Choler caused of the ☉ in ♈. 315
Purgers against the same Diseases. 316
General Purges against these Distempers. 316
Digestives against thick Melancholy and thin yellow Choler, caused of the ☉ in ♉, Melancholy predominating. 316
Purgers against the same Diseases. 316
Digestives of yellow Choler mixed with Blood, caused of the ☉ in ♊, Blood having dominion. 317
Purgers for the same Diseases. 317
Digestives of thin Water and thin yellow Choler, caused of the ☉ in ♋, Flegm having dominion. 317
Purges for the same Diseases. 317

Digestives of yellow Choler caused of the ☉ in ♌, are these following. 318
Purgers for the same Distempers. 318
Digestives of Melancholy and thin yellow Choler, caused of the ☉ in ♍, Melancholy being predominant. 319
Purgers for the same Diseases. 319
Digestives of yellow Choler, and such as thin and cool the Blood of ☉ in ♎. 319
Purges against the same Diseases. 320
Again, ... 320
Digestives of salt Flegm and yellow Choler, caused of ☉ in ♏, look in the Chap. of the ☉ in ♋ and ♓. 320
Purgers against the same Distempers of the ☉ in ♏. 320
Digestives of Red Choler caused of the ☉ in ♐, ... 320
Purgers against the same Diseases 321
Digestives of thin Melancholy and yellow Choler, Melancholy predominating, caused of the ☉ in ♑; 321
Purgers for the same Diseases. 322
Digestives of yellow Choler caused of the ☉ in ♒, are such as follows in the Chapter of the ☉ in ♊ and ♎ 322
Purgers for the same Diseases. 322
Digestives of Flegm and this yellow Choler, caused of the ☉ in ♓, Flegm predominating, ... 323
Purgers for the same Diseases of the ☉ in ♓. 323
Preparatives against Diseases caused of ♀ in ♈, of thin yellow Choler and thin Water, Choler having dominion. 323
Purgers for the same Diseases. 323
Pills... 324
Digestives of gross thick Melancholy and thin Water caused of ♀ in ♉, where Melancholy hath the dominion. 324
Purges for the same Diseases. 324
Digestives of thin Flegm or Water mixed with the Blood, Blood having dominion, caused of ♀ in ♊. 325
Purgers for the same Diseases as aforesaid of ♀ in ♉, and let blood. 325
Digestives of Flegm and cold Humours caused of ♀ in ♋, ♏, or ♓ 325
Purgers for the same Diseases 325
Digestives of yellow Choler and thin Water, caused of ♀ in ♌, where yellow Choler hath dominion. 326

Purgers against the same Diseases. 326
Digestives of Melancholy and thin Water, caused of ♀ in ♍, where Melancholy is predominant. 327
Purgers against the same Diseases. 327
Digestives of thin Water mixed with Blood, caused of ♀ in ♎; 328
Purgers for the same, and let Blood. 328
Digestives of Flegm and Water caused of ♀ in ♏, and to discuss gross and slimy Flegm; 328
Purgers of Flegm and Water caused of ♀ in ♏; 328
Against Giddiness of the Head and Apoplexia. 329
Digestives against Diseases caused of ♀ in ♐ of thick red Choler, and thin Water mixed, Choler predominating. 329
Another, when the ☽ applies to ☿. 330
Another, when the ☽ in ♉ separates from ♃, and applies to a □ of ♄. 330
A Diet. 330
Purgers against the Diseases caused of ♀ in ♐. 330
Against Pain and Ache in the Body caused of ♀ in ♐, ☽ in ♍ Separate a ♂ in ♎, & a ♀ in ⚹ of ☿, being in ♏ combust & post. App. ad ⚹ ☉ in the 12th. A Purge against the same. 331
A Preparative for the same. 331
Digestives against Melancholy and thin Flegm, caused of ♀ in ♌, Melancholy predominating, 331
Purgers of the same Diseases as aforesaid, 331
Digestive and things to cleanse and sweeten the Blood, are these that follow, and such as are in the Chapters of ♀ in ♊ and ♎, and ♃ in ♊, ♎ and ♒ 332
Pugers of thin Flegm mixed with the Blood, caused of ♀ in ♒. 332
Digestives of Flegm and Water caused of ♀ in ♓ are, as in the Chapters of ♀ and ☽ in ♋, ♏ and ♓, 333
Purgers of the Diseases aforesaid in the Chapters aforesaid of ♀ and the ☽. 333
Digestives of Diseases caused of ☿ in ♈, ♌, ♐, which proceed of thin yellow Choler and Melancholy mixed, Choler having dominion. 334
Purgers against the same Diseases of ☿ in ♈, where Choler hath dominion, hot and dry 334
Purgers against the same Diseases. 335
Digestives of Diseases caused of ☿ in ♐ 335
Purgers against the same Diseases aforesaid. 335
Digestives of Melancholy are these that follow, 336

Purgers for the same; 336
Digestives against Diseases caused of ☿ in ♍, as follow, and in the Chapters of ☿ in ♉, and ♄ in ♉ and ♍. 336
Purgers against Melancholy cold and dry, as follow, caused of ☿ in ♍, and as in the Chapter of ♄ in ♍ and ♉. 336
These following do cleanse, sweeten the Blood, and cool it. 337
These purge the Blood, ... 337
A Digestive. 337
Purges against the same Diseases. 337
Digestives of Diseases of ☿ in ♒, as in the Chapter of ☿ and ♄ in ♊ and ♒. 337
Purgers against the same Diseases caused of ☿ in ♒, of Melancholy and Blood hot and moist in the 4th degree, ... 338
Digestives of thin Flegm, Water and Melancholy caused of ☿ in ♋. 338
Purgers against the same Diseases. 338
Digestives of thick stinking Flegm and of thin Melancholy, caused of ☿ in ♏. 339
Against Diseases of ☿ in ♏, ☽ in ♎, applying to ♂ in ♎, preparative. 339
Against Diseases of ☿ in ♏, ☽ in ♎ or ♊, applying to ☿. 339
Against Diseases of ☿ in ♏, ☽ in ♋, ♏ or ♓, applying to ♀. 339
A Preparative against Diseases of ☿ in ♏, ☽ in ♎, separating from the ☉, applying to ♀ in ♐, ☉ in ♏. 339
Purges against the same Diseases of ☿ in ♏. 339
Digestives against Diseases caused of ☿ in ♓, as before-said of ☿ in the Chapter of ♋. 340
Purges against the same Diseases, cold and moist in the 4th degree. 340
Digestives of Flegm and yellow Choler caused of the ☽ in ♈, salt Flegm. 341
Purges for the same Diseases. 341
Digestives of Diseases caused of the ☽ in ♌, which proceed of salt Flegm, as in the Chapter of the ☽ in ♈. 341
Purges against the same Diseases. 341
Digestives of salt Flegm of the ☽ or ♀ in ♈, ♌ or ♐. 342
Purgers of salt Flegm caused of ☽ in ♐, of Flegm and red Choler, Choler having dominion. 342
Preparatives against Diseases caused of the ☽ in ♋, ♏ or ♓, which are of Flegm and cold Humours. 343

Purgers for the same Diseases of Flegm and cold Humours, caused of ☽ in ♋, and these purge cold slimy Flegm in the Belly. 343
Vomits to exempt the Stomach of cold Humours. 344
A Glister against Flegm. 344
Digestives against salt Flegm and stinking tough Flegm, caused of the ☽ in ♏, are such as are shewed in the Chapter of ☽ in ♋. 344
Puges against the same Diseases caused of the ☽ in ♏. 344
A magisterial Powder to purge Flegm and gross Humours withal. ..345
Against the Palsie, this following. 345
Digestives against Diseases caused of ☽ in ♓, cold and moist in the 4th degree, of stinking, tough, glassy Flegm, as in the Chapter of the ☽ in ♋ and ♏. 345
Puges against the same Diseases caused of the ☽ in ♓, of tough stinking Flegm in the 4th degree...346
Digestives of Melancholy and Flegm caused of ☽ in ♉, ♍ and ♑, 346
Purgers against the same Diseases of Melancholy and soure Flegm, caused of the ☽ in ♉. 346
Digestives against the Diseases of Flegma Acetosum in the 3d degree, caused of ☽ in ♍, as in the Chapter of ☽ in ♉...............................347
Of Sirups proper in this Case. 347
Of Waters..347
Puges against Flegma Acetosum caused of ☽ in ♍. cold and dry, .347
Or, These against Melancholy and Flegm of the ☽ in ♍, where Melancholy hath dominion. 348
Digestives of Diseases of ☽ in ♑ of salt Flegm and Melancholy, melancholy predominating. 348
Purgers against Flegm and melancholy caused of ☽ in ♑, called Flegma Acetosum, cold and dry in the 4th degree, melancholy predominating. 348
Digestives of sweet Flegm caused of the ☽ in ♊, ...349
Purgers against the same Diseases of the ☽ in ♊ 349
Digestives against diseases caused of the ☽ in ♎ sweet Flegm, are these, and such as are in the Chapter of the ☽ in ♊. 349
Pugers of the same Diseases caused of the ☽ in ♎, of sweet Flegm. 350
Digestives against sweet Glegm in the 4th degree, caused of the ☽ in ♒, and of Flegm and Blood mixed, as in the Chapters of the ☽ in ♊ and ♎, and as followeth. 350
Purgers against sweet Flegm caused of ☽ in ♒...............................350

Digestives of Flegm generally caused of the ☽ in ♋, ♏ or ♓, and of ♀ in the same. 351
Digesters of Flegm generally. 351
Purgers of Flegm generally in this case. 351
These purge putrid and rotten Flegm, being daily taken. 352
These purge rotten and corrupted Flegm, that will not yield to any Medicine, and rectifie the Complexion, and make the Patient look clear, fair, lusty and lively. 352
And these following consume Flegm in a humid Constitution and Complexion. 352
These following consume Flegm in a hot Complexion. 352
These digest cold Humours in the Breast and Stomach. 352
These purge Flegm and cold Humours in the Breast, Stomach and Lungs. 353
Medicines emptying the Stomach and Intestines............................ 353
Medicine Evacuative that purge the Head and Brain, are principally nineteen. 353
These purge especially the Head. 354
Medicines which purge Humours from the Spleen 354
Principal Medicines purging ill Humours from the Liver, and parts adjoyning. 354
Medicines which more sharply cleanse the Humours, and mundifie the Skin, are. 354
Medicines which purge Flegm from the Junctures, and draw ill Humours from the remote parts, are these. 354
These are good against ache of the Bones, Sinews, Muscles and Joynts, and draw Humours afar off. 355
Against rotten Humours, and stopping of the Breast, and Flegm in the Stomach, Head and Muscles, and against bleared Eyes, and watering Eyes. 355
Medicines that purge the Bladder from Gravel and Humours, and are good against the Strangury, and to provoke Urine. 355
Against Exulceration of the Bladder. 355
Medicines that purge the Wind-pipe of gross Humours, are these that follow. 355
Medicines which cleanse the Reins, are 355
These following are good against Pain of the Reins that cometh of cold Causes.. 356
These do purge the Reins of Gravel. 356
An Appendix 357

Some Experiments of Sickness and Death, demonstrated as a Conclusion to this Work. 357
To know whether the Sick Person shall die of his Infirmity or no...357
1. A certain Man brought his Water under this Position of Heaven following. 360
The Planets principally morbificant, are ☉, ♄ and ♂ 360
II. A Gentlemans Urine was brought under such a Position, of Heaven. 362
The Morbificant Planets are ☉, ☽ and ♀, ...362
III. The Urine of a certain Man was brought, according to this Calisebene following. 364
The Morbisicant Planets are ♂, ☿, ♀, ♄, ♃: 364
IV. A Gentleman sends for a Physitian a Messenger, which came to him about 10 of the clock in the forenoon, the Celipositiones being in manner following. 367
The Morbificant Planets ex parte Domini ascendentis, are ♂ and ☿, ex parte luna ♃, ♄, ♀. 367
V. A certain Man came to enquire of the Health of his Child, being a Son, but brought not his Urine with him. The Position of the Heavens as followeth 369
The Morbificant Planets are ♄, ♀, and ☿. 369
VI. A Question being asked concerning the state of a sick Man without Urine, The face of Heaven in manner following, &c. 371
The Morbificant Planets are ♄, ♂, and ♃. 371
VII. The Urine of a sick Man presented to Examination, under following this Position. 373
The Morbificant Planets are ♄, ☉ and ♃. 373
VIII. An old Gentleman sick sent for his Physitia, under this Position of Heaven as followeth 377
The Morbificant Planets are ♄, ♂ and ♃. 377
IX. A Question was moved concerning the state of a certain sick Man, under this Configuration following 379
The Morbificant Planets are ♄, ♂, ♃ and ☿. 379
X. A certain Man brought his Sons Water, under this Constellation following. 381
The Morbificant Planets are ♂, ☉, ☽, ☿ and ♀. 381
XI. A Man brought his Wives Water under such Celiconfiguration as followeth. 384
The Morbificant Planets are ☉, ☿ and ☽, ex parte Domina ascendentis, sed ex parte Luna ☉, ☿, ♀, ♂ and ♄. 384

XII. The Urine of a sick Woman presented to be considered under this Olympial Edification. 386
XIII. A Gentlewoman sent her Urine. Subtali Sebemate sequente:. 388
Mars, Lord of the Ascendant in the Lyon, oppressed by the Squares of ♄, ☽, ☉, ☿ and ♀, betoken great Distemperment 389
XIV. A Gentleman sent concerning his Son, The face of Heaven in manner following. 391
XV. The Urine of a Gentlewoman being sick, consulted under this following Constellation. 393
XVI. Mr. Mayn of Bassingshare-Street sent on the 2d of April, inter 7 & 8 A. M. 1640. about his Sickness, he being weak, Die Jovis Hora Martis. 395

Licensed

Jan. 8th, 1676

Roger L'Estrange.

Of the Legitimate and Laudable Use of this Art.

HE High and Incomprehensible Wisdom of Almighty God, which produced all visible and invisible Creatures from the vast and empty Womb of Nothing, replenished all things with his Goodness, communicating unto them divers and sundry Energies, Instincts and Operations, garnishing and investing them also with an admirable Pulchritude and Beauty, insomuch that the least of his creatures duely considered, doth wonderfully Extoll and Magnifie the infinite, inscrutable, incircumscriptable Wisdom and Bounty of his Divine Majesty, especially, the goodly Theatre of Heaven, being adorned with innumberable most excellent illuminating Bodys of Light, as the Sun, the Moon, and Starrs, and the Seat of God, from whence, as Saint *John* saith, *Apoc.* 22. the Christalline Fountain of Life proceedeth, influencing on this our inferiour Orb, according to the Will and Ordinance of God; as *Hosea* the Prophet witnesseth, Chap. 2. *Exaudiam dicet Dominus, exaudians Cœlos, & ipsi exaudiant Terram, & terra exaudiat Frumentunt et Mulsum et Oleum &c*: Now forasmuch as God created all things to the Honour and Praise of his Holy Name, and the further illustrating and setting forth of his Glory; it must needs follow, that the use of those said Creatures to the same End, can be no abuse or dishonour to God, but rather a means so shew forth his Divine Power and Wisdom, as long as we do acknowledge him to be *prima Causa causarum*, which giveth Influence, Energy, and Power to all things, without whose Providence a Sparrow lighteth not on the ground; For although we confess that the *Stars* have great

Power and predomination in the Elements, and all elementated Bodies, and Animals, and Vegetables, producing divers and sundry Diseases and Infirmities, yet we deny that they are the Causes of the same, *simpliciter*, by their own power, or that *per se* they have any Energie, Instinct or Operation, but that which is communicated to them from Almighty God, and by him destinated and appointed to that end; all which considered, it behoveth him that desireth to use these Presages following, to the Honour and Glory of God, and the benefit of his Neighbour; First, with a profound Humility to acknowledg on the one side his own Insufficiency, Ignorance, and promptness to erre, as altogether unable to penetrate into the secret working of the Almighty, except it please his Divine Majesty to illuminate the Caliginous darkness of his understanding, with the Light of his Holy Spirit; and on the other side, That God is the onely and essential Truth, with whom, (as St. *James* saith) *Non est transmutatio, nec vicissitudinis obumbratio.* All other Sciences of men, although never so excellent and percellebrous, yet are subject to errour and uncertainty, unless they are informed and animated from him which ruleth and guideth all things, *Librans in pondere montes, & colles in statera*: And so all curiosity and Vain-glory set apart, with a firm and stedfast confidence in Almighty God, craving his assistance in every action; and then proceed as he shall direct thee in this Science, given and bequeathed to all the Sons of Art, out of the Treasery of the Almighty, not by me, but by him, that as *Daniel* the Prophet saith, *chap. 2.* doth *retclare mysteria.* And so I doubt not, but to Gods Honour and Glory, and the Commendations of this Art, thou shalt have just cause with *David* to say, *Cœli enarrant glorians Dei sortis, & opus maxuum cjus indicat expansum corum;* and as often as it shall please God to give thee the true preseience of those things thou requirest from his...Canopy of Heaven, be sure thou forget not ..... thanks to his infinite Majesy, that he hath .... of his exceeding Goodness to create those bright lamps of Heaven, not only to shine in the firmament, and illuminate this our opacent Globe of the Earth; but also by their mediation to second it with many dowries of virtues, and ordaining them as Signs and Tokens, to guide and lead use to the knowledg of such things as it shall please him to reveal unto us: But if thou presumest otherwise of there own skill and knowledge, without confidence in God, or craving Divine Aid or Assistance, no Doubt but that will be verified on thee which the Prophet presageth to the *Caldeans, Supientia & Scientia te decepit*; for either by thy own ignorance and mistaking thou shalt be Seduced, or else Heaven it self shall yield unto thee so ambiguous an Answer, that thou shall not be able to conclude any Certainty.

Use of this Art.

Things to be observed before we give any Mathematical Presages.

This one thing I would request from the Sons of Art, that before such time as long Experience, (which is the *Lapis Lydius* to try the Truth from Falshood) hath established their opinion in the Predictions following, that they never presume to give any Judgment or Sentence of this Art, except the time of the day or night be exactly known, when the Sick person, or else some other in his behalf doth Consult with thee concerning his Disease, or the time he bringeth or sendeth his Urine to thee be assuredly known, that thereby the Ascendant, and the Angles of the figure may be exactly taken, as also the Cusp of the Eighth house, that the Lords of the Ascendant, fourth and eighth House, be no ways mistaken; for upon these, and their several habitudes and configurations, all our whole scope dependeth.

Another thing also is to be diligently observed, that there be no error commited in the calculation of the Planets, so that the true degree (of their longitude at the least) may be perfectly had, the which by way of Caveat I thought good to remember, lest this Art and my self should be both unjustly accused, or blamed without desert; and especially be Careful in the motions of *Mars* and *Mercury*, for there are Calculations now extant that have erred in the retrocedation of *Mars* above 2 degrees, and in the slow motion, and especially in the Retrogradation of *Mercury*, it is usual at sometimes to miss 3 or 4, if not 7 or 8 degrees, which intollerable Error is more than the Semidiameter of his Beams.

Astrological Judgment, And Practice of Physick

HE whole ensuing Discourse is Astrologically Composed, therefore it's necessary, by way of Introduction, briefly to give some light into the grounds thereof.

In the first place you must know that there are seven Planets, so called and charactered; Saturn ♄: Jupiter ♃: Mars ♂: Sol ☉: Venus ♀: Mercury ☿: Luna ☽: there is also the head of the Dragon, thus noted ☊: and the tail thus ☋. ☊ and ☋ are not Planets, but Nodes.

There be also twelve Signes, thus called, and characteriz'd; Aries ♈: Taurus ♉: Gemini ♊: Cancer ♋: Leo ♌: Virgo ♍: Libra ♎: Scorpio ♏: Sagittarius ♐: Capricornus ♑: Aquarius ♒: Pisces ♓: through these twelve Signs the Planets continually move, and are ever in one or other Degree of them. It's necessary you can perfectly distinguish the Character of every Planet and Sign, before you proceed to any part of this Study.

You must also know, that every Sign contains in Longitude thirty Degrees, and every Degree sixty Minutes, &c. the beginning is from ♈, and so in order, one Sign after another; so the whole *Zodiack* contains 360 Degrees; the 4 Degree of ♉ is the 34 Degree of the *Zodiack*; the 10 of ♉ is the fortieth, and so in order, all throughout the twelve Signs; yet you must ever account the Aspect from that Degree of the *Zodiack* wherein the Planet is, as if ♄ be in ten Degrees of ♊, and I would know to what Degree of the Ecliptick he casteth his sinister Sextil Aspect; reckoning from ♈ to the 10 Degree of ♊, I find ♄ to be in the seventieth Degree of the *Zodiack*, according to his longitude, if I add sixty Degrees more to seventy, they make one hundred and thirty, which answers to the tenth Degree of the Sign ♌, to which ♄ casteth his Sextile Aspect, or to any Planet in that Degree.

You must also understand, that there are five Aspects of the Planets and thus named and charactered; *Conjunction* ☌: *Sextile* ✶: *Quartil* □: *Trine* △: and *Opposition* ☍: but Conjunction is not properly called an Aspect, although for brevity sake we so term it, intending to deliver a general Explication of that with the rest. Note that there are four several kinds of every one of these Aspects, viz. *Corporalis, Partilis, Monographicus, Platicus.*

Aspectus Corporalis, is the most perfect Aspect of all the rest, and is when two Planets or more, do respect or behold each other, either of them being in the same Degree and Minute.

The Conjunction Corporal is, when two Planets are in the same degree and minute of Longitude; as if ♄ and ♂ were both in the first degree and ten minutes of ♈: with good Planets, this is the strongest good; with evil, the greatest evil.

The Sextile ✶ Corporal is, when two are distant the one from the other two Signs, or sixty Degrees, or the sixth part of the *Zodiack*; as if ♃ were in the 10 degree of ♊, and the ☉ in the 10 degree of ♌: this is an Aspect of Amity.

The Square, or Quartil Corporal is, when two Planets are remote three Signs or 90 Degrees, or the fourth part of the *Zodiack*, the one from the other, as if ♄ were in the 5 degree of ♑, and ♃ in the 5 degree of ♈: this is an Aspect of Enmity and Malignancy.

The Trine △ Corporal is, when two Planets are elongated the one from the other, four Signs, the third part of the *Zodiack*, or 120 Degrees; as if ♃ were in the first degree of ♈, and ♀ in the first degree of ♌: this is an Aspect of Friendship and Amity.

The Opposition Corporal is, when two Planets or more are distanced apart by the space of six Signs, or 180 Degrees; as if ♄ were in 20 degrees of ♈, and ☿ in 20 degr. of ♎: this is an Aspect of the greatest Hostility. And as the Corporal Aspect is most perfect, because it hapneth when two Planets do behold each other corporally, without respect to their beams, so by it all other kinds of Aspects may fitly and aptly be described.

The Partil Aspect is next in perfection to the Corporal, and in virtue and power fully equivalent unto it, only there is this difference, that the Corporal Aspect produceth his effect instantly, without succession of time, and the Partil more slowly, with succession.

The Partil Aspect is, when two Planets are distant from a Corporal and perfect Aspect, yet so that the difference doth not exceed the Semidiameter of either of them, so that they do mutually joyn by the Semiradient circle of their Beams, so that the Semidiameter of the one be not remote from the Corporal Aspect of the other; as if ♄ were in the third degree of ♈, and ♃ in the 12 of ♌, for then ♃ were but 9 degrees distant from a Trine △ corporal with ♄, and forasmuch as this difference doth not exceed either of their Diameters, therefore they shall behold each other by a Trine Partil.

The Menographick Aspect is, when two Planets do behold each other, and yet the distance between the Centre of both their Bodies doth differ from a perfect Aspect above the Semidiameter of one of them, and yet it must exceed the Semidiameter of the other of them. And this Aspect is not so powerful and forcible as the former, because the Contact between them is not so perfect, as for Example: if ♀ were in the 4 degree of ♋, and the ☽ in the 12 degree of ♈: here the difference from a perfect Aspect is 8 degrees, which is less than the ☽ her Semidiameter, and more than the Semidiameter of ♀, so that the ☽ by her beams toucheth ♀, but not ♀ the Moon, and therefore in that respect, the configuration between them is not so perfect.

The Platick Aspect is, when two Planets or more do differ from a perfect Aspect, more than the Semidiameter of either of them, yet so that this distance doth not exceed the sum of both their Semidiamters; as if ♄ were in the 7th degree of ♈, and ♂ in the 20th of the same Sign, here should be a Conjunction Platick between ♄ and ♂, because the distance they differ from a true Aspect is 13 Degrees, which is more than the Diameter of either of them, and yet less than the sum of both their Semidiameters: and this Aspect is of the least effect of all the rest, because they do not behold each other from their Centre, but by Contaction of Beams.

The Quantity of the Orbs of the Planets.

	grad.	
♄ ——	9	☌ is good with the good,
♃ ——	9	and evil with the evil.
♂ ——	8	✶ is unperfect riendship.
♀ ——	7	△ is perfect Friendship.
☿ ——	6	□ imperfect Enmity.
☽ ——	12	☍ open defiance, or
☉ ——	15	perfect Hostility.

The Semiradient Circle of

Of Applications and Separations.

Application is when one Planet doth apply toward the Aspect of some other, and Separating is when a Planet doth separate from the Aspect of another, and of each of these there are two kinds; the one is *Applicatio* or *Separatio communis*, the other is *Applicatio* or *Separatio levis*; and first of *Applications*, that which we here call *Communis*, is, when a Planet that is of a less Longitude doth Apply to the Aspect of a Planet, that according to his place in the *Zodiack* is of a greater Longitude; as if ☿ were in the 18th degree of ♋, and ♄ in the 20th of the same Sign, then should ☿ apply to ♄, because the Longitude of ♄ is greater by 2 degrees than the Longitude of ☿.

Applicatio Levis, is, when a light Planet or inferiour, doth apply toward the Aspect of another more weighty or superiour.

Separatio Communis, is, when a Planet of a greater Longitude in the *Zodiack*, doth separate from the Aspect of another having less Longitude; *verbi gratia*, the ☽ being in 10 degr. of ♓ and ♃ in the 20 of ♊, here ♃ is separated from a Sextil Partil of ☽.

Separatio Levis, is, when a light Planet doth separate from the Aspect of another more weighty than he, or an inferiour Planet from a Superiour.

Of Reception.

Reception is of two sorts, *perfects* & *imperfects*; perfect Reception, otherwise called mutual Reception, is when two Planets aspect one the other, either of them being in the Dignity of the other; as if ♂ were in ♌ and the ☉ in ♈, here ♂ receiveth the ☉ and the ☉ also receiveth ♂.

Imperfect Reception is when a Planet beholds another in his Dignity; as if the ☽ were in ♊ and ☿ in ♓, here the ☽ doth receive ☿ with a □.

Also Reception is divided into two kinds, *fortis* and *debilis*.

Fortis Receptio is, when two Planets do receive each other by the Dignity of House or Exaltation.

Debilis Receptio is, when two Planets receive each other by the dignity of Triplicity, Term, or face.

A Table of the Essential Dignities of the Planets according to Ptolemy

	♈	♉	♊	♋	♌	♍	♎	♏	♐	♑	♒	♓
Fall	♄			♂		♀	☉	☽		♃		☿
Detriment	♀	♂	♃	♄	♄	♃	♂	♀	☿	☽	☉	☿
Faces 30°	♀ 30	♄ 30	☉ 30	☽ 30	♂ 30	☿ 30	♃ 30	♀ 30	♄ 30	☉ 30	☽ 30	♂ 30
Faces 20°	☉ 20	☽ 20	♂ 20	☿ 20	♃ 20	♀ 20	♄ 20	☉ 20	☽ 20	♂ 20	☿ 20	♃ 20
Faces 10°	♂ 10	☿ 10	♃ 10	♀ 10	♄ 10	☉ 10	☽ 10	♂ 10	☿ 10	♃ 10	♀ 10	♄ 10
Terms	♄ 30	♂ 30	♄ 30	♄ 30	♂ 30	♂ 30	♂ 30	♄ 30	♂ 30	♄ 30	♂ 30	♄ 30
Terms	♂ 26	♄ 20	♂ 25	♃ 27	♃ 25	♄ 24	♀ 24	♃ 27	♄ 25	♂ 25	♃ 25	♂ 26
Terms	☿ 21	♃ 22	♀ 21	☿ 20	♀ 19	♃ 18	♃ 19	☿ 21	☿ 19	♃ 19	♀ 20	☿ 20
Terms	♀ 14	☿ 15	♃ 14	♀ 13	☿ 13	♀ 13	☿ 11	♀ 14	♀ 14	☿ 12	☿ 12	♃ 14
Terms	♃ 6	♀ 8	☿ 7	♂ 6	♄ 6	☿ 7	♄ 6	♂ 6	♃ 8	♀ 6	♄ 6	♀ 8
Trip. of the Plan. N	♃	☽	☿	♂	♃	☽	☿	♂	♃	☽	☿	♂
Trip. of the Plan. D	☉	♀	♄	♂	☉	♀	♄	♂	☉	♀	♄	♂
Exaltation	☉ 19	☽ 3	☊ 3	♃ 15		☿ 15	♄ 21		☋ 3	♂ 28		♀ 27
Houses of the Planets	♂ D	♀ N	☿ D	☽ N/D	☉ N/D	☿ N	♀ D	♂ N	♃ D	♄ N	♄ D	♃ N

A Planet without any Essential Dignities is called Peregrine.

Astrological Judgment of Physick.

Of Combustion and Subradiation.

A Planet is said to be Combust, when he is near the Sun, by the space of his Semiradient Circle, and he is *subradiis*, until he be 16 degr. remote from the Sun.

Of divers Accidents which belong to the Planets.

The *Egyptians*, *Caldeans*, and *Arabians*, do observe many curious Observations in this Art, as Translation of Light, Prohibition, Contraradiation, Restitution Frustration, Obsession, Antiscian, Cursuvacation, Cursutardation, Ferality, Augedescention, Meridional descention, Luminiminution, Numeriminution, *Via Combusta*, &c. which although I will not deny to have some small Effect, yet I have often proved that overmuch Curiosity herein doth rather deviate a man from concluding any thing certainly; for these being compared to other Observations that we mean here to express, are no more than a little spark to a great flame; for as the Light of the Sun doth hide and obscure the Stars, and as the Sea absorbeth the little Streams, so do those greater Accidents swallow up the smaller, themselves also thereby no whit, or little intended, as we may sensibly perceive.

Of the twelve Houses of Heaven, and some Names or Terms of Astrology.

The whole Sphere of Heaven is divided into four equal parts, by the *Meridian* and *Horizon*, and again into four Quadrants, and every Quadrant again into three parts, according unto other Circles drawn by points of Sections of the aforesaid Meridian and Horizon: So the whole Heaven is divided into twelve equal parts, which the Astrologers call *Houses* or *Mansions*, taking their beginning from the East.

The first Quadrant is described from the East to the Mid-heaven, or from the Line of the first House, to the Line of the tenth House, and contains the twelfth, eleventh, and tenth Houses; It's called the Oriental, Vernal, Masculine, Sanguine, Infant-Quarter.

The second Quadrant is from the Cusp of the Mid-heaven to the Cusp of the 7th House, containing the ninth, eighth, and seventh Houses, and is called the Meridian, Estival, Feminine, Youthful, Cholerick Quarter.

The third Quadrant is from the Cusp of the seventh House, to the Cusp of the fourth House, and contains the sixth, fifth, and fourth Houses, is called Occidental, Autumnal, Masculine, Melancholick, Manhood, cold and dry.

The fourth Quadrant is from the Cusp of the fourth, to the Cusp of the first House, and contains the third, second, and first House; is Northern, Feminine, Old age, of the nature of Winter, Phlegmatick.

The first tenth, seventh, and fourth Houses hereof, are called *Angles*, the eleventh, second, eighth, and fifth, are called *Succedants*; the third, twelfth, ninth, and sixth, are termed *Cadents*; the Angles are most powerful, the Succedants are next in virtue, the Cadents *poor*, and of little efficacy; the Succedant Houses follow the Angles, the Cadents come next the Succedants in force and virtue, they stand so in order; 1, 10, 7, 4, Angles; the 11, 5, 8, 2, Succedants; the 3, 9, 6, 12, Cadents, &c.

The meaning whereof is this, that two Planets equally dignified, the one in the Ascendant, the other in the tenth House; you shall judge the Planet in the Ascendant somewhat of more power to effect what he is Significator of, than he that is in the tenth: Do so in the rest, as they stand in order, remembring that Planets in Angles do more forcibly shew their Effects.

When we name the Lord of the Ascendant, or Significator of the Querent, or thing quesited, we mean no other thing, than that Planet who is Lord of that Sign which Ascends, or Lord of that Sign from which House the thing demanded is required; as if from the seventh House, the Lord of that Sign descending on the Cusp in Significator, and so of the rest: but of this more in the ensuing Judgments. The Houses and Signs wherein the Planets

Rule as Lords, and have special dominion, are thus: ♄ ruleth in ♑ and ♒: ♃ in ♐ and ♓: ♂ in ♈ and ♏: ☉ in ♌: ♀ in ♉ and ♎, ☿ in ♊ and ♍: the ☽ in ♋, &c.

The Champions for Astrology in all Ages, have by their Enemies been most gravelled, and put to a *non-plus*, (above all other parts of the Science) in this particular of the division of the *Houses*, and their *Names*; as why the Heaven might not be divided into more or fewer parts than 12? and wherefore the first House is called the House of Life, and placed in the East? why the Order and numberical succession of the Houses is from East to West? and why the second House is called the House of Riches? the twelfth of Enemies, Imprisonment, and Misery? and so why the other Houses are called by their names, and disposed in that order? Seeing (as the Enemies hereof pretend) as well their Order as Names, observe no Order at all, but are rather a *Chymæra* of Confusion, a plain hotch-potch of Fiction and Foolery, as *Picus Mirandulus*, a bitter and Learned Antagonist, in his 10th Book, and *Alexander ab Angelis* in his 4th Book and 27th Chapter, and indeed not without reason; for all who have endeavoured formerly to give the reasons of these Houses, (though very Learned) as *Lucius Bellantius, Julius Firmicus*, and others, have produced nothing orderly, nothing of truth, but meer Figments onely: so that if any where they brought a Reason which seemed but to defend one House, the very same really destroyed all the rest; and therefore *Alexander ab Angelis*, lib. 4. cap. 19. after his *Monstre* of all the Arguments brought by *Julius Firmicus* concerning these Houses, he justly resells them in these words; *Ridiculus fit, quisunque ridiculas has rationes nostra resutatione egere existimaret*. Thus this Noble Science, (to the great discouragement of her Professors) hath rested under this obloquy, to the great encouragement of its virulent Adversaries, till of late years, these Doubts have been cleared, and this Doctrine most Elegantly justified by the worthy Pen of *Jobannis Baptista Morinus* in his *Astrologia Gallica*, lib. 17, to the end of the 7th chap. and excellently Englished by our Honoured Countryman Capt. *George Wharton*, and highly honoured and applauded by that Famous Mathematician of our times, Mr. *Will. Oughtrid*, recorded in

Wharton's Almanack 1659, to which I refer my Reader, it being too copious for me in this place.

Seeing this Doctrine of the 12 Houses hath been so oppugned by Adversaries, and so weakly defended by Friends, I will take the Liberty, *de novo*, to make a small Addition in reference to its justification and probation.

And because there are many think the division of the 12 Celestial Houses to be a vain and frivolous invention, I thought it good here to shew some Physical and Mathematical reasons for the grounds thereof, besides what others have said; which although they are not subject to the gross understanding of those which measure every object by the palpable feeling of their muddy brains, yet to the Sons of Art I doubt not but they will be as clear as the day. And to the end, that we may the better express our mind herein, we will use the help of *Number*, because there are many Mysteries contained therein; for as Holy Writ testifieth, God hath disposed all things in Number, Weight, and Measure: and the *Babylonians* were wont to say, *Cur Homo Animal Sapientissimum? Quia Numerare potest.*

You shall understand that there are four Numbers analogizing with the four first Physical Qualities; and that, like as all things are made and do consist of divers combinations and mixtions of the said Elemental Qualities, so likewise by the Composition, and union of these Numbers, all other Numbers do result and arise.

For *One* is the beginning of Numbers, yet of it self properly is no Number, and hath for his Energie Unity, Peace, and Life; Unity, because One is indivisible, and contrary to Death, which is a division of all things complectionated. It doth Analogize with Moisture radical, which hath more Entity, or is *circa esse*, more than any other Elemental Quality; Moisture uniteth and conglutinateth things together, it is the Radical Moisture of Life, that nourisheth and feedeth both Animals and Vegetables.

One hath for his Contrariety or Opposition, *Two*; for Duallity is contrary to Unity, and therefore it hath contrary Energies; for Two signifieth Enmity, Discord, Hate, and Diseases, and Two doth Analogize with Siccity; for Dryness consuming Humidity makes the Subject fall to Dust and Cinders.

And by the Union of One and Two is three produced, and therefore Three resembleth *actus inter agens & patiens*; and because *omnis actus est cum motu*, therefore it signifies the operation and motion, &c. It analogizeth with Heat, for Heat is produced between Moisture and Dryness, as may be seen in a Lime-stone put into Water; also Heat is most actual of all Elemental Qualities; and Three hath for his Duallity or Opposition, Six; and therefore Six being contrary to Three, hath also Energies oppugnant thereunto, *Actio* signifieth immobility, rest, because *Quies oppenitur motui*; also it signifieth the end of things, for things do in *fine Quicscere*. It analogizeth with Cold, for Moisture that is flexible, and apt to move, by Cold is congealed and made stable, and unapt to flow, In Latitude all things are determinated in Six, but according to Longitude in 12, because 1, 2, 3, and 6 added together, resulteth or amounteth unto 12; so likewise the whole Sphear of Heaven in Latitude containeth six Divisions, and in Longitude 12, which we call Houses, whereof the first (beginning at the East) hath *One*, for his Conformity; for as One is the beginning of Number, so the first House is the beginning of all the rest, and hath like Energies, as Unity Identity, Peace, and Life.

As *One* hath *Two* for his Opposition, so the first House hath the West Angle for his Opposition, being also the second part of the whole Sphear, and that is the reason, that the 7th House being oppugnant to the first, hath repugnant Energies as the Logician saith, *Contrariorum Contraria est consequentia*: therefore it signifieth Strife, Hate, Enmity, Solution of Continuity, and Discratie; also it signifieth Wives or Women, for *Siccitos* doth *appetere Humiditatem*; as between *One* and *Two* is ingendred *Three*, between *Agens* and *Patiens* is *Actus* produced, being a *medium* as it were, *inter terminum a Quo & ad Quem*; therefore the South Angle, or Tenth House signifieth Action, Operation, and Motion, and hath for his Opposition the Angle of the North, or 4th House, which signifieth the end of Things, and all things that desist to move, because *Quies opponitur Motui*. Some *Astrologians* say that these two last rehearsed Angles do represent the Father and Mother; for as *Artesius* in *Libro primo Sapientie majoris*, saith, *Temper avit enim — scil.una pars caloris cum parte frigiditatis sibi equali, & evenit ex ea Temperamenta, Matura Humiditatis;* which said Humidity doth analogize with the first House; and thus much in brief as touching the Significations of the four Angles: the other Houses consurge of like Reasons, but parallel'd to bystical Demonstrations passing the Capacity of the Common sort, which for brevities sake, here we omit; accounting this sufficient to give the incredulous a Tast of our mathematical *Cœlischemation*, and to shew that the Division of the Houses, and the Signification of them, is no frivolous invention, built upon the fantastick imagination of mens idle brains, but grounded upon sufficient demonstration, both *Mathematical*, *Physical*, and *Cabalistical*.

How to find the Significators of the Sick Person, and the Morbificant Planet.

The time aforesaid being truly had, and the points of the twelve Houses answerable thereunto, with the Position and Situation of the 7 Planets; then for the Significators of the Sick Patient, take the Ascendant, his Lord, and the Moon, and that Planet or Planets, which by ♂, □, or ☍, afflicteth those Places, shall be the true Morbificant Planets, or Signifcators of the Disease; yet here it is to be noted, that the principal Effect herein is to be referred to the Planets that afflict the Lord of the Ascendant, next the ☽, and lastly the Ascendant; for a Planet afflicting the Ascendant, brings no notable Detriment, except it be by Conjunction, as I have by long experiment proved; and although the ⚹ Aspect of ♄ and ♂ do also bring swome Distemperance to the Sick, yet it is so small, that it is not equivalent to a □ of ♃ or ♀, and therefore not much to be regarded, for overmuch scrupulosity in this Art doth rather deviate a man from the true Scope, than bring him *ad Tramitem rectam*.

How to find in what part of the Body the Semem Morbificum is, together with the Diseases in the Members.

Those things are very hard to find without the help of the Parties Urine, or relations in some sort from the Party, for although the Starrs do insinuate unto us these things more precisely than either Urine, Pulse, or Excrements, yet the Significators in this behalf are many, and thereof Ambiguity often ariseth, except some farther help assisteth that may direct our Judgment herein; for sometimes the *Semen Morbificum* is in those parts of the Body that are governed by the Lord of the Ascendant, sometime in those parts which are attributed to the Dodecatemory Ascendant, sometimes to the Sign the Lord of the Ascendant or the Moon is in, and sometimes according to the domestical Situation of the Lord of the Ascendant, or the Moon. And in one of these places it never faileth the imbecillitated members or parts of the Body wherein pain or grief is felt: sometimes it is in those places aforesaid, and sometimes in those parts attributed to the morbificant Planets, their Situation in Longitude, or Domestical Location, and in one, or more of these it never faileth, as may appear in divers Examples, at the end of the Book following.

For what Cause the Sickness is, generally observe

The Significators in fiery Signes, and the Sign ascending in the first, and descending in the sixth of the same Nature, shew Hectick Fever, and that Choler principally is predominant in this Sickness.

The Significators in Earthy Signs, argue long and tedious Agues, or Fevers of great continuance, or such Diseases as may occasionally proceed from Melancholy, as *Consumption*, &c.

The Significators in Aiery Signs shew the Blood putrified corrupted, Gouty Diseases, Leprosies, and *Hand* and *Foot-Gout*.

The Significators in Moist Signs, declare the Disease to proceed from some Cold and Moist Cause or Causes, and shew

Coughs, Rottenness in the Stomach, and that those parts are afflicted and disaffected.

The Parts of the Body attributed to the Seven Planets

Saturn{ The right Ear, the Spleen, Bladder, Paunch, Bones, middle Finger and Teeth.

Jupiter{ The Liver, Lungs, Seed, Ribs, Sides, Veins, Arteries, Grissels, Navel, Muscles, Pulse, and the fore-finger of the hand.

Mars{ The left Ear, Gall, reins, Veins, Testicles, right Nostril, and the plane of *Mars* in the Hand.

Sol{ The right Eye, the Heart, Brain, Sight, right Side, Sinews, Head, Nerves, with the Ring-finger of the Hand.

Venus{ The Matrix, Belly, Reins, Sperm, Loyn's, Fatness, Genitals, Buttocks, Paps, parts of generation, Throat, Flesh, left Nostril, Liver, Stomach, Smell and Taste, and the Mount of the Thumb.

Mercury{ The Memory, Phantasy, Spirits, Imagination, Brain, Voice, Speech, Tongue, Pipes and Organs of Voice, Sinews, the Gall, Hands and Feet, and the little Finger.

Luna{ The Left eye of a Man, and the right of a Woman, the Stomach, Belly left side, Bowels, Bladder, Taste, Appetite, Stones, the Liver of a Woman, Brain, Marrow of the Back, Intestines, Entrals, and the ferient or brawny part of the hand.

The Parts of the Body attributed to the 12 Signs

Aries and the first House	The Head, Face, Nose, Brows, Cheeks, Chin, Eyes and Ears, and all other parts of the Head.
Taurus and the 2d House	The Neck, the Throat, Pole, Wesand, and Parts under the Chin.
Gemini and the 3d House	The Shoulders, Arms, Hands, Fingers, and Wrists.
Cancer and the 4th House	The Breast, Mediastine, Sides, Liver, Ribs, Præcordiacks, Lights, Spleen, Paps.
Leo and the 5th House	The Heart, Liver, Gall, Stomach, the Back between the Shoulders and præcordiacks, the left Pap.
Virgo and the 6th House	The Midriff, Bowels, Belly, Guts, Gall, Mesenterion, and bottom of the Stomach.
Libra and the 7th House	The Reins, Loyns, Navel, small of the Back, Liver, part of the Belly, Buttocks, Groin, and Bladder.
Scorpio and the 8th House	The Privy Members, Stones, Bladder, Cods, Matrix and parts adjoyning.
Sagitarius & the 9th House	The Hips, Thighs, Buttocks, lower part of the Back, and *Os Sacrum*.
Capricorn & 10th House	The Knees, Hamms, and upper part of the Legs.
Aquarius & 11 House	The Legs from the Knee downward, and the Shins.
Pisces and 12th House	The Feet, Ankles, Instep, and Toes.

Diseases attributed to the 12 Signs, and their proper Significations.

♈ Is a masculine Diurnal Sign, moveable, Cardinal, Equinoctial: in nature fiery, Hot and Dry, Cholerick, Bestial, Luxurious, Intemperate, and Violent; the Dirunal House of ♂, of the fiery Triplicity, and of the East. Of Diseases these;

All Pushes, Whelks, Pimples in the face, small Pocks, Hare-lips, Polypus, (*Noli me tangere*) Ring-worms, Falling-Sickness, Apoplexies, Megrims, Tooth-ach, Head-ach, and Baldness.

♉ Is an Earthly, Cold, Dry, Melancholy, Feminine, Nocturnal, Fixed, Domestical, or Bestial Sign; of the Earthly Triplicity, and South, the Night-house of *Venus*. It signifieth, Of Diseases,

The Kings Evil, Sore Throats, Wens, Fluxes of Rheums falling into the Throat, Quinzies and Impostumes in those parts.

♊ Is an Aerial, Hot, Moist, Sanguin, Diurnal, Common, or double-bodied Humane Sign; the Diurnal House of *Mercury*, of the Aery Triplicity, Western, Masculine.

This signifies all Diseases and Infirmities in the Arms, Shoulders, Hands, corrupted Blood, windiness in the Veins, distempered Fancies, &c.

♋ Is the onely House of the Moon, and is the first Sign of the Northern and Watry Triplicity; is Watry, Cold, Moist, Flegmatick, Feminine, Nocturnal, moveable, a Solstice Sign, mute, and flow of Voice, Fruitful and Northern. In Diseases.

It signifies Imperfections all over, in the Breast, Stomach and Paps, weak Digestion, cold Stomach, Ptisick, salt Flegms, rotten Coughs, dropsical Humours, Impostumations in the Stomach, Cancers, which ever are in the Breast.

♌ Is the only House of the Sun, by nature Fiery, Hot and Dry, Cholerick, Diurnal, Commanding, Bestial, Barren,. of the East and Fiery Triplicity, Masculine. Of Diseases,

All Sicknesses and distempers in the Ribs and Sides, as Plurisies, Convulsions, pains in the Back, Trembling, or passion of the Heart, Violent burning Fevers, all Weaknesses or Diseases in the Heart, sore Eyes, the Plague, the Pestilence, the yellow Jaundies.

♍ It's an Earthly, Cold, Melancholick, Barren, Feminine, Nocturnal, Southern Sign; the House and Exaltation of ☿, of the Earthy Triplicity. In Diseases,

The Worms, Wind-Cholick, all obstructions in the Bowels and Meseraicks, croaking of the Guts, infirmities in the Stones, any Disease in the Belly.

♎ Is a Sign Aereal, Hot and moist, Sanguin, Masculine, Moveable, Æquinoctial, Cardinal, Humane, Diurnal, of the Aereal Triplicity, and Western; the chief House of *Venus*. It signifies,

All Diseases, or the Stone or Gravel in the Reins of the Back, Kidneys, Heats and Diseases in the Loyns or Haunches, Impostumes or Ulcers in the Reins, Kidneys, or Bladder, weakness in the Back corruption of Blood.

♏ Is a Cold, Watry, Nocturnal, Flegmatick, Feminine Sign; of the Watry Triplicity, fixed, and North, the House and Joy of *Mars*. In Diseases it represents,

The Gravel, the Stone in the secret Parts, Bladder, Ruptures, Fistulaes, or the Pyles in *Ano*: Gonorrhea's, Priapism's, all afflictions of the privy Parts either in Man or Woman, Defects in the Matrix.

♐ Is of the Fiery Triplicity, East; in nature fiery, Hot, Dry, Masculine, Cholerick, Diurnal, Common, Bicorporeal or Double-bodied, the House and Joy of *Jupiter*. In Diseases,

It signifies all Fistula's, or Hurts falling in the Thighs or Buttocks, and generally denoteth Blood heated, Fevers pestilential, Falls from Horses, or hurts from them, or other four-footed Beasts; also prejudice by Fire, Heat and Intemperateness in Sports.

♑ is the House of *Saturn*, and is Nocturnal, Cold, Dry, Melancholick, Earthy, Feminine, Solstitial, Cardinal, moveable, Domestical, Four-footed, Southern, and the Exaltation of *Mars*. It signifies,

All Diseases incident to the Knees, either by Strains, or Fractures; it notes Leprosie, the Itch, the Scab.

♒ Is an Aereal, Hot and moist Sign, of the Airy Triplicity; Diurnal, Sanguine, fixed, Rational, Humane, Masculine, the principal House of *Saturn*, wherein he most rejoyceth, Western. In Diseases,

It signifieth all manner of infirmities in the Legs and Ancles, incident to those Members, all melancholick Winds coagulated in the Veins, or disturbing the Blood, Cramp, and the like.

♓ Is of the Watry Triplicity, a Northern, cold Sign, Moist, Phlegmatick, Feminine, Nocturnal, the House of ♃, and exaltation of ♀, a Bicorporeal, Common, or double-bodied Sign, an Idle, Effeminate, sickly Sign, or representing a Party of no action. In Diseases, it signifies,

All Diseases in the Feet, as the Gout, and all Lameness and Aches incident to those Members, and so generally salt Flegms, Scabs, Itch, Botches, Breaking out, Boyls and Ulcers proceeding from Blood putrified, cold and moist Diseases.

Diseases Attributed to the Seven Planets.

Saturn in a Chronical Disease is the Author of such as proceed of Melancholy, as Quartan Agues, Black Jaundies, obstruction of the Spleen, Deafness, Madness proceeding of Melancholy, Palsie, Swimmings in the head, ringings and noise in the Ears, Anorexia, Hyposarca, Gouts, Ptisis, Cruditics, and Flux. In acute Diseases ♄ being the Morbificant Planet, the Disease shall proceed of superabundance of Flegm, and crude Humours, Surfeits, stuffing of the Pipes with Flegm, toughness of the Stomach, a lassitude and weariness in all the Limbs, lothness to speak, the Pulse slow and remiss, all Impediments in the right Ear and Teeth, Leprosies, Rheums, Consumptions, Palsies, Tremblings, vain Fears, Fantasies, Dropsy, the hand and foot-Gout, Apoplexies, Dog-hunger, too much flux of the Hemorrhoids, Ruptures, if in ♍ or ♌, in any ill Aspect with *Venus*: Note ♄ corrupts the Blood by Melancholy, ♂ by Choler.

Jupiter, of Chronical Diseases, signifieth Inflammation of the Lungs, Heat of the Liver, Convulsions, Aposiemations, Flegmons, Itch, Ring-worms, Apoplexy, Arthritis, Headach proceeding of Blood, Spitting of Blood, Passions of the Back-bone, Swelling and Inflammations proceeding of Blood, &c. In Acute Diseases, ♃ being the Morbificant Planet, , be signifieth such as proceed of Blood, as Plurisies, Peripneumonia, Squinances, Inflammations, Pocks, Measels, Plague, continual Fevers, *Synochus putrida*, Distempers of the Liver, starting of the Members, heaviness of the Head, Sleepiness without perfect rest; the Pulse strong and lofty, infirmities of the left Ear, palpitation and trembling of the Heart, Cramps, pain in the Back-bone, all Diseases lying in the Veins or Ribs, and proceeding from corruption of Blood, windiness, all putrefaction in the Blood, or Fevers proceeding from too great abundance thereof.

Mars, of Chronical Diseases, importeth such as proceed or red Choler, hot Apostemations, overflowings of the Gall, Jaundies, Madness, Frenzies, hot Gouts, Exulcerations, Fistulaes, Carbuncles, Fluxes of Blood, breaking of Veins, Agues, Burnings, Vomiting of blood, &c. In Acute Disease, ♂ being the Morbificant Planet, the Disease shall proceed of Choler, as Burning Fevers, Tertians, Cholerick ejections upward and downwards, Jaundies, Inflammations of all the Body, proneness to Anger, great Thirst, redness of the Face, Pestilent burning Fevers, Megrims in the Head, Carbuncles, the Plague, and all Plague-Sores, Ring-worms, Blisters, mad sudden Distempers in the Head, Bloudy-flux, all Wounds and Diseases in mens Genitories, the Stone both in the Reins and Bladder, Scars or small Pox in the Face, all hurts by Iron, the Shingles, and such other Diseases as arise by abundance of Choler, ♂ affects the Gall, and left Ear, the Pulse high and swift.

Sol governeth yellow Choler, butning Fever, Semitertian and Tertian Fevers, Beating and palpitation of the Heart, Swooning, Opthalmia, redness of the Eyes, and blood-shot, but Rheums, Tussis, Catarrh, &c. In Acute Diseases, such as proceed of Choler, like unto *Mars*, but more remiss, Consumptions, Collick, pricking under the Sides, bastard Plurisies, Pimples in the Face, trembling of the vitals, or any Disease of the Brain or Heart, Tympanies, infirmities of the Eyes, Cramps, sudden Swoonings, Diseases of the Mouth, and stinking Breaths, rotten Fevers; principally in Man he governeth the Brain, the Heart, and right

Eye, and Vital spirit; in Women, the left Eye; the Pulse uneven, swift, and intended, &c.

Venus, being the Morbificant Planet of Chronical Diseases, signifies such as proceed from Flegm, as Astmacs, stuffing of the Pipes, the Liver and Stomach with crude Humours, Suffocation of the Matrix, Swellings, *Leucophlegmatia*, pain in the Reins, Gonorrhea's, French Pox, all Diseases of the Matrix, and Members of generation, in the Reins, Belly, Back, Navil, and those parts; any Disease or Distemper arising by inordinate Lust, Priapism, Impotency in Generation, *Hernias*, the *Diabetes*, or pissing Disease. Of Acute Diseases, such as proceed from abundance of Flegm and cold. *Venus* combust signifies Diseases proceeding of Torture, as Agues, Collick, Stone, Pain in the Limbs or Side, Gravel, and loss of Appetite, the Pulse low and remiss, but somewhat intended.

Mercury denoteth Diseases proceeding of mixt Humours, according to whom he is configurated, Distraction of Sense, Madness, all Vertigo's, Lethargy, or Giddiness in the Head, Lightness, or any Disease of the Brain, Ptisick, Stammering, and imperfection in the Tongue, vain and fond Imaginations, all defect in the Memory, Hoarsness, dry Coughs, super-abounding of Spittle, all snaffling and snuffling in the Head or Nose, the hand and foot Gout, Dumbness, Tongue-evil, all evils in the Fancy and Intellectual parts, Suggestions of Evil-spirits, foolish and irrational Conceits, troubled Thoughts, stuffing of the Pipes and organs of Voice, black Jaundies, Wind in the Bowels, lightness of Mind, Deliration, aridity of the Tongue, Swellings in the Legs, Hands and Fingers.

Luna, being the Morbificant Planet, in Chronical Diseases, signifies the Falling-sickness, Apoplexies, Palsies, the Cholick, the Belly-ache, Arthritis, Sciatica, Leucoflegmatia, Worms, Rheums, Lunatick passions, Quotidian Fevers, Diseases proceeding of Oppilations, Retention of Menstrua, and all other Excrements, as Ordure, Urine, and Sweat, and the inordinate evacuation of them; Diseases in the left Side, Stones, the Bladder, and Members of Generation, the Menstrues, and Liver in Women, Dropsies, Fluxes of the Belly, and cold Rheumatick Diseases, cold Stomach, the Gout in the Wrists and Feet, Sciatica, Rheums or Hurts in the

Eyes, *viz.* in the left of Men, and the Right of Women, Surfeits, rotten Coughs, Convulsion-fits, Kings-evil, Apostemes, Small Pox, and Measels. In Acute Diseases, the Moon prognosticateth such as proceed of Watry Humours, Citrine Water, and Salt Flegm, for the most part with Swellings and Breakings out, annexed with Heat and Inflammation, Drought and appetite of Drink,

In young Maidens, the ☽ being the Morbificant Planet, in Chornical Diseases signifieth the Green sickness; in old Women, Passions of the Matrix, the Mother, and such like.

    Now having briefly (yet fully) shewed what manner of Infirmities are most usually attributed to the 7 Planets; yet here is to be noted, that many of these, and divers others of like nature and condition, may happen, as well under any other Planet, as the same Planet they are here attributed unto, the Causes that produce them being divers; therefore the surest ground is not altogether to depend upon Astrology in the investigation of the Disease, but also to require the help of Pathologial mean, and the Disease once found, the Morbificant Planet will assuredly, without fail, demonstrate the true Cause of the Disease, and of what Humour it proceedeth, far more directly than any Urine, Pulse, or Excrement whatsoever; and this is the true Scope herein, not to rely only upon this Art to find out the Disease, but the true Cause thereof, which being removed, or taken away, the effect will also cease; *nam sublatâ Causa deficit Effecius.*

In the next place we shall briefly (yet fully) Treat of the Crisis in Diseases, as being a principal Subject Relating to this Treatise: And first what Crisis signifies.

    Crisis is no other thing, than a Duel or Contention betwixt Nature and the Infirmity; if Nature at the time of the Crisis overcome the Malignity of the Disease, it's a good *Crisis*; if the Sickness prevail, it's a pernicious and ill *Crisis*. Or,

    Crisis is no more than this, *viz.* a sudden alteration of mans body when he is sick, tending either to health, or further sickness; for when this *Crisis* is, there's a sharp fight, as it were, betwixt Nature and the Disease, whether of them shall overcome.

Days Critical, Decretory, and Crismal are all one, and intend no more than a certain and more sure Judgment of the Infirmity afflicting, either more powerfully, or in a less measure, at those time when the true *Crisis* is.

The true *Crisis* is best of all taken from that Moment of time when first the sickness invaded the infirm; which if it cannot be had, then it may be taken (but not so certainly) from the very hour when first the water is brought to the Physician to advise for recovery; but if no Urine come, then when the Doctor, first speaks with the sick Party, and is demanded by the infirmed what he thinks of his sickness, and what course he would advise for cure thereof.

Every sudden and vehement motion of the Disease, may be called a *Crisis*, or it is not a local motion altogether, but an alteration of the Disease.

Or Crisis imports Judgment in the Disease afflicting, and which way it will terminate, *viz.* for good or evil; and according to *Avicen*, *Crysis et velox motus morbi ad salutem bel ad mortem.*

Next how the true Crisis may be found; or the Hour, Day, Month, or Year, in which the Disease may be perfectly judged.

The true *Crisis* is the time in which the Disease is most intended, insomuch that the Part either dyeth at that instant, or the Disease at that time imports Death; or from that time forwards amendeth, and hath the symptomes alleviated: and how to find this same time there are many opinions among *Physicians* and *Astrologians*, but all of these that ever I could yet read of, are full of ambiguity and uncertainty, and many times swerving from the truth, partly, and oft times wholly; as those that observe the *Hora decubitus*, and from thence account the 7th day as Critical; or those that think they come nearer to the mark (as I my self did sometimes think, although long experience proveth both to be far distant) which observe the time the Moon cometh to a Quartile Aspect of the place she passed under at the *decubitus*; for although the *Crisis* sometimes doth happen upon the same times, yet it is doubtful or uncertain whether it be upon the next 7th day, or the 14th, or the 21st, or the 28th day, &c. or at the time the ☽ cometh next to aspect the place she possessed at the *Hora decubitûs*, either by a □ or ☍, &c. which cometh nearest to the truth of any former given Rule, and for which I shall annex a Table at the end of this Discourse, to find the true time according to the motion of the *Moon* and *Sun*, &c. Yet sometimes the *Crisis* happeneth upon none of these times, whereby it appeareth, that these Observations are uncertain, and not to be depended upon; therefore he that would be more perfectly resolved concerning this main point, let him give ear to these our *New* refined Principles and Grounds; the which by Gods Aid and Assitance, and many painful Observations, we have proved, and found to be of such truth, that I cannot choose but admire the wonderful Providence of Almighty God herein, which sweetly disposeth all things in *Numero, Pondere, & Mensura*, prescribing to the whole œconomy of Nature, such a *Law, Order*, and *Dependency*, that it were easier for Heaven and Earth to annihilate and turn to nothing than to break or infringe the same, unless it shall please his Divine Majesty, miraculously, at his Will and Pleasure to command it any new kind of Service; but yet for all this, neither I, nor any man else, is able to give any such Rules that shall never fail: although I dare boldly affirm, that the like for verity in all respects are not to be found: for howbeit I am assured, that there is *in rerum natura, lex, & immutabilis ordo*, yet with *Solomon* I must confess, that *omnium Operum Dei, nullus possit bomo invenire rationem*. Admit that *Natura sit vera, Ars vera, yet raro verus Artifex*, a true Artist rarely found: therefore to come to the matter; He that would be certified when the *Crisis* shall happen, let him observe whether the Lord of the Ascendant doth apply to the corporal Conjunction □ or ☍ of any Planet, *per applicationem communem*, or no; and if he apply to more than one, look to which of them he is nearest, and then count how many Degrees of Longitude are between them, and for every Degree add so many Days, Weeks, Months, or Years, to the time the Disease was first related to thee, or to the time the Urine was first brought unto you, and you shall have the time exactly in which there will be a *Crisis* of the Infirmity; yet here is to be noted, that when the

Disease is mortal, that neither ♃, ♀, ☿, nor the ☽, are able to make a perfect *Crisis*, although they do in some respect *Crisisie*, as I have seen by experience; for the Lord of the Ascendant at such time coming to any of these by deduction aforesaid, will at that instant intend the Disease, and afterwards the Party shall for a time seem to amend, and the symptomes of his Disease abate, and yet for all that, at the next Crisisication with ♄, ♂, or the ☉, the Party shall dye; and you shall here understand, that the Lord of the Ascendant doth not only shew the time of the Crysis, in manner aforesaid, by the distance from some other Planet *per applicationem communem*, but also *per separationem communem*; when he shall be elongated from a ☌ □ or ☍ Corporal, the space of the semidiameter of his Beams, or of the afflicting Planets, and for every degree he lacketh of that distance, add as before so many Days, Weeks, Month, or Years. Some Astrologians have curiously taken upon them to determinate the time of the *Crisis* in manner following, *viz*. If the Significators be in a moveable Sign, for every degree of longitude they add a day; in a common Sign a week, and in a fixed Sign a month, or a year; others in Angles, a day, in Succedant Houses a week, and in Cadent a month or year. But how vain and superstitious these Observations are, daily experience teacheth. And although I dare not warrant at all times this Rule following to be currant, yet for the most part I have found it true, and very seldome otherwise; that is, to look whether the Disease be *Acute* or *Chronical*, (I term them *acute*, which be *quick* Diseases, and have had no long time before in breeding; and them I term *Chronical* which be long and inveterate;) if the Disease be acute, then for every degree add a day; if chronical, a week, a month, and sometimes a year.

Let the Reader take notice, that there are Acute and Chronicle Diseases. Of Acute Diseases, some are simple Acute, others Peracute, *id est*, very Acute, others are Perperacute, or exceeding Acute. Those which are simple Acute, are finished in 8, 10, 11, 14, 20, or 21 dayes, they are terminated in the time the Moon traceth the 12 Cœlestial Signs of the *Zodiack*, which is in 27 dayes; some odd hours and minutes.

Those acute Diseases which suffer changes, are very fickle; for sometimes they increase, sometimes they are remitted, according as the Lord of the Ascendant or (according to others) as the Moon, meets with the beams either of good or evil Planets; and sometimes they change out of acute Diseases into chronick Diseases, and so a continued Fever may change into a Hectick Fever; and these Diseases terminate in forty dayes.

Very acute Diseases are such as terminate and are concluded in 5, 6, 7, or 8 dayes; amongst which is the Disease called *Peripneumonis*, an inflammation of the Lungs.

Exceeding acute Diseases are such as end in three or four dayes at farthest, as Pestilences, Apoplexies, &c.

Chronick Diseases follow the motion of the Sun, and 'tis about ninety dayes before the first *Crisis* appears, for in that time the Sun comes to the proper Quartil of the place he was in at the Decumbiture, as appears in Hectick Fevers, Dropsies, and the like; but when he comes to those Degrees from the Decumbiture, which are called Judicative, or Intercidental, which are both one, or Judicial, (as shall be seen in the Table following) some motion appears, whereby a man may judge of the *Crisis* to come. It falls out well, if the Sun be well aspected by good Planets; and werse, if by evil Planets; and this holds true, if you consider it from the nativity, throughout all the whole course of a mans Life: for Diseases are particular attendants on a mans Life.

Moreover, of the *Crisis*, some are perfect, some are imperfect; A perfect *Crisis* is when the Disease appears plain and intirely, and perfectly to be judged of, and this is sometimes hopeful, sometimes desperate; Hopeful, when there is a great probability of Health and Recovery; Desperate, when there are palpable signs of Death.

An imperfect Crisis, is, when the Disease is changed upon every light occasion; as if *Mars* be author of the Disease, and in a double-bodied Sign, without fail the Crisis is variable.

That Crisis is safe, which comes without great pernicious Aspects.

It is doubtful and dangerous, which comes with great pernicious Aspects. The Disease is fit to be judged, when signs of

Concoction come the fourth day, and then certainly the Crisis will appear the ninth; the ☽ moves not upon an equal motion, therefore it's safer to trust to her motion, rather than to the tradition of days, for herein is a great error, by reason of the inequality of the Moons motion; for, according to the best extant opinions, the Sun hath dominion in Chronick Diseases, (as is said before) and the Moon ion Acute; and therefore I have spoken to this end to them. It is the motion of the Sun and Moon, and Lord of the Ascendant, that produce the Crisis, and not the number of dayes, &c.

When any notable Disease comes, if you would discern whether it tends to Health, Death, Mutation, or continuance, it is necessary that you begin at the first punct of time of the invasion of the Disease. This *Galen* saith is very hard, if not impossible to find; 'tis taken *pro confesso*, that it may be easily known when a man takes his bed in his sickness, but when the beginning of the sickness is, that's the Question; for a lusty Body bears the Disease longer, and is longer before it submits to take Bed, than a weak, infirm, sickly Body; a meer suspition of Disease will send a fainthearted person to bed, you may perswade him he is sick, though otherwise. But the true time to be taken for the beginning of the Disease, is that in which a man finds a manifest pain or hurt in his Body; for instance, when a man hath got a Fever, usually the head akes certain days before; this is not the Fever, but a messenger, or fore-runner of the Fever; the true beginning of the Fever is, when the Disease appears sensibly, or when a horrour or trembling invades the sick, as does usually in the beginning of a Fever; this is the beginning of the Disease, when the Disease appears manifest to sense; and this was the Judgment of *Hippocrates*, the best of Physicians. And you shall find this always, that the more acute the Disease is, the more manifest the beginning of it is to sense, yea so manifest, that it is almost impossible, that the beginning should lye hid from any one, though he want Reason, if he have but Sense; but if it should so fall out that you cannot take a beginning from the first invasion of the Disease, then take your ground from that very time the Parties Urine was first brought, or the time when first they consulted with the Physician about the Disease and cure, and account that the first *Crisis*.

Now the time called *Critical* is always evil, because of the contrariety of the Sign the Moon is in then, to the Sign she was in before, or the contrariety of her nature to the opposite place, at such a time there ariseth a controversy and contest between the Disease and Nature; the Moon maintains Nature in Acute diseases, and hence is the reason, that if she be afflicted upon a Critical day, by the Bodies or ill Beams of ♄ or ♂, or the Lord of the House of Death, (which is always Lord of the eighth House, and sometimes Lord of the fourth House, if he be a Malevolent, because he signifies the grave) the Disease increaseth, and sometimes the Sick dyes, but if the Moon at the time of *Crisis* behold the Lord of the Ascendant, or the Fortunes fortunately, Health ensues; for the malady is vanquished, and overcome in the conflict.

If the Disease terminate not upon the first *Crisis*, see how the Moon is configurated on the second *Crisis*, and judge then by the same Rules, &c.

If it terminate not then neither, as sometimes such a thing happens, view the third *Crisis*, and judge by that the same way; if your Jundgment, ballanced by Reason and the former Rules, certifie you that the Disease will not end, one way nor other, neither in Health nor Death; see what you can say when the Moon returns to the place she was in at the Decumbiture, which is about twenty seven days, eight hours, and some minutes, and see how the Moon is then seated and affected, and to what Planets she is configurated then: and this of necessity must be the end of all Acute diseases.

Thus you see an Acute disease can last but a Month at longest, not one in a hundred lasteth so long; nor one in twenty lasteth above half so long.

If the Disease end not then, the Acute disease is turn'd into a Chronick disease;' and all Chronick diseases must be judged of by the Sun: the Rules of Judging of Chronical diseases by the Sun, are the same by which we judge of Acute diseases by the Moon.

Now to come to the matter and conclusion of this Subject, you must know, that the times considerable in Diseases are three principally; the principal is the *Crisis*, or Critical day,. which is when the ☽ hath gone 90 degrees from her place at the decumbiture, or last *Crisis*; and this is so called because then Nature will manifest what the Disease is; and at this time it will assuredly be more fully discerned in one kind or other, for good or bad, according to the Aspects the Moon applies to, as hath bee said. The next time is called *Indicial*, which is half a *Chrysis, viz.* the motion of 45 degrees, at what time the Disease doth more or less manifest it self, according as the ☽ is aspected, which prognosticates a good or bad *Chrysis* to ensue.

The third denomination of time, in reference to critical Observation, is called *Indicative*, wherein the Physician may expect Indications how the Disease will shew it self. This by some is called Intercidental: upon these intercidental and indicative dayes, the Disease is usually remitted and mitigated.

Now for right distinction and calculation of Time, observe in what degree of the *Zodiack* the ☽ was at the decumbiture, and to that degree add 22 degrees and 30 minutes, which is half the time between the Crisis and Indicial time, and this shews (when the Moon comes to that degree) the first Indicative, or intercidental time; then to this former time add 22 degrees 30 minutes more, and that makes the Indicial time; to which, when the Moon comes, it is accounted a Judicial day; which is when the ☽ is gone 45 degrees or half a Quadrat from the first Crisis; then to this last Indicial time add 22 degrees, 30 minutes more, which makes 67 deg. 30 min. from the first Crisis; and this is the second Indicative day, or Intercidental time, as falling between the Crisis and Judicial day; to which again add 22 degrees 30 minute more, and you have the first perfect Crisis from the decumbiture, *viz.* 90 degrees; and adding 22 degrees 30 minutes more, makes the next Judicative day, when the ☽ comes to it, and so on through the whole *Zodiack*, and over it again, if the Disease Terminate not in that time, as will plainly appear by the following Table, in a familiar Example, when the ☽ comes to an Indicative, or Intercidental time, when to a Judicial day, a semiquadrat, or half a

Crisis, and when to a true □, and when to an ☍, which is called a full Crisis, and so to all the Indicative and Judicial days during the Sickness, &c. as for Example; Let the true place of the ☽ at the decumbiture, and beginning of the Disease, be supposed to be 15 degrees, 44 minutes of ♊, and because 44 minutes almost make one degree, I enter with 16 degrees under the Sign ♊, in the 4th Column, so that 16 degrees of *Gemini* is my *Radix*, or true place of the ☽, over against 16 degrees, to the right hand, I find 8, 30, over the head thereof ♋; so that when the Moon came to 8 degr. and 30 min. of ♋, it was the first Indicative, or Intercidental day, wherein the Physician might expect how the Disease would shew it self; upon every Crisis, or Indicative day, have consideration with what Planet the Moon is in Configuration; if with a benevolent, expect some remisness in the Disease, if with a malevolent, a bad indication.

Next on the right hand to 8, 30 of ♋, you find 1 ♌; *viz.* when the ☽ comes to the first degree of ♌, she was then in semiquadrate to her first place; and this is as if it were half a Crisis, at what time the Disease might more or less manifest it self, according to that Aspect the ☽ found at her being in that first degree of *Leo*; in the next Column on the right hand you see 23, 30, over it ♌; it was a second Indicative day, whereby the Physician might further judge of the increase or decrease of the Disease: in the next Column you find 16, over it ♍, when the ☽ came to the 16th degree of *Virgo*, there was then a true Crisis, at what time the Disease assuredly might be more fully discerned in one kind or other, and then according to the Aspects, the ☽ in that degree had to the Planets, good or ill, so might the Patient or Physician expect a better or worse Crisis: and so in the same continued line or Column you run round the Heavens, ever observing the ☽ her coming to those places of the *Zodiack* wherein she makes the Indicative, Indicial, or Critical day, and what Planet or Planets she is then in Aspect with, and whether in the figure they promise good or ill; besides this you shall observe, what dayes she, or the Lord of the Ascendant transits the Cusp of the sixth, seventh, and eighth Houses, and how then she is aspected of the benevolent or ill Planets; and observe, if she be combust, or in *via combusta*, which is from the 20ᵗʰ degr. of ♊ to the first of ♋, in the North part of the *Zodiack*; and in the South from the 6ᵗʰ degr. of ♐ to the 16ᵗʰ of the same, and from the 24ᵗʰ of ♐ to the fifth of ♑, or in ☌, □, or ☍ of ♄ or ♂, or of a Combust Planet, or of some hurtful fixed Star, of malignant nature, it is evil, and a sign of death or of long sickness, &c.

And note, whatsoever the Moon doth work in Acute and sharp Diseases by Critical dayes, Indicatives, and Intercidents, in 27 dayes and 8 hours, the same is to be accounted in Chronical distempers, by the yearly motion of the Sun; when the Sun comes to the □, or ☍ of the place in which he was at the beginning of the Disease; therefore mark all the Aspects of the Sun to that Degree, and of the Moon, as aforesaid, &c.

Critical degrees from the place first are	*The Indicial Degrees are half the Critical, as*	*The intercidents or Indicative are half the Judicial, as*	
		deg.	min.
□ 90	45		
☍ 180	135	22	30
□ 270	225	112	30
☍ 360		202	30
		292	30

Of Judgment.

These are carefully to be considered before you give any Judgment;

First, That you make your Prayer to Almighty God, that he would give you the grace that you may most faithfully perform that which you take in hand, to his Glory and to your own Credit.

Secondly, If thou findest the Cusp of the Ascendant to fall in the very latter end of a Sign, or the beginning, as it were, between two Signs; then doubtless the Quærent comes but to tempt thee.

Thirdly, If the Question be not Radical, that is, if the Lord of the Ascendant, or the Lord of the Hour be not of one Triplicity, this signifies the carelessness of the Quærent, and that he cares not whether you hit or miss. Therefore thy Figure thus found, proceed no farther to any Judgment, unless it were Radical; which being so, it noteth an universal desire in the Quærent to be resolved in the Question propounded.

Fourthly, You ought not to erect a Scheme for your self, but it is more proper to commit it to another, lest you flatter your self in choice of your Ascendant, or the like.

Fifthly, Consider the place of the Moon, whom if you find in the end of a Sign, chiefly in a common Sign, in a double-bodied Sign, or a moveable Sign, then I wish thee to take heed to thy self, and to be very wise and careful what communication of Speech you do use with the Quærent, for doubtless he comes of malice to tempt thee, that he may find some occasion to do thee villany.

Sixthly, If the Ascendant and his Lord, and the seventh House and his Lord be afflicted, deferr that business at that time, for fear lest thou receive some blame for thy labour, or else shame for thy false Judgment.

Seventhly, If thou presume to give Judgment, not being skilful therein.

Eighthly, If thou be affectionate to the Quærent, whereby thou art loth the truth should be delivered: for as *Ptolomæus* worthily saith, Love or Hatred do wrest a man from the truth; for where Love is there if Favour (oftimes) in Judgment, many times making the matter better than it is; and if Hatred, then he will discourage the Quærent more than need is.

Ninthly, If the Quærent come to thee in the Hour of ♄, or ♂, or if the Dragons tayl be in the Ascendant, or with the Moon, or the Moon be in *Scorpio*, then there will be Lying on all sides; or if the Lord of the 6th, 7th, 8th, or 10th Houses, be Lord of the Hour, or the Lord of the Hour in those Houses, or Combust, or Retrograde, I counsel thee not to meddle therewith.

That Sickness that shall happen the Moon being in that place of the figure or degree wherein a Malevolent Planet was in the time of his Nativity, it is most dangerous; if in a □, or ☍, it will prove a most dangerous infirmity; but if she be in the place of a Benevolent Planet, or in good Aspect, then the sick Party is nothing to be feared at all; if the Radical Ascendant of the Sick do behold the Ascendant of the time wherein the sick Person began to be sick, or evil at ease, the Patient will be in great danger, or if they be in a □ or ☍ Aspect.

The Patient shall be in great danger by the means of the Physician, if the Sick have or had ♃ or ♀ in those degrees wherein the Physician had or hath ♄ or ♂ in their Nativities; if in a □ or ☍ very hurtful, but not evil as in Conjunction, for that and Opposition are the worst.

The Physician shall be right welcome to that Patient whose Ascendants or Lords do agree, or be in any good Aspects together, or if the Luminaries be in any good Aspect together, or if the Lights of the one do behold the Lights of the other with a favourable Aspect; or if the Lights of the one do behold the Ascendant, or the Lord of the other, with any friendly and amicable Aspect.

When thou shalt find the seventh House, or the Lord thereof afflicted with ♄ or♂ being therein, or beholding it with a □ or ☍, change thy Physician, for he shall do no good, but be crafty in his Actions and Judgment, and to thee unfortunate.

But if thou find ♃ or ♀ in the seventh House, or in any good Aspect with the House, or with the Lord thereof, then refuse not in any wise the help of the Physician, for he shall by Gods help Cure thee, to Gods Glory, and his Credit.

The Physician ought to take heed that he visit not the Sick in the hours of ♄ or ♂, or in the hour of the Planet that was Lord of the 8th House at his Nativity; as for Example: if in the hour of ♄, the Physician shall be blamed for being too slow or negligent; if in the hour of *Mars*, great brawling and strife shall happen between the Patient and the Physician, with small gain to the Physician. The hours of ♃ and ♀ are greatly commended of the Learned: the ☉, ☿, and the ☽ are accounted indifferent, except they be proper Significators of Sickness or Death. The ☽ within four or five degrees of the ☊ or ☋ in Conjunction, signifieth Death to the Sick. If good Planets be in the Ascendant, the sick Party shall be easily ruled, and the Physician and those that be about him shall be right-willing to do him good; chiefly, if they be not combust or Retrograde; but if any evil Planet be there, then judge the contrary, both to the Physician and the rest about the sick Person; for the Sick shall be forward and unruly: if in the tenth House there be any evil Planet, the Medicine shall not profit the Sick; and let the Physician do what he can for his life, yet he shall receive great blame of the common sort of people.

If the first House and the sixth House belong both to one Planet, or the Lord of the House where the Lord of the 6th House shall be found, he shall be the occasion of his own Sickness or Infirmity; if the first and eighth House, he shall be the cause, or will procure his own death; if the Ascendant and the Moon be unfortunated, and their Lords free, the Patient is sick in his Body, and quiet in mind; but if the ☽ and the Ascendant be fortunate, and their Lords unfortunate, then the sick Party is greatly vexed or grieved in his mind, and not sick in his Body; but if the Moon, and the Ascendant, and their Lords be afflicted, then he is sick both in Body and in Mind; or if a fortunate Planet do behold the Ascendant and not the Moon, he is sick in mind and not in Body; and if the Moon only, and not the Ascendant, then the contrary. The Lord of the 6th House in the Ascendant or 8th House, it sheweth that the Disease is easy to be known, and in the 7th or fourth House, then it is hard to be known of what kind it is: and in the 9th, or 11th House, the Infirmity is to be known, and in the other Houses hardly to be known.

Ganivettus, in his *Amicus Medicorum*, affirms, that the Ascendant and his Lord, and the Lord of the House where he shall be found, are to be given to the Sick, the 10th House and his Lord to the Physician, the fourth House and his Lord to the Medicines, and those that are about the Sick as Helpers. The 6th House, and his Lord, and the Lord of the House that he is in, but the Moon must herein be considered. The 6th House doth signifies the Disease, and the Cause thereof; as for example: if a Terrene Sign be upon the 6th, then he took his Distemper of Cold, and look where the Lord thereof is, and the Moon, and such are the peccant Humours; and for the Air, Water, or Fire, if the 6th House be afflicted with any Malevolent Star, or if the Lord thereof be afflicted in any sort, so judge of the Humours, and look to the fourth House from the 6th House; for it hath a secret Signification of the end of a particular Disease. In like manner, forget not this, that in any Question whatsoever, if you find the Lord of the Ascendant, not to be in the Ascendant, neither to behold it; then he is not to be accounted as Lord, but the Lord of the Exaltation is to e reckoned as Lord, if he do behold it; if not, then the Lord of the Triplicity; if not he, then the Lord of the Term; if not he, then see if the Lord of the Hour, chiefly if he have any authority in the Ascendant, then he is to be accounted as Lord of the Ascendant.

Not this, that the Lord of the Hour is to be reckoned in as full power as is the Lord of the Ascendant, if he be not Retrograde, nor Combust, and such like.

Hermes says in his 88 Aphorism, *Erit impedimentum circa illam partem corporis quam significat signum quod suerit Nativitatis tempore impedimentum:* There will be some impediment in or near that part of the Body which is signified by the Sign that shall be afflicted at the time of the Birth. The use of all comes to thus much:

That if you would know where any Disease is, I mean, in what part of the Body, see in what Sign the Significator of the sick Party is, and what part of mans Body that Planet signifies in that Sign, which you may do by the ensuing Table, in that Member or part of the Body shall you say the sick Party is grieved or diseased.

A Table shewing what Members in Mans Body every Planet signifieth in any of the Twelve Signes.

	♄	♃	♂	☉	♀	☿	☽
♈	Breast Arm	Neck Throat Heart Belly	Belly Head	Thighs	Reins Feet	Secrets Legs	Knees Head
♉	Heart Breast Belly	Shoulders Arms Belly Neck	Reins Throat	Knees	Secrets Head	Thighs Feet	Legs Throat
♊	Belly Heart	Breast Reins Secrets	Secrets Arms Breast	Leggs Ancles	Thighs Throat	Knees Head	Feet Shoulders Arms Thighs
♋	Reins Belly Secrets	Heart Secrets Thighs	Breast Thighs	Feet	Knees Shoulders Arms	Legs Throat Eyes	Head Breast Stomach
♌	Secrets Reins	Belly Thighs Knees	Knees Heart Belly	Head	Legs Breast Heart	Feet Arms Shoulders Throat	Throat Stomach Heart
♍	Thighs Secrets Feet	Reins Knees	Legs Belly	Throat	Feet Stomach Heart Belly	Head Breast Heart	Arms Shoulders Bowels
♎	Knees Thighs	Secrets Legs Head Eyes	Feet Reins Secrets	Shoulders Arms	Head Small-guts.	Throat Heart Stomach Belly	Breast Reins Heart Belly
♏	Knees Legs	Thighs Feet	Head Secrets Arms Thighs	Breast Heart	Throat Reins Secrets	Shoulders Arms Bowels Back	Stomach Heart Secrets Belly
♐	Legs Feet	Knees Head Thighs	Throat Thighs Heads Feet	Heart Belly	Shoulders Arms Secrets Thighs	Breast Reins Heart Secrets	Bowels Thighs Back
♑	Head Feet	Legs Neck Eyes Knees	Arms Shoulders Knees Leggs	Belly Back	Breast Heart Thighs	Stomach Heart Secrets	Reins Knees Thighs
♒	Neck Head	Feet Arms Shoulders Breast	Breast Legs Heart	Reins Secrets	Heart Knees	Bowels Thighs Heart	Secrets Legs Ancles
♓	Arms Shoulders Neck	Head Breast Heart	Heart Feet Belly Ancles	Secrets Thighs	Belly Legs Neck Throat	Reins Knees Secrets Thighs	Thighs Feet

As if ♄ be Significator of the sick Party, and (at the time of your Question) in ♊, have recourse to your Table, and you see ♄

in ♊ signifieth a Disease in the Belly, or Heart, &c. Do so in the rest.

And this is to be noted, that look what Planet the Moon separated from last, so judge of the Infirmity in his beginning; and whomsoever she is conjoyned withall; so judge of the present state thereof; and look who she doth apply to, so judge of the end.

Life and Death.

The Moon moving from the ✶ of the Lord of the Ascendant to the ☌ of the ☉ Lord of the 8th House, must prognosticate Death; and being Combust, doth much augment the evil whereupon Death must needs follow; and the rather, if the Lord of the 6th House be Retrograde, and behold the 7th House by a □ Aspect.

Though the ☽ be in the 8th House with the Lord of the Ascendant, and beholding 3 or 4 Planets more, the Party will escape; for this is a general Rule, The ☽ beholding 3 or 4 Planets, whether good or bad, or with what Aspect soever, it betokeneth Life.

The ☽ separating her self from the Lord of the Ascendant, and applying, to the Lord of the 8th House, sheweth Death; so doth the Lord of the Ascendant in applying to the Lord of the 8th House. If ♃ be Significator with ♂, and ♂ in Application to the ☍ of ♄, it is a tedious lingring Sickness; for this is always a general Rule, that if the ☽ or any Planet be in the end of any Sign, it is to be accounted as in the next Sign.

The ☽ being in the Ascendant in ♓, and separates her self from a friendly Aspect of ♃ Lord of the Ascendant, and applies her self to a good Aspect of ♂ in the 6th House, and Lord of the 8th House, and then shortly after beholds with a Malignant Aspect, must needs signifie Death, though the first was a Trine; for this is always a general Rule, that the ☉, the Moon, and the Almuten of the Ascendant, are Significators of Life.

The Moon in the 4th House in ♌, afflicted by the ☉, and ♂, *Mars* being in the 6th House, signifies Death. This is a general Rule, the ☽ in the 4th House in ♌, ill affected, declares Death.

Mercury Lord of the 8th House, the Moon also combust, betokeneth Death. *Ganivettus* giveth it for a general Rule, that the Lord of the Ascendant in the 8th House, or in any of the Houses of ♄ or ♂, or chiefly beholding them with any ill Aspect, it denounces Death.

♃ in the 8th House, Lord of the Ascendant, and ☽, the Moon separating therefrom, and applying to ♂, betokeneth Death; for it is held a general rule, the Lord of the Ascendant in the 8th House, beholding ♄ or ♂ with any Aspect, though it be by translation, signifies Death.

The ☉ being Lord of the Ascendant, and unfortunately placed in the 8th House, and beholding ♄, though but by translation of Rayes, it signifies Death, and if *pars mortis* be within 3 degrees of the Ascendant, aspected by ♄ and ♂, by ☍ or □, if either be Lord of the 4th House, he will not linger above three dayes.

☽ in ♏ being the Ascendant, the Sun Lord of the hour in the 8th House, ♄ Lord of the 4th in the 3d, ☽, ♂ Lord of the first and 6th Houses, aspecting ♄ or the Sun, the Party is cause of his own death, by unseasonable drinking, or drinking at a Pond.

This is held for a general Rule, that the Moon within 5 degrees of the 4th House, is a testimony of Death, and so is ♄ in the third House, ☽, and beholding ☿ by opposition.

The Moon Lady of the Ascendant, placed in the fourth, applying to a ♂ with a Retrograde Planet, though ♃, if ♄ be Lord of the 8th House, and in the 10th from the 8th, and the terms of ♄ ascend, it signifies Death.

The ☽ being in □ to *Cauda Draconis*, doth signifie Death, unless it e a Critical day, then it is not death, but a vehement vexing, in a most horrible sort, of the Patient; neither is her ♂ or ☍ with ☊ or ☋ in a Critical day, a Judgment of Death, but a grievous vexing of the Patient, especially in the Head, Breast, and Heart.

The ☽ in ♏ in the 10th House, being in Aspect with ♄, ♃, ♂, and the ☉, shews the Patient to escape Death but yet shall vomit much Blood, and corrupt Matter, which shall endanger the sight.

The ☽ being in the 8th House, removed one degree from the ☉ at the Parties falling sick, doth signifie a sore time of Sickness, for a Months space, but not Death, though she be in the 8th House; for her Separation is nothing so noxious in any Distemper as the Application.

The ☽ in *Scorpio* in the 4th, beholding ♂ with a □ in ♌, and opposing the ☉, ♀, and ☿ in the 10th, causeth Blood greatly to abound in the Face; yet after vomiting of Blood the Party will escape.

Mar afflicting the ☽ by a □ or ☍, and ☿ being], and combust in the 4th House from the 8th, it signifies the party to become frenzy, and especially if the ☽ be within 5 degrees of ☊ or ☋, in the 4th from the 8th, or 4th from the 7th House, it signifies Death: for this is a general Rule, that the ☽ at the decumbiture, within 5 degrees of ☊ or ☋, portends Death.

The ☽ in ♉, with the Pleiades in the 8th House, (though Aspected with any Planets, good or bad) it is a shrewd sign of Death, and the Patient to be troubled with many Fancies and fears.

A general Rule, if ♄ be within 5 degrees of the Ascendant, and Combust, it intimates Death; and ☿ in like manner signifies Death.

It's very necessary in this manner of Judgment, that you always have respect unto the Question; for if the Question come direct, that the Party sick did send, or was acquainted with the coming of the Messenger, or Urine, then ought you always to have respect to the Ascendant, the Lord thereof, to the Moon, to the 8th House, and Lord thereof; as thus, for brevity sake, some Examples in our own experience.

The Lord of the Ascendant in the 4th or 8th, not too far remote, as viz. not above five degrees from the Cusps of the Houses, and being in his fall or detriment, denotes Death; if the Party do escape, it will be very hardly; if the ☽ withall aspect the 8th, or his Lord, or be in the 8th not remote, it is Death without doubt.

The Lord of the Ascendant in Combustion, or *sub radiis* of the ☉, signifies Death, whether Applying or Separating;

especially if the ☽ be ill affected, or do Apply to the Lord of the 8th, or be in the 8th.

The Lord of the Ascendant Cadent, Angular, Aspecting the 8th House, or his Lord, and the ☽ evil-affected, it is Death.

The Lord of the Ascendant, and Lord of the 8th both one Planet, and beholding the 8th House by any Aspect, being Cadent, and afflicted by ♄ or ♂, and the ☽ ill aspected, it is Death without doubt.

The Lord of the Ascendant, and Lord of the 8th House both in one Sign, both Combust, and both in a Cadent House, the Moon applying to the Lord of the 6th or 8th, it is Death.

The Lord of the Ascendant and the ☽, if both behold the 8th House and Lord thereof, it is Death.

The Lord of the Ascendant and Lord of the 6th, both Combust or Retrograde, aspecting the 8th House, or the ☽ ill-aspected withall, it is Death.

But always have regard to the Lord of the Ascendant, and the Moon, and see in what state they be, and in what place of the Heavens, and how they do behold the 8th House, and Lord thereof, for thereafter shall the Judgment of Death be.

Pars Mortis, or the part of Death, is taken by day from ♃ to ♄, and projected from the Ascendant in the same manner the part of Fortune is taken, from the Sun to the Moon; of this I think few are ignorant.

And also, whereas you may desire to know where the Ascendant shall be taken, when the Father or Mother do make the Question for their Son or Daughter, without consent of the Sick, This you shall observe after our Experience in such a case:
The 4th House shall be the Ascendant for the Quærent, and for the Urine.
The first House and Lord thereof, shall be the Ascendant for the Son or Daughter sick.
The 12th House and the 8th shall be for death.
The 10th House for the Infirmity, whether long or short, or no.
The 9th House and Lord thereof for the Liver.

In such a case you must have always a double consideration, that is to say, to take the Ascendant of the Figure, and of the Question for Life, and note how their Lords be aspected to the 8th House of the Question, and of the Figure, and their Lords, and how the Moon doth behold them; and so in all other Questions, where the Question comes without consent of the Sick.

The ☽ in ☌ or Aspect of the Lord of the 12th House, the Lord of the Ascendant in ☌ or Aspect of the Lord of the 12th, the Lord of the Hour in ☌ or Aspect of the Lord of the 12th; any of these in the 12th in ☌ with ♄ or ♂, then it is a shrewd sign the party is bewitched, or fore-spoken, or hurt by some ill Person or Spirit.

If the Lord of the Ascendant, the Moon, or Lord of the Hour be in ☌, □, or ☍ of the Lord of the 10th House, and neither of them Lord of the sixth House, then the Finger of God is on the Party, and the Distemper is supernatural.

If the Lord of the Ascendant be in the 6th, or the ☽ or Lord of the Hour be in the sixth House, the Party is cause of his own Disease, by Surfeit of ill Diet.

If the Lord of the 6th be in the Ascendant, or the Lord of the Ascendant in the 6th, or in ☌, □, or ☍ with the Lord of the sixth, the Sickness is natural. If the Lord of the Ascendant, the Lord of the Hour, or the ☽ do apply to the Lord of the 6th, the Disease is not at the highest.

Take heed in Administring Physick, that the Lord of the 6th House be not in the 12, 3, or 9 Houses, or within 5 degrees of any of them; because the Physician will be slighted, and the Medicine appear loathsome.

Take heed also, that the Lord of the sixth House be not in the Ascendant, the 10, 6, 4, 7, 5, or 11th Houses, nor that the ☽ apply to the Lord of the 6th House.

As before I have written, so it resteth yet to proceed for to shew more at large whether the Sick be likely to live or dye upon the Question made; for if he be like to live, then may you with comfort give Physick, but the first thing that belongs thereto is, to give him counsel to repent him of his sins before committed, and call to God for Mercy and Grace, and that he would forsake the World, and rely only on the Mercy of Jesus Christ; not perswading through vain hope to live, knowing that we must all dye, and we know not how soon, except God give us knowledge by such as he hath chosen and appointed to be Judiciaries of Sickness and Diseases, and of Life and Death: as Physicians skilful in the motion of the Heavens, and courses of Natural causes, seeing the ends and effects thereof by the said Heavenly motions, and Cœlestial glorious Bodies, by which, under God, we and all the Creatures on Earth are ruled and Governed, &c.

Now therefore to our purpose; Thou shalt understand that the 8th House of the Figure and Question is the House of Death.

The 4th House and 8th House of the Question are witnesses to the 8th House of the Figure.

The first House, or Angle of the East, or Ascendant, is always naturally the House of Life.

The Ascendant of the Questions, *viz.* the House that is for the Quærent, is witness to the House of Life, and is *Domus Vitæ accidentaliter*, for the Sick joy in both together.

The lord of the Ascendant and the ☽ are the Messengers and signifiers of Life. If the Father of a Child make the Question, then the 4th House is the Ascendant.

it is a sign of Death when the lord of the Ascendant and lord of the 8th are found together in ☌ or Aspect, then the Patient shall dye of that Infirmity.

The lord of the Ascendant in the 4, or 8th House, not remote, viz. or within 5 degrees of the Cusps, ill-aspected, or in his fall or detriment, signifieth Death, and if the Party do escape, it will be very hardly.

The lord of the Ascendant Combust, or *sub radiis solis*, signifies Death, whether Applying or Separating.

The lord of the Ascendant Cadent from an Angle, aspecting the Ascendant of the 8th House, signifies Death.

The lord of the Ascendant and 8th House, both one Planet, and beholding the 8th House by △ or any Aspect, being Cadent, and afflicted by ♄ or ♂, it is Death.

The lord of the Ascendant, and lord of the Hour, in ☍ or □ to the House of Death, and the lord of the 7th beholding the

Ascendant of the 8th House, there is a probability the Patient may not dye, but recover. If they do not behold the 8th House, though they be in ☍ to the lord of the 8th, although the ☽ be in the 4th, he may live. But if the lord of the Ascendant and lord of the hour do behold the 8th House, and the ☽ in the 4, or 8th, though the lord of the 7th behold the 8th House, he shall dye; or if the ☽ do behold the Ascendant of the 8th House, or his lord, he shall dye.

If the lord of the Ascendant be in □ to the Ascendant of the 8th House, and not beholding the lord of the 8th House, and the lord of the hour in ✶ to the 8th House, and not beholding the 8th House, and the Moon in the 6th and not beholding the 8th, nor his lord, though the lord of the 4th be in the 8th, the Party shall not dye, but be sorely grieved, and hardly escape.

If the lord of the Ascendant do apply to the lord of the 8th, and the ☽ be afflicted, it sheweth Death.

If the lord of the Hour be also lord of the 8th,], in a cadent House, and the Moon apply to a combust Planet, or that is *sub radiis*, though the lord of the Ascendant be in the Ascendant, if the lord of the 8th afflict the Ascendant, or if *Saturn* be joyned to the House of Death, the Party shall dye.

The lord of the Ascendant under the Earth, and the lord of the 8th in the 8th or 4th, or the lord of the Ascendant apply to the lord of the 8th, it signifies Death.

If the lord of the Ascendant give his light to the lord of the 8th, and the lord of the 8th be in an Angle, and the lord of the Ascendant cadent, it signifieth Death.

The lord of the Ascendant above the Earth, applying to the lord of the 8th, the lord of the 8th in the 8, or 4th House, it is Death.

The lord of the Ascendant, and the ☽ with evil Planets, it is Death.

The lord of the Ascendant free from affliction, and free from the 8, and 4th House, and from their lords, and from ♄ and ♂, and an evil Planet in the Ascendant, every man shall say he will dye, and yet he shall escape.

The lord of the Ascendant, or ☽, or 6ᵗʰ being Combust or], and the lord of the Ascendant in the 8ᵗʰ, conjoyned to ♂ or ♄, the sick shall dye of that Disease.

The lord of the Ascendant, lord of the hour, and lords of the 6, 7, and 8ᵗʰ, all combust in a Cadent house, though ♃ be in the Ascendant, the Party shall dye.

The lord of the Ascendant, and lord of the 6ᵗʰ together, and no good Planet in the 6ᵗʰ, nor in a fortunate place, he shall dye.

If the lord of the Ascendant and the ☽ do both behold the 8ᵗʰ House, he shall dye.

The lord of the Ascendant, and lord of the 6ᵗʰ, both Combust or Retrograde, he shall dye.

The lord of the Ascendant in the 8ᵗʰ, joyned to ♂ or ♄ by ♂ or Aspect, it is great danger of Death.

The lord of the Ascendant in the 4ᵗʰ, and the ☽ in ♋, in the 6ᵗʰ, applying to ♀ in ♎ in the 8ᵗʰ House by □, it is Death.

The lord of the Ascendant Cadent and Retrograde, and beholding the Ascendant of the 8ᵗʰ House by ⚹, and the ☽ in the 4ᵗʰ, separating from the lord of the Ascendant, and applying to the lord of the 8ᵗʰ, by a △ aspect, the Party shall dye of that Disease.

If one Planet be lord of the Ascendant, and lord of the 8ᵗʰ, and Combust in the House of the Quærent, and the ☽ in the 8, or 4ᵗʰ, if ♂ be lord of the Ascendant, and 8ᵗʰ, and Combust, it is Death.

If ♑ be in the Ascendant, the lord of the Ascendant, and also lord of the 8ᵗʰ; both in one Sign, and both Combust in a Cadent House, ☽ applying to the lord of the 6ᵗʰ in ♊, it is Death.

If the lord of the Ascendant do not behold the 8ᵗʰ house, nor his lord, although the ☽ do behold the Aspect of the 8ᵗʰ house, and apply to the lord of the 4ᵗʰ in the 8ᵗʰ house, the Party shall live, and not dye at this time.

If the lord of the Ascendant of the Nativity be in the 8ᵗʰ in the Question for the Sick, and in the same Sign that was Ascendant at the Birth, and the ☽ apply to the lord of the 8ᵗʰ, it is Death. ♏ ascending at the Birth, ♂ in ♏ in the Question, in the 8ᵗʰ House.

If one Planet be lord of the Ascendant, and also lord of the 8th, as ♀ in ♋ in the 9th, and the ☽ in ♏ in the 5th House, and separate from ♄ and ♃, and apply to the lord of the 8th, or Lady, being ♀, and the ☉ lord of the hour in the 8th, it is death without doubt.

If the lord of the Ascendant do apply to a Planet in the 8th, as to ♂, and the lord of the 8th be in the Ascendant, as ♄, the Party will dye shortly of that Infirmity, although ♀ be in the Ascendant, and also in ☌ with the lord of the 8th, and between the Ascendant and him, this signifieth a Lightning before Death.

When the lord of the Ascendant is in the 8th, and the ☽ in a full Aspect of ♃, and leaving ♃, and applying by □ or ☍ to the lord of the Ascendant in the 8th, and the lord of the 8th in □ or ☍ to ♃ at that instant, and the Almuten of the Ascendant in his fall,] in a Cadent House, as ♂ in ♉, in the 3d], then it seems the Party shall be very sick, like to dye, and yet shall amend, and be reasonable well again, and presently relapse and fall sick again, through his own folly, and so dye.

♂ Lord of the Ascendant, and in the 6th, within 30 degrees of the lord of the 8th, and within 30 degrees of the Ascendant of the 8th House, and the lord of the 7th in the 7th, then the Party shall dye of that Infirmity.

The lord of the Ascendant cadent, in a ⚹ to the 8th House, and the lord of the hour in a △ to the 8th House, and a ⚹ to the lord of the Ascendant, and the ☽ in the 6th, separating from the lord of the 8th, it is Death without doubt.

The lord of the Ascendant and lord of the hour being combust, both of them in a Cadent House, although ♃ be in the Ascendant, and the ☽ separate from the lord of the 8th, yet it is Death.

Whensoever you find the lord of the Ascendant, the lord of the hour, and the ☽ in the last degrees of the Signs they be in, as if ☿ 29 in the 4th, ☽ 27 in the 9th, ♀ Lady of the hour, 29 degr. in the 5th, in ♊, or the like, and the lord of the 8th be joyned to the Ascendant, applying or separating within half the degrees of his Orb, it prognosticates Death shortly after.

Again, if the last degrees of a Sign, as the 29 degr. of ♋, or the like, be in the Ascendant, and the lord of the Ascendant, or the lord of the hour, or the ☽ going from one House to another, it is a sign of Death.

Wherefore be wise in giving Judgment, when thou findest ♑ in the Ascendant, for if ♂ be either in ☌, ✶, □, △, or ☍ of the Ascendant, it is Death; for he hath his Exaltation in ♑, and I never found it so but it was Death; or if he did aspect the lord of the 8th by ☌ or ✶, he being peregrine.

If ♑ be in the Ascendant, and ♄ lord of the hour in ♈, or peregrine, and ♂ in ♉, in the 4th, or in any place of debilities at any Aspect to the lord of the 8th, the lord of the 8th being peregrine, and the ☽ peregrine in a Masculine Sign, it is Death very shortly after.

If the lord of the hour be lord of the 8th, and in his Detriment or Fall, and in the 8th, or in a cadent House, and the ☽ separate from the House of ♄, and apply to him again before she come to any other Planet, though the lord of the Ascendant, being in the 7th in his fall, and ☽ in the 7th, and ♃ in the Ascendant; if with this the Ascendant, it is Death without doubt.

If one Planet be lord of the Ascendant, and also of the 8th, and be in △ to the Ascendant of the 8th House, or the Ascendant of the 8th House apply to that Planet, and the ☽ separate from the lord of the Ascendant and 8th, and apply to the lord of the 4th being in the 10th, though in his Detriment, it is Death without all doubt after 14 dayes: you shall account for every degree lacking of the full Aspect of the ☽ to ♄ 60 dayes.

If the lord of the Ascendant be in his Fall or Detriment, although in Succedants or in Angles, and the Ascendant of the 8th House apply to him by ✶ or △, and the ☽ be Lady of the hour in the 8th, separate from ♄ in the 9th, and apply to the lord of the 8th by △ or ✶ in the 11th, though there be a △ between ♄ and ♂, yet the Party will dye without doubt.

If the lord of the Ascendant be in his Detriment or Fall in ☍ to the Ascendant of the 8th House, within the moiety of their Orbs, or do behold the 8th House by □, △, ✶, or ☌, or be also lord of the 8th, and in □, ☍, or ☌ of the lord of the 4th House, and though the ☾ do not behold the 8th House, nor his lord, but apply to the lord of the 6th, then the Disease will wax stronger and stronger on the Party, and he will dye without doubt.

If the lord of the Ascendant be lord of the hour, in his fall or detriment, and in the 6th, and go from ♂ to ♄ by ☌ ▱ □, or ☍], though they do not either of them behold the 8th, nor his lord applying, but separating, yet it is Death.

If the ☾ go from the lord of the Ascendant by ☌ or Aspect, and next apply to the lord of the 8th, by ☌ or Aspect, the Party shall dye.

If the ☾ be in the 4th or 8th, and behold the Ascendant of the 8th, or his lord, it is Death.

If the ☾ give the light of the lord of the Ascendant to the lord of the 8th, it is most usually Death.

If the ☾ and lord of the Ascendant be both in Cadents, and the ☾ do apply to the lord of the Ascendant by △, and after she leaveth the lord of the Ascendant, she apply by ☌ or Aspect to the lord of the 8th, or the lord of the House of the lord ascending, or both, the Party will dye.

If the ☾ or lord of the Ascendant have any Malignant Aspect to the lord of the 8th, it is Death; especially if the Question be by night; for then the Moon governs the time.

If the Moon be in the 7th, separating from ☿ lord of the 8th in the 9th combust, and the lord of the Ascendant combust, and the ☾ applying to ♀, being Lady of the 6th or 7th, going out of the Sign she is in, in a cadent House, and if she be Combust or afflicted, it is Death, though ♃ be in the Ascendant.

If the ☾ do separate from the lord of the hour by ✶, and apply to the lord of the 4th being in the 8th, by △, and the lord of the 8th in the 8th, also] in □ to the ☾, the Sick cannot escape, but shall shortly dye.

If the ☾ be in the 4th in ♏, and apply to ♄ being lord of the 8th, though there be 29 degrees of ♒ in the 8th, the ☾ separating from ♀. and ♄ also being lord of the hour, it is Death without fail,

If the ☾ be Lady of the 8th, and in a cadent House, and apply to the ☉ in the 7th, and the lord of the hour in the 8th, and the lord of the Ascendant in his Fall and Retrograde in ☍ to the 8th House, it is Death.

If the ☽ do separate from the lord of the Ascendant, though the lord of the Ascendant be in his own house, and apply to the lord of the 8th by ☍, the Moon existing in the 4th, and ♀ in the Ascendant in her fall, it is Death without fail.

If the ☽ separate from the Ascendant, and from the lord thereof, and apply to the lord of the 8th, it is Death.

If the ☽ be in the Sign of the 8th, in the 7th, going from the Ascendant of the 8th, and did last separate from the lord of the 8th, the lord of the 8th being in the Sign ascending, in the 12th house, and the lord of the Ascendant] in the 9th, going from the Ascendant of the 8th, the Sick shall escape and not dye, though every man think he will dye.

If the ☽ be in the Sign of the 8th, and the lord of the 8th Combust, and the Moon apply to the lord of the Ascendant by △, or the like, all being Cadent, though the Moon do not behold the Ascendant nor the 8th House, the Party will dye.

If the ☽ be in the Sign of the 8th, and the lord of the 8th Combust, and the Moon apply to the lord of the Ascendant by △, or the like, all being Cadent, though the Moon do not behold the Ascendant nor the 8th House, the Party will dye.

If the ☽ do separate from a Planet in the 6th, though ♃; and apply to a Planet in the 8th, as to ☿ being lord of the 4th, and the ☽ in ☍ to the 8th House, the Party will dye of that Disease.

If the ☽ do separate from a Planet in the 6th, and apply to a Planet in the 8th, the ☽ existing in the 4th, and the lord of the 4th in the 8th, and so soon as the separates from the lord of the 4th she apply to the lord of the 8th by □, being Retrograde, the Party cannot by any means escape.

If the ☽ do separate from the ☉ by △, the ☉ being lord of the hour, and the ☽ applying to ♀, being Lady of the 8th, and combust or *sub radiis*, it is Death without any remedy.

If the ☽ separate from the ☌ of the lord of the Ascendant, and apply to the Sun by ☌, and after that apply to the Conjunction of *Mars*, so soon as she is separate from the Sun, being lord of the 8th, the Party undoubtedly will dye.

If the ☽ do separate from the lord of the 10th, the lord of the 10th existing in the 6th, applying to the lord of the 4th being in the 8th, and the ☽ in ☍ to the 8th, and the Ascendant of the 8th apply to the ☽, she being lady of the hour, the Sick will dye shortly.

If the Moon be in the 6th in ☍ to the Ascendant, separate from the lord of the Ascendant being in the 10th, and applying to the lord of the 8th, in the 7th], in the Sign of the 8th, and the lord of the 4th in the 8th, the Party shall dye of that Disease.

If the Moon do separate from the lord of the Ascendant, the lord of the Ascendant being combust, and in the 6th, in his Fall, going to the Sun, it is Death.

If the ☽ be in the 4th, and do separate from the lord of the Ascendant, and from the lord of the 7th, and apply to the ☌ of ♄ in the 4th House], it is Death.

If the ☽ be in the Ascendant void of Course, and the lord of the hour in the 8th, and being lord of the 6th, and next apply to the lord of the 8th House, he will dye shortly, and the Sickness will more and more fortifie until he dye.

If the ☽ be in the 6th, and separate from the lord of the hour in the 7th, and apply to a Planet in the 8th, the lord of the Ascendant being in the 4th, it is Death without fail.

If the ☽ do separate from the lord of the 7th and 8th, and apply to the ☉ by △, and the lord of the 8th in the same Sign with the Sun, and the Moon after she doth go from the Sun do apply to the lord of the 6th by □, it is Death.

If the ☽ do separate from the lord of the 8th, and apply to a Planet in the 10th by △, and after she leave that Planet she find the lord of the 6th by □, and the lord of the hour aspect the 8th House, or if the the lord of the Ascendant aspect the 8th by △ or ✶, it is Death.

If the Moon do separate from the lord of the Ascendant, and be void of Course, and the next Planet she applies to be the lord of the 8th from the Quærent, then the Party shall dye; and if ☿ be lord of the 8th, in such a case the Party will be Frantick, and Melancholick, mad, and so dye.

If the ☽ do apply to ♄ lord of the 8th, in the 2d, in ☍ to the 8th, and also to ♃ by a △, being in ♑ in the 8th], the Party dyes of that Infirmity.

If the Moon be Lady of the Ascendant, and the last degree of ♋ in the Ascendant, and the Moon be in ☌ or Application to the lord of the 4th, being in the 8th House of the Question, it is Death.

The ☽ in ♏ in the 4th, in ☌ with ☋, separating from the lord of the hour, and the lord of the 4th, and applying to ♃ lord of the 8th, and aspecting the Ascendant of the 8th, also, the lord of the Ascendant being the ☉, and in the 10th, not aspecting the Ascendant nor the 8th, it signifies long Sickness, or Death within 13 dayes.

If the Moon be Lady of the 8th, the last degrees of ♋ being in the 8th, and the Moon in the 6th applying to an ☍ of the ☉, the ☉ being in the Ascendant, falling into the 12th House, and the ☽ did last separate from ♄ in the 8th, and the lord of the Ascendant in a cadent House, it is a sign of Death.

If the ☽ be Lady of the 8th, and in the 8th, and apply to the Sun by ✶, △, or □ in the Ascendant, and the lord of the Ascendant cadent out of Angles, as in the 3d, and Aspect the 8th, it is Death without doubt.

If the ☽ do separate from ♃, being lord of the Ascendant in the Ascendant, and apply to ♄ in the 6th, ♀ being Combust it is Death; because ♀ us exalted in ♓ the Ascendant.

When the ☽ is in a cadent House, *in vis combusta*, and doth apply to the lord of the 8th, as the ☉, and to the lord of the 6th also, though the lord of the 8th and 6th be both in the Ascendant in ☌, yet the party will dye without doubt, even when they think he will live, he will dye suddenly.

If the ☽ do separate from ♃ or ♀ in an Angle or Succedant, and apply to a Planet in a cadent House, in his Fall or Detriment, the lord of the Ascendant also in his Fall, although he behold the Ascendant, it is Death; the lord of the Ascendant being lord of the 8th, especially if the ☽, the lord of the Ascendant, or the Planet which the ☽ applies to, be going out of the Signs or Houses they are in.

If the ☽ do apply to the lord of the 8ᵗʰ, and the lord of the Ascendant in the 8ᵗʰ both at once, the lord of the Ascendant in a full aspect of the lord of the 8ᵗʰ, with reception, it is Death. I have found it so. ♄ lord of the 8ᵗʰ in 7 degr. of ♍,], ☿ lord of the Ascendant in the 7ᵗʰ if ♑, in the 8ᵗʰ, and the ☽ in the 3d of ♏ in the 6ᵗʰ House.

If the ☽ be in the 6ᵗʰ House, or in the Sign of the 7ᵗʰ, and do separate from ♄ in the 12ᵗʰ, in the Sign of the Ascendant, and do apply to ♂ by a □, being lord of the 8ᵗʰ, in the 10ᵗʰ; the lord of the Ascendant and lord of the hour in the 8ᵗʰ House, in the Sign of the 8ᵗʰ, not remote, it signifies the Sickness will grow more and more on the Party until he dye: as suppose 16 of ♍ to ascend, ☿ lord of the Ascendant, and the ☉ lord of the hour in ♈, both in the 8ᵗʰ House, ♂ lord of the 8ᵗʰ House in ♊ in the 10ᵗʰ, ♄] in ♍ in the 12, ♀ in ♉ in the 8ᵗʰ, ☊ in ♈ the 8ᵗʰ, the ☽ separating from ♄ and applying to ♂.

The lord of the Ascendant, and the lord of the hour in the 8ᵗʰ House, not aspecting the lord of the 8ᵗʰ, and the ☽ in the 6ᵗʰ applying to the lord of the 8ᵗʰ, it is Death.

If the ☽ do separate from ♂ lord of the 6ᵗʰ, ♂ being joyned to the Ascendant, and the ☽ and lord of the Ascendant do both apply to the lord of the 8ᵗʰ, it is Death to the Mother of the Child.

If the lord of the Ascendant be lord of the 8ᵗʰ in the 8ᵗʰ, and the ☽ combust applying to, or separating from the ☉, but separating from the Sun, and applying to ♄ or ♂] in the 11, 5, 2, or 8 Houses, it is Death, in what place of the Heavens soever the ☽ be.

If the lord of the Ascendant be also lord of the 8ᵗʰ, and in the 8ᵗʰ, not remote, but within 30 degrees of the Ascendant of the 8ᵗʰ, it is a sign of Death.

Lord of the Ascendant, and lord of the hour in the 8ᵗʰ, and in the 8ᵗʰ, not aspecting the lord of the 8ᵗʰ, and the ☽ in the 6ᵗʰ applying to the lord thereof, it is Death.

If the ☽ do apply to ♂ in the 8ᵗʰ, in the Sign of the 8ᵗʰ, going out of the 8ᵗʰ into the 7ᵗʰ House, within one degree, and the ☽ do apply to the Ascendant of the 8ᵗʰ, within 12 degrees, and the lord of the Ascendant do not behold the 8th, but is Angular, then the Party shall be in great peril of Death, and be as 'twere dead for a time.

If there be an evil Planet joyned to the lord of the Ascendant, by ☌, □, or ☍, then the Sick shall hardly escape, except that ill Planet do receive the lord of the Ascendant, which if he do, then with much ado he may escape in the end.

The lord of the Ascendant in partile Aspect, applying to the lord of the 8th with any Aspect, with Reception, it is Death.

If the lord of the 8th be lord of the hour, and combust, and the Moon within 3 degrees going out of the Sign she is in, and applying to a Retrograde Planet, it is Death.

If the last degrees of a Sign be in the ascendant, as 27, 28, 29, or 30, and the ☉ be lord of the 4th, and the lord of the Ascendant be combust, it is Death, though the Moon apply to ♃.

If the lord of the 8th be in the 10th, and do behold the lord of the Ascendant, and do apply also to the Ascendant of the 8th House by Aspect, it sheweth Death./

If *Mars* be within one degree of the Ascendant in a moveable Sign, beholding *pars Mortis* by a □, and ☿ be lord of the House of the Moon, and in the 8th, both Retrograde and Combust; then will the Party be Mad, and dye within a day or two after, and will be the cause of his own Death.

If the lord of the Ascendant be also lord of the hour, as the ☉ in the 11th with ♀, and lord of the 8th, as ♄ in the Ascendant at a ✶, △, □, or ☍ to the lord of the Ascendant, and ♃ in the 8th; though the Moon do not behold the 8th, nor his lord, the Party shall dye of that Infirmity before it goes from him.

The lord of the Ascendant cadent without an Angle above 8 degrees, and the Ascendant applying to him by ✶, △, □, ☌, or ☍, the ☽ in the 8th in ♌, and applying to the ☉ in the latter degrees of ♐ in the Ascendant by △ or ✶, and the lord of the hour cadent, and the lord of the 6th combust, it is Death.

The lord of the 8th and of the 6th in the Ascendant in the Sign of the Ascendant, beholding the lord of the Ascendant with ✶ or △, though ♃ be in the 8th, it is Death.

If ♄ be lord of the 8, 7, or 6ᵗʰ, and in the Ascendant and Sign ascending, casting any Aspect to the lord of the Ascendant, it is Death; for the Sickness will fortifie till Death do ensue.

If ♀ be Lady of the Ascendant, and also of the 8ᵗʰ, and the ☽ separate from the lord of the 4ᵗʰ, and apply to ♀ by ☌ or Aspect, it is Death without doubt.

When the Planet that is Exalted in the Sign ascending is combust, or going to combustion, and cadent, and the ☽ goes from the lord of the Ascendant and be opposite to the 8ᵗʰ house, and apply to ♄ or ♂ in the 6ᵗʰ, it is Death without fail.

♄ Lord of the Ascendant in the 8ᵗʰ in ♍, ♂ in ♉] in the 3d, and the ☽ at □ to the Ascendant of the 8ᵗʰ, going from ♃ to ♄, ♂ being lord of the hour, it is a sign of Death.

When the first degree of any Sign is in the Ascendant and the lord of the Ascendant in the 8ᵗʰ, within half is Orb of the Ascendant of the 8ᵗʰ, and combust, though ♀ be in the same Sign between the Sun and the lord of the Ascendant, ♀ going from the ☉ and applying to the lord of the Ascendant by ☌, being], and the ☽ in a full △ to ♂, and leaving ♂ she apply to the ☍, ☌, or □ of ♃, it is Death.

When the ☉ is lord of the 4ᵗʰ, and cadent, and the lord of the 8ᵗʰ combust, and the lord of the Ascendant and the ☽ also cadent, and there be Reception by translation of Light between the ☽ and the lord of the 8ᵗʰ by Exaltation or Houses, then the Party shall dye without fail.

If an evil Planet be in the Ascendant, and another evil Planet with the lord of the Ascendant, then no medicine will do the Sick good, but Death follows.

If in the 6ᵗʰ House be an evil Planet, and also in the first House, and some other Planet joyned with them, it is Death. But if the malice of the Planet be strong, and from strong places, as Angles, then is the Sickness very strong.

The lord of the 6ᵗʰ in the first, or the lord of the first in the 6ᵗʰ, it is very evil.

And universally, so often as the ☽ and lord of the Ascendant be letted, impeded, or afflicted, it's a sign of long Sickness or Death.

If ♄ do apply to the lord of the Ascendant by ⚹ or △, he shall live, but ♄ must not be lord of the 8ᵗʰ then.

If ♄ be] from the lord of the Ascendant, he shall dye.

If the principal lord of the 8ᵗʰ do apply to the lord of the Ascendant by ⚹ or △, he shall live; if he go] from the lord of the Ascendant, he shall dye.

When the ☉ is lord of the Ascendant, it is a good sign of Life.

When the ☽ doth apply to the ☉ by ⚹ or △, it's a good sign; but if the ☽ do separate from the ☉, it's an evil sign, be it by what Aspect soever.

The lord of the Ascendant, lord of the hour, and the Moon in cadent Houses, or in the 8ᵗʰ, and some of them aspect the 8ᵗʰ, and some the lord of the 8ᵗʰ House, it is Death.

If ♀ be Lady of the Ascendant, and aspect the lord of the 8ᵗʰ, entring into combustion, and the Moon combust, and separating from the lord of the 8ᵗʰ, being in the Ascendant, the Party shall not dye, yet every one will despair of his life.

Although the Moon do separate from the lord of the 4ᵗʰ, and apply to a Planet in the 8ᵗʰ, if the Moon do not behold the lord of the 8ᵗʰ, although she do behold the Ascendant of the 8ᵗʰ afar off, the Party shall not dye of this Infirmity, but shall hardly escape; although ♂ be in the 4ᵗʰ, in □ to the Ascendant.

If the ☽ be Lady of the 8ᵗʰ, and the Ascendant of the 8ᵗʰ apply to the ☽ by ⚹, the lord of the Ascendant and lord of the hour both in the 8ᵗʰ remote, not in the Sign of the 8ᵗʰ, though the Moon apply to ♄ by △, and to ♂ by □, being lord of the 4ᵗʰ, and in the 7ᵗʰ, the Party shall not dye, but hardly escape.

If the ☽ be Lady of the Ascendant, and go from the lord of the 4ᵗʰ by aspect, and the Ascendant of the 8ᵗʰ go from the Moon, and the Moon do not behold the lord of the 8ᵗʰ House, the lord of the 4ᵗʰ being lord of the hour, and the Ascendant apply to the ☽ by ⚹, the Sick shall not dye of that Disease.

If the Moon do last separate from the lord of the 8ᵗʰ, and next after apply to the ☉ by ⚹ or △ in the 9ᵗʰ House, then the Party shall not dye of that Infirmity.

If the Moon do separate from the lord of the hour last, being in the Ascendant, weak and Retrograde, and apply to the lord of the 8th by ☌ at that instant, the Moon being Lady of the 4th, and the lord of the 8th being Retrograde in the 5th, and neither the Moon nor lord of the 8th behold the 8th, but the Ascendant by □, the degree ascending going from the Moon, and lord of the 8th, though the lord of the Ascendant do behold the 8th by ⚹, the Ascendant of the 8th going from the ⚹, the sick Party shall not dye.

If the Moon do separate from the lord of the 8th being Retrograde in the 5th, and apply to a Planet that is in his Exaltation in the 8th House by ☍, and the ☉ lord of the hour in the 6th, the Party shall escape, even beyond expectation.

If the Moon be combust in a cadent House, and the lord of the hour also, and not beholding the lord of the 8th, but separate from him, and the ☉ lord of the Ascendant; the Party shall not dye, but miraculously escape after much sickness.

If the Moon do go from the lord of the 8th to the lord of the Ascendant, he shall escape.

Whosoever falleth sick near the time of an Eclipse, and the Ruling Planets in the Eclipse be in the Ascendant of his Nativity that so falleth sick, or in the Ascendant of his Revolution, or in the place of his Hyleck, or of his Signifier of Life, that Disease then taken will be perilous and deadly.

If at the time of the first falling sick, or in the time of the Question, or first beginning of the Sickness, the ☽ be in the 4th with ♂, and the good Planets be cadent, it is a sign of Death.

How greatly is the Sickness to be feared, if in the time of the Question, or first beginning of the Sickness, both the Luminaries by under the Earth!

In the beginning of any Sickness, or in the time of any Question for the Sick if the Moon be Oriental, within 12 degrees of the Sun, it is a Sign of Death, and the nearer the Sun the worse.

If in the degree ascending, or near unto it within 2 degrees, be an evil Planet, it is an argument of Death, as well in the Question as when he first falleth sick. If it be in a fixed Sign, reckon for every degree a month; if in a common Sign, then reckon for every degree 7 dayes, but be sure that Planet be direct, and apply to the Ascendant.

If the ☉ be lord of the Ascendant, and the ☽ combust, and the ☽ separate from the lord of the 8th of the Question, and apply to the ☉, the lord of the 8th in the Ascendant, viz. ♃, the Party shall escape, being well looked unto.

If the ☽ be in the Ascendant in ♋, and do separate from the Ascendant, and apply to the lord of the 8th] in the 4th, and the lord of the Ascendant in the 7th House, going out of the Sign he is in; as ☿ lord of the Ascendant in 29 degrees of ♐ the 7th, and the lord of the Ascendant and lord of the 8th do behold the Ascendant of the 8th within the moity of their Orbs, the Sick shall not dye at this time.

If the ☽ do separate from the lord of the 8th, the lord of the 8th being in the 12th in the Sign of the Ascendant, and apply to the □ of ♂ in the 2d, and ♄ lord of the Ascendant be in the 7th], and the ☽ in the 6th, the Party will not dye, but be long sick before he perfectly recover.

If the lord of the Ascendant and the Moon be joyned by ☌ or Aspect to the lord of the House of Death, then the Party shall dye of that Infirmity, except the lord of the 8th do receive the lord of the Ascendant or the Moon: and if the lord of the House of Death be joyned to the lord of the Ascendant, he will dye, except there be some strong Reception between them.

It's a very evil sign when the lord of the Ascendant is joyned to an evil malignant Planet, or is unfortunate and weak, or if he be joyned to the lord of the 8th.

Also if an evil Planet, or if the lord of the 8th be in the Ascendant, or joyned to the Ascendant, it's very evil sign.

When the Ascendant at the time of first falling sick shall be the 7th House at the birth, you may fear Death, unless the profection of that year be the same Sign; those Signs which are adverse in a Nativity, are the Signs of the 6th, 7th, 8th, and 12th.

When the 5 Hylegiacal places at the hour of birth, at the time of decumbiture of the Sick, as also the lord of the Ascendant are oppressed, judge death immediately to follow, unless Reception intervene betwixt the Infortunes, and the Fortunes interject their comfortable Aspects; for then, by a Divine Miracle, as it were, the Party sick may escape.

He will be infinitely oppressed, who in the hour of ♂ shall first get an Hot Disease and in the hour of ♄ a Cold one.

The lord of the Ascendant, and of the Figure, Combust, do undoubtedly declare Death, unless some Reception be between the Sun and them, such a chance hapning, and the ☽ proving fortunate, after all hopes of escape, a little hope remains.

The lord of the 8th in an Angle, the lord of the Ascendant in a Cadent House, is always Mortal, the rather if he be an Infortuane.

The lord of the Ascendant and the ☽ in ☌ with the lord of the 8th, without the interposing Aspects of the Fortunes, threatens Death.

The Application of the ☽ to a Planet in the 8th is always dangerous; the Application of the lord of the Ascendant unto the lord of the 8th, or unto malevolent Planets therein, the ☽ being any manner of way afflicted, denotes Death.

The ☽ transferring the Light and Influence of the lord of the Ascendant to the lord of the 8th brings usually Death: so also when the lord of the 8th is in the Ascendant, the lord of the Ascendant and the ☽ being both afflicted. It always proves fatal, when the lord of the Ascendant is infortunate in the 8th, and the ☽ being then afflicted, and very weak, and in no Essential Dignity. The lord of the Ascendant being subterranean, and in any Aspect to the lord of the 8th in the 8th, or if he be in the 4th, and the lord of the 8th in the 4th, and they both in a ☌, argue death. It's a very ill sign of Life, when the lord of the Ascendant is corporally joyned with the lord of the 4th, 6th, 7th, or 12th, it seldome succeeds well with the sick Person then.

Have special consideration to the Luminary of the time, for according to the well or ill affection thereof, you may improve your judgment; the lord of the Ascendant afflicted of an evil Planet in the 8th, without the benevolent Aspects of the Fortunes, the ☽ also then vitiated, shew great peril of death; and usually be reason of the ill government of the sick Party, or some errour in his ordering, or course in Physick: it's a powerful Argument that the sick Party will dye, when at the time of his first Question to his Physician you find the lord of the Ascendant combust in the Ascendant.

The lord of the Ascendant and of the 8th unfortunate, denote Death.

The lord of the 8th in the 10th House, and lord of the Ascendant in the 4, 6, or 7th, afflicted of the malevolent Planets, argue Death.

A Planet very strong, and placed in the Ascendant, if he be lord of the hour, and of the 8th, portends Death. If the lord of the 8th be], and in ☌, □, or ☍ of the ☽, it shews Death; the lord of the 8th in the 7th, the ☽ and lord of the Ascendant in cadent Houses, infested with the ill Aspects of Infortunes, and more certain if one of the Malevolents be lord of the 8th, or posited in the 8th: some say, if the ☽ be in ☌ with ♄ or ♃, the sick Party will have little good thereby; nor will he escape, unless ♄ be Retrograde, and ♃ direct.

When the lord of the Ascendant is in ☌ with the lord of the 8th, or in □ or ☍ of a Planet posited in that House, or in the Antiscian of the lord of the 8th, without the benevolent ⚹ or △ or ♃, and at the same time the Moon be any ways afflicted, it's probable the Sick will dye; but if the lord of the Ascendant be in reception with the Planet in the 8th, it's possible he may avoid Death: however let him be assured of a very long and grievous Disease.

If the ☽ be with ♄ or ♂, without the assistance of some good Aspect from ♃ and ♀, and if ♄ be slow in motion, or is going Retrograde, it's so much the worse, and it's one Argument the Sick will dye at that time; if other testimonies concur, it's more certain.

The lord of the Ascendant in the 7th, in his Fall, or under the Earth in the 4th, or 6th, or in other cadent Houses, afflicted by the Malevolents, and the lord of the 8th in the 7th, these are testimonies of Death.

A Malevolent Planet near to the Degree ascending, or a violent fixed Star, *viz. Antares* in the 4th degree of ♐, *Lance Australis* about the 9th of ♏, *Pallilicium* in 4 of ♊, *Caput Medusa*, in 20 of ♉, these prenote Death.

The lord of the Ascendant in ♌ or ♒, in any bad configuration of the lord of the 6th or 12, shews little hopes of recovery.

Both the Lights afflicted of ♄ in Angles, give testimony of a tedious long Sickness; so do both the Lights being ill dignified, and under the Earth, signifie the same.

When as also the Sun from the beginning of the Disease shall be corporally afflicted, or by the □ or ☍ of ♄ or ♂ impedited, or be in the perfect Antiscian of a Malignant Planet, and shall apply and not separate, either Death, or an extraordinary long Sickness succeeds.

The ☽ after the beginning of the Disease coming to ☍ of the lord of the Ascendant and he] or combust, argues Death, or a sharp Disease, not easily curable; ♄ in ☍ with the lord of the 8th, the ☽ in the 4th with ♂, or the ☽ in the Ascendant, and near the Degree ascending, are Arguments of Death. The Moon besieged by the Infortunes, or between the ☉ and ♂, or between ☉ and ♄, are ill Omens of Death.

Who falls sick whilst the Moon is under the Sun-beams, viz. departing from Combustion, his Disease shall increase till she hath passed the ☉ his ☍; but then if she prove ill-affected, and come to an ill Aspect of the lord of the 8th, it threatens Death, otherwise he or she will escape.

Any Malevolent in the 6th, or any Planet peregrine and unfortunate in that house, shew great danger in the Disease; the combustion of the ☽ in the 8th House, and in ♌ or in ♎ in □ or ☍ to ♄ or ☿, or in ☌ with the Pleiades in 24 ♉, or other violent fixed Stars, argues Death: the ☽ being Lady of the 6th or of the Ascendant in combustion, and the lord of the 8th at the same time afflicted by ☌ or ill Aspect of ♄ or ♂, shew Death.

Both the Luminaries afflicted by ♄ denote a chronical and long Distemper, but being afflicted by ♂, the Sickness is short, and Death speedy.

Sings Vita. *Signs of Recovery.*

1. Jupiter, ♀, ☉, and ☽ in the Ascendant, not beholding the lords of the 8ᵗʰ or 6ᵗʰ Houses, free from the affliction of the Malevolents, and in good Signs; good signs of Recovery.

2. The ☌ of the ☽ with ♃ is fortunate, especially if it fall in ♋, where either of them have Dignities; but it hath the least of goods in it if it fall in ♑, because there they are both debillitated.

3. The Moon free from the lords of the 6ᵗʰ and 8ᵗʰ Houses, and applying to the lord of the Ascendant, *salutem significat.*

4. The ☽ in an Angle well affected, or in a Succedant, increasing in Light and Motion, and free from ♄ and ♂, *solutem judicat.*

5. The ☽ posited in a good House of Heaven, *viz.* as the Ascendant, 10, 5, 11, 9, 2, or 3d Houses, in ☌, ✶, or △ with the lord of the Ascendant, or in his Antiscian, although he be a Malevolent, and the ☽ and he increasing in light and motion, *salutem pollicentur.*

6. In the beginning of the Disease, though the ☽ make no Aspect, yet if upon a Critical Day she well apply, it is good. In like manner, the ☽ applying by □ or ☍, without any good Aspect, she being in her own House or Exaltation, it is good.

7. The Moon in her own House, in the House of ♃ or ♀, and being beheld by either of them, without the noxinoxious Rayes of the Malevolents, *Morbus ad salutem tendit.*

8. In the beginning of the Disease, the Sun, Moon, and Lord of the Horoscope, being free from any affliction of the lord of the 8ᵗʰ, and the lord of *pars mortis, nulla aderit mortis sequentis suspitio.*

9. If the Benevolents are generally more strong and powerful (at the decumbiture) than the Malevolents, and that they behold the Ascendant or the Moon, *Sanitatem ager consequetur.*

10. Although the Moon be with ♄ or ♂, yet if ♃ or ♀ friendly aspect her, *liberabitur ager.*

11. If the ☽ shall separate from a weak Malevolent, and apply to a powerful and strong Benevolent, *Sanitas agroto retituetur.*

12. *Saturn* Oriental from the Sun, if the Disease proceed from Cold, the Party shall recover, but be long weak. In like manner, if ♄ be Occidental of the ☉, and the Disease be from a hot Cause, he recovers likewise.

13. *Mars* after his Opposition with the ☉, is not so malignant as before the ☌; the Conjunction of ♂ with the Moon is very noxious and pernicious, the ☍. or □, or any Aspect by Rayes, beholding each other, are not so hurtful, the Moon is more noxious in her Increase than Decrease of Light, and ♂ is more mischievous being Oriental than Occidental.

14. The Lord of the Ascendant received by the Lord of the 8th, and both free from the malevolents, *post sanitasem desperatam ager convalescei.*

15. The Lord of the Ascendant in reception of Houses with the lord of the 8th, *Auxiliantur beneficiis, Evasionem morb denotas.*

16. If you find the Lord of the Ascendant benevolent, in a good House of Heaven, and free from the rayes of the Malevolent, *maxime ad sanitatem conducit.* In like manner, it's of little moment to consider the Position of Heaven, at the time of the decumbiture, or beginning of the Disease, though Benevolents are in the Ascendant, or 10th House, or behold the same, if the ☽ in the mean time be afflicted by ☌, □, or ☍ of the Malevolents, *non crit inde auxilium leve ad salutem consequendam.*

Of the twelve Houses of Heaven, so far as they concern our business of Sickness.

Understand that the whole Heaven is divided into 12 parts, according to the Longitude and Latitude of every Place, City, or Town; and these 12 parts are called the 12 Houses of Heaven, which are not fixed, but in respect of every several place; and we are to consider these 12 Houses under a treble notion.

Four of these Houses, which are called Angular, are likewise esteemed good, and do signifie Health, Strength, long Life, and good Fortune: and these are the 1, 4, 7, 10, Masculine.

Four other are called Succedant, and mean, and do signifie both Health and Sickness, Strength and Weakness, long

Life and short, Life and Death, good Fortune and bad, for they are common to both; and these are called Cadent Houses: which are the 3, 6, 9, and 12th Houses.

Understand also, that there are 12 Signs in the *Zodiack* of Heaven, and these are Fixed, and are circumvolv'd round about, the World once in 24 Hours, by virtue of the first Mover.

Of these 12 Signs some be Moveable, some Fixed, and some Common, &c. for they are to be understood under these three considerations.

♈, ♋, ♎, and ♑, are moveable, in them Sickness will change.

♉, ♌, ♏, ♒, are fixed Signs, and intimate long Sickness.

♊, ♍, ♐, ♓, are common to Sickness and Health both.

Again, these Signs are divided into four Parts or Triplicitics, as thus;

♈, ♌, ♐, are Hot and Dry, Cholerick and Fiery.

♉, ♍, and ♑, are Cold and Dry, Melancholick, of the nature of the Earth.

♊, ♎, and ♑, are Hot and Moist, Sanguine, of the nature of the Air.

♋, ♏, and ♓ are Cold and Moist, Flegmatick, of the nature of Water.

Of the Seven Planets, so far as concerns this Subject of Sickness.

There are Seven Planets, whose ordinary motions are in their several Spheres under the Zodiack, of the which,

♄ is Cold and Dry, Melancholick, resembling the Earth, with a superfluous cold Flegm, naturally Noxious and Evil, Unwholsom, Unpleasant.

♃ is Hot and Moist, Sanguine, of the nature of the Air, Fortunate, Healthful, Temperate, and naturally good and friendly unto Life.

♂ is Hot and Dry, Cholerick, Fiery, Untemperate, Unfortunate, an utter enemy to the Life of Man, and good Estate thereof; increasing Choler, Hot and Dry, Active, Increasing.

☉ is Hot, and more Dry than Moist, friendly to the Life and Nature of Man, increasing and cherishing good Blood, causing yellow Choler, Simple, of the nature of Fires, Asscending, Active, Sharp and Subtile.

♀ is Temperate in Heat and Cold, in Moist and Dry, but yet more Cold than Hot, and more Moist than Dry, Decreasing, and Descending, Passive, Flegmatick, causing thin Flem and Water.

☿ is naturally more Cold and Dry than Hot and Moist, but of superfluous Humidity, and is Moveable, Quick in Melancholick causes, Thin Melancholick and Subtil.

☽ is Cold and Moist, of the nature of Water, Decreasing and Descending, passive, causing a saltish, thick Water, and Flegm.

☊ *Caput Draconis* is of the nature of ♃ and ♀ Good and Fortunate, Temperate in Heat and Cold, but moist in the first, &c. Both Masculine and Feminine, Active and Passive, Ascending and Descending, friendly to the Life and nature of Man, causing few Diseases, but apt to help all Diseases, when the ☽ is therewith.

☋ *Canda Draconis* is of the nature of ♄ and ♂, and is most Evil and Unfortunate, Untemperate, Destructive, Active, Masculine, Ascending, an Enemy to the Life and Nature of Man, causing many Sicknesses and Diseases.

Now we have spoken of the Houses, the Signs and Planets of Heaven, which are Bodies Cœlestial, and do dispose and rule the Motions and Actions of our Bodies Elemental and Terrestrial; you shall also understand, that the 12 Houses of Heaven are stronger, and of more force and effect in operation, than the 12 Signs, and the 12 Signs are of greater force and efficacy in their operation, than the 7 Planets; and the natures of the Planets do alter and vary according to the Signs that they be in; and the Signs do alter and vary according to the Houses they are in.

Now to leave Bodies Cœlestial, and speak of the Elementary, whereof the Bodies Terrestrial are compounded, constituted, and made; you are to understand that there are 4 Elements, *viz. Fire, Water, Earth, Air.*

Guido Bonatus understandeth them thus;

Caliditatem, que est causa Generationis.
Frigiditatem, que est causa Destructionis.
Humiditatem, que est causa Corruptionis.
Siccitatem, que est causa Durationis.

Et Elementa sunt nt in suis Spheris pura & Sumplicia, babent Simplices Qualitates Quatuor vincentes, viz.

☉ *Ignis Caliditatem generative,* ☉, ♃.
♃ *Aer Humiditatem corruptive,* ♃, ☽.
♄ *Terra, Siccitatem durative,* ♄.
☽ *Aqua, Frigiditatem, destructive.* ☽.

Whatsoever therefore is Hot, as the Fire is in his Simple and Elementary Quality, doth heat, open, digest, attenuate, ripen, subtilitate, and make thin, and simple, and maketh soft.

Whatsoever in his Simple and Elementary Quality and nature is Moist, as the Air, doth moisten, putrifie and corrupt, make slippery, lighten and conglutinate.

Whatsoever is Dry, as the Earth is in its Simple Quality and nature, drieth, maketh barren, attracteth and setleth, and is the worst in decreasing.

Whatsoever is Cold in his Simple Nature and Quality, as the Water, doth make cold, thicken, and causeth indigestion, congealeth, destroyeth, maketh hard, knitteth together: it doth not pierce and open, but shutteth, incloseth and stoppeth, and nourisheth not, but astonisheth and extinguisheth the Radical Heat and Breath of Life.

Of Compound Qualities.

Whatsoever is Hot and Dry of Nature, is cholerick, generative, attractive, durative, and conservative, drying, heating, and attracting; doth harden, and cause watchfulness, because of heating and drying of the Brain and Head; they do also exhaust and draw, gather together and collect, they do also cleanse and purge, provoke to siedge, and make sweet, they do cleanse and scour the Body replenished with cold and moist Humours.

Whatsoever is Hot and Moist, generates by reason of Heat, and corrupteth by reason of Moisture, and bringeth not to perfection.

Whatsoever is Cold and Dry participateth of duration and destruction; for if the Dry exceed the Cold, then it will be durative; but if the cold Quality in the same subject exceed the dry, the *destruit, & et siout Lignum arridum.*

Whatsoever is Cold and Moist, *est indigeste materia, coruptat, & omnino destruit, non generat, neque durat, neque frucium fort, sed obiupet, espellit, infrigat, lumisciat, corrumpit, mortificat;* creates heaviness, dulness, and slowness in all things provokes to sleep and drowsiness, and Rots, consumes, separates and divides, is of the nature of the ☽ and ♀, ingenders moist and watry Humours and Imposumations, and repells Humours by congelation and thickning, dispersing them in sundry places.

First therefore, understand, that the Body of Man, and all other Elementary things, are composed of the 4 Elements, *viz.* of Air, Water, Fire, and Earth; two active, and two passive matters; one active and one passive ascending, and increasing, and one active and one passive matter descending and decreasing, for Guido saith, *omne coepus ex quatuor Elementis constar.*

Secondly, understand, that the Body of man is divided into twelve parts, according to the twelve Signs, and then into 36 parts, according to the division of the 12 Signs into 36 Faces and Triplicities.

Thirdly, understand, that the 12 Signs have Dominion over and in the Body Humane, as well as in other bodies and things; and these Signs are divided into 4 several Triplicities, as followeth.

♈, ♌, ♐, are hot and dry, cholerick, bitter, of the nature of Fire, consuming, yet generative, durative, attractive, by reason of Heat and drowth; for by reason of their heat they are generative and attractive, and by reason of drowth they are durative; and by reason both of heat and drowth they are consuming: for the Fire doth consume all imperfect matter and substance, that is not united in a just Temperature.

♉, ♍, ♑, are cold and dry, of the nature of the Earth, and of ♄, melancholick, durative, by reason of Drowth, and destructive by reason of Cold, for there is no destruction but by ♀ and ☿; they are also astringent and durative in themselves, and destroyers of others externally; for ♄ in his own being once revived, doth give long life, and is durable, by reason of his dry Quality; but if ☿, ♀, and ♄ be put together, then is destruction by over much cold.

♊, ♎, and ♒, are hot and moist, of the nature of the Air, Sanguine; and because they are more moist than hot by nature, and do participate with Fire in heat, and Water in moisture, and are digestive and generative by reason of heat, and corruptive by reason of their moisture, ☿, ♀, and ♄ therefore alter the meat, digest, and increase the blood.

♋, ♏, and ♓, are cold and moist, of the nature of the Water, Feminine, Passive, like the Moon, Flegmatick salt in taste, ☽, ♂, ♃, corruptive by reason of their moisture, and destructive by reason of their coldness; they are more cold than moist, and are called the expulsive Signs, for they do corrupt, destroy, and expell: *Luna ergo percurrens in Signis suis multa admiranda possunt fieri ad corperum destructionem.*

And here note, that these four Elements twelve Signs, and seven Planets, do induce in all mortal Bodies four Humours, viz. Blood, which is sweet, Choler, which is bitter, Melancholy, which is sour, and Flegm, which is saltish: but these four Humours are so united in the Body of man, and mixed and knit in such sort, that there is no separation thereof until the dissolution of the Body, and separation of the Spirit from the Body, the which dissolution is done many ways; but here it is to be understood but of one way, that is, by natural Death, and not by unnatural Death; and according to that Humour which is most prevalent, and predominant in the Body of man, thereafter is the man called, either Sanguine, Cholerick, Flegmatick, or Melancholick, and every one of these Humours have their proper times of Rule, and different times of Working in their several times, as occasion is given. Their general times of distinct Rule, as thus; Sanguine rules from 9 at night till 3 in the morning, Choler from 3 to 9 forenoon, Melancholy from 9 to 3 afternoon, Flegm from 3 to 9 at night. Thus briefly touching on things as they may in the progress of this Work concern us, but now to proceed.

Experimented Judgments of Life and Death, and of Diseases.

As touching the true knowledge hereof, it is by the motions of Heavens, and Aspects of the Planets, therefore in erecting of your Figure and before you give any Judgment, certain things are to be considered, and divers Questions to be asked.

The first thing to be noted is, the instant time when the Question is made, or the Urine brought; for sometimes one bringeth it when the Physician is not at home, and the Party leaveth it with some of his Servants, or with some friend, or with a neighbour, to be delivered unto him; then in such a case, he shall take the Question at the delivery of the Urine, or when the Party cometh for an Answer; but if you find the Urine by chance left in some place for you, then you shall take that Question of the Urine when the Party comes to you for his Answer.

The second thing by way of Question is, you shall ask the Name of the Party that is sick, and the Age; for by the Name you shall know whether it be man or woman, by the Age you shall know whether the Party be young or old; for there are divers things to be considered in the differences of Diseases of men and women, and of old folk and young.

If it be a Woman, the third Question is, whether she be married or not? for if married, she may be with child, or she may have pain in her matrix by child-birth, the which Maids have not. Again, if she be young, she may have the Green-sickness, by reason of Nature's Obstructions; and this is incident both to Women, Children and Maids, obstructions of Nature, their natural Courses, either they may not have them at all, or else not in their due order and course; and then they experience pains in the Reins, in the Side and Stomach, and often incline to vomit, and have much pain in the Head, and this seldome or never faileth.

The fourth Question is, you shall ask, who sent the Urine, or by whose motion or command the Urine was brought or sent? for sometimes the Sick saith, go to such a Doctor and ask my Disease; and sometimes the say, ask him whether I shall live or dye; and sometimes whether he can help me; and sometimes again some of the Friends of the Sick, unknown to the Sick, do come and ask his Disease; whereupon you shall ask the bearer of the Urine, who bad him or her come with it? or whether the Party that bringeth the Urine came with it of his or her own accord, or not? for if the bearer of the Urine, or any such like that maketh the Question, come unto you, not being of his blood or kindred that oweth the Urine, but as his friend or neighbour, moved with pity, or of good will, or being desired thereunto, or if it be the Husbands Brother's Wife that bringeth the Urine, or asketh the Question, then the first House (which is the Angle of the East) and his Lord, is the House of Life, and is also lord of the Urine, and the lord of the 5th House is lord of the Liver, and the first House shall be the Ascendant for the Asker, and the 7th House for the sick Person, and the 8th House and the 4th shall be Significators of Death; the 4th House is the end and determination of every Question, and therefore also of Life and Death, as hereafter shall be shewed more plainly. And finally, know this for a general Rule, that whosoever brings the Urine, or asketh the Question by consent of the sick Body, whether it be Father, Mother, Brother, Sister, or Child, or the Wife or Husband of any Sick, if the sick Party bid them go, or consent unto their going to ask the Question, then the first House shall be the Ascendant of the Question, as before.

If some secret fellow, or councellour to the Sick in private matters, whom he trusteth much, which reapeth benefit at his hand, or that trusteth to have something by the death of the Sick (be it he or she, man or woman, not being of his kindred, nor sent by the sick) bring the Urine, or ask the Question, then the second House and his lord is for the Quærent, and for Life, and the 8th House is for the sick Person, and the 9th House is the House of

Death, and the 6th House is for the Liver. This was the Opinion of Dr. *Foreman*, very knowing this way.

If the Brother, the Sister, the Uncle, Aunt, or Kinsman of the Sick, bring the Urine, or ask the Question for the Sick, not being sent by the Sick, then the third House and his lord is the Ascendant of the Question, and for the Asker; and the 7th House shall be for the Liver, and the 9th House shall be for the sick Person, and the 10th House shall be the House of Death, and the 8th House shall signifie the Infirmity, and the first House shall shew the remedy, and how it is to be done, and this must be without consent of the sick Body, of the Brothers or Sisters own accord, or proper motion.

If the Father or Mother of the Sick, unknown to the Sick, bring the Urine, or ask the Question for the Sick, then the 4th House shall be the Ascendant for the Question, for the Quærent, and for Life, and for the Urine, and the 8th House shall signifie the Liver, and the 10th house shall be for the sick Body, and the 11th House shall be the House of Death, and the 2d House shall shew the Remedy, and the 9th House shall shew the particular Infirmity; as sometimes the Father of a young child doth bring the Urine, or ask the Question for the child being sick, sometimes the Mother.

If the Son or Daughter of the Sick bring the Urine, or make the Question for the Sick, then the first House and his lord shall be the Ascendant of the Question for the Quærent, for Life, and the 9th House shall signifie the state of the Liver, and the 11th House shall be for the sick Person, and the 10th House shall signifie the Infirmity, and the 12th House shall be the House of Death, and the third House shall shew the Remedy: and this is, if the Question be asked by such a one unknown, and without consent of the Party sick.

If the sick Person himself bring his own Urine, or make the Question for himself, or say to someone, take my Urine, and go and know my Disease, &c. then the Question is by the sick, or by the command of the sick himself; then the Ascendant of the Sign and his lord shall be significators of the sick Party; the 6th House and lord thereof, the Planets therein placed, the place of Heaven and the Sign wherein the ☽ is, shall signifie the Disease and part afflicted; in reference to the Ascendant the 7th House shall represent the Physician, and the 10th his Medicine; if the Lord of the 7th be unfortunate, the Physician shall not care; if the 10th House or lord thereof, his Physick is improper; the 4th House signifies the end of the Sickness, and whether it will terminate quickly, or indure long.

If the Husband of the Sick, or Wife of the Sick make the Question, or bring the Urine, then the 7th House shall be the Ascendant of the Question, for the Quærent, for the Urine, and for Life, and the 1st House shall be for the Sick, and shall signifies the Distemper, the Sickness and part afflicted, the 11th house for the Liver, and the estate thereof, the 1st house the Physician, and the 4th his Medicine, or means, the 2d house shall be the house of Death, and the 10th house for the end and determination of the Sick, and the Disease. And here note also, that if the Wife come for the Husband, if he bid her go, the first house shall be for the Quærent, &c *è contrà*, for thw Wife saith sometimes, I will go, and the Husband saith no, yet she goeth, then the 7th House is for the Quærent, and so of the Husband in reference to the Wife.

If the Master or Mistris of the sick bring the Urine, or make the Question for the Sick, saying my Servant is sick, then the 10th house shall be for the Quærent, for the Urine, and for life, and the 4th house for the sick Person, and the 2d for the Liver, and the 8th house (according to some) for the Medicine, the 3d house for the Infirmity, and the first house for the end thereof; and the 5th house for Death.

If the servant of his own accord make the Question for his Master or Mrs. being sick, then the 6th house shall be the Ascendant of the Question, for the Quærent, for the Urine, and for Life, and the 12th House for the sick Party, the 10th house for the Liver, and the 11th for the Disease, the first house for Death, and the 9th house for the end and determination of the Sick and his Disease, and the 4th house for the Medicine.

If a man come, saying, my brother sent me to you to know what Disease his Servant hath that is sick; whether he will live or dye? here the 11th house is the Ascendant of the Question, for Life, for the Quærent, and the Urine, the 5th house for the Sick, the third house for the Liver, the 4th house for the Sickness, the 6th house to know whether he will live or dye, the 9th house for the Medicine, and the second for the end of his Disease; except the Urine do come by the consent of the sick Person, if it do, then the sixth house shall be the Ascendant for the Quærent.

And sometimes also the Master or Mrs. saith unto their Servant, go to such a one, and ask what Disease &c. Here in such a Question I take the 1st house for the Quærent, for life, and for the Urine, and the 7th house for the Sick, because the Messenger came by commandment of his Master or Mrs, Father or Mother, and not of his own accord; the 5th house for the Liver, the 6th for the Infirmity, the 8th for Death, the 11th for the Medicine and Remedy; the 4th house for the end, the 2d house how thou shalt be paid for doing thy Cure, and what Expence he shall be at for his health, whether much or little.

And here note, that naturally the 1st house is the house of Life, the 4th house signifieth the end, the 5th the Liver, the 6th the Infirmity, the 7th the sick Person, the 8th whether it be Death or no, the 9th the Physician, the 11th the Cure and Medicine, the 10th the Finger of God, the 12th a secret Enemy, or Witchcraft. Though this Method do somewhat differ from what I proposed before, which was the way of the Ancients, yet I thought necessary to mention likewise what hath been verifie by experience; let each Student and Practitioner try and trust.

And furthermore, observe, that by whomsoever the Question is made, and what House soever thou dost find Ascendant for the Question, for the Urine, and for Life, thou shalt in thy Judgment joyn him and his lord with the 1st House Natural and his lord, for Life; and the 5th House of the Question, and the 5th House of the Figure for the state of the Liver, and the 6th House of the Figure, and 6th House of the Question for the state of the Sickness, whether it shall be long or short; and the 7th House of the Question, and 7th House of the Figure for the sick Person, and the 8th House of the Figure, and 8th House of the Question for Death; the 11th of the Question for the Medicine; the 4th House of the Question and 4th of the Figure for the end of the Disease; and whosoever bringeth the Urine or maketh the Question either he doth it by consent of the sick Person, or without the consent of the sick Person; and if it be by and with the consent of the sick Person, and with his or her good will, or if the Sick say go, then the first House alwayes shall be for the Quærent, &c. as aforesaid; but if he say go not, or that he know not of it, then the Party that is the cause thereof shall make the Ascendant of the Question; as if it be the Father, then the 4th House is for the Ascendant; if the Brother, then the third house; if the Servant, then the 6th House, and so forth, as aforesaid.

When any one therefore comes to you with any Urine, or doth make any Question for the Sick, the premises before-said considered, and the instant time of moving the Question being noted, you shall mark especially his demand, for sometimes the Party that cometh saith,

Sir, I am come to you to have your counsel on this Urine of one that is sick, and saith, I would know his Disease, or whether he will live or dye.

Sometimes also they say, I would know what Disease he hath.

Sometimes they say, I would know whether he will escape it, or whether he will dye thereof.

Sometimes they ask none of these things, but the say, I would know what is good for him.

Sometimes again they will ask, whether you can help him that is sick?

Sometimes they ask for a Woman, whether she be with Child or no?

And sometimes they ask, whether the Party hath not such a Disease as is suspected, or no?

So that sometime they ask one Question, sometimes another; for the minds of People are variable and divers, even according to the motions of the Heavens, and aspects of the Planets and Stars, and a man shall have no power to go to ask a Question for the Sick, though many times they desire and determine it, neither to ask any thing touching the Sick, but when his mind doth accord with the Heavens, and when the Heavens do accord to the end of his intent, to shew the just end thereof;

for I have known oft-times by experience, that some have been in the mind to come to me, as themselves have confess'd, for their infirmities, a quarter of a Year together, yet have had no power to come to me until they have been past remedy; upon which coming I have told them such a time they would dye of their infirmity, and they have died, as I have said; and sometimes because my self would not deal with them, they have gone to others for Physick, yet all hath not served: this have I proved many a time and oft, as well on young folk as on old and middle aged, and as well on women as on men, and children of both sexes; for by the figure many things are seen and known that are not to be known by Urine, in mine opinion, at first time. Amongst the old Philosophers, it was advised to be brought to the Physician to know the Disease; not for that the Disease, or Life, or Death can be perfectly discerned by the Urine, but by bringing the Urine, it is a token from the Sick to know his Disease, by making the Question for the Sick; for no man ought to study Physick except he be well seen in Astrology; for it is impossible to give a just Judgment of the state of a Disease only by seeing the Urine, or by feeling the Pulse, or Siedge, or seeing the Sick; for a man by Astrology will say more by a Question demanded for the state of the sick, for his sickness and Disease, and touching Life and Death, for curing of the Party hurt or sick, than ten other Physicians that shall see the Urine, and speak with the sick Body; for many are sick that know not their own Disease, nor the Cause, nor the Degrees thereof, and by Astrology it is to be known, and by no means else, because the Bodies of men are subject to Diseases, according to the influence of the Heavens; for, *à superieribus inferita reguatur*; for is a man mark well, all Diseases are either Natural, Supernatural, or against Nature; if it be Natural, it is by the Influence of the Heavens in his Nativity; if is be Supernatural, it is the Finger of God on a man, or on his generation, for some offence committed, which remaineth on a man, and sometimes on his Posterity, through many generations to come; by which means they are more or less subject to some certain Disease, as some to dye suddenly, some to have the Kings Evil, some the Stone, the Gout, some the French Pox, some the

Leprosie, and such like hereditary Distempers, and all to die of one Disease, and these are said to have such a Disease by Nature, but it is Supernatural, and Natural also.

If it be against Nature, it is by Surfeiting, or drinking or eating something that makes them sick, or by Witchcraft, or Sorcery, or by Inchantment, or by the punishment of the Devil, or some Spirit, by the permission and sufferance of God; and all these things cannot be known but by Astronomie, and therefore we conclude, that if he be not a good Astronomer and Astrologer withall, he can be no good Physician; this I have often hinted in my Almanacks, and shewed the same from the most Learned.

Again, the proportion of Medicine and of the Body, and the degree of the Disease, and of Medicine, and commixtion of Humours, and the diversity thereof, are not known by any means but by Astronomy; for who can make a just proportion of Medicine for any Disease, except he be a good Astronomer? neither can he tell the times proper for healing the Disease, nor whether it be to be cured or no, even as the blind man hits the Hare; *nam Astrologia est oculus medici,* saith *Aristotle, sine qua cæctus appellabitur.*

Next we are to know and observe, which of the four Virtues or Humours is weaker or stronger than the other, or than it should be, whereby the distemper of the Body doth grow.

In the Bodies of Natural Men are four Radical Virtues, holding a due proportion by Nature, by the which the Health and Strength of the Body is always maintained, and when any of these four do predominate and get dominion over the other, then doth the body wax sick and languish in pain, or else is utterly frustrate of the Radical Humidity, and so surprised, and overcome by Death. The first of these four Virtues is Digestion, the second Retention, the third Attraction, and the fourth Expulsion; and these four Virtues are always sustained by four Principal and Radical or Natural Humours.

I. Digestion hath its operation, and is maintained by Blood, making his operation in the Stomach by the Liver, for so long as the Liver keepeth his natural proportion, by heat and moisture of good blood, so long shall the Body be in Health; and if the Part distemper himself by his Diet or otherwise, whereby the Liver is oppressed with much Moisture, Drowth, Heath or Cold, then the meat in the stomach for want of Decoction, by too much cold, or overmuch heat, fouleth and corrupteth the Blood, and breedeth distempers and diseases in the Body, proceeding unnaturally from the excess of Choler, Melancholy, Blood, or Flegm.

The natural Blood, or spirits of Life, relate to the Liver, the Vital to the Heart, the Animal to the Brain, to which the Sperm and Seed is much relative.

The second of the four Virtues aforesaid is Attraction, this operation is performed by natural Heat and Choler, which is ingendred by good digestion, of the Liver, and hath its principal residence in the Gall, and if this Humour become adust or abound, the Blood is infected thereby, and many distempers and infirmities are caused, as shall be shewed more plainly when we come to treat of Choler.

The third of these Virtues is Retention, which conserveth the Nutriment in the Body till it be digested, and it is maintained by Melancholy, naturally cold and dry, and hath its proper residence in the Milt or Spleen, as shall be seen hereafter.

The fourth and last is natural Flegm, which is expulsive, and partly miseth in the Veins with the Blood, is cold and moist, and thereby is maintained the Expulsive faculty, whose office is to expell the Exrements that annoy the Body, as after will farther appear.

And now to return to our former matter again, to know which of these four Virtues or Faculties is diminished, or which of them doth abound beyond his natural Order, you shall understand, the Virtue Retentive belongeth to ♄, the Virtue Digestive to ♃, the Virtue Attractive to ♀, and the Virtue Expulsive to the ☽.

Observe diligently therefore which of these four Planets, ♄, ♃, ♀, or the ☽ have most dignities in the Sign of the 5ᵗʰ House of the Question, which alwayes signifieth the state of the Liver, that Planet according to his potency or debility in the Figure of Heaven, in the Sign, and Degree, and Place where he is, shall signifie the strength or debility of the Liver, and of that Virtue which he governeth.

If ♄ be strongest in the Sign of the 5ᵗʰ House of the Question, then the fault is in the Virtue Retentive, that either it is too strong or too weak, by too much unnatural Melancholy abounding therein, or for want of natural Melancholy to retain the meat in the Body, and then the Muscles of the Stomach being oppressed with too much moisture, the Party remitteth up the meat and drink he taketh, so soon and as often as he doth take it; for that the Liver is oppleted with moisture, which weakeneth and overcometh the Virtue Retentive.

If ♄ be strong in an earthly Sign, as ♉, ♍, or ♑, which are cold and dry, melancholy, then is the Virtue retentive too strong in the Liver, through too much Melancholy abounding in the Liver, stopping and oppressing the Liver, causing Oppilations, Faintings, Heaviness, black Jaundies, with the Spleen swelling, Wind and Indigesture, and the Party hath a stomach to eat meat, and when he hath it, he eateth very little, for having eaten it, it is long before it be digested, and lieth hard and heavy in the Stomach.

And if the said Melancholy descend into the Bowels, then the Partie are Costive, and cannot go to stool; if into the Muscles of the Bladder, then he cannot make water; if into the Milt, then the Party becometh Splenetick, and waxeth lean, and sometimes, the Veins being stopped, swelleth in the Body and Members, or consumeth, and sometimes hath much Stitch in the Sides.

If the said Melancholy enter into the Cells of the Heart, the part affecteth Solitude, and avoids talk and noises, shuns the light, and delights to be in dark places, and will sometimes incline to rave and curse, and is prone to all mischief, and to mischief himself or some others.

Furthermore, Melancholy is cold and dry, soure and sharp, of the nature of the Earth and of Saturn, dark, pale, and wan, the dregs of all the Humours; for soureness and sharpness are from cold and dry Qualities, as from ♉, ♍, ♑, and ♄, and it is oftentimes like Allum-water in taste.

Bitterness proceeds from the Qualities of Hot and Dry, and relates to ♈, ♌, ♐, and the ☉, and ♂ in them.

Saltness comes of Cold and Moisture, as from ♋, ♏, ♓, and the ☽ in any of them, cold and moist, Flegmatick.

Freshness of taste comes of ♄ in ♉, ♍, or ♑, or of ♄ in ♊, ♎, ♒.

Sweetness comes of Heat and Moisture, ♃ in ♊, ♎, or ♒.

Unfavouryness in taste come of ♋, ♏, ♓, especially ♓, and therefore we say, ♄ is cold and dry, sour and sharp; so are ♉, ♍, ♑, Melancholy.

♃ is hot and moist, Sanguine, sweet in taste, pleasant; so are ♊, ♎, and ♒.

♂ and the ☉ are hot and dry, Cholerick, bitter; so are ♈, ♌, and ♐.

♀ and ☽ are cold and moist, Flegmatick, saltish and unsavoury; and so are ♋, ♏, and ♓.

☿ is indifferent according the Planet he is joyned unto, or Sign he is found in: for if he be in ♈ he is bitter, if in ♉ soure, if in ♊ sweet, if in ♋ saltish and unsavoury.

If ♄ be in ♋, ♏, or ♓, having most Dignities in the 5th House, then is the Retentive Faculty weakned in the Liver, by too much cold Flegm, and the Party hath a cold Liver and vomiteth much, and hath no lust to eat, and eateth little, and the Party is fearful and timorous; and ♄ in ♋ doth cause the black Plague of Melancholy and Flegm, then must you purge Flegm and Melancholy, and help the digestive Faculty with warm things.

If ♄ have most Dignities in the 5th House, and be in ♈, ♌, or ♐, which are hot and dry, Cholerick, then is the Liver oppressed with too much Choler and Melancholy, mixed with a very dry, hot, bitter, sharp, hard, and yellowish Humour.

If ♄ be in ♈, it is of slender, thin, yellow Choler and Melancholy: if in ♌, it is of gross, thick, yellow Choler, and reddish, and is hot and burning, and very dry, causing cholerick Passions in the Bowels, and much vomiting, and hot burning Agues of long continuance, and the Plague (if the Season be infectious) of green Choler, tough Flegm, and Melancholy, with a wonderful drought in the parts, that they can scarcely speak often times.

If ♄ be in ♐, then it is of red Choler, strong and potent, burnt, mix'd with melancholy, causing Plagues, hot burning Fevers, with Madness. If ♄ be in ♌ Retrograde, and in the 4th House, then this Choler oppresseth the Stomach, and the Party doth vomit much, by reason of that excess of drowth in the Stomach supernaturally.

If ♄ be in ♊, ♎, or ♒, then is the Liver oppressed with Melancholy mixed with Blood, and maketh the blood thick and fæculent; if Melancholy have the upper hand, and be predominant, then it is more dry than moist, and more cold than hot, and more soure and sharp than sweet. And if Blood have the better, it is more hot than cold, and more sweet than sharp.

If ♄ be Lord of the Ascendant, and in ♊, ♎, or ♒, and ♂ ascend in the 5th House, or any Sign where the ☽ hath most Dignities, by reason the ☽ hath most Dignities in ♉, or in the Sign of the 5th House, ♄ being lord of the Ascendant, and in the 5th as is aforesaid; in ♊ it signifies the Stomach is weak, and the expulsive Virtue is too strong: and the Party vomiteth much, and cannot keep his meat, by reason of much cold and moisture in the Stomach and Liver, Melancholy and tough Flegm mixed with the Blood in the Liver and Tunicles of the Stomach above *Zirbus*, but the Retentive Virtue or Faculty below *Zirbus*, in the Belly, Bowels, and Bladder, is too strong, and the Party is very costive, and cannot go to stool nor make water.

If ♄ have most Dignities in the 5th, and be in an Angle not remote, although he be Occidental and], and in ♋, yet the Retentive faculty is too strong; and if it be in a Woman, her Terms are stop't.

If ♃ be strong, and have most Dignities in the 5th house, or Sign of the 5th, then the Virtue Digestive is too strong, or too weak, according to the strength or ♃ in the Figure of Heaven at that time.

If ♃ then be in Airy Signs strong, as in ♊, ♎, ♒, then the Blood aboundeth in the Liver, and the Digestive faculty is swift and quick, by reason of the heat and moisture of Blood which is in the Liver. Blood overmuch abounding causeth Pleurisies and Diseases, and heat of the Lights, and impostumations of the Liver and Lungs; if then the Blood ascend to the heart, it choaketh the vital spirits, and causeth Syncope and Faintness, Palpitations and Swoonings; if it ascend to the Brain, it causeth Head-ache in the *Sineiput*, or fore-part of the head, with Lunacy oft-times and Frantickness; if it pass out to the extreme parts of the Body, it causeth impostumations; but if ♃ have no Dignities, but be in a Cadent House, as in the 6th, Combust, or oppressed by ♂ by a □, ☍, or ☌, then it causeth Sickness, very oft the Dropsie in the Belly.

If ♃ be weak in ♉, ♍, or ♑, which are Earthly Signs, cold and dry, contrary to Nature, then is the Liver oppressed with Choler, *Præssina* and *Cholera fuliginosa*, that is, green or sooty Choler mix'd with Melancholy, and mix'd with the Blood in the Liver, which doth thicken and cool the Blood, causing Oppilations and Stoppings in the Liver, with Indigestion, as when a man hath seemingly a stomach to eat, yet cannot eat.

If ♃ be strong in the 5th House, and in ♈, ♌, or ♐, then is the Liver corrupted with Choler, vitiating and infecting the Blood; if in ♈, with thin yellow Choler; if in ♌, then with thick yellow Choler, hot and dry, causing great, hot, fæculent Fevers; if in ♐, of red Choler mixed with Blood, causing Madness and pestilence, and hot burning Fevers.

If ♃ be in ♋, ♏, or ♓, and have most Dignities in the 5th House, then the Digestive Virtue is weakened by too much cold and moisture, especially of much moisture, called *Cholera Vitellina*, which is of Flegm and Blood mixed, and is slimy, tough, moist and viscous, and the Party, hath a cold Stomach, and digests not his food, for the abounding of this viscous, flegmy matter in the Liver, corrupts the Liver and the Blood, and causeth Dropsies, and such Diseases: in this Distemper administer not Physick in the hour of ♃, the ☽, nor ♀, neither let them be strong in the

Figure of Heaven, but minister in the hour of ♂ and the ☉, when they be in ♈, ♌, or ♐, or in the hour of *Saturn*, when he is in ♊, ♎, or ♒, fortunate and strong, putting in the Ascendant ♈, ♌, or ♐; and let the ☽ be in ♈, ♌, or ♐, applying to the Sun or Mars by △ or ✶, and it must be cured by and with things that are very dry in operation, and hot in *primo gradu*.

If ♃ be lord of the 5th, and have most Dignities in the 5th, and be in his own Sign, or where he hath many Dignities, and be strong in Angle, free from the malevolent Aspects of ♄ and ♂, *viz.* the □, ☌, or ☍, then it signifies the Liver and the Virtue digestive is strong.

If ♃ be lord of the 5th, and have most Dignities in the 5th, and be in ♒ in the 6th, sub radiis or combust, having no Dignities at all, and be oppressed with the □ of ♂ out of ♉ in the 10th, then it signifieth the Party hath a pain caused of Choler and Melancholy, and that the Digestive Virture is weak for want of good Blood, and the like is also if he be oppressed by the ☍ of ♄ out of ♌, but hten yellow Choler hath the Dominion.

If ♀ have most Dignities in the 5th House of the Question, and be in ♋, ♏, or ♓, then is the Attractive Virtue weakened by much cold and thin watry Flegm, and Water caused of ♀ in ♋, ♏, ♓, and it is salt Flegm; and if she be in ♋ the water is thin Flegm, and salt, and cold; if in ♏ thicker, salter, more stinking, tougher, and colder; if in ♓ most stinking, and more tough, thicker and colder, causing Dropsies, cold Oppilations, Fevers, and Swellings; and in such a case Administer not in the hour of ♀ nor the ☽, but in the hour of ☉ or ♂, or in the hour of ♃, he being in ♈, ♌, or ♐; or put ♈, ♌, or ♐ in the Ascendant, or when the ☽ is in ♈, ♌, or ♐, applying to ♂ or the ☉ by ✶ or △, and then purge Flegm and watry Humours, and let the Cure be done with hot and dry things, and the Diet hot and dry.

If ♀ be in ♈, ♌, or ♐, then the Attractive Virtue is too strong, and draweth many ill Humours to the Liver, of Flegm and Choler, which is salt and bitter withall, caused of ♀ in ♈, ♌. or ♐; if ♀ be in ♌, then of thick and fæculent yellow Choler, and subtil, bitter, and saltish; if ♀ be in ♐, then it is caused or red Choler and

Flegm, hot and dry, very bitter and brinish, causing salt flegmie faces.

If ♀ be in ♊, ♎, or ♒, it comes of thin Flegm and Water mixed with Blood; if ♀ be in ♊, of Blood and thin Flegm, sweetish and saltish; if ♀ be in ♎, thicker Blood and Flegm, more sweet and saltish; if ♀ be in ♒, then of very thick Blood and Flegm, most salt and sweetish; withall hot and moist, with shivering, causing oftentimes impostumations; minister not in the hour of ♀ nor the ☽, but in the hour of ♃ in ♑, ♍, or ♉, or in the hour of ♂ or the ☉ being in ♉, ♍, or ♑, ♋, ♏ or ♓, ☽ in ♉, ♍, or ♑, applying to ☉, ♂, or ♃, with ✶ or △, and ♉, ♍, or ♑ in the Ascendant.

If ♀ be in ♉, ♍, or ♑, then the Virtue Attractive is distempered by cold and dry Qualities, and by Melancholy and thin Flegm, cold and dry, sour and saltish, mixed with the Blood in the Liver, stopping the Stomach, causing a loathing of meat and indigestion, and it is saltish and sharp like Allum-water; if ♀ be in ♉ then of thin Melancholy and thin Flegm, and is sharp, cold, and saltish al little; if ♀ be in ♍, then thicker Melancholy and more thin Flegm, and it is more sharp, and somewhat saltish, like Allum-water; if ♀ be in ♑, then of thicker, blacker, grosser Melancholy, and thin Flegm, and it is very saltish and sharp withall, like Allum-water; in this case minister not in the hour of ♀, ☽, nor ☿, nor ♄, but in the hour of ♃, ♂, or the ☉, when ♊, ♎, or ♒, applying to ♂, ☉, or ♃, by ✶ or △, and purge Melancholy and Flegm strongly, If the ☽ have most Dignities in the Ascendant of the 5th house of the Question, and be in ♋, ♏, or ♓, then the Virtue Expulsive is too strong in the Liver by reason of too much Flegm and Moisture oppressing the Liver, especially if the ☽ be in the 5th; if the ☽ be in the 4th house, then the Virtue Expulsive is too strong in the Stomach, and the Party Vomits much, and hath much gnawing in the Stomach; if the ☽ be in the Ascendant, then the Expulsive Virtue is too strong in the Head, and then the Eyes do run and drop, or Scabs come out, or the Ears run, or some other impediment comes out in the Head, or the Nose bleedeth; if the Moon be in the 10th house, then the Party hath the running of the Reins, or Gonorrhea Passion, or some flux or weakness in the Reins, or cannot hold his Urine; if the ☽ be in the 7th house, then the Expulsive Virtue is too strong in the Limbs, and there be Scabs, Pushes, Carbuncles, Botches, Impostumations, or other sores; if the ☽ be in the 9th, then the Expulsive Virtue is too strong in the Liver, and the Party bleedeth at the Nose, or at the Mouth; and if the Question be for a Woman, the Expulsive Virtue is too strong in the Matrix, and she hath the Running of the Whites, or shew extraordinary of her Flowers, or a Lask; if for a man, then it is too strong in the inwards, and there may follow a Lask or Dysenteria.

If the ☽ be in ♋, then the Flegm and Water is thin and cold, saltish and unsavoury.

If the ☽ be in ♏, then it is thicker, stinking, unclean and venomous, with viscous Flegm, corrupt.

If the ☽ be in ♓, then it is caused of thick Flegm, very cold, moist, and saltish,

In such a case minister not in the hour of the ☽, nor ♀, but in the hour of ♂ or the ☉, being in ♈, ♌, or ♐, and put ♈, ♌, or ♐ in the Ascendant, and the ☽ in ♈, ♌, or ♐, when the ☽ doth apply by ✶ or △ to the ☉, ♂, or to ♃ being in ♈, ♌, or ♐, or to ♄ in ♈, ♌, or ♐, or to ♀ in ♈, ♌, or ♐, with the ☽ in △ or ✶ out of a fiery Sign, then purge Flegm, and give a dry Diet: and if ♉, ♍, or ♑ be in the Ascendant, and the ☽ in ♈, ♌, or ♐, applying to ♂ or the ☉ you may give the Party a Vomit; and let the lord of the 6th be weak, and the lord of the Ascendant strong, fortunate, and direct.

If the ☽ be in ♊, ♎, or ♒, having most Dignities in the 5th, then the Expulsive Virtue is too strong, through too much moisture of sweet Flegm abounding in the Liver, which is caused of Flegm and Blood mixed; but if the Blood have the dominion, the Party is moist and Rheumatick, and the Spittle is whitish, and somewhat clammy, and a little sweet, but rather tasts a little saltish.

If the ☽ be in ♊, the Spittle and Flegm are thin, and little sweetish and hot; if the ☽ be in ♎, it is more sweetish, hot and thick; if the ☽ be in ♒, very sweet, thick and clammy.

In such a case, minister not in the hour of ♃, the ☽, nor ♀, but in the hour of ☿ or ♄, they being (if it may be) in ♉, ♍, or ♑;

neither shall you put ♊, ♎, or ♒ in the Ascendant, or the ☽, or ♃, but let them be weak; but you may put the ☽ in ♈, ♌, or ♐, applying to ♄ or ☿, or in ♉, ♍, or ♑, applying to the ☉ or ♂ by ✶ or △; then purge sweet Flegm, and give things that do dry and cleanse.

If the ☽ have more Dignities in the 5th, and be in the 5th, in ♉, ♍, or ♑, then is the Expulsive Virtue weakened through too much cold and drowth of Melancholy and Flegm, infecting the Blood, and stopping the Liver, and it is called *Acetosa Phlegma*, and *Vitrea Phlegma*, by reason of the Analogy it beareth in colour and taste to Glass and Vinegar, as being a little saltish, but soure and sharp like Allum-water, and it is wonderful cold, tough and dry, making oppilations and indigestion in the Liver, and little lust to meat, and the Party is heavy, dull, earthy, and melancholy; if this *Vitrea Phlegma* ascend to the Stomach, the Stomach will be cold, hard, heavy, and soure, inclining to vomit, and yet cannot vomit, but hath much pricking, reaching tearing and gnawing in the Stomach; for such it is good to vomit: if this *Vitrea Phlegma* affect the Lungs it causeth shortness of Wind, Ptisick, and extreme Coughs: if it ascend, and affect the Brain, it causeth heaviness, yet little sleep, but prickings, and cold, and aches in the Head; and this shall you know, if the ☽ be in ♉, ♍, or ♑, and in the Ascendant, then it is *in eapite*; if she be in the 10th, then it is in the Reins, and causeth the Stone; if she be in the 4th, it is in the Stomach; if in the 7th, the Limbs, causing dry Scurfs and Scabs; if the ☽ be in the 5th, the Question being for a Woman, then this Humour is in her Matrix-veins and causeth Retention of her Flowers; if it be in the Bowels, it obstructs going to stool.

If the ☽ be in ♉, it is cold, dry, sharp, stiff and soure.

If the ☽ be in ♍, it is more cold, dryer, sharper, stiffer and sourer.

If the ☽ be in ♑, then all these exceed in the Superlative degree.

In such a case minister not in the hours of the ☽, ♄, or ☿, but in the hour of ♃, the ☉ or ♂, they being in ♊, ♎, or ♒, ir it may be; nor give the Party any thing that may breed Flegm or Melancholy, but things to digest and purge Melancholy, and to increase the Blood, and administer things hot in the third degree. And in administring to cure this Distemper, put not the ☽ in ♉, ♍, or ♑, not the ☽ ♄, nor ☿ in the Ascendant; but let them be weak and unfortunate: but you may posite ♎, ♊, or ♒ in the Ascendant, and the ☽ in ♊, ♎, or ♒, or in ♋, applying to ☌ or the ☉ by △ or ✶; or in ♓, applying to ♂; or in ♈, ♌, or ♐, applying likewise to ♀, and let the lord of the 6th be weak and infortuante, and the lord of the Ascendant strong and fortunate.

If the ☽ in such a case be in the 5th, and in ☌ or Aspect with ♄, it causeth the black Jaundies; if with ☿, it causeth Madness.

If the ☽ have most Dignities in the 5th, and be in ♈, ♌, or ♐; then it signifieth the Expulsive Virtue is weakened by too much heat and dryness, caused of Flegm and Choler mix'd, and it is very hot and dry; if the ☽ be then in the 5th House, this salt Flegm resteth in the Liver and inwards of a man, and Matrix of a Woman.

If the ☽ be in the 4th House, then it is in the Stomach, bitter, clammy, salt and dry: if the ☽ be then in the Ascendant, it is then in the Head and Face, and will cause Redness and Pimples, and the Eyes will look, red and yellowish, full of red Veins.

If the ☽ be then in the 10th House, it is in the Reins, and will cause the Stone, and stopping in the Reins and Kidneys: if she be in the 4th, it affecteth and afflicteth the Stomach: If the ☽ be in the 7th house, then it is in the Limbs and extreme Parts, and will break out in Scabs and Flux.

And this note, if Flegm predominate in this commixtion, it is more salt than bitter, and causeth great dryness and burning, and a red face, with smarting and swelling, if it be in the Stomach, and soreness in the Womb; and if Choler predominate, it is saltish, but more bitter than salt; and if it rise to the Head, you shall perceive it by the Eyes, for they will be yellowish full of red Veins.

The ☽ in ♈, it is caused of thin and subtil yellow Choler and Flegm; if the ☽ be in ☌ or application with ♂, or if ♂ be lord of the 12th in the New of the Moon, or lord of the 6th in the Wane;

it causeth the yellow Jaundies, and over-flowing of Choler in the Liver from the Gall.

The ☽ in ♌, it is caused of thicker yellow Choler and Flegm, and is drier an salter, causing the yellow Jaundies generally, and St. *Antbonies* fire, Carbuncles and Shingles, and hot burning Fevers and Itches.

The ☽ in ♐, it is caused of red Choler, hot and dry in the 4th degree, hot and burning, causing *Noli me tangere*, Cankers, salt hery Faces, and aches in the Body, Gouts, and many Diseases hard to be cured.

And when it happeneth so, that ♂ or the ☉ be lord of the 6th, 10th, or 12th House, or lord of the hour, it is so much the worse, and harder to be cured, or not to be cured at all, because it is in the extremity of the 4th degree; and if you go about to cure it, you must beware you minister not in the hours of the ☽, ♂, or the ☉, but in the hour of ♀, she being in ♊, ♎, or ♒; or in the hour of ♃, being in ♋, ♏, or ♓; or in the hour of the ☉, he being in ♊, ♎, or ♒; the ☽ in ♏ or ♓, applying to ♀ or ♃. Neither must you put ♈, ♌, or ♐ in the Ascendant, nor the ☽ in ♈, ♌, or ♐, but in a weak Sign and place of the Heavens, where she doth not behold the sixth House, nor the Ascendant nor the lord of the 6th House, but she may behold the lord of the Ascendant. Neither shall you put ♈, ♌, or ♐ in the 6th, but in some cadent House, for this kind of Flegm is salt, hot and dry, clammy and burning, and the Party must be cured with cold and moist Medicines in the 4th degree, if it be in ♐, and in the third degree, or in ♈ or ♌; for it is of Flegm and Choler commixt.

First, prepare the Party four or five dayes, then purge three dayes strongly; and if it be a Woman, diet her with a Dietary drink to that intent, and let her blood after it, if occasion serve.

General Judgments on the House which is the place of the Liver.

If the Planet that hath most dignities on the 5th House of these four Planets, *viz.* ♄, ♃, ♀, and the ☽ be fortunate and strong, or apply to fortunate Planets, then he shall help the same Virtue which he governeth, if you minister means in his hour, when the ☽ applieth to him, and give things to increase the Virtue diminished, and to diminish the peccant faculty abounding; but if the said Planet be unfortunate and weak, he shall then be unfit to help or succour the said Virtue or Faculty which he governeth, if you administer in his hour, or if the ☽ do apply to him when you do minister.

But in all your first ministrations to any for any Disease, let the lord of the 6th House be weak and infortunate, in his Fall or Detriment, in a Cadent house, or in ☍ to the 6th House; but if the lord of the 6th be Retrograde, or a Retrograde Planet in the 6th, or in the Sign of the 6th House, it is a sign that the Sickness will return again; or if it be a Sore or Wound, that it will relapse and break out again.

And if any two of the four Planets, ♄, ♃, ♀, ☽, have equal Dignities in the Sign of the 5th House, and be in equal places of the Heavens, (as both in Angles, or in Conjunction, or if one of them be lord of the Ascendant, and the other of the hour, or if the ☽ apply to one of them, and the other be lord of the Ascendant or hour) then is the fault in those two Virtues which those two Planets do signifie.

And note also, if you find a Sign in the 5th House, in the which two of the aforesaid Planets have equal Dignities, as ♈ in the 5th, considering ♄ and ♃, then shall you look which of those two Planets is weakest in the figure, and if ♃ be in ♑ in the second, and ♄ in the 9th in ♌ Retrograde, or in the 8th, he shall signifie according to the Sign and Place wherein he is, the Humour abounding, as ♄ in ♌ signifies thick yellow Choler and Melancholy, with waterish Flegm, or ♃ in ♑, which there doth signifie thick Melancholy mixed with the Blood, causing Oppilations.

And generally note, that if the Planet that signifies the strength and virtue of the Liver, or weakness thereof, if the said Planet be in a Sign of his own nature, he signifieth the abounding, and overmuch of this Humour and virtue; and if he be in a Sign contrary to his nature, he signifieth the weakness and debility of the said Virtue, as for example; If ♄, which signifies the Virtue

Retentive, be in a Sign cold and dry, of the nature of the Earth, like unto ♄, as ♉, ♍, or ♑, and in his Triplicity, Term or Face in an Angle, then the Virtue Retentive is too strong, by reason of too much natural Melancholy in the Body; as if ♄ be in the 4th house, then it is too strong in the Stomach; if in the 5th, then in the Liver or Matrix of a Woman; if in the Ascendant, then in the Head and Brain; if in the 10th, then in the Reins; if in the 7th, then in the limbs and extreme parts of the Body.

But if ♄ be in ♋, ♏, or ♓, and have no Dignities at all, then the Virtue Retentive is weakened for want of natural Melancholy, by too much cold and moisture abounding: if ♄ be in the 5th house, then the excess of Moisture is in the Liver, and in the inwards of a man, and in the Matrix of a Woman, causing the issuing of the Whites in a woman; if it be in the Liver, it causeth the Dropsie and Indigestion; if ♄ be in the 4th, then there is too much cold and moisture in the Stomach, causing vomiting; if ♄ be in the Ascendant, then there is too much cold and moisture in the Brain and Head, causing Head-ache and humours, and running of the Eyes; if ♄ be in the 10th, then there is too much cold and moisture in the Reins and Bladder, causing *Gonorrhea Passio*, or issuing of Nature, or much pissing; if ♄ be in the 7th, then there is overmuch cold and moisture in the Legs and extreme parts, causing Impostumations of cold Humours, and Dropsies.

And this is generally to be observed, that if the lord of the Ascendant, or lord of the hour be in any of the four Angles, and signifier of the grief and Disease; or if the Planet that hath most Dignities in the 5th be lord of the Ascendant, or lord of the hour, or lord of the 6th, or the Planet to whom the ☽ doth apply, and be angular; look which of the four Angles he is in, and there is the most grief; as if he be in the Ascendant, then is the greatest grief and pain in the Head; if in the 10th, then in the Reins; if in the 7th, then in the Legs and extreme Parts; if in the 4th, then in the Stomach; if in the 5th then in the Liver and Matrix of a Woman, and in the Liver and Inwards of a Man.

And note, the nearer the said Planet is to the Cusp of the Angle of the House wherein he is, the nearer is the Disease to the extremity of that place of the member; as if the Planet be near the Degree ascending, or within a degree or two then is the pain in the upper part, or mould of the Head; if he be in the 10th or 12th degree of the Sign ascending, then it is in the Brain, or middle of the Head; and if he be in 24 or 26 degrees, then is the grief in the lower part of the head, near the separation of the Head and Neck, as in the Pole, or under the Chin.

And if the Planet in the 10th House be near the Cusp of the 10th House, then the pain is below the girdle, in the Reins, if it be 10, 12, or 14 degrees from the Cusp, then it is in the Kidneys: if 20, or 24 degrees then above the Kidneys; if he be in the 4th near the Cusp, then the pain is in the upper part of the Stomach near the Throat; if in 10, 12, or 14 degrees, then is the grief in the midst of the Stomach; if in 20 degr. to 30, then in the bottom of the Stomach; if he be near the Cusp of the 5th House, the Distemper is in the upper part of the Matrix or Liver; if in the midst of that Sign, in the midst of the Liver or Matrix; if in the latter degrees of the Sign, then the Distemper affects the lower parts of the Liver or Matrix.

And generally note, that if there be no Planet found in any of the 4 Angles, or in the 5th House, or within 5 degrees of any Angle, nor within 25 degrees of the Ascendant of an Angle, or of the 5th House, then the Party hath no Disease, but is found, except it be of some extraordinary or superficial cause beyond Nature.

And in as many of these Angles or places as you shall find any Planet not remote from the Cusp, in that place which it signifieth, there is pain and Disease in the Body more or less; and these Rules fail not.

Again, if one Planet be lord of the Ascendant and lord of the hour also, angular and not remote, or in the 5th, or within 5 degrees falling from the Angle, the chief pain and grief shall be in that place which the House he is in doth signifie; if he be in the Ascendant, then the Head; and it never faileth.

The better to imprint this Doctrine in the mind of the Reader, behold the Figure following; and note that every House hath 30 degrees, 25 degrees within the Ascendant, and 5 degrees past, or virtually in the next house.

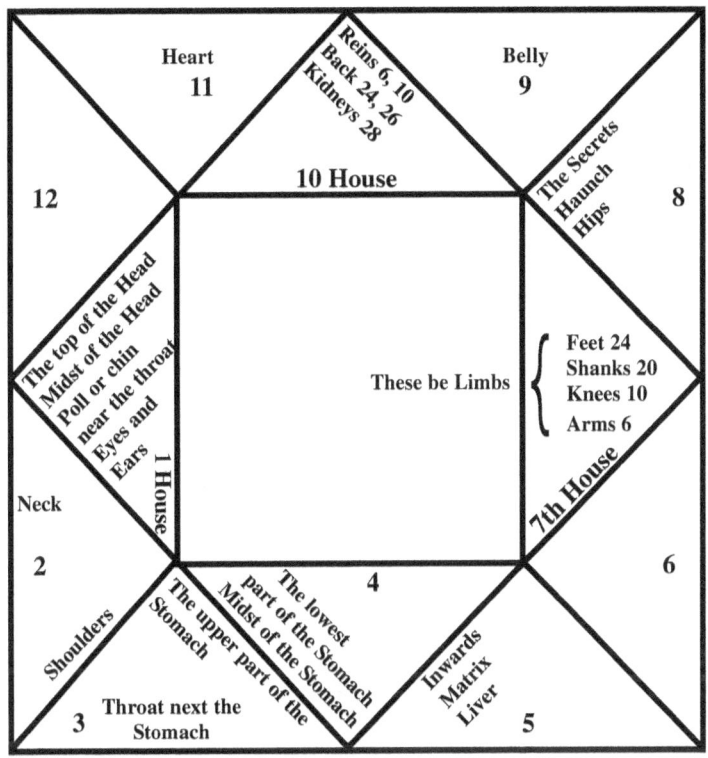

Figure showing that every House hath 30 degrees, 25 degrees within the Ascendant, and 5 degrees past, or virtually in the next house

The 4th House.

These are the five principal Houses, that shew the principal Parts of the Body, if there be any Disease in them.

The Figure being erected, it is very necessary to ask four Questions of the party touching the Sick.

1. As first, What the Name of the sick Person is?
2. Inquire of the age of the Party.

3. If a Woman, whether married or no?

4. The 4ᵗʰ Question, and most necessary of all, is, At whose procurement the Urine was brought, whether by the sick Person himself, or that some of his Friends or kindred procured the Urine to be brought, as aforesaid, for the Question made.

Judgments of the 4 Angles of the Question, and the first House.

Any Planet whatsoever, or ☊ or ☋ in the Ascendant, not remote in the 12ᵗʰ House, but in the 12ᵗʰ within 5 degrees of the Ascendant, signifieth pain in the Head, according to the strength and weakness of the Planet, or of ☊ or ☋ whatsoever he be.

Any Planet whatsoever, or *caput* or *cauda Draconis* in the 4ᵗʰ House, or in the 3d not remote from the Cusp above 5 degrees this signifies pain and distemper in the Stomach.

Any Planet, or ☊ or ☋ in the 7ᵗʰ House, or in the 6ᵗʰ within 5 degrees of the Cusp of the 7ᵗʰ, signifies pain and weakness in the limbs, in some part between the huckle-bone and the top of the toes.

Any Planet, or ☊ or ☋ in the 10ᵗʰ house, or in the 9ᵗʰ not remote from the Cusp of the 10ᵗʰ above 5 degrees, signifies pain in the Back, Reins and Kidneys.

Any Planet, or ☊ or ☋ in the 5ᵗʰ, if the Question be for a Woman, the Planet either in the 5ᵗʰ, or remote not above 5 degrees, then that Woman hath impediment in her Matrix, and her Terms be stopt, or else she hath them too much, or the purging of the Whites; and if the Question be for a Man, he hath some pain in his Liver and Inwards. *Cauda Draconis* in the 5ᵗʰ, in a fixed Sign, signifieth the Retention of Terms.

The first ten degrees of the first House have the upper part of the Head, the second ten degrees have the Fore-head and the Poll, the 3d ten degrees and last, contain the Nose, Cheeks, Mouth, Tongue, Teeth and Chin; and so forth of the 12 Houses as of the 12 Signs, for every House and Sign hath 30 degrees, which are divided into 3 triplicities, and every triplicity is 10 degrees. Also the Neck and Throat is divided into 3 parts, as before is said of the Head; that is, the first 10 degrees for the upper part, the second ten degrees for the middle part, and the last 10 degrees for the nether or lowest part of the Neck and Throat, and then the 3d House for the Shoulders and Arms, and the 4th for the Breast and Stomach, and so forth with the rest.

Some Ancient and Modern Physicians very eminent, have considered the 12 Houses thus, in reference to the Temperaments, which in Practice will be found necessary, the better to judge of the nature of the Disease; as will appear more plainly in the sequel: every one of these Temperaments admits of 4 degrees.

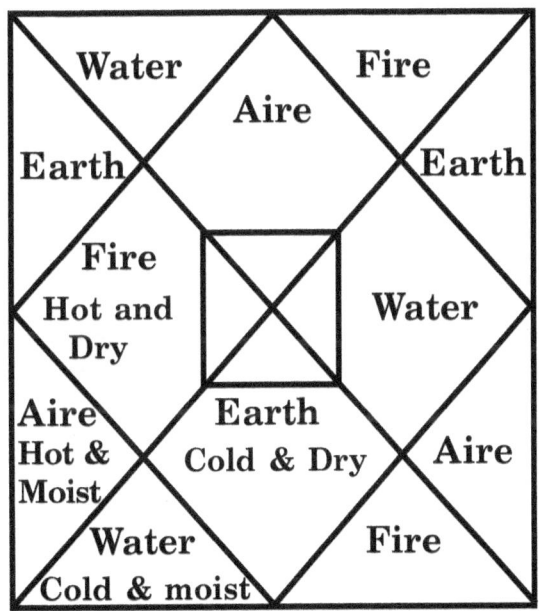

In the next place it will be necessary to give a brief touch of the principal Diseases that are to be understood upon every House, to which all the other may be referred; as in the first House which signifies the Head, we may consider all Head-pains and aches, all infirmities of the Eyes, distempers of the Brain, Falling-evil, weakness of the Nerves, and decay or default of the spinal Marrow; al impediments incident to the Animal faculty, pains of the Jaws and Teeth, the Nose, Face, and Ears, and *Alopecia*. In the second House consider the Diseases incident to the Throat, as Squinancy, Kings Evil, and the like. In the third House consider all impediments incident to the Arms and Shoulders. In the fourth *Pleura*, as *Peripneumonia*, rising or rottenness of the Lungs, Coughs, Plurisie, Vomitings, Impostumations, and the like. In the 5th House consider false Conceptions, the evil accidents of the Womb, suffocation of the Matrix, fits of the Mother, the Whites, and excess of Flowers. In the sixth House consider the Sciatica, and the like. In the 7th house consider the accidents of the Limbs, *Podagra*, all pains and accidents belonging to the Feet and Toes. In the eighth House consider the Dropsie and the like. In the 9th, griping of the guts, the Cholick, of Wind and otherwise, and all like Distempers. In the 10th House consider all accidents of the Reins and Bowels, as Scowring, Gonorrhea, pain of the Back, Gravel and Sand. In the 11th House the affection and afflictions of the Heart are to be considered, as Cardiack Passions, Tremblings, Palpitations, and the like. In the 12th House are understood the Herpes, Palsie, and all afflictions of the Nerves and Sinews.

Farther note, that the whole circumference of the Heavens is 360 degrees, which are in every Figure contained in the 12 Houses, and every House properly hath 30 degrees: if 12 degrees go before the Line or Section of the House, then 18 follows after; and also in our Latitude of 52 degrees or thereabouts, by reason of the obliquity of the Zodiack, in some houses may be contained more than 30 degrees; nay, a whole Sign intercepted, and in other Houses less that 30 degrees; but be it more or less, the degrees must admit of equal Division; as if 40 degrees be in one House, they are to be divided equally into 3 parts, or more; so if 20 degrees be in another house, the same; and the Planets placed in the same, to be considered as in the following figure, by way of supposition.

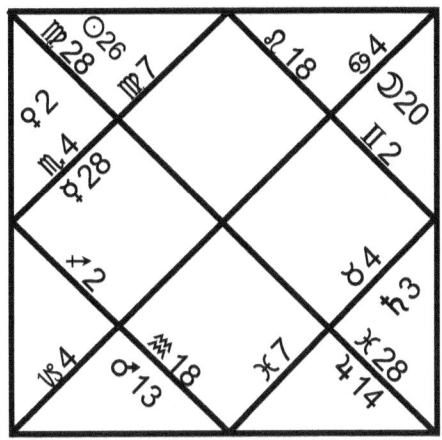

Here in this Figure of Supposition, ♀ is in the 2d degree of ♏, in the 12th House, therefore you shall account ♀ in that place, in respect of the House, to be hot and dry in the first degree, because she is not out of the verge of the first House, by reason in this sence of Temperaments, 12 degrees before are accounted within the House: ☿ is in 28 of ♏, though ☿ be there in the first House, yet you shall reckon him in the beginning of the second House; and in respect of the place where he standeth in the House, he is hot and moist in the first degree, because he is not 12 degrees above the Ascendant of the 2d House; and if ☿ had been 16 degrees in ♐, then he should have been said to be hot and moist in the beginning of the second degree, in respect of the House, and not of the Sign; and if he were 25 degrees in ♐, then he should be said to be in the third House, and should be said to be cold and moist in the first degree: ♂ in the 13th of ♒, is said to be in the beginning of the fourth House, and is said there (in respect of the House) to be cold and dry in the first degree.

Now it followeth to speak of the Retentive Faculty.

Retention is one of the principal Virtues in the Body of man, and belongeth to *Saturn*, which is cold and dry, Earthy of nature, and Melancholick, and hath dominion of the Mite or

Spleen, wherein the natural Melancholy is contained, and fortifieth and strengtheneth the Body of Man and his Members, and hath its operation in ♉, ♍, and ♑, terrene Signs, as *Guido Bonatus; Tantum agit in Terram, & in corpore bunsano.*

And this Retentive Faculty may be considered as Natural or Unnatural, before, and after Digestion; Natural according to the Body, for the support and maintenance of Nature; Unnatural, against the Body, distempering and injuring the same.

Retention before Digestion in the upper part of the Stomach, which is the place of the first digestion, which keepeth the meat it cannot descend, by reason of unnatural melancholy remaining in the Stomach, nor yet digest for want of natural Heat and Moisture, whereby a man is forced to cast up again, or doth retain and keep it in his Stomach with great pain, except he force it up again; For naturally it will not come up, because the Expulsive Virtue is weakned in the Stomach, by reason of the said unnatural Melancholy there remaining.

Retention in digestion is to detain the meat in the proper place of Digestion, till it be throughly digested to the conserving an strengthening of Nature.

Retention after Digestion is performed in all the members by operation of natural Melancholy, and his office is to retain and keep the nourishment that is appropriate to nature for the maintenance and upholding the Body in health, after due separation in the Liver after Digestion, whereby every part and member of the Body may receive that which properly and peculiarly belongeth thereunto.

Retention after Digestion is of two sorts, Natural and Unnatural; this unnatural is performed two ways, *viz.* as well in the outward parts of the Body, as in the Arms, Legs, or Flesh, Muscles or Sinews; as inwardly in the Belly, Liver, Stomach, Bowels, &c.

Unnatural *Retention* is caused of unnatural Melancholy, whether it be in the extreme parts, or in the inward parts; and be reason of this unnatural Retention a man falleth into a Consumption, especially when it is in the extreme parts: when the Consumption is either particular, or general, in one Member, or throughout the whole Body, by reason of unnatural Melancholy impacted in the Veins in some particular place or spread abroad generally in all the Body, which kind of Melancholy is more dry than that which is natural and by reason of the great dryness thereof, stoppeth the Veins and passages, that the Blood cannot have free course as it ought, to give nourishment to the Body, or to the Members; and this unnatural Melancholy overcometh the natural Melancholy, even as the greater quantity of stinking water doth overcome a little quantity of sweet and fresh water; for it is to be considered, that cold and dryness are enemies to heat and moisture, which, if they get the mastery of hot and moist, then they do expell them; and if heat and moisture by consumed in the Liver or other parts of the Body, how can the Digestive Virtue do his Office? for cold and drowth causeth indigestion.

Therefore know this, that the whole state of the Body in Sickness and in Health standeth and consisteth in a right good and natural Digestion, and in the maintenance of Radical heat and humidity in the Stomach, Liver, and other parts of the Body. Also know this, that a hot Liver never causeth a consumption of the Body, but a cold Liver; and a cold Liver and a cold Stomach never cause a hot Disease, and a moist Liver never ingendreth a dry Disease, but a Dropsie and such like: for the Liver is as the root and foundation of the whole Body and according to the good or bad digestion of the Liver, shall the state and health of the Body be, either good or bad. And when this unnatural melancholy Retention is in the Body it self, and not in the extreme parts, then is the Expulsive Virtue weakned in the Liver, Milt, Lungs, Stomach, Body and Bowels, in which soever of them it doth abound. When one doth receive meat or drink into this Body, and vomit it up again, then it is a sign that the Retentive Virtue is weakned in the Stomach, and the natural Faculties in the Stomach are overcome by too much moisture, or by too much heat and drowth.

When one doth vomit blood, and bleed much at the Nose or Mouth, then is the Retentive Virtue or Faculty weakened in the Liver and Veins by over-much heat and moisture.

When the Lask or bloody Flux prevails, then is the Retentive Virtue weakned in the Bowels and Muscles, and in the Belly, and the Expulsive Faculty is too strong. But if it be the bloody Flux, then is it weakned in the Veins and Reins of the Back, and then there is too much heat or moisture in the Reins and Veins; when Nature passeth from a man, and that he waxeth weak in the Reins of his back, it is caused of too much moistness and heat in the Reins, or of one of them, and in the Veins that pass from the Reins to the *Dutus*, which Veins are called the Seed-bringers, for the lust of a man is in the Reins, and the lust of a Woman in her Navel.

When one staleth Blood, or that his Water doeth from him more often then it ought, or otherwise then it should, then is the Retentive Virtue weakened in the Muscles of the Bladder, and Conduits that come from the Reins to the Bladder, by too much moistness.

When a Womans Flowers or Terms be stopt, so that she hath not her natural Course as she was went, or as she of right ought to have, then it is a sign that the Retentive Virtue is too strong in the Veins of the Matrix, which are stopt and shut up by too much dry and hard Melancholy, or Choler adust, that resteth in them and in the Matrix.

When a Womans Flowers or Terms do pass from her unnaturally, or otherwise than they ought, as sometimes it chanceth, whether they be the white Flowers or the red, though it come sometimes by a squat, a fear, a fall, or howsoever it cometh, yet is the Body below *Zirbus* and the Matrix and her Veins, oppress'd by too much moistness thither resorting to the Muscles transverse, or to the five Veins of the Matrix, whereby the said Veins cannot shut and close, but open, and being open by reason of the moistness, the Matrix being weak openeth her self oftentimes more or less, according to the Humour, day by day, or sometimes in two or three days, sometimes in longer and shorter space, and in such a case the Party hath pain and heat in the Back and Reins, and pain of the Head and Sides. When the red Flowers do issue unaccustomedly, it is a sign of perfect digestion in the Veins, and the cause of their so issuing if, overmuch unnatural heat and moisture in the Veins of the Matrix, and that the Retentive Virtue is thereby weakened in the said Veins.

When the white Flowers do issue, it is a sign of imperfect Digestion, and that the Retentive Virtue is weakened in the Matrix and Veins thereof, by too much cold and moisture, and the more they do flow, the more moisture is there, and the more cold in the Matrix; and in such a case a Woman hath a great pain in her Sides and Flanks, and is very weak in the Reins, pained in the Stomach and Head.

Signs that the Retentive Virtue is weakened are these, much bleeding at the Nose or Mouth, much vomiting up Blood, Flegm, Choler, or meat undigested, or digested in part or in all, or if a man be given to, or forced to vomit, or that his Stomach doth turn (as they say) at the sight of any meat or other thing, in this the Retentive Faculty is weakened above *Zirbus*, by over-much moisture resting in the Stomach, or in the Liver, or in the Muscles of the Stomach.

But if one have the bloody Flux, the Lask, the running of the Reins, Gonorrhea Passion, or that his Urine pass from him against his will, or more often than it should, or if the Terms, Flowers, or Menstures, white or red, flow or pass from the Woman out of due time, or otherwise than they should, or if the Milk in a Womans Breast pass more than it should of natural course, then is the Retentive Virtue weakened by too much cold and moisture below *Zirbus*, in the proper places aforesaid, except the milk which is above *Zirbus* in respect of the Paps, but the generation of milk is from the Menstrues.

The four transverse Muscles which were spoken of before, that are in the Belly, which are called the Retentive Muscles, because the meat and dregs are by them retained and kept in the Body, two of them spring from the Ribs on the right side, and pass over-thwart the Belly, the one on the one side of the Navel, and the other on the other side, close almost by the Navel, and they pass to the left side to the bones of the Haunch or of the Pecten: and the other two spring from the Rib on the left side, in manner and form as aforesaid, and they pass over the Womb by the Navel cross to the Haunches, as the other do on each side of the Navel, as in the Anatomy of the Muscles you shall see more plainly: and by these 4 Muscles the Retentive Virtue in the Womb is retained in due proportion, to the upholding of Nature, &c. And these are debilitated and hurt by too much superfluous humidity and moisture oppressing or filling them; and it is helpen again by administring of Medicines, by Cataplasmes, Oyls, Unguents, Purges or Clysters, and such like.

For Suffocation or strangling of the Matrix, when it is caused of Retention of the Flowers, for that the Retentive Virtue is too strong by overmuch dryness.

Remedies when the Retentive Virtue is weakened in the Stomach, or that one doth Vomit much or often by reason of too much Moisture.

Oyl of Mints, oyl of Mercury, oyl of *Psillii*, and rub therewith the Stomach, the soals of the Feet, and Members, or take Syrup of *Pentaphyllon*, Syrup of bitter Almonds, Syrup of Nenuphane, *alias Nymphea, cum ypognittidas mixtura:* or take the Water of Mints drunk, Syrup of Mints eaten, in a reasonable Quantity, as from half an ounce to an ounce.

Remedies when the Retentive Faculty is weakened in theLiver by over-much Heat.

℞ *Oleum Psyllii, oleum Jusquiami oleum Sem papaveris*, or such like, for these are cold and moist, Retentive; and anoint the Stomach and Region of the Liver therewith; or give him to take some of these Syrups for the same.

Syrup. Acetosus, Syr. Ausygdalar. amar. Syr. Pentaphylli. Syr. Violar. cum ypognisidos. Aqua Pentaphylli, aqua Acetos. for these Waters are Cool, Retentive, and Consortative in such a case. Or with this Unguent anoint the Stomach and Region of the Liver.

℞ *Virga Pastoris, ypognistidos. simpertitae, ana M B.pentaphylli, psyllii laturae agrestis, ana, pug. B. herb. Acetos. Seariolae, ana Mj. & cum axungia porcina siat unguentum,* and put thereto a little Vinegar.

A Remedy where the Retentive Faculty is weakned in the Belly by cold and moisture, viz. A Clyster to purge and scowr the Belly and Bowels, and purge out Water and Flegm.

℞ *Origani, Camomile, Melilota, Fenugr, ana, Mj. coquantur in aqua usque ad consumptionem tertia partis, de colatura accipe ib j. cui adde diaphaeniconis, Electr. indima, benedicta laxativ. bicrapig. ana 3β: olei Camomilli 3. Rutarei latia 3.,see, fiat Clyster.* and then anoint the four transverse Muscles with some of these oyls, *viz.* Oyl of Mints, oyl of Mercury, oyl of Bayes, oyl of Mace, oyl of Foxes, or with such like oyls that are hot and dry, and let them drink the water of Mints or of Mercury, with some other appropriateSyrup.

In *materia frigida & vehementi auctoque dolore,* consult Wickerus on this subject.

A very good Clyster in these Causes.

℞ *Hordei, violaria, mercurialis ana M j, fiat decoctio, de calatura accipe 3xjj, quibus adde Diacatbolicon 3, Electuarii de succo Rosarum 3, olei violarum 3, salis 3β, misce, fiat Clysterium.*

A Remedy when the Retentive Virtue is weakened in the Belly, and the Party hath the Flux of a Hot Cause.

Take some of these Oyls and anoint the Back and the Reins, and the Muscles transverse, *viz.* Oyl of Henbane, oyl of Psyllii, oyl of Poppy, or the Unguent aforesaid; and let him drink Syrup of Violets, or of *Acetosus,* or *amigdalarium amarum, pentaphyllibypognistidos,* and such like Syrups, in waters appropriate, and in such a case of weakness there is nothing better than the middle Bark of an Oak boyled in milk, and drunk oftentimes; the Acorns and Cups are very good boyled, or taken in powder, in any weakness, or pain, or stitch.

Camphire drunk with the juice of Water-lillies, stoppeth the running of the Reins, and white flux of the Flowers passing from Women. It is cold and dry in the third degree.

A Remedy when the Retentive Virtue is too strong in the Matrix, by too much cold and dry Melancholy of ♄, and the Expulsive Virtue too weak, as followeth.

℞ *flor. Borag. bugloss. ocimi, malvarum ana M j, radic. buglos. radic. assari, rad. doricnii, rad. raphani ana 3j, sem. anisi 3j, som. fenigre, Raphani, ana 3ij, fiat Decoct. Coletur, & tolle 3viij, addantur pulp. Cassia 3ij. olei sem. lini, olei ocimi ana 3h fiat Clyter pro matrice & vulva;* this Clyster is hot and moist, expulsive in the second degree.

If you will make a Cataplasme thereof to lay on the belly, then when it is boyled put all in a mortar, and beat it well after the oyl is strained out, and thicken it with the flower of Venerick or Lineseed beaten, and make a Cataplasme or bag for the belly, but then you must put in twice as much of the herbs at first to boyl therein, or else there will be too little to make a Cataplasme.

♄ is superiour of the seven Planets, signifies blackness, darkness, and all uncomfortableness, is heavy and slow in his motion, of nature cold, and dry of temper, Enemy to the Earth, and to the Nature and Health of human kind, inclining more to evil than good; melancholick of nature and complexion, passive, descending, wasting, and consuming evil of himself by nature, and is more evil than ♂ by reason of his cold and dry temper, whose special enemy and opposite is ♃; for what Disease or evil is caused by ♄ under his Ascendant or hour, or when the Moon applies to ♃, he being lord of the Ascendant, and by such things as belong to ♃; and likewise whatsoever is bound in the hour of ♃, may be loosed in the hour of ♄; when ♄ is lord of the Ascendant, and the ☽ applying to him by ☌, ✶, or △, the ☽ separating from ♃, and it is to be done with those things that belong to ♄; and here note, that ♄ hath of the humane body, the Milt, the Spleen, and the fleshy part of the Stomach, the inner part of the right ear, and above it, and the bladder, and the melancholick Humour mixed with Flegm, that is viscous and tough, and he ruleth the virtue Retentive, and the retentive Muscles, and naturally he causeth Leprosies, Morphews, and the Gout in the Feet, the Canker, and all Diseases that come of viscous Flegm, as the Fever hectick, the Flux, the Dropsie, the Ptisick, *Catarrha, ventris solutio*, the spumatick and melancholick Humour, both natural and unnatural, and also against nature; of the which Melancholy we will here shew the generation, and the particular natures and properties thereof before we pass any farther.

Melancholy Natural is one of the four principal Humours ruling and reigning in the Body of Man, and tendeth to the natural supportation and subsistence of the Body of Man in Health, and it hath its principal residence under the Milt, on the left side, and is termed black Choler, and is the Dregs and *faces* of all other Humours, and it self; for if one be born under ♄, he being in ♑, then shall he be naturally Melancholy in the 4th degree, and will be very wise and deep in Judgment; but if one be born in the 3d degree of Melancholy, and come to be melancholick in the 4th degree, against Nature, then he waxeth mad, and is as if Diabolically possessed, because it is against Nature.

When the Spleen is oppressed with Unnatural Melancholy, the Party be he young or old will wax very sad, pensive, solitary and heavy, and his Belly will wax hard and tough, and swell as though he had a Tympany, which will be destructive in the end, if it be not remedied by anionting the Party on the Region of the Milt with oyl of Bayes or oyl of Camomile, of Foxes, of Swallows, of Lillies, of Dill, or such like oyls, hot, and somewhat moist withall.

If this Unnatural Melancholy be mixed with Flegm, or remain in the Belly, in the Muscles transverse, or in the Muscles *Latitudinater*, then is the Virtue Expulsive weakened, and the Virtue Retentive too strong, by reason of the great drowth, and then is the Body bound, and the Party cannot go to stool, and in such a case a Clyster is to be used; or else anoint the Muscles aforesaid on the Belly with oyl of Mercury, and Violets, and Nimpharum mixed together.

When one doth receive meat and drink into their Body, and vomit it up again, or is troubled much with vomiting, then it is a sign that the Retentive Virtue in the Stomach is much weakened for want of natural melancholy, or that there is in the Muscles too much unnatural melancholy or superfluous moisture; in such a case if the Part by hot in the Stomach, or very cold, make him vomit well first, and then give comfortable things for the Stomach, to allay it if it be too hot.

This noxious and unnatural Melancholy is caused three kind of ways; either of melancholy mixed with the blood in the Veins of the whole Body, hurting the Brain, or of the blood in the Brain onely, being infected with melancholy, or of inflammation, or evil affect in the Stomach, &c.

The common signs of this Disease be carefulness, sadness, solitariness & hatred; they have strong imaginations, and withdraw themselves from Company; moreover, they desperately desire death, or to kill or drown themselves; and some fear left they should be killed, and then is the Humour in the Heart; some do laugh, and some do weep, and some think themselves to be inspired with the Holy Ghost, and prattle or prophesy of things to come; such are melancholy either naturally born, or else against nature, as is aforesaid, born under ♄ in ♍ or ♑, for in them the state of the Body is slender, black, rough, and altogether melancholick; *Saturn* cold and dry, they are full of great and fearful apprehensions, addicted to, and loving evil meats, and studying and devising great and deep matters, and occupy themselves about unknown things, and slight or regard not common things, for their Judgment and Capacity are above ordinary.

If the Melancholy rest in the Sides, you shall know it by this, they will have rawness and much windiness, sharp belchings, burnings, and grief of the Sides; also the Sides are plucked upwards, and many times they are troubled with inflammations, especially when Choler is mixed with Melancholy; also there is costiveness ion the womb, little sleep, troublesome, fearful and naughty dreams, swimmings in the head, and soundings in the ears, &c.

If you would know whether natural or unnatural Melancholy do abound in the Liver, you shall know it first by the Urine; if the Urine be grayish, blue, or white, it signifieth that natural melancholy doth abound, and also such Urines have they that have splenetick passions, and those that are troubled with Quartan Agues, and those that are troubled with Indigestion, and cannot digest their meat.

Unnatural Melancholy causeth the Urine to be of two sorts, sometimes without Quantity and Quality, and then is the Urine pale and thin, for that it is caused of melancholy that is more cold and more dry than Natural melancholy. Sometimes Unnatural melancholy changeth the substance of the Urine, and then the Urine looketh black.

If Blood be mixed with Melancholy, and Blood have the predominancy, then the Urine looketh reddish, but of a deep colour tending to black or darkness.

If Melancholy have the predominancy, then the Urine looketh dark and gray, tending somewhat to redness.

If Melancholy be mixed with Choler, and have the preheminence, then the Urine looketh dar and waterish, but yellowish withall.

If Choler abound, then the Urine looketh of a deep Amber-colour, cleer, and most commonly is much in quantity.

If Melancholy be mixed with Flegm, and have the predominancy in the commixtion, then the Urine looketh gray and whitish, slimy, and somewhat darkish withall.

If Flegm exceed in the commixtion, then it looketh thick and whitish, full of Flegm, like the whites of eggs, and of a dirty colour.

If Melancholy be equally mixed with Flegm, the colour of the Urine shall be like unto Hemp. or like to small Ale, clear and thinnish and full of froth; and such an Urine signifieth a great stopping in the whole Members and Milt, caused of a strong Melancholick Humour, which causeth, through a great drowth, a general swelling throughout all the Members of the Body, from the Head to the Foot, the Veins are full of Wind, and the Blood wholly corrupted; give no vomit to such a one, for then he dieth.

Urine of an aged man clear and whitish, like good Sack or white Wine, and full of small motes boyling in the middle Region, and seething very round upward, and yet remain in the middle sparking like bright Stars, and full of Froth withal; signifieth great Obstructions of the Milt and Liver; a great Rheum, is pained in the Head, Stomach, and Reins, and digesteth not his meat, hath Wing in his Body running from place to place, and is caused of Melancholy stopping the Milt; which causeth also Stitches, Prickings, and the Spleen

And finally all Urines in Men or Women that look very clear like White-wine, brownish dark, or black, or grayish do signifie Melancholy to abound in the Body, and a great cold and dryness, and stopping of the Liver, Milt, or Reins.

Hairs long or short in Urine signifie swelling of the Milt, and pain of the Side in a Man, and stopping of the Terms in a Woman.

Sparkles like Stars, or sparkes of fire in a mans Urine, signifie Rheum; in a womans, that she is with Child, or else Rheumatick.

Of the Astronomical Judicial of Diseases.

Before I have shewed of Melancholy by the Urine; and now I will shew you how you shall judge of it by the Figure of Heaven, but first I will shew what Diseases ♄ doth cause, and how he doth alter his Nature, and commix himself with the other Humours in the Body of Man, and how you shall know his degree of Heat and Cold, more or less, his temperature and distemperature, by which the Diseases which he doth cause generally are shewed; and for the better understanding of what is said, I will note down the nature of the twelve Signs of the *Zodiack*, and the rest of the Planets, and *Saturn's* commixing in the Signs with the Planets, and that he runs his course in 30 years; and first we will speak of ♈, ♌, and ♐, which are the three Oriental Signs, of the fiery Triplicity, hot and dry.

Aries is a Sign of the heart of the East, moveable and quick, and ascendeth swiftly, and is most moveable of all the Signs; bitter in Taste, and weak in Nature, and causeth yellow

Choler thin and sharp, Biles, Leprosie, red Spots, Itches, Scurfs, Deafness, Baldness or little hair, small Beard, is hot and dry, cholerick, of the nature of Fire, the Day-house of ♂, the Exaltation of the ☉, the Fall of ♄, the Detriment of *Venus*, and is hot and dry, temperate in the first degree, &c.

The first 18 degrees of ♈ are temperately hot and dry, equal; the last 12 degrees of ♈ are hot and dry in the beginning of the first degree.

Saturn therefore in the first 18 degrees of ♈ is temperate in cold and heat, but dry in the first degree, and the Diseases that he causeth are of yellow Choler and Melancholy mixt, which is neither cold nor hot, but very dry inward, bitter and hard, causing Agues; in the last 12 degrees of ♈ *Saturn* is hot in the beginning of the first degree, and dry in the second degree, causeth Diseases: ♄ lord of the 12th or 6th, or being lord of the hour, and in ♈ in ♂ with ☽ in the Ascendant, causeth the falling-sickness, black Choler and Leprosie, Morphew, Fistulaes, and *Podagra*.

The Cure of Diseases caused by Saturn in Aries and in Leo.

Now you shall understand, that if in the Question for the sick the ☽ do apply to ♄ or ☿ being in ♉, ♍ or ♑, and ♄ in ♈ or ♌, or if the ☽ apply to ♄ in ♈, ♌ or ♐, then the Melancholy exceeds in the Conjunction, and the yellow Choler is least, and then is the Humour tough.

The like is if ♄ be in ♌, but then the yellow Choler is more thick, and then will it require a Digestive before it be purged.

If ♄ be in ♈ or ♌, and the ☽ apply to ♂ or the ☉, then is the Choler augmented, and is most in the Conjunction; but if the ☽ apply to ♃, then is the Blood infected with Choler, and the Heat is increased in the Liver, then after Digestion and Purging it is necessary to let Blood, and to give things that cool the heat of the Body: but if the ☽ applies to ♀, if she be in Signs cold and moist, she allayeth part of the heat and dryness of the Choler; but if she be in Signs hot and dry, the augmenteth the Choler; if she be in Signs hot and moist, then the tempereth the dry quality of the Disease, but augmenteth the heat; and if she be in Signs cold and dry, then the allayeth the heat partly, but she augmenteth the drowth. Now in curing these Diseases caused of ♄ in ♈ or ♌, take heed that you minister not first to the Party in the hours of ♄, ♂ or the ☉, or of ♃, if he be in ♈, ♌ or ♐, or of ☿, if he be in ♈, ♌, ♐, ♉, ♍, or ♑, but in the hours of the ☽ pr ♀, being in ♋, ♏ or ♓, and beware that when you minister first the ☽ be not in ♈, ♌, or ♐, and that she do not apply to ♄, ♂, or ☉, but to ♀, if it may be, and put in the Ascendant ♋, ♏, ♓, or ♎, if possibly you can.

But you may make ♄ lord of the 6th House, and put him in the 12th, or 11th, or 9th House, in his Fall or Detriment, especially in the 11th combust, the ☽ separate from ♄, because he is cause of the infirmity, and let the ☽ apply to the Lord of the Ascendant, and for a need you may put ♊ in the Ascendant, but you must make the Lord of the 6th House weak, and in any case let not the Moon apply to ♄.

These things before-said observed and considered, you may purge without Preparatives if ♄ be in ♈, because the Humours be thin, but ♄ in ♌ requires Preparatives, because the Humours are more condense, and thicker, and causeth yellow thick Choler.

Preparers and Digesters of yellow Choler are these.

Violet leaves and flowers, cold in the 2d degree, *Nenuphare*, cold in the 4th deg. Poppy, cold in the 4th degr. Lettuce cold in the 3d degr. Nightshade cold in the 3d deg. Roses, cold and dry in the 3d deg. *Acetosa*, cold in 2d gr. Orange, cold in 1 gr. and 2 degr. *Blitum*, cold in 2 degr. Cichory-roots, cold in 2 gr. *Citri caro* cold in 1 degr. *Curcubitae semen*, cold in 2 degr. *Cucumeris semen*, cold in 2 degr. *Cichorii folia*, cold in 2 degr. *Endivia* cold in 2 degr. *Succi limonior.* cold in 2 gr. *Semen Melenum* cold in 2 gr. *pruna Damascen.* cold in 2 degr. *Scamonia* cold in 4 degr. *tria Sandula* cold and dry in 3 degr. *Syrupus Violar. Papazer. Nenuphar. Acetos.. Rosar. Endiv. Ciccor. Oxinel pontic. Limoniorum, Solani, Atriplicis, Malorum granat.*

These Digest Melancholy.

Borrage, Bugloss, Bugle, Bugloss-roots, all hot in 1 gr. Beets, hot in 2 gr. black Bizantie, temperate, Basil hot in 2 gr. *Cassia fistula*, hot in 1. moist in 1. *Radix dulcis.*, temperate, hot and moist, *Dragacantbum*, hot in 2d, moist in 1st, Flowers of Bugloss, hot and moist in the 2d gr. Flowers of Borrage, hot and moist in the 1st gr. Flowers of Ciccory, moist in the 1st gr. *flores malin*. moist in 1st deg. *Jujubes* h. 1st m. 2d gr. *Maces* hot 3d degr. *Macropiper*, h. m. 2d. long Pepper white and black, hot in 4th degr. Peacocks flesh, h. and moist in the 4th gr. *rad*. Zap, hot and moist in the 2d, *rad*. Bugloss, hot and moist 1 deg. *rad*. Acori, hot and moist 3d. *rad*. Asari, hot and moist 3d. *rad*. Dervini, hot and moist 3d. *rad*. Raphani, hot in 3d, moist in 2d degr. *Sacharum*, hot in 1st, moist in 2d. *Uva passa*, temperate hot and moist.

These Syrups do properly digest Melancholy.

Boraglnis, bugloss. *de stecados, epithimi, Ciccorii, endivia, Decoctionis Polypodii, limonior. oximel pontia. Elect. plaris, efdra, saira magna, oppopica, musa anea, metridate, philantrhopus diacutum, diacastorium.*

These prepare Melancholy.

Borrage, bugloss, bugle, *blitarum, oximel, cicorii, endivia, malvarum, mirab, in die & nocte.*

These Digest both Melancholy and Choler.

De stecados, Epithimi, Lupialorum, Endivia, Cicorii, Oximel pontic. cap. Veneris, Nymphea, lemoniorum, malor. granatae.

You may prepare yellow Choler an Melancholy caused of ♄ in ♈ or ♂ in the first or second degree thus.

℞ *Syrup. Endiv. Cichor.* ana 3j. *Syrup. Epithym. & Fumitorii,* an. 3β. *Syr. buglos.* 3j. *Aqua borrag. Endiv. Fumitorii* a. 3iiij. *fiat potus pro* 6 Dos.

Or thus:

Tamarindorum 3β, senna, aniseed, foenic. a. 3j. polypodii 3, ligni sancti 3, florum violarum, borag. bugloss. ana 3vj, fiat decoctio, adcolatur 3xvj. Addantur Syr. Fumitorie, capillarum Vener. ana 3j. Syr. acetos. oxysarcha. ana 3j, fiat potus pro 7 Dos.

Or thus:

℞ Oximel simple 3vj, Aectos. 3ij, pulveris Jeralogodii 3β, Aqua borag. endiv. absintbii ana 3, fiat potus pro 5 Dos.

Purgers of yellow Choler.

Manna, alancalon, tamarinds, Rhubarb, confection of Manna; Elect. succ. Rosar. Diagridion, Scammonii.

Purgers only of Melancholy.

Polipody, lapis Lazul. lapis Armen. Esdra.

Haustus Melancholicum Humorem concoquens, & ad Evacuationem præparans.

℞ Syr. de Epithymo, de fumo terra, de lupulo, ana 3, Aqua boraginis, origani, ana 3, misceantur, fiat potio, cujus exhibeantur pro uno haustu, 3.

To purge yellow Choler and Melancholy in the second degree.

℞ Diaprunorum, Elect. Succi Rosar. lax. ana 3β, Aqua fumitor. absynthii ana 3j, pulveris Jeralogodii 3β, fiat potus pro una Dose. It purgeth yellow Choler and Melancholy in the third degree almost.

Or thus:

℞ Senne orient. 3β, polipodiae 3j, Rad. fœnic. petrof. 3ij, thymi, borrag. bugloss. ana p. j. fiat decoct. ad consumpt. dimid. partis ad colatur. 3niij. addantur diacathol. confectio Hamech, diapranorum solutivorum, ana 3β, pulveris Jeralogodii 3β, Syr. Rosarum, Boraginis, *ana* 3j, *fiat potus pro tribus Dos.* It purgeth Melancholy and Choler in the third degree.

Of *Saturn* in *Leo*.

Saturn in the first six degrees of *Leo* is hot in the first degree and dry in the second, causing strong Pestilential Fevers, hot and very dry, of yellow Choler mixed with Melancholy and superfluous Flegm, causing much vomiting, and strong Fits of twelve hours, six hot and six cold, in which they burn mightily, and are wonderfully dry, and in the end of the Fit they swoon, much like one that hath the Falling-sickness; and when the Fits are gone a Week, two, or three, the least distemper causeth a relapse, and it also causeth many times the black Plague on them that have this Fever: in this Disease Choler hath the Dominion, but it is mixed with much Melancholy, causeth the Piles and Hemorrhoids, and pain of the Back. ♄ in ♌ causeth the Passion and trembling of the Heart through thought and fearfulness.

Saturn in the next 18 degrees of *Leo* is hot in the second and dry in the third, causing Diseases of thick yellow Choler, and of Melancholy; but Choler hath the dominion, with a superfluous Flegm, causing Pestilential, and hot burning Fevers, and so dry that the Speech is hindred, stopping of the Liver and Stomach, forcing to vomit with pains, and if the ☽ be in ♊, and apply to ♂ in ♐, ♄ in the 6th, it causeth the Strangury, and the Fever Hectick.

Saturn in the last six degrees of *Leo* is Hot *in principio tertii*, and Dry in *principio quarti grad.* causing the Plague and hot Pestilential and burning Fevers, of thick yellow Choler mixt with Melancholy, and superfluous Flegm, the dry temper doth exceed, and it also causeth the Fever Hectick, which is consuming Fever, and reigneth in the Belly with a pain or stitch in the side.

These following do digest Melancholy and yellow Choler of ♄ in ♌

Violets, Nightshade, Lettuce, Purslane, Limons, Whey, Vinegar, Butter-milk, Sorrel, Endive, Succory, cold Water,

Verjuyce, Poppy, Orage, *Absinthium,* Fumitory, *Cortex ligni sancti,* Bugloss, Burrage, Nenuphar. *Semen Melonum, semen cucrbit. 4 fem. frigid. major, 4 fem. frigid. minor, semen lactuce, sem. Atriplicis,* Tamarind. Senna, Polipod. Capil. *Veneris, Stecados, Adiantbes,* all the sorts of Mirabolanes, *Sanicula,* Roses. *Syrup. fumarum, violarum, absintbii, papaver. cicor.* Syrup of Roses, *syr. solani, acetos. endiv. syr. capill. Ven. Scolopend.* Syrup of Stecados, Oximel Pontick, Oxisachara, *syr. Epaticae.*

A Digestive against Drowth of ♄ in ♋, the ☾ applying to ♀ in ☉.

℞ Syrup of Violets, Burrage, Succory, *ana* 3iβ, *aquarum violarum atriplic. betarum, rosarum, borag. bugl. ana* 3iij, *fiat potus pro* 6 Dos.

Or thus:

℞ *Syrup. perthemii, borag. violarum ana* 3iβ, *aquarum perthemii, violarum, fumitor. absinthii, solani, ana* 3iij. *fiat potus pro* 3 Dos.

Digestives of Choler that is thick and yellow, and of Melancholy, with tough Flegm caused of ♄ in ♋, that is hot and dry in the 3d degree.

℞ *Fol. violarum, acetos. blite, cichorii, jujub. ana* M. j. *rad. Cicorii,* p. j. *fiat Decoctio ad colaturam* 3x. *addantur de Syrup. cicorii, violarum, papaveris ana* 3, *fiat potus pro* 5 Dos. This is cold and moist in the third degree, digesting yellow Choler and Melancholy caused of ♄ in the third degree.

Moreover;

℞ *Syr. papaveris, syr. nenupharis, violarum ana* 3ij, *aquanox solani, portulacæ, fumitoria ana* 3. *fiat potus pro* Dos. 6. This doth digest Choler in the extremity of the third degree, and doth moisten much against ♄ in ♋, in the 3d degr.

℞ *Syr. papaxris, syr. nenupharis, violarum ana* 3, *aquanox solani, portulacæa, fumitoriæ ana* 3. *fiat potus pro* Dos. 6. This doth digest Choler in the extremity of the third degree, and doth moisten much against ♄ in ♌, in the 3d degr.

℞ *Ligni sancti* 3iiij, *corticis ejusdem* 3jβ, *infundantur in 3lb aqua buglos. cichorii, absintbii; coquantur igne lento, ad medias, & in colatura dissolve syrup. fumitoriæ* jlb, and let the Party drink hereof 3vi morning and evening to the end. It digesteth the cholerick and melancholick Humours corrupting the Blood, wonderfully, even in the extream of three degrees.

Purgers of yellow Choler and Melancholy caused of ♄ in ♌, hot and dry in the 3d degree.

℞ Flowers of Violets, Borrage, Bugloss, *Nenupharis ana* p.j. *Cicorii, blitæ, lactuce, acetos. endiv. ana* p.j. *sonicum atriplicis, lactucæ, melonum, cucutbit. ana* 3ij, *sonicum Anisi, fanic. petroselini ana* ӡjβ, *passular, mundstar.* 3β, *polipodii* 3iiij, *Rbabarb.* 3ij, *prunorum pernor. numero* xij. *tamarindorum* 3j, *senne* 3β, *coloquintida* 3β, *fiat decoctio in collaturs* ij lb, and with a sufficient quantity of Sugar, *fiat potus pro 5 Dosibus.* Clarifie it, and Aromatize it, *cum Diatragacantha, frig.* 3β, *aqua Rosæ cochlear.* This doth purge Choler and Melancholy almost in the fourht degree, and doth moisten and refresh the Body very much.

Again,

℞ *Pill. fætidar. pill. sagap. ana* ӡiiβ, *pulveris Tberalogodii,* 3ij, *agaric. trochis.* ӡβ, *miser, & cum Syrup. betonic. fiant pill.* xvj. whereof (the Body before prepared) give sight for a Dose; they do purge the Back, Arms and Legs, of Choler and Melancholy in the 3d degree, and do thrust out broken bones in Wounds, purging all the extreme parts exceedingly.

A Purge against Choler and Melancholy in the third degree, caused of ♄ in ♌.

℞ *Polypodii* 3β, *passularum* 3β, *prunorum, sebesten ana* p.v. *Tamarindorum* 3. *Sannicle* 3β, *violarum,* p.j. *mercurialis, borrag. ana,* Mβ. *fiat decoctio, & in collatura* 3v. *dissolve Confectionis Hamech* 3ij,

Electuarii diacarthami 3j, *syrup. Ros. laxat.* 3ij, *fiat potus pro ij dos.* Clarifie it, and it purgeth Choler and Melancholy in the third degree, caused by ♄ in ♌.

Another.

℞ *Florum borag. buglos. violarum,* ana p.j. *pulp. tamarind.* 3j. *polipodii* 3ij, *sennæ orient.* 3ij, *ligni sancti, sem. feniculi petroselini, anifi, liquirit. agaric.* ana 3j, *Rhabarb.* 3j, *prunorum Damase. numero* ix. *passularum mundatarun* 3β, *fiat decoctio ad collatur.* 3ij. *addatur manne Elect. syrup. Ros. lax.* ana unc. j. *fiat potus pro una dosi, clarificatur & arotiz. cum aqua Rosarum* unc.β. This potion is gentle both in taste and working, and yet purgeth Chlor and Melancholy in the third degree, and giveth commonly 20 stools.

Again,

℞ *Polipod, passular. mundatar.* 3β, *prunorum sebest. numero* v. *Tamarindarum, sennæ,* ana 3β, *florum violar. borag. buglos.* ana p.j. *mercurialis* Mβ, *fiat decoctio ad colatur.* 3v. *dissolve confect. Hamech* 3ij, *Electuar. Diacarthami,* 3j, *Syrup. Rosar. laxat.* 3ij. *fiat potus pro* 2 *dos.* Clarifie it; it purgeth Choler and Melancholy in 3 degrees, caused of ♄ in ♌.

℞ *Polypodii* 3β, *senna* 3β, *flor. violar. borag. buglos.* ana pj, *mercurialis,* Mβ, *fiat decoctie ad colaturam* 3v; *addantur nonfectionis Hamech, Elect. Diacartbami,* ana 3iβ, *syrup. rosa laxa.* 3iβ, *fiat potus pro duabus dosibus.* This purgeth Choler, Water, and Melancholy in the third degree, and worketh wonderful well and gently, giving a dozen or 14 stools, this dissolveth hard congelations in the Belly.

℞ *Flo. borag. buglos. violar.* ana pj, *fumitor. lupulor. scolopendr.* ana Mj, *senne oriental.* 3iij, *polypodii* 3iβ, *prunorum Damascen. numero* 9, *passular. mundatar.* 3β, *sem. fænic. petrosel.* ana 3β, *sem. anisi, liquorit.* ana 3j, *fiat decoctio ad colatut.* 3ijβ, *addantur confection. Hamech* 3j, *diaprunorum solutivor.* 3ijβ, *Electr. succi Rosar. laxat.* 3j, *fiat potus pro una dosi.* Clarifie it. It purgeth Choler and Melancholy in 3 deg. and gently giveth 14 or 15 stools.

℞ *Confect. Hamech, diaprunorum* ana 3ij, *Elect. succi rosar. lax.* 3β, *aqua fumitor. borag.* ana 3iβ, *fiat potus pro una dos.* It purgeth Choler, Melancholy and Flegm, in the 3d deg. and is good against the Plague caused of ♄ in ♌.

℞ *Florum borag. buglos. nymph.* ana p.j, *lupulor. stecad. hepatic. scabios.* ana ℈ j, *sem. petroselini, fæniculi, cummini, anisi, brusci,* ana 3j, *seemeu aneti* 3j *zinziber. Cinnamon,* ana ℈j, *Rad. polypod.* 3iβ, *senne* 3iij, *tamarindar.* 3β, *passular. mundatar.* 3j, *prunorum* 9, *de mirabol. nitrinor. Indi kebule* ana 3iij, *Rhabarb.* 3β, *ligni sancti* 3j, *mccboacan.* 3β, *fiat decoctio ad colatur.* 3vij. *Addantur Electr. succi rosar. laxat.* 3j, *diaprunorum* 3β. Let it stand six hours, then clarifie it for three doses, and aromatize it with *pulv. diatrag. frigid.* ana ℈j, *aqua rosar.* 3β, *detur mane cum custodia borar.* 2. this doth purge Melancholy and Choler strongly in the 3d degr. caused by ♄ in ♌, and it purgeth the Head, Liver, Stomach and Milt, and worketh gently.

Of the pain of the Side and Belly caused by Saturn in Leo.

This pain afflicteth often the right Side, and sometimes the Belly, like the Cholick, and sometimes it is perceiv'd like a Wind or Stitch under the right Side, and there is no better Remedy for it than to drink Bay-berries beaten and to eat Limons, or to drink the juyce thereof with Vinegar, or Vinegar and Sugar-candy, or Butter-milk, or any sharp or sour things; look in the Chapter of *Mercury* in ♑.

Saturn in the first 12 degrees of ♐ is hot in the third degree and dry in the 4th, causing Diseases of red Choler and Melancholy, with a superfluous Flegm mixed, and red Choler hath the dominion, as appears by the Diseases it produceth; as the *Noli me tangere*, the Plague, Pestilential Fevers, Carbuncles, salt Flegm, hot and dry Diseases hard to be remedied, Piles and Hemorrhoids, Canker, and contraction of the Sinews.

Saturn in *Sagitary* being lord of the hour, lord of the 12th or 6th, causeth the dry and hot Gout, and swellings in the Feet remediless.

Saturn in the last 18 degrees of *Sagittarius*, is hot in the 4th degree, and dry in the extremity of the 4th; above Nature destructive and mortal, uncurable, of red Choler and Melancholy, utterly consuming the Radical Humidity of the Body, breeding violent Fevers, *Noli me tangere*, Piles, Hemorhoids, and contraction of the Sinew, and such dry Diseases as are without Remedy.

The Cure of Diseases that are caused of *Saturn* in *Sagitary*, so far forth as they may be cured, insomuch as they are of thick, hot, and dry burning Choler and Melancholy, with a superficial tough Flegm, but Choler predominates, and causeth these Distempers vehemently hot and dry in the extremity of 4 degrees, as is said before.

To these Distempers administer not Physick in the hours of ♃, ♂, nor ♄, but under ♀ or ☽, putting ♋, ♏, or ♓ in the Ascendant, and Luna in one of them.

Digesters of red Choler and Melancholy, caused of ♄ in ♐, Hot and dry in the extremity of 4 Degrees.

Cold Water, Nightshade, Whey, White-wine-Vinegar, and Vinegar of Squills, juyce of Limons, Lettuce, Purslane, Violets, Jujubes, Atriplex, oxisachara, Syrup of Fumitory, syrup. *violarum, acctos. syr. papaver. flor. borag. & buglos.*

℞ *Syrup. fumitor. acetos. oxisachar. violar. ana* 3j, *Aqua acetos. violar. jujubi ana* 3iij. *fiat potus pro tribus dosibus.* It digesteth red Choler and Melancholy in the 4th degree.

Or,

℞ *Succi acetos. succi blitæ, succi seamoniæ, succi papaveris, ana* 3ij, *succi limonior.* 3iiij. *Aquarian solani, violarum, lactuce, aceti albi vini, ana* 3iiij. Boyl them softly, strain them, and add thereunto two Ounces of Oxisachare, of white Sugar-candy two ounces, & *fiat potus.* Of the which let him take 4 ounces at a time, two or three times in a day. It mightily digesteth Choler aforesaid, in the 4th degree.

Purgers against red Choler and Melancholy caused of ♄ in ♐, Hot and Dry in the 4th degree.

Syrup. acetos. syr. violar. syr. acetosit. citri, syr. solani, syr. de infuione.

Aqua solani, aqua papaveris, violarum, laciuc. aqua betæ, aqua nenupæ, angelicæ, aqua cardui benedicti, aqua serpentariæ.

Tberiaca Galeni, Methridatum, pulvis contra pestem, Oyl of Scorpions, *baccæ bederæ, triforasenicæ. Electuarium frigidum, oxipharmicum, cum decoctione mirah. cassia fistula,* tamarinds, magnes, violets, hops, Juyce of Limons, *epithimum, stecados, mirabolan. nigr. polypodii, sennæ, rosarum virid. poppy, fumitory, volubilis, mirab. Indii, calamentum, folia jujubi, endiv. pruna perfica, solanum. Lapis laxuli, lapis Armen. pill. de lap. laxul. pill. de 5 gen. mirab. pill. de jeralogod. pill. Russini, confect. bamech, anacard. biera picra simpl. rhabarb. diaprunes.*

These purge red Choler.

Pistulæ elateriæ, pill. de turbith, pill. de coloquintida, electuarium psiliticum, electuar. Ducis.

℞ *Diasennæ* 3ij, *pill. de lapide lazul. de fumitor. ana* 3j, *pill. lucis major,* 3ij, *Aqua boragin. hysopi, solani, ana* 3iiβ. Commix them for two Doses, they purge Melancholy and Choler adust in the 4th degree.

℞ *Hysopi, scabiosæ, fumitor. calamenti, endiv. ana* Mj. *Capil. Vener. Scolopendr. Rad. fænicul. petros. ungulæ, ana* p.j. *tamarindar.* 3j, *mannæ* 3β, *sennæ* 3v, *polypodii* 3iij, *mirabol. Ind. & beber. ana* 3β, *absintbii* Mβ, *fiat decoctio adcolatur.* 3viij, *addantur de pill. Elaterii, pill. de turbith. ana* 3j, *confect. hamech* 3ij, *disturb. stomatic. laxativ. diasennæ, ana* 3v, *fiat potus pro tribus dosibus.* It purgeth the Stomach, Lungs, Breast and Bowels strongly, in 4 degrees, *Cholera æruginosa,* and red Choler and Melancholy, and *Cholera prasrva* caused of ♄ in ♐, and of ♂ in ♑.

Saturn in the first 18 degrees of ♉, is cold and dry *in primo gradu,* and causeth Diseases of Melancholy, hard, cold and dry, with a superfluous flegm possessing the heart, raising many fantasies, and madness.

Saturn in the last 12 degrees of ♉ is cold and dry in the beginning of the 2d degree, causing Diseases of Melancholy, cold and dry, with a superfluous flegm possessing the heart, causing visions and fantasies, melancholick passions, solitariness, heaviness, and sadness, with Cankers, Gouts, and stiffness of the Limbs and Sinews.

Of ♉, ♍, ♑, that are cold and dry, of the nature of the Earth, Melancholick, &c. ♄

Taurus is a Sign of the South, towards the West, cold and dry, of the nature of the Earth, melancholick and fixed, Nocturnal, Feminine, slow, sharp, rheumatick, hurtful, unfortunate, the Night-house of ♀, the Exaltation of the ☽, the Detriment of ♂, and causeth Diseases cold and dry, of Melancholy, as Cankers, dry Scabs, and Itches.

♄ In the last 12 degrees are caused melancholick passions, as before is said, with Cankers and Sores caused of an Humour cold and dry in the second degree, of very thick and fæculent Melancholy, bitter and unsavoury, somewhat sharp, like Allom water.

Saturn in the first six degrees of *Virgo* is cold and dry in the extremity of 2 degr. causing Diseases of Melancholy, cold and dry, mixed with a certain superficial and tough Flegm, the which, if it possesseth the Liver, it causeth indigestion and a cold and dry stomach, and maketh oppilations and indigestions in the Liver; and if it affect the Milt, it causeth swellings of the Milt, pain of the side, Stitches, with Consumptions. If it affect the heart, it causeth heaviness and evil thought; if it reach the Brain, it drieth the Brain, prevents Sleep, so that one shall be ever musing, melancholick and solitary; and when it falleth into the great guts, as it doth often, it causeth exceeding pain in the guts, like the Cholick, and it breedeth much wind in the Belly, and griping in the Bowels, and pain of the Haunches, and small of the Back, and an exceeding desire often to the Stool, and yet to void nothing but Flegm, and hard knobs like Nuts.

Saturn in the next 18 degrees of *Virgo* is cold and dry in the third degree, causing strong Diseases of Melancholy, Solitariness, Griefs and Sadness, Fearfulness, Fansies, Madness, Watching, and all Melancholick distempers, with Quartan Agues cold and dry, consuming the Radical Humidity of mans Body, and the Wind-cholick, and great gripings in the Bowels, with weakness in the Haunches and small of the Back, and oft provoking to the Stool, and nothing done, by reason of so much cold in the great guts, in the which is gathered great store of black Melancholy and tough Flegm which makes the Retentive Faculty so strong in those guts, that they will not let the Excrements pass through them, and the Expulsive Faculty is exceeding strong in the Muscles of the Fundament, to expell the dregs which rest above, and come not down; the Party so afflicted, his best way is to sweat and lye still, and to purge Melancholy; if ♄ be in ♍, and the ☽ apply to ♃ in ♓, then it is caused of much tough Flegm mixed with Melancholy, in the places aforesaid.

 Saturn in the last 6 degrees of ♍, is cold and dry in the beginning of the fourth degree, causing Melancholy, Madness, the Wolf, Cankers, and the like; dead Palsies, Quartan Agues, cold Gouts, Sciaticaes, and pain of the Hips, from strong, thick and tough Melancholy, and Wens, Warts, and such like; and this Melancholy is mixed with a superfluous dry Flegm, and tough withall, stopping the Veins and passages.

 Virgo is a Sign of the South, and by East, cold and dry, of the nature of Earth, Melancholick, Common, Feminine, Nocturnal, and more cold and dry than ♉; Barren, Reasonable, Tractable, Beautiful, equal in Body, having a convenient Voice, Dark, Fearful, the House, Joy and Exaltation of ☿, the Fall of ♀, the Detriment of ♃, and causeth Diseases of cold and dry Melancholy in the Belly and Bowels.

♄ *in* ♑

 Capricorn is a Sign cold and dry, of the nature of the Earth, melancholick, of the heart of the South, but he is more dry and more melancholick than ♍ or ♉, Feminine, Nocturnal, oblique, weak and vicious, slow, sharp, violent rheumatick, hurtful, unfortunate, heavy, luxurious, of few Sons, *sed multi usus tum muliere*, and is the House of ♄ by night, the Exaltation of ♂, the Fall of ♃, the Detriment of the ☽, and causeth Diseases of thin Melancholy, cold and dry in the 4th degree, and ingendreth Biles and Botches, Leprosie, red spots, Itches, Scurfs, Deafness,

Melancholy, Madness, Stammering, and a small Beard, by reason he is generally cold and dry.

  Saturn in the first 12 degrees of Capricorn, is cold and dry in the 4th degree, causing Melancholy, Madness, the Goat, Leprosie, Cankers, Quartan Fevers of long continuance, and Consumptions.

  Saturn in the last 18 degrees of ♑ , is cold and dry in the extremity of 4 degrees, and above nature, causing such melancholick Diseases as are not to be cured, as possession by Devils, desperate Madness, Leprosies, Wolves and Cancers, of thin Melancholy and Flegm, infecting the Brain, Head and Eyes, drying up and consuming the Body, and Quartan Fever not to be cured. And such as be born under this Sign, either they be Prophets, or very good men, or commanders of Devils, and diabolically affected, and wax mad, or do not live long in the world, they eat little, and watch much, and study, they love to live alone in deserts or obscure places, and either the Angels of God fetch them away, or the Devil in the end, if they live to years, and do not dye before they come to 30 years of age. Under such a constellation was *Henoch* and *Elias* born: for it makes them wise and zealous, and deep in understanding of Mysteries. And so likewise, if *Saturn* be at that time in the 9th House, and be Lord of the Ascendant, or in some Angle of the heaven well-aspected, then he shall incline to God, if ♄ be in some evil place, Retrograde, Combust, or with ♂, he will incline to Evil, and be dealing with Devils, and neglect his God and his Service.

Of Gemini.

  Gemini is a Sign hot and moist, of the nature of the Air, sweet in taste, sanguine, common, oblique, fair, and reasonable, having a small voice, and is strong in the Southwest and by West, a barren Sign, great and long, mighty of stature; he governeth of the Body humane the Arms and Shoulders, and causeth hot and moist Diseases of Blood, as Impostumations, Plurisies, fluxes of Blood, and much bleeding, he is the Day-house of ☿, the Exaltation of the Dragons head, the fall of the Dragons tayl, and detriment of *Jupiter*.

Saturn in the first 18 degrees of ♊ is hot and moist, sanguine, temperate, not distempering the Body with Melancholy and Flegm, comforting and increasing Nature and the Radical humidity in the body, and causeth few Diseases, or none at all, but in the Belly and Bowels.

♄ in the 12 last degrees of ♊ is hot and moist in the beginning of the first degree, ingendring sweet and tough Flegm, of Melancholy and superfluous moisture mixed with the Blood, causing Diseases of the Belly and Bowels, ingendring worms.

Of Libra.

Libra is a Sign of the Airy triplicity, Occidental, hot and moist, the heart of the West, moveable, fortunate, and Masculine, a direct, fair, reasonable, and Æquinoctial Sign; is sweet in taste, and is light, the Day-house of *Venus*, the Exaltation of ♄, the Fall of the ☉, and the Detriment of ♂, an causeth Diseases in the Reins, Navel and Buttocks, of hot, thick and fæulent Blood, and governeth the Reins and Kidneys.

Saturn in the first six degrees of *Libra* is hot and moist in the first degree, causing Diseases of Blood infected with Melancholy, apt to ingender Frenzies, Impostumes, and fluxes of Blood, the Hemorrhoids, in cold Sweats and flushing Heats.

Saturn in the next 18 degrees of ♎ is hot and moist in the second degree, causing infection of the Blood of Melancholy and superfluous Flegm, but Blood predominates, causing Fevers and Impostumes, the Measels and Small Pox, Fluxes, Plurisies, Scowrings, Coughs, Rheums, Plague, and Pox in Children, Grief, Thoughts and Discontent, and pain of the Side.

Saturn in the last six degrees of *Libra* is hot and moist in the beginning of the third degree, infecting and thickning the Blood with Melancholy and superfluous Flegm, causing the Meazles, Small Pox, Hoarsness, and heat of the Lights, runnings and slowings of Nature, Gonorrhea-Passions, Impostumations and Pleurisies under the Diaphragma, pain of the Side, rising of the Lungs ready to stop the breath, the Dysentery, the Plague, the Piles and Hemorrhoids, Grief and Discontent, Fevers of two fits, and a trembling in the Body.

Of Saturn in Aquary.

Aquary is a Sign hot and moist, of the nature of the Air, light and fixed, vain, North-west, and is more hot and moist than ♊ or ♎, and is more fixed than *Scorpio* or *Leo*, and not so much fixed as ♉; he is Masculine, fortunate, diurnal, Hyernal, sweet in taste, a violent, humane, and strong double-bodied Sign, sound and reasonable, of few Sons, long of Body, and weak Spirited, and crooked withall, addicted to Women; he is the Day-house of *Saturn*, the Detriment of the ☉, and causeth Diseases and distempers of the Shanks, Legs and Throat, of hot and moist causes, of Blood hot and moist, thick and abounding, as Impostumations, Kings Evil, Squinancy, Infammations, Pimples, with fluxes of Blood.

Saturn in the first 12 degrees of ♒ is hat and moist in the third degree, in gendring and multiplying Blood, as aforesaid, mixed with Melancholy and superfluous Flegm, breeding Fevers of two fits, with heat inward, and cold outward, small Pocks, Meazles and Cankers.

Saturn in the last 18 degrees of ♒ is hot in the beginning of the fourth degree, causing Diseases of Blood abounding mixed with Melancholy and Flegm, producing the *French* Pox, Impostumes, Cankers and Itches, and divers such Diseases.

Saturn in Cancer.

Cancer is the heart of the North, and is a Sign cold and moist, of the nature of the Water, corruptive and expulsive, Nocturnal and Feminine, direct, vicious, heavy and salt in taste, of the Summer, hurtful, sound, and of many Sons, and doth give divers and unequal proportions of the Body, signifiying creeping Vermin, and Beasts of the Water, and noble, gentle, yet unstable Women, without voice, and is the Day and Night-house of the ☽, the Exaltation of ♃, and the Fall of ♂, the Detriment of *Saturn*, and hath of the Body humane the Stomach, Breast, the Lungs and the Appurtenances: and of Diseases he causeth Biles, Leprosies, Dropsies, Fistulaes, Red spots, Itches, Scurfs, Deafness, Baldness, and small Beard, the *French* Pox and Impostumations of cold: of

Humours it signifieth waterish and thin saltish Flegm and corruptive.

 Saturn in ♋ in the first 18 degrees is cold in the first degree, and temperate in drowth and moisture, ingendring Diseases of much Flegm and Water mixed with thin Melancholy, causing Coughs, stopping of the Stomach, oppilations, with pains and prickings, of cold causes, in the Stomach, with shivering; and it produceth also the black Plague, by reason that the Blood is overcome with Flegm and Water, and it will be long e're the Sores will come out, and they come forth with much pain; but this Plague is not infections. This Plague, by the testimony of Dr. *Foreman*, reigned in *London* in the years 1592, and 1593, (who had it himself, and saw the depth of this Diseases) some were taken in the Heads and they did sleep much, for the brain was then much infected; and they did oft escape, being well back'd to, and purged with *Confection* of *Hamech*: some were infected both in the Brain, and at the Heart and Liver, and these would vomit much, and sleep much, and were very drowth, and these did most commonly dye the fourth day, and were without Remedy: some were infected in the Liver, and their Sores came forth in the Groyns, and these did neither sleep nor vomit, and did always escape, being well looked unto, being purged well with *Confection* of *Hamech* and *Diacarthamus*.

Of the *Black Plague* caused of *Saturn* in *Cancer*.

 You must understand that the cause of this Plague is, as aforesaid, of Flegm, thin Water, and Melancholy mixt, Flegm and Water having the dominion; and they that are taken with this Plague have much heaviness, weakness, and faintness, with a cold shivering three or four dayes, and sometimes seven or eight dayes before they be sick, and they cannot eat their meat, but are cold inward; and if the Humours apply to the Brain, then they are heavy and drowsie with sleep, and the Sores do come forth and appear commonly about the ears or neck, or in the face; and if the Humours settle to the Heart, then the Parties are fearful, timorous and faint, and the botch cometh forth under the Armpits, Breast and Shoulders, or Back; if the humour rest in the

Liver, and something affect the Heart withall, then they vomit, and the Sores will come forth in the Groyn, Buttocks, or thighs, and in this case it is good to vomit much, and to purge; and if the Brain and Liver be both infected, then the Party vomiteth much, and is very sleepy, and most commonly they dye within three or four dayes after they be taken with it, and there is seldome remedy, or none at all.

And you shall understand that this Plague was not infectious, because it came of a cold cause; and there was nothing that bred it so soon as eating of fresh Herrings and Cucumbers, and fruit, and such things as breed slimy Flegm and Water; and most commonly where it took a house, it went round amongst children and servants, that were all of one kind of feeding; and those two years was great plenty of fresh Herrings, and much fruit; and there dyed in the year 1593 eighteen hundred a week, and most of the Doctors of Physick did fly from *London*, and Dr. *Foreman* staid by it, and thanks God he saved many.

He farther saith from his own experience, that as there are two sorts of Plague, *viz.* from *Saturn* and *Mars*, so there are two sorts of Gods Tokens, the one black, and the other red; if the red spots do appear on them that have the black Plague, they may escape and live; and if the black spots do appear on them that have the red Plague, then they usually escape; but if the red spots appear in the red Plague, and the black spots in the black Plague, there is no other to be expected but death. He also saith, he saw this in himself and many others. And moreover he observes, that the farther *Saturn* went into *Cancer*, the more the Plague did increase, and when he was in the latter end of ♋ the Plague raged vehemently, and was at the highest.

Saturn in the last 12 degrees of *Cancer*, is moist in the beginning of the first degree, and cold in the beginning of the second degree, ingendring Diseases, and the black Plague, of thin Water and Melancholy, with heaviness and faintness, three or four dayes before they feel the Plague, and have no lust to their meat, and yet they are in reasonable temperature, and if this Humour settle and affect the Brain, the Party will be very heavy with sleep; if into the Stomach, then apt to cast.

Saturn in Scorpio.

Saturn in the first six degrees of *Scorpio* is moist in the first degree, and cold in the second, ingendring Diseases of much Flegm and Melancholy, but Flegm is predominant, as the French Pox, Swine Pox, Fistulaes, Gouts, Impostumes and cold Agues, and in this cold and moisture beareth sway; and it is tough, stinking, and slimy Flegm, causing cold, and the Parties shall be cold both inward and outward, with trembling and shaking; and *Saturn* in ♏ causeth also the black Plague, as he doth in ♋, but more strong and more forcible, of slimy Flegm and stinking Water; and the spittle is sharp and sour, especially if the Humour be gathered in the Stomach, but if it be gathered in the Liver, then there is heaviness in the Hypocendries, in the right side; and if the Humour be gathered in the inwards, it will grieve him to fetch his breath, but if it be in the Milt, there will be grief and heaviness in the left side; if it be in the Matrix, then there will be grief in the Reins and place of the Matrix; and if it be in the Lights and spiritual Members, then there followeth a Cough, and a hard fetching of breath, and dulness in the Stomach and Liver; it causeth evil digestion, and little appetite to eat, and most commonly this runneth out into the extreme parts, and causeth much pain of the joynts and *arthritica passio*, and the *French* Pox, and sometimes the Party hath a Fever withall, and then the Urine is duekish white, of an Iron colour, grayish, near unto white, with a mean substance; and this signifieth *Acetosum: id est*, Flegm tart, sour and cold.

Saturn in the next 18 degrees of *Scorpio* is moist in the second degree, and cold in the third, causing Diseases of filthy Flegm mixed with Melancholy, causing the French Pox, Fistulaes, cold and moist Gouts, Impostumations, and cold Fevers, or *Artbritica passio*, and Fevers of *Phlegma Acetosum*, as is said in the first six degrees of *Scorpio*.

Saturn in the last six degrees of ♏ is cold in the beginning of the third degree, causing Diseases of tough, slimy and filthy stinking Flegm, mix'd with Melancholy, causing Fistulaes, cold Goats, Impostumations, cold Fevers, the *French* Pox, &c. and this Flegm is called *Phlegma Acetosum*, which is tart, sour and cold;

and the Party shall be cold both inward and outward, with trembling and shaking, and causeth also the black Plague, more forcible than in *Cancer*, and of a more slimy and stinking Humour, and in such a case the Urine is white and yellowish, or of an Iron gray, near unto white, with a mean substance, and this signifieth *Acetosum phlegms* to abound without a Fever.

Of Pisces.

Pisces is a Sign cold and moist, of the nature of the Water, flegmatick, and is more cold than *Cancer* or *Scorpio*, and is the moistest of all the Signs, and is of the North-west, Nocturnal, Feminine, common, oblique and crooked, infortunate, lacking voice, signifying Birds, Fowls, and Fishes of the Sea and other waters; is double-bodied, unsavoury, salt of taste, and more salt than ♋ or ♏, unequal of proportion, of mean beauty, hurtful, burst, broken, rent, torn, wayward, and a Sign of many Daughters, and much use and company of Women, and signifieth thick and tough Flegm, the Gout in the Feet, the wet Gout and Dropsie, Biles, Botches, Impostumations, *French* Pox, Meazles, red Spots, Fluxes, Scurfs, Itches, Deafness and Baldness, and a small Beard, he is the Night-house of ♃, the Exaltation of ♀, the Fall and Detriment of ☿.

Saturn in the first 12 degrees of *Pisces*, is moist in the 3d degree, and cold in the 4th, ingendring Diseases cold and moist, of much tough and stinking Flegm mixed with Melancholy, as the French Pox, Aches in he Bones, *Artbritica passio*, the cold and moist Gout, Fistulaes.

Saturn in the last 18 degrees of *Pisces*, is moist in the beginning, and cold in the extremity of the 4th degree, above Nature, corruptive and digestive, extinguishing the radical Humidity of the Body by much cold, and inferring death and corruption, and mortification of the Members, ingendring Diseases, as Gouts, dead Palsies, Falling-sickness, *Epilepsia*, *French* Pox, Aches in the bones, *Artbertica Passio*, Dropsies, and the black Plague, as in *Scorpio*.

Of Jupiter.

Jupiter is next unto *Saturn*, and he passeth the 12 Signs of the *Zodiack* in 12 years; By nature he is hot and moist, temperate, of the nature of the Air, sanguine, light, sweet in taste, Ascending, nourishing and increasing. He hath in the Body humane the Liver, the Blood and the Stomach, the Vital spirits the left Ear, and the Belly; the inward part of the Brain-pan, the Navel, the Intestines, the Ribs, the right Hand, and Cartilages, with the Grissels, and ruleth the Virtue Digestive and the Natural Virtue, and is friendly to the Life of Man.

Of Diseases, *Jupiter* causeth the increasing and abundance of Blood, Impostumations and Plurisies, the Squinancy, Impostumes of the Lungs, the Cramp, the Apoplexy, the Lethargy, the Cephalick and Cardiack Passion, the Fever *Synochus* and *Synocha inflatima*, and all Impostumations of Blood, and Diseases that come of superabounding of blood.

If the Blood be mixed with Melancholy, the water looketh somewhat dark or blackish, swarthy and heavy.

If Blood and Choler adust be mixed, the colour of the Urine will be like unto Hemp.

If Blood and Choler adust be mixed, and Blood be predominate, then is the Urine *subrubicurida*.

If Blood be mixed with Choler, and Blood predominate, then the Urine is reddish, and the Party is troubled and tormented most with his Disease from nine of the clock at night till three in the morning, and is dry, and drinketh much and sleepeth little.

But if Blood and Choler be mixed, and Choler have the predominancy, *subrufam facit Urinam*.

If Blood and Choler be equally mixed, *tune rusam facit Urinam*; but the Choler sheweth yellow in the Urine, and the Urine is very red and thin.

If Blood be mixed with Flegm, and Flegm have the upper hand, then the Urine looketh of a dark reddish colour, heavy (as it were) a deep yellow, and the Party eateth little, and is dry inwardly, yet drinketh but ordinarily; but is in most pain from three a clock at afternoon till nine at night.

If the Urine be thick in substance, and red in colour, then Blood hath the predominancy in the Distemper, and is cause of the Disease.

If Urine e thin of substance, and red of colour, then Choler hath the predominancy, and causeth the Disease.

If the Urine be thin of substance, and darkish white in colour, then Melancholy ruleth, and causeth the Disease.

Cold causeth whiteness in colour, and doth thicken, and is passive and ponderous, congealing an destroying, indigestive, stopping, and making oppilations, in the Body, extinguishing the Radical Heat and Breath of Life.

Heat causeth redness and thinness, attenuating, digestive, preparing and opening, active, increasing and ascending, light and quick in, moving, nourishing and preserving the Radical moisture and humidity of the body.

Moistness causeth blackness, darkness and thickness, corruptive, putrifying and rotting, and is decreasing and descending, heavy, slow in motion, dissolving and expelling.

Drowth causeth thinness, blackness or darkness, yellowness and cleerness, as it is mix'd with Choler or Melancholy; if with Choler, the Urine looketh yellowish; if with Melancholy, black and darkish; and Drowth is passive, descending, decreasing light, and quick in moving, drying and drawing, thirsty, sucking, preserving, making to abide and indure, knitting and joyning together.

Cold and drowth cause thinness and whiteness, but if the melancholick Humour be fæculent, or of burnt Choler, then the Urine sheweth somewhat thick and dark, or brown like deep Sack or Bastard; and if the melancholick Humour be ery dry, not burnt, then is the Urine very thin and cleer, like Rhenish-wine or White-wine, and sometime like Water.

Heat and Moisture of Blood make the Urine red and somewhat thick, or between thick and thin, but red.

Heat and Drowth of Choler make the Urine glowing red, and somewhat thin.

Of ♃ in ♊, ♎, and ♒.

Jupiter in *Gemini, Libra* and *Aquary,* is of the nature of the Air, sanguine, hot and moist, increasing of the blood, and causing Diseases from blood superabounding, &c. as follows.

Jupiter in Gemini.

Gemini is a Sign hot and moist, of the nature of the Air, sanguine, of the South-west, common, long and large, the House of *Mercury,* and the Fall of *Cauda,* the Detriment of *Jupiter,* and Exaltation of *Caput Draconis,* is oblique in Ascending, reasonable, and of small voice, masculine, sweet in taste, light, vernal, humane, fortunate.

♃ in the first 18 degrees of ♊ is hot and moist in the first degree, encreasing good and natural blood, mightily causing Pleurisies and Impostumes, *Peripneumonia* and Issues of blood.

Jupiter in the last 12 degrees of ♊ is hot in the beginning of the second degree, and causeth the blood to increase and surmount in moisture and heat, causing Pleurisies and Impostumes (as before) and Issues of blood, and flowings in Women, and oft Spitting of Blood.

Of *Jupiter* in *Libra.*

Libra is also a Sign hot and moist, and more hot and moist than *Gemini,* is the heart of the West, of the nature of Air, sanguine, increaseth blood, is moveable, masculine and fortunate, direct, reasonable and dark, having a great voice, double-bodied, joying in company of Women, a humane Sign, the Day-house of ♀, the Exaltation of ♄, the Fall of the ☉, and the Detriment of ♂; and causeth Diseases in the Reins and Kidneys, issuing of Nature and *Gonorrhea Passio;* increases Blood and Impostumations, and Pleurisies, *Peripneumonia,* and the like.

Jupiter in the first six degrees of ♎ is hot and moist in the second degree.

Jupiter in the next 18 degrees of ♎ is more intent, hot and moist in the second degree, much increasing blood, causing

Diseases of Blood, as beforesaid, Impostumes, Pleurisies, and such like.

Jupiter in the last six degrees of ♎ is hot and moist in the beginning of the 4ᵗʰ degree, causing much heat and moisture, and abundance of blood, breeding many Diseases of blood in the Liver and lungs, as Pleurisies and Impostumes, the Matrix with much bleeding and the like.

In these Diseases caused of ♃ in ♎, minister not in the hour of ♃, but in the hour of ♄ or ☿; neither let ♊, ♎, or ♒ be in the Ascendant, but ♉, ♍ or ♑, and cure the Party with cold and dry things, first letting him blood in the Liver-Vein, and give him things to cool the blood, and to diminish the quantity, and abate the quality thereof, as is specified before.

Of Aquarius.

Aquary is a Sign of the Airy Triplicity, more hot and moist than ♊ or ♎, ingendering Blood, sweet in taste, masculine, fixed, fortunate, occidental, towards the North, Diurnal, Hyemal, violent, double-bodied, humane, light, sound and reasonable, of few Sons, gentle, long of body, some crookedness, the Day-house of ♄, the Detriment of the ☉, and causeth Diseases in the Liver, Reins and Lights, through the excess of blood, hot and moist, and the rising of the Lights in the Throat through much hot blood stopping the Lights.

Jupiter in Aquarius.

Jupiter in the first 12 degrees of ♒ is hot and moist in the 4ᵗʰ degree, ingendring much fæculent blood, very hot and moist, producing distempers in the Lights and Liver.

♃ in the last 18 degrees of ♒ is also hot and moist in the 4ᵗʰ degree, causing much fæculent thick blood, stopping the Lungs and Lights, making rising in the Throat ready to stop the Wind, and affecting the face with swelling and redness; it multiplyes blood in the Liver and Veins, causing Pleurisies, Impostumes, Fluxes, and Spitting of blood. *Jupiter* in the 8ᵗʰ, and the ☽ in ♓, applying to ☍ of ♂ in ♊, causeth the Fever Hectick, great pain of the back, the stone in the Kidneys, and Indigestion, and botches in the Liver.

♃ in the first 18 degrees of ♈ is temperate in drought and moisture, but hot in the 1ˢᵗ degree, causing Diseases of yellow Choler, thin and sharp, corrupting the blood, causing Pimples, Itches, Scabs, small Fevers and Heart-burning, vomiting up of clots of blood, and bleeding at the Nose.

Jupiter in the last twelve degrees of *Aries* is hot in the beginning of the first degree, ingendring Diseases of yellow Choler mixed with the Blood, Choler having predomination, causing Pimples, Itches, Scabs and heat of the blood, and Fevers.

Of *Jupiter* in *Leo*.

Jupiter in the first six degrees of *Leo*, is dry in the second, and hot in the first degree, ingendring Diseases of thick, yellow Choler and Blood mixed; and the Choler having predominancy, causeth Impostumations and Fevers, Itches, Scabs, Heat of the Liver, yellow Jaundies, pains of the Thighs, Sciatica, salt Flegmy fæces, and the like.

Jupiter in the next 18 degrees of *Leo* is dry in the second degree, and hot in the third, causing Diseases of thick yellow Choler and Blood mixed (Choler predominating;) as Impostumes, Fevers, Botches, the Sciatica and pain of the Thighs, and heat of the Lungs, and Itches, and Heart-burning, and the yellow Jaundies.

Jupiter in the last six degrees of *Leo* is hot in the beginning of the 4ᵗʰ degree, and dry in the beginning of the third degree, ingendring Diseases of thick yellow Choler mixed with Blood; Choler hath the dominion, and causeth hot burning Fevers, the Kings Evil, Impostumes, heat of the Lungs, stopping of the Liver, the yellow Jaundies, the Sciatica, pain of the Thighs, and salt flegmy fæces.

Of *Jupiter in* Sagitary.

Jupiter in the first twelve degrees of *Sagitary* is dry in the third, and hot in the 4ᵗʰ degree, causing Diseases hot and dry, of red Choler mixed with Blood; and the red Choler having dominion causeth dryness of the Liver, red and high colour in the Face, strong Fevers, Impostumes and strong pains of the Head and left Ear, dryness of the Brain, Frenzy, Griping pains in the belly, *Collica Passio*, Impostumes in the Liver, pains in the Grissels, giddiness of the Brain, sore Eyes, heat of the Lungs, and such like.

Jupiter in the last 18 degrees of ♐ is hot in the extremity of the 4th degree, and dry in the beginning of the 4th degree, causing Diseases of red Choler mixed with Blood, that are without Remedy; as *Noli me tangere*, the Kings Evil, Impostumes and dryness of the Liver, Frantickness, yellow Jaundies, salt Flegmy-fæces, and Diseases of exceeding heat and drowth, consuming the Radical moisture and Humidity of the body.

Of *Jupiter* in *Taurus*.

Jupiter in the first 18 degrees of *Taurus* is temperate in all the four Qualities but makes the Blood apt to convert into Melancholy, and to turn into *Cholera æruginosa*, and *Cholera prassiva*.

♃ in the last 12 degrees of ♉ is cold and dry in the beginning of the first degree, ingendring Diseases of Melancholy mixed with Blood, Melancholy having the dominion, causing *Cholera prassiva* and *Æruginosa*, making oppilations and stoppings in the Liver and Milt, and causing costiveness and pains of the Bowels and about the Navel, and Cartilages, and left ear and throat, and in the veins and bones; a Fever in the bones, indigestion, and much wind and blood, melancholy running up and down the Body from place to place.

Of *Jupiter* in *Virgo*.

Jupiter in the first 6 degrees of *Virgo* is cold and dry in the first degree, ingendring *Cholera æruginosa* and *prassiva*, that is, a Humour mixed of Melancholy and Blood, Melancholy having the dominion, causing Chaps, Wens, Warts, Knobs, Measels, Small Pox, stiffness and ache in the Knee, Belly and Sinew, with costiveness and oppilations.

Jupiter in the next 18 degrees of ♍ is cold and dry in the second degree, ingendring *Cholera æruginosa* & *prassiva*, which is a

Humour compact of Melancholy and Blood, Melancholy having the Dominion, causing, as beforesaid, in all things, and the wind cholick, and much pain in the bottom of the belly; especially if ♃ be in the 8th or 9th, and be signifier of the Disease, and great pain and cold in the knees.

Of *Jupiter* in *Capricorn*.

Jupiter in the first 12 degrees of *Capricorn* is cold and dry in the third degree, causing Diseases of Melancholy mix'd with Blood, Melancholy having the dominion; as Diseases in the throat and muscles, and it is called, as before, *Cholera prassiva & æruginosa*; and it is somewhat a thin Humour causing Knobs, Warts and Wens, and hard Impostumes.

Jupiter in the last 18 degrees of *Capricorn* is cold and dry in the beginning of the 4th degree, ingendring Diseases of thin Melancholy, corrupting the blood, and Melancholy having the dominion, causing Diseases in the Throat, and swelling in the Jaws and Glandules.

Of *Jupiter* in *Cancer*.

Jupiter in the first 12 degrees of ♋ is cold in the beginning of the first degree, and moist in the beginning of the second; ingendring *Cholera vitellina*, that is a Humour mixed of Flegm, Water and Blood, and Flegm hath the dominion; and it is very tough and slimy, and very moist, ingendring Diseases in the Stomach, and in the privy parts and Matrix, and stopping of the Conduits of the Bladder, and pain in the left side under the Ribs, and under the left Pap like a Pleurisie, the Worms in Children, and the French Pox and ache in the bones.

♃ in the last 18 degrees of ♋ is temperate in cold and heat, but moist in the first degree, ingendring *Cholera vitellina*, that is an Humour mixed of Flegm, Water and Blood, where Flegm hath the dominion; causing Diseases in the Bladder and privy parts, in the Yard, and stopping of the Urine, Gonorrhea, the Dropsy in the hands and other parts, and Impostumations in the bottom of the Stomach, a great Rheum and Cough in the Lungs, faint and weak sleeps, and the falling evil. ♄ in ♋, and ♂ in ♎, causeth Gonorrhea, and Impostumes in the Reins; ♃ in ♋, and ♄ in ♎, causeth the Pox of a venomous Humour.

♃ in ♋, and ♂ Lord of the Horoscope, and ♄ in ♎ causeth the *French* Pox, the Gonorrhea, and sharpness of Urine.

Of *Jupiter* in *Scorpio*.

Jupiter in the first 6 degrees of *Scorpio* is cold in the first degree, and moist in the second, ingendring Diseases of thick and stinking Flegm, corrupting the Blood, and Flegm predominates in the commixtion, ingendring *chlera vitellina*, with Gouts in the Feet, swellings and pains in the Feet, and in the privy Members, Fistulaes, Pox and running sores.

♃ in the next 18 degrees of ♏ is cold in the second degr. and moist in the 3d; ingendring *cholera vitellica* of Flegm, stinking and corrupt Blood, but Flegm is most in the commixtion, causing the French Pox, Fistulaes, running Sores, swelling of the Feet, the wet Gout, and such like.

♃ in the last 6 degrees of ♏ is cold in the beginning of the third degree, and moist in the beginning of the 4th degr. ingendring *cholera vitellina*, causing the Pox, the wet and cold Gout, swellings of the Feet, Fistulaes and running sores, and many evil and moist Diseases, as the Dropsie, &c.

Of *Jupiter* in *Pisces*.

Jupiter in the first 12 degrees of ♓ is cold in the third, and moist in the 4th degree, causing many Diseases of Water and Flegm mixed with the Blood; as the cold and moist Gout, the Pox, aches, Fistulaes, Itches, and Dropsies, with rotting and corruption of the Liver indigestion, a pricking and gnawing of the Stomach, a great Rheum, stuffings of the Stomach and Liver, the Dropsie and quotidian flegmatick Fever, which seize the Party in the extreme parts with great cold, and create pains in the belly and under the short ribs, and hips, and reins, neck and stomach.

♃ in the last 18 degrees of ♓ is cold in the beginning of the 4th degree, and moist-above nature, in the extremity of the 4th degree, causing Diseases of Flegm and Water mixed with the Blood, but Flegm and Water have dominion, and the Diseases are remediless, as the *French* Pox, Dropsy, wet Gout, rotting of the Liver, gnawing, pricking and tearing of the Stomach, with incessant pain, pricking, and affliction to the Head.

Of *Mars* in ♈, ♌ and ♐.

Mars is a Planet hot and dry, of the nature of Fire, unnatural to the life and health of man and humane kind; untemperate, burning and scorching, more hot in his nature than the Sun, full or red Choler, and is Active by reason he is hot and masculine: *Mars* hath of the Body humane the *Cistos*, the Gaul it self, and also hath a part in the Blood, the veins, reins and kidneys; as also the back and the buttocks, and the *Decuesus speraiatis*, and *vim irascibilem*, the reins, and worms in the head, the side, the blood of a wound; and to him belongeth cutting and scarifying of wounds of men, and burning with Cauteries either actual or potential.

Mars causeth Head-ache, Frenzies, and hot cholerick Agues of long continuance, the Fever tertian and quotidian, the hot Pestilence and Plague, hot Apostemes, Megrims and Inflammations of the Liver, Tetters, and St. *Anthonies* fire, and the Stone in the Reins, Canker, *Noli me tangere*, Abortion. *Mars* rules the cholerick Humour, his House is *Aries* and *Scorpio*, his Exaltation is ♑, his Fall is ♋, his Detriment ♎ and ♉.

Of the cholerick Humour subject to Mars.

Choler is one of the four Natural Humours in the body of Man, and is ingendred in the Liver, and hath its residence in the Gall; and by Natural Choler is maintained the Virtue Attractive in the members of Man, which is hot and dry, and is of the nature of ♀ and the ☉, if it be Natural; but if it be Unnatural and burnt, then it is of the nature of ♂, which is hot and dry, by Nature untemperate; and so much the more if he be in ♈, ♌ or ♐, breeding Diseases and Infirmities in the body humane.

Choler hath most power and dominion in Summer, from the 8 Ides of *May* until the 8 Ides of *August*, whereby are ingendred hot Agues and sharp Fevers, and is of most force from three a clock in the Morning till nine before Noon: and as by

Natural Choler the Body humane is maintained and kept in temperance, so by Unnatural Choler it is destroyed and killed; for there are four degrees of Choler, according to its Heat and Drowth, more or less, and the first is the mean wherein the full proportion of Natural Choler doth consist, the which being distempered, the Body becometh diseased more or less, according to the Distemper and Humour abounding.

Of Natural Choler.

Natural Choler is hot and dry, temperate, and maintaineth the Attractive Virtue in all the Members of the Body, to the maintenance of Life and Health; and the right Natural Choler is reddish, cleer and pure.

Of Unnatural Choler.

Unnatural Choler, if it abound in the Gall, it overfloweth the Liver, and causeth the yellow Jaundies, and there are caused many bitter belchings in the Stomach; if Unnatural Choler in the Liver commix it self with Blood in the Veins, and ascend to the Brain, it maketh the Party light-witted, and frantick, and drieth the Radical moisture and humidity of the Brain, preventing sleep and rest.

If this unnatural Choler remain in the Liver and Stomach, it causeth great drought and oppilations in the Liver, breeding the yellow Jaundies, and divers other Diseases, and so much the more when it once spreadeth through the Veins into the Body, and then it causeth Fevers, Pimples, Ringworms, and sometimes Impostumations, especially in those places of the body where the Attractive Virtue is very strong, and the Expulsive very weak.

And when this unnatural Choler doth fall into the Liver, and mix it self with Melancholy, then mixing, it self with Blood, and running out into some particular place or part of the Body through the Veins; it is there then the cause of wonderfull ill Diseases, as Cankers, Fistulaes, Wolves, *Noli me tangere*, and suck like.

Of Urine.

The Urine of Natural Choler should be red or subruse, *Rubes* and *subrubes, per totam tenuem*; and such Urines do signifie Natural Choler without a fever, but if there be a fever, these are the tokens:

Bitterness of the mouth, anger, thirst, little sleep, pain of the head, hardness of the belly; and in the houres of Choler, which are from three of the clock in the morning till nine before noon, the Party hath much grief and pain, and the fever usually seizes the body in these hours.

But if Natural choler doth abound with a Fever, then the colour of the Urine *est magis rubea vel rusa, ut ignis expresst*, and hath all the signs aforesaid, but more strong.

Of *Unnatrual Choler* there are four sorts;

First, *Cholera citrina*, caused of the ☉ in ♈ or ♌. Then *Cholera vitellina.* Thirdly, *Cholera prasuia*; and fourthly, *Cinlera aruginosa.*

Cholera citrinia is caused of ♂ and ☉ in ♈ or ♌, especially of ☉ in ♈ or ♌, and maketh the Urine of Citrine colour, like perfect Amber, and but meanly thin, as after shall follow. *Cholera vitellina* is caused of ♃ in ♋, ♏ or ♓, and of ♂ and ☉ in ♋, ♏ and ♓, *& reddit urinam subeitrinam mediocriter tenuem*, and is ingendred of the congelation of Flegm and cleer Choler, and is viscous an clammy, whitish, like the white of an Egg.

Cholera prasina is caused of ♃, ♂ and ☉, in ♉, ♍, ♑; and this doth seldom change the colour of the Urine, except in sharp Fevers, and this is greenish of colour, and is ingendred of the distemperature of the Stomach.

If adust be mixed with blood, then the colour of the Urine is like unto Hemp.

If Citrine colour be mixed with Melancholy, and Choler have the upper hand, then the Urine looketh yellow.

Cholera æruginosa is of a dark greenish colour, and doth burn in the Stomach, being ingendred from adustive Humours, by the influence of ♃, ♂ and ☉, in ♉, ♍, and ♑.

Mars in the first 18 degrees of ♈ is hot and dry in the first degree, ingendring hot and dry Diseases of yellow Choler and red mixed, but the yellow is most in the commixtion, which causeth Agures, Itches, Jaundies and Oppilations, and pains in the right side of the Head, and Pimples in the face, redness of the Eyes, with Lunacy and Franticness.

Mars in the 12 last degrees of ♈ is hot and dry in the beginning of the second degree, ingendring yellow Choler and red, but the yellow Choler is most in the commixtion, and causeth Pimples in the face, pain in the right side, the Head, Kidneys, and dryness and stiffness of the Eyes, over-flowing of the Gall, the Jaundies and Oppilation of the Liver, Shingles, Agues and Itches, Alopecia, Frenzy and Madness.

For the curing of such Diseases caused of Mars in Aries, minister not in the hour of ♂ nor the ☉, nor in the hour of ♃ being in ♈, ♌ or ♐: neither let ♈, ♌ nor ♐ be in the Ascendant, nor ♉, ♍ nor ♑, if ♂ or the ☉ be therein, but ♋, ♏, ♓ or ♊, ♎ or ♒, if ♀ or ☽ be therein, and the things that must cure must be cold and moist; and first it were good to bathe the Party, to digest the Humours; then to purge, and prescribe a cold Diet for a season.

Of Mars in Leo.

Mars in the first six degrees of Leo is hot and dry in the second degree, ingendring red and yellow Choler, and the yellow predominates, causing Diseases of the heart and back, stopping of the Liver, and *Cardiaca passio, Synocopen*, hot Fevers, Plague and Pestilence, with great heat and drowth.

Mars in the next 18 degrees of Leo is hot and dry in the third degree, causing Diseases of thick yellow Choler, of red Choler causing pestilential Fevers, the Plague and Pestilence infective, and pains of the heart and back, the yellow Jaundies and oppilation of the Liver, Piles and Hemorrhoids.

Mars in the six last degrees of ♌, is hot and dry in the beginning of the fourth degree, ingendring much yellow, thick and red Choler, very hot and dry, causing pestilential Fevers, the Plague and Pestilence infectious, *Syncopen* and trembling of the Heart, and great pains of the Heart and Back.

For Cure hereof, minister not in the hour of ☉ or ♂, but in the hour of ☽, ♀, ☿, being in ♋, ♏ or ♓; ♋, ♏ or ♓ being in the Ascendant.

Of Mars in Sagittarium.

Mars in the first 12 degrees of ♐ is hot and dry in the 4th degree, infecting the body and blood with much thick, red choler that is hot and very dry, causing the Plague and Pestilence, and hot pestilential Fevers, Carbuncles andsuch like, Hemorrhoids and Piles, Wolves, Cancers, Impostumations, and such Diseases as eat and consume the flesh and Radical Humidity of the Body, and swelling of the Legs.

Mars in the last 18 degrees of ♐ is hot and dry above nature, consuming and drying up the Radical Moisture and Humidity of the Body, and utterly extinguishing the Life of Man; causing also Botches, Carbuncles, Plague, Pestilence, consuming Agues, and the like; as the violent Sciatica, and great extream pain in the joynts and huckle-bone, with extreme heat and burning. If the Moon be in *Gemini* and apply to *Mars* in the last 18 degrees of ♐, and ♄ in ♌, and be Lord of the 12th, in the 6th, it causeth the Stone and Stangury, pissing of Blood, and intolerable pain; for ♂ in ♐ causeth hot and dry Diseases of red Choler; and in such a case, if ♄ be in ♉, ♍ or ♑, and joyned to ♂ by ☌ or aspect, or the Moon apply to ♄, or if ♄ be Lord of the hour, it causeth *Noli me tangere*, Canker, Wolf, or such like; for the Humour is venomous, consuming and corroding above nature.

Of the Cure of Mars in Sagittary.

Minister not to any in this case in the hour of ♂ or ☉, but in the hour of ☽, ♀ or ☿ being in ♋, ♏, ♓, and put ♋, ♏, or ♓ in the Ascendant, and make the lord of the 6th weak, then bathe the Party in cold Water, and let him blood out of hand, and give him things to quench his great heat and drought and anoint his Body with *infrigidans Galeni*, and such like cold Ointments, and purge red Choler strongly, for these Diseases are infective.

Of Mars in Taurus.

Mars in the first 18 degrees of *Taurus* is temperate in heat cold, and dry in the first degree, ingendring Diseases of red Choler and Melancholy equally mix'd, causing Diseases cold and dry in the neck and throat, as Wens, hard knobs, dryness of the Sinews, Cramps, oppilations of the Liver: ♂ in ♉ in Aspect to ♄ in ♉, ♍ or ♑, causeth hardness of the Spleen, the Stone, pain in the belly and side, and dry Melancholy Diseases, and Consumptions, putrefaction in the Matrix, Diseases in the Head, like to vomit, but cannot, and pain of the Back and Stomach.

Mars in the last 12 degrees of ♉ is cold in the beginning of the first degree, and dry in the beginning of the second, ingendring Diseases of dry, thick and tough Melancholy and red Choler, and Melancholy predominates, and causes Diseases hot and dry in the Neck and Throat; as Warts, Wenns, stiffness of the Sinews, Cramps, oppilations of the Spleen and Liver, and Diseases that do breed Wind, and do pine and consume the flesh away, by reason of many oppilations and stoppings in the Body, the Stone in the Reins and Gravel, and provocation of vomiting, but ineffectual; and if ♂ in ♉ behold a Planet in a fiery Sign, he causeth Gonorrhea, and if ♂ aspect ♄, and ♄ in ♍, then it causeth a venomous sharp Humour, rising in the flesh, like stinging of Nettles, and will cause the Meazles or Pox.

Administer not to any where the Disease is caused of ♂ in ♉, ♍ or ♑, in the hour of ♂, ♄ or ☿, but in the hours of ♀, ♃ or the ☽, and put ♈, ♊ or ♎ in the Ascendant, or ♋ if ♃ be there, and the ☽ in ♊, ♎ or ♈, applying to ♃ or ♀, and the Cure shall be by digestion first of the Humours, then purge the bathe.

Of Mars in *Virgo.*

Mars in the first six degrees of ♍ is cold in the first degree, and dry in the second, causing Diseases of Melancholy and red Choler, Melancholy having dominion, causing oppilations of the Liver, pains and gripings in the Belly, the Stone in the Bladder, the Stangury and Cholick, pain of the Milt, the Piles and Hemorrhoids, with Tympanies and such like.

♂ in the next 18 degrees of ♍ is cold in the second, and dry in the third degree, causing, oppilations and stopping of the Liver, of Melancholy and red Choler fæculent and thick, Melancholy predominating, causing stoppings and swelling of the Milt, pains and gripings in the Belly, the Wind Cholick and Strangury, the Stone in the Bladder; and ♂ with ♄ the Piles and Hemorrhoids.

♂ in the last six degrees of ♍ is cold in the beginning of the 3d, and dry in the beginning of the 4th deg. causing Diseases of thick Melancholy and red Choler, Melancholy exceeding, causeth Diseases and Oppilations of the Liver and Milt, pain and gripings of the Belly, the Strangury, the Wind-Cholick and Stone in the Bladder, the Hemorrhoids, Piles, and Meazles in children.

The Cure.

Administer not in the hours of ♄, ♂ or ☿; but in the hours of ☽, ♃ and ♀, and put ♈, ♎ or ♊ in the Ascendant, or ♋ or ♒, if ♃ be in either of them, and the ☽ in ♊, ♎, ♒, if ♃ or ♀; then digest, vomit, bathe and purge, for this Humour will not be well purged without a digestive be given before.

Mars in Capricorn.

Mars in the first 12 degrees of *Capricorn* is cold in the 3d, and dry in the 4th degree, causing Diseases of much tough and dry Melancholy and red Choler; as the Leprosie and Cankers, *Noli me tangere*, Consumptions and such like; stiffness of the Joynts, dryness of the Sinews, and many dry and cold Diseases in the extremity of Nature.

♂ in the last 18 degrees of ♑ is cold in the beginning of the 4th degree, and dry above nature, causing Diseases of much Melancholy and red Choler; as Consumptions, Cankers, *Noli me tangere*, the Wolf, and such like, with stiffness in the Joynts and Sinews, and the dry Goat, red spots in the Legs and Arms, and other places; and the Party is dry, and pineth and consumeth away.

The Cure.

The Diseases of ♂ in ♑ are very hard to be cured, and dangerous, or not to be cured at all; for the Humour is red Choler and Melancholy mix'd, and dry in the extremity of the 4th degree, drying up the Radical humidity, and stopping the passages and parts of the Humours that maintain nature.

To these Distempers administer not Physick in the hours of the ☉, ♂, ☿ nor ♄; look in the Chapt. of ♂ in ♉ and ♍; and in the Chapt. of ♄ in ♐; and let him vomit well, and purge strongly after digestion, for this will not be well purged, but it must be first strongly prepared.

Of Mars in Gemini.

Mars in the first 18 degrees of *Gemini* is temperate in moisture and drowth, and hot in the first degree, causing Diseases of red Choler mixed with Blood; but Blood is predominant, causing the Shingles, Tetters, Ring-worms, Piles and Hemorrhoids, Impostumes, Fevers, Scabs and Itches.

Mars in the last 12 degrees of ♊ is moist in the beginning of the first degree, and hot in the beginning of the second, ingendring Diseases of red Choler and Blood, Blood exceeding in the commixtion, and the Diseases are hot and something flegmatick withall, and hereof breeds the Shingles, Tetters, Ring-worms, the Piles and Hemorrhoids, Impostumes, Fevers, Scabs and Itches.

The Cure.

In these Diseases minister not in the hour of ♂ nor ♃, neither shall you put ♊, ♎ nor ♒ in the Ascendant, but minister in the hour of ☽, ♀, ☿, or in the hour of ♃ being in ♉, ♍ or ♑, and cure it by cold things that purge red Choler, as aforesaid; for in this case the blood will look exceeding red: Try it by blood-letting.

Of Mars in Libra.

Mars in the first 6 degrees of ♎ is hot in the second and moist in the first degree, ingendring corruption and infection of the Blood by red Choler, causing Importumations and pains of the Reins and Kidneys, Fluxes and Gonorrhea-Passion, Biles, Carbuncles, and the Water hot and scalding, much pain the Head would break in pieces; and the pain is most felt on the right side of the Head, and in the Neck also, and a Cough withall, and pain of the Lungs and Stomach, of much red Choler corrupting the Blood, and small Pox, if the ☽ apply to ♄ or ☿; if the ☽ apply to ♀, it causeth pain of the Belly, coldness of the Stomach and indigestion.

♂ in the next 18 degrees of ♎ is moist in the second, and dry in the third degree; ingendring corruption in the Blood by red Choler, through dryness thickning the same, causing Impostumations, Tetters, Ring-worms, Pestilential Fevers, Diseases of the Lungs and heat thereof, Biles, Carbuncles, Piles and Hemorrhoids, the Flux and *Gonorrhea Passio*, Water hot and sharp, pain and heat in the Reins, and pain of the Side, the green Sickness, and a rising of the Lungs into the Throat ready to stop the Wind.

Mars in the last 6 degrees of ♎ is moist in the beginning of the third degree, and hot in the beginning of the fourth; ingendring much thick and fæculent blood, caused by red dry Choler, producing heat and pain of the Reins, wasting of Nature, Gonorrhea, Fluxes, Scalding-water, Impostumes, Carbuncles Biles and Botches, Hemorrhoids and Piles, oppilation of the Liver and Lungs, with retention of the Flowers, the Mother also and the Small Pox.

The Cure.

The times and manner of Curing are rehearsed in the Chapter of ♂ in ♊, but in this there ought to be some digestion used before purging, and then let blood, and you ought to digest three dayes at least, for else a Purge will not effectually work (as I have proved) and your Purges must be very strong, as ℥ij of Pills, or ℥jβ of Electuary, else they will not sufficiently work out this

Humour; these Parties being let blood, the blood doth look exceeding red, and it is good after purging to let blood, for the blood is thick; and then give drink to purge the blood, and to cleanse it of red Choler.

Of Mars in Aquarius.

Mars in the first 12 degrees of ♒ is moist in the 3d, and hot in the 4th degree, causing Diseases of hot, thick and fæculent Blood and red Choler mix'd, as Impostumes, the Kings Evil, Carbuncles, Pleurisies, Botches, heat of the Lights, much Choler, and stuffing in the Stomach, Faintness, Trembling, heat of the Reins, and Water, stopping of the Urine and pain of the Yard, with pains in the side and stopping of the Terms; if ♂ be in ♒, and the ☽ in ♐ applying to ♀ in ♓, then it causeth a general weakness in the body, and indigestion, coldness of the Liver, thick corrupt rottenness of the Blood, and pain of the Cods, and the Humours be equally mixed.

Mars in the last 18 degrees of ♒ is moist in the beginning of the 4th degree, and hot above nature, causing Diseases of hot, thick and fæculent blood and red Choler, and the Blood hath the dominion, producing Impostumations, Botches, the Kings Evil, Plague, &c. the Scurvy and swelling of a venomous Humour, and the Meazles; for Blood of ♂ in ♒, and ♃ in ♉, causeth the Meazles.

The Cure.

Minister not to any of these Diseases of ♂ in ♒ *in hora Martis*, nor of ♃ if he be in ♈, ♌ or ♐; nor of ♄ nor ☿ if they be in ♊, ♎, ♒, ♈, ♌ or ♐; but in the hours of the ☽ or ♀ in ♋, ♏ or ♓; prepare him, purge him, and let blood speedily, but first let blood.

Of Mars in Cancer.

Mars in the first 18 degrees of *Cancer* is temperate in all the four Qualities, yet causing Diseases of red Choler and thin Flegm, causing biles, botches, and leprosie, pimples, red spots, itches, scurf, deafness, and worms in the Stomach, and hardness in the Belly, and it is the beginning of salt Flegm, whence Flegm hath the dominion; hot and dry.

Mars in the last 12 degrees of ♋ is cold and moist in the beginning of the first degree, causing Diseases of red Choler, and thin saltish Water and Flegm, and Flegm hath the dominion, causing Diseases of the Stomach, Coughs, Rheums, Scabs and Itches, of salt Flegm, red Choler, and thin Water mixed together; the Water or Flegmatick Humour having the dominion.

Mars in the last 12 degrees of ♋ is exceeding moist, dark and heavy, temperate between hot and cold, and a little windy, and breeding much Water and flegmatick Humours.

The Cure.

Minister not in *hora Martis*, or ☉, nor the ☽, but in the hour of ♀, she being in ♈, ♌ or ♐; or in the hour of ♃, he being in ♈, ♌ or ♐: ♊, ♎ or ♒ being in the Ascendant, the ☽ applying to ♃, and vomit the Party, and let him blood, then purge red Choler and Flegm in the first degree.

Of Mars in *Scorpio*.

Mars in the first six degrees of *Scorpio* is cold and moist in the 1ˢᵗ degree causing Diseases of thick Flegm and stinking, and of red Choler mix'd, but Flegm hath the preheminence; causing Itches, Pimples, saucy flegmy fæces, salt flegm, pains of the privy parts and Matrix, and Reins likewise; and ♂ in ♏ causeth Small Pox, and ♂ in the last face of ♎ causeth Small Pox of salt Flegm, that having the dominion; and causeth the French Pox and aches and pains in the bones, Nocturnal as well as Diurnal.

Mars in the next 18 degrees of ♏ is cold and moist in the second degree, causing Diseases of thick stinking Flegm and Water, with red Choler, Flegm predominating, causing Diseases of the privy parts, *Vulva* and Matrix, stopping the Urine that a man shall not piss, and the Small Pox in young and old, and long worms in the Stomach and Belly, and vomiting, with a Fever of Choler and Flegm.

Mars in the last 6 degrees of ♏ is cold and moist in the beginning of the third degree, causing Diseases of thick stinking

Water and Flegm mixed with red Choler, Flegm having the preheminence, causing, Diseases of the Bladder and privy parts, of the Matrix, and stopping of the Urine.

The Cure.

Minister not in *hora Martis*, ☉ nor ☽, but in the hour of ♀, being in ♈, ♌ or ♐; or in the hour of ♃ being in ♈, ♌, or ♐; ♊, ♎ or ♒ being Ascendant; ☽ applying to ♃, make him vomit, let him blood, and purge him of red Choler, and digest if occasion serve: This kind of salt Flegm is very tough and stinking, for it is commixed of red Choler and flegm, flegm predominating; therefore digest flegm and purge it most, and the red choler will evacuate with the flegm; for this kind of salt flegm is more cold and moist.

Of *Mars in Pisces.*

Mars in the first 12 degrees of ♓ is cold and moist in the 3d deg. ingendring Diseases of thick and tough Flegm mixed with red Choler, Flegm having dominion; as the French Pox, pains of the Feet, the Gout and Sciatica, *Podagra, Genugra, Chiragra*; the Lethargy, pricking and gnawing of the Stomach, oppilations of the Liver, the Dropsy and dead Palsie, benummedness of the Members and the black Plague, of salt flegm; for it is a king of tough and strong flegm, salt, cold and moist, mixed of three parts flegm, and one of red choler, causing also Fevers, salt flegm in the Stomach and bitter belchings.

Mars in the last 18 degrees of ♓ is cold and moist in the beginning of the 4th degree, causing Diseases of flegm thick and tough mix'd with red choler, flegm predominating; as all kinds of Gouts aforesaid, Aches, the Lathargy and Dropsie, pains of the Feet, the dead Palsie, and such like; pains and bitter belchings of the Stomach, of salt Flegm, of ♂ in ♓, of red Choler and Flegm having dominion: four parts of Flegm and one part of red Choler.

The Cure.

The manner and form of Curing is set down before in the Chapters of ♈ and ♋; but here you are to sweat the Party mightily, and to prepare and purge Flegm and red Choler; but herein it is not good to let blood, but to give a drying drink.

Of the Sun in Aries, and of his Nature.

Which is hot and dry, temperate, and is scituate in the midst of the Planets as a King, and is the Life of all things by his approximation and ascension, and the Death of all things by his descention and elongation; and therefore he is said to rule the Heart of Man, which is scituate ion the midst of the Members in the lesser World, which is the Body of Man: and is the first part in Man living, and the last dying. He ruleth also the Spirit of Life, which consisteth in the Heart. He hath also the right Eye, the Sight and the Nerves, the Marrow and Virtue Attractive, and causeth dry Diseases. He hath also the Thighs, the roof of the Mouth, and Organs of the Senses inwardly, the Hands, the Feet, the Sinews, the Fantasiacal Virtue, the left eye in a Woman, and the right eye in a man, and causeth the Rheum to descend from the Eyes, the hot Rheum, the hurts of the Eyes, and all sicknesses of yellow Choler, hot and dry, thin and sharp, and causeth the yellow Jaundies, itches, Scabs and the Flux.

Of the Sun in Aries.

SOL in the first 18 degrees of ♈ is hot and dry in the beginning of the first degree, ingendring Diseases of much yellow Choler sharp and thin, causing Pimples, Heat in the Breast, Head-ache, yellowness in the Eyes, swelling in the Legs, Scabs, Itches, Ring-worms, Inflammations thereof, Fevers, Strangullion, Deafness and darkness of the Eyes, Rheums, itching of the Eyes, stopping of the Terms, with faint languishing and the Gout.

☉ in the last 12 degrees of ♈ is hot and dry in the first degree, ingendring Diseases, of thin, yellow and sharp Choler, in the Eyes, Itchings, Pimples, Scabs, Heat in the Stomach and breast, Head-ache and pains of the Head, the Strangury and pain in the Thigh and Huckle-bone, Sciatica, much yellow water in the Stomach, Liver and Belly, with faintness and Dropsies.

The Cure.

The Cure of Diseases proceeding from the ☉ in ♈, caused of much thin yellow Choler: Minister not in *hora* ☉ nor ♂, but in the hours of ♀ or ☽, especially being in ♋, ♏ or ♓; or at least being in ♉, ♍ or ♑, putting ♋, ♏ or ♓ in the Ascendant, and the ☽ applying to ♀, and let the lord of the 6th House be weak, and perform your Cure with cold and moist things, few digestives do serve in this cause, because the Humour is thin; but first purge the Patient of yellow Choler, then let him blood, and give him drinks cold and moist, and if the Rheums fall much to the Eyes, then purge the Head, and make an Issue backwards, or a Seaton on the 3d *Vertebra* of the Neck, and draw a silk through it, to draw and divert the Rheum from the Eyes, often moving the string, and you may wear it as long as you think good, and you shall find it profitable.

Of *Sol* in *Taurus.*

SOL in the first 18 degrees of ♉ is temperate in cold and heat; but dry in the first degr. ingendring Diseases of Melancholy and thin yellow Choler, Melancholy predominating, causing Diseases in the Legs; as Itches, Warts, and Knobs.

☉ in the 4th degr. of ♉ being Lord of the house and in ♈ in the 2d, causeth Biles, Botches, Swellings and Impostumations in the Throat between the Neck and Head and under the Chin.

☉ in ♉ in the 7th with ♀ causeth Botches, Sors and Swellings in the Throat and in the Limbs.

☉ in the last 12 degrees of ♉ is cold in the beginning of the first degree, and dry in the beginning of the second degree, causing Diseases of thick Melancholy and thin yellow and sharp Choler, Melancholy predominating, and the Humour is soure and bitter withall, causing Diseases in the Knees, and stiffness of the Sinews and Joynts.

The Cure.

Minister not in *hora* ☉ nor ♂, if he be in ♉, ♍ or ♑, but if he be in ♊, ♎ or ♒, you may ; neither in the hour of ☿ nor ♄, being in ♊, ♎ nor ♒; but you may minister in hora ♃, ♀ of the ☽, being in ♊, ♎ or ♒, and put ♊, ♎ or ♒ in the Ascendant, the ☽ applying to ♃; and you must cure with things moist and temperate in heat and cold; but somewhat heating; and in such a case it is good to bathe the Parties, and to digest the Humours well before you purge, for that it is caused of gross Melancholy and thin yellow Choler, Melancholy predominating.

Of *Sol* in *Gemini*.

SOL in the first 18 degrees of *Gemini* is temperate in heat and moisture, but hot in the first degree, ingendring Diseases of Blood, and sharp thin yellow Choler, Blood prevailing, causing Pimples, Itches, Scabs, and stopping of Womens Terms. The Sun in ♊ either Lord of the hour, of the 6th or of the 12th House, causeth the Stangullion and the Stone.

Sol in the last 12 degrees of ♊ is hot in the beginning of the 2d degree, and moist in the beginning of the first ingendring Diseases of thin, sharp, yellow Choler and Blood; as Scabs Itches, Pimples, Heat of the Liver; and pain in the Knees.

The Cure.

Minister not in the hour of the *Sun*, nor *Mars*, nor *Jupiter*, but in the hours of ♀, ☿ or ☽, or ♄ being in ♉, ♍ or ♑, or in ♋, ♏, or ♓, and purge yellow Choler, and let blood; but few digestives serve in this manner and case.

Of *Sol in Cancer*.

SOL in the first 18 degrees of ♋ is temperate in all the four Qualities, causing Diseases of thin Flegm, and thin, sharp, yellow Choler, Flegm abounds in the commixtion, causing Itches, Flux, Scabs, saltish Humours in the Face and Stomach, and pains of the Feet, faintness, pain and weakness in the Reins, and languishing Diseases, with faintness of the Limbs, salt flegmy fæces, and a spice of the Pox.

☉ in the last 12 degr. of ♋ is cold and moist in the beginning of the first degr. ingendring Diseases of saltish Water and Flegm, and sharp thin yellow Choler, and Flegm hath the dominion, and produceth Scabs; Itches, Ptissick and straitness of Breath, and Diseases of Flegm in the Lights and Stomach, and exceeding languishing and faintness, and pain of the Heart, and they cannot eat, nor relish their meat, and oft-times the Strangury withall.

The Cure.

Minister not *in hora* ☉ nor ♂, except he be in ♋, ♏ or ♓, but *in hora* ♃, or in the hour of ♀ or the ☽ being in ♈, ♌ or ♐, and put ♈, ♌ or ♐ in the Ascendant, and let the Party sweat well and vomit, and then purge him well.

Of Sol in Leo.

SOL in the first 6 degrees of ♌ is hot and dry in the beginning of the 2d degree, and causeth Diseases of thick yellow Choler, and thin sharp yellow Choler, causing the yellow Jaundies, hot burning Fevers, Scabs, Pimples, stopping of the Liver, and heat of the Liver.

Sol in the next 18 degr. of ♌ is hot and dry in the extremity of the 2d degree, causing Diseases of abundance of yellow Choler; as the yellow Jaundies, stopping of the Terms, vomiting, indigestion, dryness and heat of the Liver, pain of the Heart, faintness, weakness, pining away and consuming.

Sol in the last 6 degrees of ♌ is hot and dry in the 3d degr. causing hot and dry Fevers, yellow Jaundies, stopping of the Liver, pain of the Head, overflowing of the Gall, pain in the Groin, with kernels like and near unto the Pestilential and infectious Plague; the red Plague is also caused of much Choler, and also causeth the running of the Reins, and Gonorthea-passion in men, and vomiting up of much blood in Women, through corruption and stopping of their Terms, and consuming and pining away of the flesh, with overmuch heat and drowth, of Choler, pain in the head and back, weakness and faintness.

The Cure of ☉ in ♌ of much yellow Choler.

Minister not in *hora* ☉ nor ♂, neither put ♈, ♌ nor ♐ in the Ascendant, but minister in *hora* ☽, ♀ or *in hora* ♃ in ♋, ♏ or ♒; or *in hora* ☿. or ♄ in ♋, ♏ or ♓, when the ☽ is in ♋, ♏ or ♓, applying to ♀, or ☿, or ♄; and digest Choler first, then purge yellow Choler; for this kind of yellow Choler is somewhat thick, and give things to cool and quench drought.

Of Sol in Virgo.

SOL in the first 6 degrees of ♍ is cold in the first degree, ingendring Diseases of Melancholy and thick yellow Choler, and Melancholy hath the Dominion; and the Humour is cold and dry, soure and sharp in taste, causing Kernels and Scabs in the neck and throat, stiffness of the Sinews, Cramps, Small Pox, Meazles and strong Fevers, oppilations in the Liver and Milt.

Sol in the next 18 degrees of *Virgo* is cold in the second degree and dry in the third; causing Diseases by the ingendring of Melancholy and thick yellow Choler, and Melancholy hath the Dominion, and the Humour is soure and sharp, causing Scabs in the Neck, and Kernels, stiffness of the Sinews, the Squinancy, the Kings Evil and *Angina*.

Sol in the last 6 degrees of ♍ is cold in the beginning of the 3d degree, and dry in the beginning of the 4th degr, ingendring Diseases of Melancholy and thick yellow Choler, Melancholy being in the excess, the Humour is four and sharp, causing oppilations in the Liver, pains in the Almonds in the Throat and root of the Tongue, and the Kings Evil, Kernels and *Noli me tangere*.

The Cure.

Look in the Chapter of the ☉ in ♉, for the manner of Curing; but here it is not amiss to sweat the Party, and to let blood if need required, but you must first digest, and then purge him well, and then let blood.

Of *Sol in Libra*.

SOL in the first 6 degrees of ♎ is moist in the first degree, and hot in the second, ingendring Diseases of thick Blood and thin yellow Choler, causing Diseases in the Arms, Shoulders and Hands, Scabs, itches, Biles, and heat in the Reins, and Scalding of the Water, with running of Nature.

Sol in the next 18 degrees of ♎ is moist in the beginning of the 2d degree, and hot in the beginning of the 3d degr. ingendring Diseases of thick Blood, and thin yellow Choler, Blood having the dominion, causing pains and Diseases in the Reins, Arms, Shoulders and Hands, Biles, Botches, yellow Jaundies, sharp Urine, and wasting of Nature.

Sol in the last 6 degrees of ♎ is moist in the 2d, and hot in the 3d degree, causing Diseases of thin Blood and thin yellow Choler. Blood predominating; as pains of the Reins, scalding of Urine, wasting of Nature, Bloddy Flux, pains of the Hands, Arms and Shoulders, Kings Evil, *Angina, Squinantia,* Fluxes of the Terms, Biles, Scabs and Itches.

The Cure.

Minister not in *hora* ☉, ♃ nor ♂, but in the hour of ☽, ☿ or ♀, if they be in ♉, ♍ or ♑, ♋, ♏ or ♓; but first you ought to clarifie the Blood, and cool and thin it, and then breathe a Vein.

Of *Sol* in *Scorpio*.

SOL in the first 6 degrees of ♏ is cold and moist in the first degree, causing diseases of tough Flegm, stinking, and of thin yellow Choler, Flegm having the Dominion; as Dropsies, benumming of the Members, Palsies and griping and pricking of the Stomach, oppilations of the Liver, stuffing of the Light, Coughs.

Sol in the next 18 degrees of ♏ is cold and moist in the 2d degree, ingendring Diseases of stinking corrupt Water and Flegm, and of thin yellow Choler, Flegm bearing sway; as Dropsies, Rottenness and oppilations of the Liver and Lungs, Coughs, Fevers, great pricking and tearing at the Stomach, Palsies and Impostumations.

Sol in the last 6 degrees of ♏ is cold and moist in the beginning of the 3d degree, ingendring Diseases of tough stinking Flegm and Water, and of thin yellow Choler, Flegm having the predominancy; as Palsies, Dropsies, Fistulaes, Issues, pains of fretting and tearing at the Stomach, stopping and rotting of the Liver and Lungs, with Coughs.

The Cure.

Minister not *in hora* ☉, *vel* ♂, but in the hours of ♄ or ☿, when they be in ♊, ♎ or ♒; or in the hours of ☽ or ♀, being in ♉, ♍ or ♑, ♊, ♎ or ♒, and sweat and purge, and digest the matter well, for it is a kind of salt tough Flegm mixed with yellow Choler, Flegm having the dominion, and therefore will ask good and often digestion and purging. Look in the Chapter of ☉ in ♋ and ♓.

Of *Sol in Sagittary*.

SOL in the first 18 degrees of ♐ is hot and dry in the beginning of the 4th degree, ingendring much thick red *Choler*, causing *Ethica passio*, swelling of the Limbs, heat and pain of the Back and Heart, *Cardixa passio*, and heart-burning great drought, pains in the Head and Brain, Rheums in the Eyes, and a flux of hot Humours falling thereinto, Frantickness, pain of the Gums and roof of the Mouth, Tooth-ache and pain in the Feet, the Piles, Hemorrhoids, and impediments in pissing.

Sol in the last 18 degrees of ♐ is hot and dry in the extremity of the 4th degree, ingendring Diseases of thin yellow Choler, and thick red Choler, increasing pestilential Fevers, *Noli me tangere*, Carbuncles, pains at the Heart, and in the Back, in the Head and Brain, and roof of the Mouth, Frantickness, pain in the Feet and Hands, Heart-burning, Syncope, stopping of the Liver, overflowing of the Gall, yellow Jaundies and Green-sickness.

The Cure.

Minister not in the hour of the ☉ nor ♂, but in the hour of ☽, ♀, ☿ or ♄, being in ♋, ♏ or ♓, and put ♋, ♏ or ♓ in the Ascendant; and must prepare this kind of red and yellow Choler, for it is red, gross and thick, red Choler predominating, and it is hot and dry, consuming the 4th degree.

Of *Sol in Capricorn*.

SOL in the first 12 degrees of ♑ is cold in the 3d degree, and dry in the 4th degree; ingendring Diseases of fæculent Melancholy and thin yellow Choler and the Melancholy hath the dominion, causing Cramps, contractions of the Sinews, Warts, Wens, Knobs, Cankers, Gripings and pain in the Belly and Bowels, the Wind-cholick and Stone in the Reins, Palsies and benumming of the Members, the Stangury, the Swine Pox and the *French* Pox, Meazles, Piles and Hemorrhoids.

Sol in the last 18 degrees of ♑ is cold in the 4th degr. and dry above Nature, ingendring Diseases of Melancholy and thin yellow Choler, Melancholy predominating, causing Cramps, contraction of the Sinews, Wens, Knobs, Warts, Piles, Hemorrhoids, Strangury, griping and pain of the Belly and Guts, Small Pox, and *French* Pox, and Meazles; and if ☽ be in ♑ and apply to ☉, it is the *French* Pox, with ache in the bones, nocturnal pains, pricking and knobs in the flesh.

The Cure.

Minister not in the hours of ♂, ☉, ♄ nor ☿, but in the hours of ♃, ♀ or the ☽, being in ♊, ♎ or ♒, or in ♈, ♌ or ♐, putting ♊, ♎ or ♒ in the Ascendant, the ☽ applying to ♃ or ♀; and give digestions, and bathe the Party well to moisten the Humours; for it is a subtil kind of Melancholy mixed with thin yellow Choler, Melancholy having the dominion, and if occasion serve, open a Vein; but it is always better to open a Vein in hot causes than in cold, and better to purge and vomit in cold causes than in hot.

Of Sol in Aquarius.

SOL in the first 12 degrees of ♒ is moist in the beginning of the 3d degree, and hot in the 4th, ingendring Diseases of Blood and thin yellow Choler, causing Impostumations in the Reins, wasting of Nature, *Gonorrhea Passio*, Water hot and smarting of the Yard, Strangullion and Gravel in the Kidneys, the Green Sickness, and stopping of the Terms.

Sol in the last 18 degrees of ♒ is moist in the 3d, and hot above Nature, causing Diseases of thick Blood and thin yellow Choler, Blood having the dominion, causing Impostumations, Carbuncles, the Rose-swelling, *Gonorrhea Passio*, sharpness of Urine, pains of the Reins, Kidneys and yard, wasting of Nature.

The Cure.

Minister not in the hour of the ☉ nor ♂, but in the hour of ♀, ☽, ☿ or ♄, ♉, ♍ or ♑ being in the Ascendant digest yellow Choler, thin Blood, and open a Vein.

Of Sol in Pisces.

SOL in the first 12 degrees of ♓ is hot and moist in the 3d degree, ingendring Diseases of thick stinking Water and Flegm, and the Flegm hath the dominion, and is saltish and bitter, causing Dropsies, rotting of the Liver, Coughs, Impostumations, dead Palsies, and many Diseases in the privy parts, fluxes of the Flowers, and such like, benumming of the Hands and Fingers, Legs and Arms, of a venomous Humour, and in the joynts like stinging of Nettles, causing the dead Palsie.

☉ in the last 18 degrees of ♓ is cold and moist in the beginning of the 4th degree, ingendring much thick stinking Flegm and Water, and thin yellow Choler, and the Flegm hath the dominion, causing Diseases and pains in the privy parts; also fluxes of the Flowers, *Hernia Aquosa*, Dropsies, Indigestion, and rottenness and coldness of the Liver, Strangury, &c.

The Cure.

Minister not in the hour of ♂ or ♃, being especially in ♋, ♏ or ♓, nor in the hour of ☽ or ♀, being in ♈, ♌ or ♐, but minister in the hour of ♄ or ☿ being in ♊, ♎ or ♒, as it is said in the Chapter of ☉ in ♋ and ♏; and sweat and digest, and purge them strongly.

Of *Venus* in *Aries*.

Venus in the first 18 degrees of ♈ is temperate in all the four Qualities, yet causing distemperature of thin yellow Choler, and thin flegm equally mixed, Jaundies and Itches, the Whites and running of the Reins, Rheums and Biles.

♀ in the last 12 degrees of ♈ is hot and dry in the beginning of the first degr. ingendring Diseases of thin Flegm and yellow Choler; the Choler is strongest, causing Itches and Agues, &c.

The Cure.

Minister not to any that are grieved with the Diseases of ♀ in ♈, in the hour of ♀ nor the ☽, especially if the ☽ be in ♈, ♌ or ♐; nor in the hours of ♂ nor the ☉, if they be in ♋, ♏ or ♓; but if ♂ or ☉ be in ♊, ♎ or ♒, putting ♋, ♏ or ♓ in the Ascendant you may minister otherwise; as in the hour of ♃, being in ♉, ♍ or ♑; or in the hour of ☿ or ♄, if they be in ♊, ♎ or ♒, and make the Parties to sweat well, and purge, and let blood, for few digestions serve for inward causes, because the Humour is thin and sharp, yellow Choler and thin Water, Choler having preheminence, &c.

Of *Venus* in *Taurus*.

Venus in the first 18 degrees of ♉ is cold in the first degr. and temperate in drowth and moisture, ingendring Diseases of Melancholy and thin Flegm, Melancholy preceding, causing Diseases of Head and Brain, with Deafness, and pain of the ears; in the side and Reins with stitches, &c.

Venus in the last 12 degrees of ♉ is cold in the beginning of the 2d degree, and dry in the beginning of the first, ingendring Diseases of thick Melancholy and thin Flegm, Melancholy predominating, causing pains of the Head, and deafness of the Ear, pain of the sides and Stitches.

The Cure.

Minister not in the hour of ♀, ☿ nor ♄, but in the hour of ♃, being in ♈, ♌ or ♐; or in the hour of ♃, being in ♊, ♒ or ♎, digest the Humour, and sweat the Party, then purge him well, and if need require, then open a vein, and the Cure must be done with hot and moist things.

Of *Venus in Gemini.*

Venus in the first 18 degrees of *Gemini* is temperate in heat and cold, but moist in the first degree, ingendring Diseases of Blood and thin Flegm, Blood having dominion causing Impostumations, Pleurisies and swellings, Rheums and Kernels, and pains of the Throat, the Squinancy and *Angina*.

Venus in the last 12 degrees of ♊ is hot in the beginning of the first degree and moist in the beginning of the second; ingendring Diseases of Blood and thin Water, the Blood prevailing, causing Impostumes, Pleurisies, Scabs, Swellings and Rheums, with pains of the Throat, *Angina*, Squinancy, *Abotium*, and such like.

The Cure.

Minister not in the hour of *Venus* nor the ☽, if she be in ♊, ♎ or ♒, but if she be in ♉, ♍ or ♑ you may; and in the hour of ♃, he being in ♉, ♍ or ♑, or in the hour of the ☉, ☿ or ♄, in ♈, ♌ or ♐, purge, sweat, and let blood, and make the Lord of the 6th weak, and cleanse the blood.

Of *Venus in Cancer.*

Venus in the first 18 degrees of ♋ is moist and cold in the first degree, ingendring Diseases of much Flegm and salt Water, causing Pains and Aches in the Arms and Shoulders, Fistulaes, Dropsies and Palsies, and pains and making of the Stomach, Giddiness of the Head and Apoplexia, with the French Pox, and Swelling in the Stomach.

♀ in the last 12 degrees of ♋ is cold and moist in the beginning of the second degree, causing Diseases of much cold Flegm, and saltish thin Water, in the Arms and Shoulders, Hands and Fingers; as, Chilblains, Imposthumations, Dropsies, palsies, Fistulaes and French Pox.

The Cure.

Minister not in the hour of ☽, ♀, ♄ nor ☿, if they be in ♋. ♍ or ♓. but if they be in ♊, ♎ or ♒, you may administer; and you may also in the hour of ☉ or ♃, being in ♈, ♌ or ♐, or ♊, ♎ or ♒, and let the Party sweat well, and then purge, Flegm, and vomit, and avoid all things that breed Flegm or cause cold.

Of Venus in Leo.

Venus in the first 6 degrees of *Leo*, is hot and dry in the first degree, ingendring Diseases of yellow Choler and thin Water, in the Stomach, Matrix and Reins, with Cataraches, Choler predominating, causeth Pimples and Scabs.

♀ in the next 18 degrees of ♌, is hot and dry in the 2d degree, ingendring Diseases of thin Water and thick yellow Choler, Choler being the stronger, causing the Piles and Hemorrhoids, Rheums in the Stomach, yellow Jaundies, oppilations in the Liver, evil digestions, Fevers, Impostumations in the Stomach; and in children the small Pox, if the ☽ separate from the ☉ in ♌, and much Flegm and stuffing in the Stomach, with sleepiness and heaviness.

♀ in the last 6 degrees of ♌ is hot and dry in the beginning of the 3d degree, ingendring Diseases of thick yellow Choler and thin Flegm, soure and saltish, and unsavoury taste, and Choler exceeds in the commixtion, and the Party is hot inwardly, and outwardly cold, shivering with Fever, pains of the stomach, oppilations, ill digestion, Hemorrhoids, Piles, Itches, Scabs, Flux, Chilblains, Swellings and Sciatica.

The Cure.

In the Diseases caused of ♀ in ♌, minister not in the hour of ♀ nor in the hour of the ☽, if she be in ♈, ♌ or ♐, nor in the hours of ♂ or the ☉, being in ♋, ♏, ♉, ♓, but in the hours of ☿ or ♄ being in ♊, ♎ or ♒, or in the hour of the ☽ being in ♋, ♏ or ♓, and digest the matter well, and purge and let blood.

Of *Venus in Virgo*.

Venus in *Virgo* in the first 6 degrees thereof is cold in the 2d degree and dry in the first, ingendring Diseases of Melancholy, and thin Water, Melancholy predominating was Melancholick Passions Diseases of the Heart, pain of the Back-bone, and the *Illiaca Passio*, with Diseases in the Bowels and Navel, and trembling and faintness of the Heart if the ☽, ♋ from the ☉ to ♀, it causeth the Strangury, Heat of the Urine and pain of the Reins, with great smarting in the Yard, and Gonorrhea passion, and a Fever, the ☽ being Lady of the hour.

♀ in the next 18 degrees of ♍ is cold in the 3d, and dry in the 2d degree, ingendring Diseases of Melancholy and thin Flegm, with trembling and faintness of the Heart, fearfulness, and pain of the Back-bone, Diseases of the Bowels, and about the Navel, Biaca *Passio*, the wet and dry Gout, *Chinagna* and Swellings.

♀ in the last 6 degr. of ♍ is cold in the beginning of the 4th degree, and dry in the beginning of the 3d, ingendring Diseases of Melancholy and thin Flegm, as Rheums, catarrhs, Melancholick passions and faintness, trembling of the heart, Biaca *passio*, griping pains of the Bowels, and about the Navel, the Wind-cholick and pain of the Back-bone.

The Cure.

Minister not *in hora* ♀, ☿, ☽ nor ♄, but in the hour of ☽, or in the hour of ☉ or ♂, being in ♊, ♎ or ♒; sweat the Parties well, digest and purge, as in the Chapter of ♀ in ♉.

Of *Venus* in *Libra*.

Venus in the first 6 degrees of ♎ is hot in the first degree, and moist in the 2d, ingendring Diseases of thick and hot Blood, and of thin Water, Blood having Dominion, causing the Cholick, the Strangury, pains and gripings in the Belly, and about the Navel, Worms in the Maw, Iliack Passion and suffocation of the Matrix, bleeding at the Nose in a Man, and Vomiting of Blood in a Woman, the Pleurisie and Impostumations, and a Wind running up and down the Body, that is sometimes in the Bowels, and sometimes in the Stomach, and sometimes under the short ribs in the left side, with great pain; purge and let blood.

♀ in the next 18 degrees of *Libra* is hot in the second and moist in the third degree, ingendring Diseases of thin Water and thick Blood, Blood predominating, causing many Diseases, as Chilblains, Cholick, Strangury, pain and griping in the Belly and about the Navel, and Worms in the Maw, *Iliaca Passio*, suffocation of the Matrix, and continual issuing of the Terms, and much Blood in the Liver, and much bleeding at the Nose, or vomiting of Blood; most commonly in a Woman, and bleeding in a man at the Nose, much pain in the left side by Wind, and it is apt to breed a Pleurisie, or Impostumations in the Liver, or the Fever *Synochus*.

♀ in the last 6 degrees of ♎ is hot in the beginning of the 3d degree, and moist in the beginning of the 4th, ingendring Diseases of thick Blood and thin Flegm, causing pain and gripings in the Belly, and about the Navel, Iliack Passion, Worms in the Maw, and suffocation of the Matrix, with fluxes of Womens Terms.

The Cure.

Minister not in the hour of ♀, nor in the hour of ☽, if she be in ♊, ♎ or ♒, but if she be in ♉, ♍ or ♑ you may; and also minister in the hour of ♃, ♄, or ☿, if they be in ♉, ♍ or ♑; look in the Chapter of ♀ in ♊, and let blood.

Of Venus in Scorpio.

Venus in the first 6 degrees of ♏ is cold and moist in the 2d degree, ingendring Diseases of much thick stinking flegm and water, causing Diseases in the Reins and Kidneys, the Whites in Women and stopping of the Veins and conduits of the Urine, that one cannot piss, if ☽ be in aspect of ♄ in ♉, ♍ or ♑, she causeth in Women the Mother, in Men the Wind-cholick and Indigestion, weakness of the Liver, and much Water in the Stomach and Matrix, if she be joyned to ♃ in ♓, with venomous Humours causing suffocation of the Matrix, and the Dropsie.

♀ in the next 18 degrees of ♏ is cold and moist in the 3d degree, ingendring Diseases of stinking tough Flegm and Water, causing Indigestion, rottenness in the Liver, Dropsies, flux of the Whites in Women, stopp[in gof the Urine, pains of the Reins, and Kidneys, and issuing of Nature; when ♀ is in ♋, ♏ or ♓, and is Lady of the 12th House, or 6th, it signifieth that the Expulsive Virtue, or Faculty, waxeth strong in the Bodies of Women, and that if their Terms were stop'd before, they will come down shortly; for the Expulsive Virtue is maintained by cold and moisture, and to such, where Venus is Lady of the 12th, and the ☽ applyes to ♀, especially if the ☽ separate from Saturn, then give them to bring down their Terms Milk boyled, and drink Ale or Beer put in it without Sugar, and let them oft eat it, and it will bring down much congealed Blood, and their Terms from them, Venus in the 7th in ♏, and the ☽ in the 12th applying to Venus and separating from ♄. probat.

Venus in the 6 last degrees of ♏ is cold and moist in the beginning of the 4th degree, ingendring Diseases of much cold, stinking and tough Flegm and Water; as Dropsies of much cold, stinking and tough Flegm and Water; as Dropsies, Indegestions, rottenness of the Liver, Coughs, tickling of the Lights, pains of the Reins and Kidneys, stopping of the Urine, fluxes of the Whites in Women, Cramps.

The Cure.

Minister not in the hour of ♀, ☽, ☿ nor ♄, being in ♋, ♏ or ♓, but in the hour of ♃ or the ☉, and put ♈, ♌ or ♐ in the

Ascendant. Look in the Chapt. of ♀ in ♋. Sweat, vomit and purge, and forsake all cold and moist meats.

Of *Venus in Sagitary*.

Venus in the first 12 degrees of ♐ is hot and dry in the 3d degree, ingendring Diseases of thick red Choler and thin Flegm, Choler predominating, causing Diseases in the privy parts, in the Matrix and *Vulva*, as burning with Women, Botches, Carbuncles, the Gonorrhea and Piles in the Fundament, Fistulaes in the lower parts of the Belly.

♀ in the last 18 degrees of ♐ is hot and dry in the beginning of the 4th degree, ingendring Diseases of much thick red Choler and thin Water, Choler exceeding; as Diseases of the Testicles and privy parts, the *Vulva*, Matrix and Green-sickness, Hemorrhoids and Piles, Heat of the Reins and Fever, Botches and Carbuncles, claps and heat of Urine, hot burning Fevers of long continuance; breeds great pains in the Stomach, Head and Back, comes sometimes with cold, other-whiles with hot fits for 12 hours, and much rising in the Throat, like to stop the breath, like heart-burning of salt Flegm, and breeds pain under the Ribs, under the region of the Liver, of salt Flegm, and pain round about the Body, girding them round about the Paps, especially when the ☽ in the 6 last degrees of ♐ applies to the ☉ in ♏, or to ♂ in ♎; or if the ☉ or ♂ be lord of the hour, then there is much pricking and tearing, and pain about the Heart, and under the left Breast and right Side.

The Cure.

Minister not in the hour of the ☽, nor the hour of ♀, being in ♈, ♌ or ♐, nor in the hours of the ☉ and ♂ being in ♋, ♏ or ♓, ♈, ♌ or ♐; but in the hour of ♃ being in ♊, ♎ or ♒; or in the hour of ♄ or ☿ being in ♋, ♏ or ♓; and first digest the Humour well, then purge him strongly, for here Choler hath the Dominion, and your preparatives in this must be as strong as purgers of ♀ in ♈, and therefore here I hold it good to purge with Scammony, Diagridion, Coloquintida or Turbith, as you shall find most convenient, and give no Purges against any Diseases caused of ♀ in ♐, but prepare three dayes first strongly, for it is of strong salt Flegm. Your diet in this Cure must be fresh Beef, Mutton or Veal, or Birds, and sometimes fresh Butter, and Beer or Ale, but no Wine, Spice nor salt Meat.

Of *Venus* in *Capricorn*.

Venus in *Capricorn* in the first 12 degrees is cold in the 4th degree, and dry in the 3d, ingendring Diseases of Melancholy and thin Flegm, causing pains and aches in the joynts, in the Thighs and Huckle-bones, and Buttocks, some times the Sciatica: if ♀ be in ♑, she alwayes signifies a Woman weak and lean by Nature; being Lady of the Ascendant, or signifier of the Party, then she is very suspicious, full of care and thought, and by nature subject to much sickness, which pain of the Side and Heart, pining and consuming, and of ill thoughts, thinking themselves to be bewitched, and indeed are subject to the power of ill persons, as being timorous and weak of Faith; they languish in Sickness much, and fret quickly, and take thought and conceits, are often puling-sick, and not long well, yet apt to have many children; they are conceited of themselves, thinking themselves fair, and indeed are fair enough, but full of tongue and passions, especially if ♀ be in ♋, and the ☾ apply to ♄.

♀ in the last 18 degr. of ♑ is cold in the extremity of the 4th degree, and dry in the beginning of the 4th, ingendring much cold Melancholy and thin Flegm, Melancholy exceeding, causing Diseases, as aches and pains in the Joynts, Thighs and Huckle-bones, Sciatica, Impostumations.

The Cure.

Minister not in the hour of ♀ nor ♄, but in the hour of ♃, being in ♊, ♎ or ♒, and do as is said in the Chapter of ♀ in ♉ and ♀ in ♍.

Of *Venus in Aquarius.*

Venus in the first 12 degrees of ♒ is hot in the 3d, and moist in the 4th degree, ingendring Diseases of thick fæculent

Blood, and thin Flegm, blood prevailing; as Impostumations, and Dropsies in the Knees, and aches and swellings of the Flesh, Chilblains, the Kings Evil, and Lunar-passions.

♀ in the last 18 degrees of ♒ is hot in the beginning of the 4th degree, and moist in the extremity of the 4th, ingendring much thick Blood and thin Water, blood prevailing, causing Pleurisies, Impostumations, Chilblains, Dropsies, aches in the Knees, the Kings Evil, and Lunatick passion.

The Cure.

Minister not in the hour of ♀, nor in the our of ♄ nor the ☽, if she be in ♉, ♍ or ♑; you may in the hour of ♃ being in ♉, ♍ or ♑; or also in the hour of the ☉ or *Mercury*; and let blood, and cleanse the blood. Look in the Chapt. of the ☽ in ♊.

Of Venus in Pisces.

Venus in the 1st 12 degr. of ♓ is cold and moist in the 4th degr. ingendring Diseases of much thick, tough, stinking Flegm and Water; as Indigestion, rottenness of the Liver, Dropsies, Fistulaes, *Hernia aquosa*, Impostumes, loss of the members, putrefaction, and great Rheums, and stoppings and stuffings at the Stomach, Coughs, and pains of the Belly, with the Quotidian flegmatick Fever.

♀ in the last 18 degr. of ♓ is cold and moist in the extremity of the 4th degr. above Nature, causing mortal Diseases, of much tough, cold, slimy Flegm and thin Water, causing the *French* Pox, Dropsie, Indigestion, rottenness of the Liver, Fistulaes, and many Diseases in the Legs and Ankles of putrefaction and mollification, pains of the Belly and Hips, with the Quotidian flegmatick Fever and Gout in the Hands and Fingers, ache of the Bones, and swelling of the hands and feet, the Scurvy, the *French* Pox, of venomous Humours and corruption of Blood, by venomous water and rotten blood.

The Cure.

Minister not in the hour of ♀ nor ☽, nor ☿ nor ♄ being in ♋, ♏ or ♓, but in the hours of ☉, ♃ or ♂, being in ♈, ♌ or ♐. Look in the Chapter of ♀ in ♋: vomit, sweat and let blood.

Of the Properties of Mercury.

Mercury is said to rule the Tongue and Memory, because of his Eloquence, and hath attributed to him the Speech and Deliberation, the Lungs, the Spleen and Milt, the Lights, the Stomach, the Bladder, the Matrix, the right Ear, the Brain, the Nostrils, the instruments of the Senses, and the Virtue Receptive, the Animal Spirits, the Thighs, the Belly, the Flank and the Hands, the Throat-bole, the Navel, the Pecten, the Veins, the Nerves, the Thoughts and Diseases of the mind, the third sort of Madness, and the third kind of Falling-sickness, the Cough, the precipitation of the Matrix, and the perturbation of the mind, abundance of Spittle and Rheums, and divers dry Diseases.

Of Mercury in Aries.

Mercury in the first 18 degrees of ♈ is temperate in heat and cold, but dry in the first degree, causing Diseases of subtile, thin, yellow Choler, and of thin, subtile and sharp Melancholy equally commixed, causing Itches and froth, and Rheum in the Stomach.

☿ in the last 12 degrees of ♈ is hot in the beginning of the first degree, and dry in the beginning of the 2d, ingendring Diseases of thin yellow Choler, and thin and subtile Melancholy, Choler predominating; and the Urine will book like Sack, but somewhat greenish, and it causeth Diseases of the Brain, hot Fevers, Pimples and risings of the Blood, the Canker and the Kings Evil, *St. Anthonies* Fire, darkness and dimness of the Eyes, stoppings of the Flowers, and suffocation of the Matrix, horrible and fearful thought and vexation of the mind, especially if ♂ behold ☿; He causeth also Agues to come by fits, and soreness of the Tongue and Mouth through Rheum, Choler, and Melancholy mix'd, which come from the Lungs and Stomach, ascending into the Head, the rising of the Lungs into the Throat, especially if he aspect ♃ in ♒, and the ☽ separate from ☿ and apply to ♃.

The Cure.

Minister not in the hour of ☿ nor ♄, but in the hour of ♃ or ♀, being in ♊, ♎ or ♒, and put ♊, ♎ or ♒ in the Ascendant, or ♋, ♏ or ♓, if ♃ or the ☉ be therein, and sweat the Parties well, digest the Humour, and purge and let blood.

Of *Mercury* in *Leo*.

Mercury in the first 6 degrees of ♌ is hot in the first degree and dry in the second, ingendring Diseases of thick yellow Choler and thin Melancholy, but Choler predominates, causing pains and aches in the Shoulders, Arms and Sinews, straitness of the Lungs, Rheum and stopping of the Lungs and Stomach, Fearfulness and Frenzy if he be in Conjunction or Aspect with ♄, Faintness and languishing.

☿ in the next 18 degrees of ♌ is hot in the second degr. and dry in the third; ingendring Diseases of thick yellow Choler and thin Melancholy, with pains in the Arms and Shoulders, and aches in the Muscles, &c. the Piles, if ☿ be Lord of the Ascendant, and the ☽ go from the ☉ in ♋, it causeth sleepiness, heaviness and vomiting, and much Water mixed with Melancholy in the Stomach, and the Small Pox, and much pain in the Head, Lungs and Stomach stuffed with Flegm; the Party is cold inward, hath pain of the Belly, with shaking, fearfulness and trembling, especially if the ☽ go from ♀ in ♌, with a Fever.

☿ in the last 6 degrees of ♌ is hot in the beginning of the 3d degree, and dry in the beginning of the 4th degree; ingendring Diseases of thick yellow Choler and thin Melancholy, pains in the Shoulders and Arms, Aches in the Sinews.

The Cure.

Minister not in the hour of ☿, the ☉ nor ♂, being in ♈, ♌ or ♐, but in the hour of ♃; as before in the Chapter of ☿ in ♈.

Of *Mercury in Sagittary*.

Mercury in the first 12 degrees of ♐ is hot in the 3d degr. and dry in the 4th, ingendring Diseases of red Choler and thin Melancholy, Choler having dominion, and causeth strong, dry, and hot burning Fevers, and pains in the Reins, and the Stone in the Reins, the Piles and Hemorrhoids, and pains about the Navel, and Cankers, and scorching dryness and hardness of the Liver, stopping of the Menstrues and dryness of the mouth with clammy Flegm, tough, thick, and sour withall, and it resteth in the lungs and Throat, causing Consumptions, and drying up the Radical humidity of the Body, and wasteth Nature.

☿ in the last 18 degrees of ♐ is hot almost in the 4th deg. and dry in the extremity of the 4th degree, ingendring Diseases of thick red Choler and thin Melancholy, red Choler predominating; causing dry and hot mortal Fevers, which do consume the Radical humidity of the Body, the Stone and pains of the Reins, the Piles and Hemorrhoids, and pain about the Navel, the Canker and corroding Diseases that are without Remedy. Further, he stirreth up subtile Humours and venomous, causing a kind of the *French* Pox, with much twinkling, and pricking, and aking in the Head and Fore-head, and in the Arms and calves of the Legs, pain of the Side and convulsion in the Bowels and Belly, and griping of the Guts, and the Humour aforesaid caused of thin Melancholy and red Choler is saltish, and fretteth the Tongue, and especially pain of Wind in the right Side, in the Region of the Liver, both in Man and Woman, in one of the Sides, and benumming of the Head and Brain.

If ☿ be combust, and the ☽ separate from ♀ in ♏, and apply to ♂ in ♐, it causeth consumption of the Body and Members, and dryness of the mouth, Throat and Lungs, and stopping of the Terms, of a clammy thick Flegm, of red Choler and Melancholy; and it is sharp and sour withal, and stops the pores of the Body, causing great weakness, and consumeth the Radical humidity by heat and drowth, causing death suddenly.

If ☿ be in ♐ in 11 or 18 degr. and Lord of the Ascendant, and the ☽ separate from ♀ and apply to ♄ in ♍, it causeth the great Pox, with extreme aches and pains; it breaks out in the

Head and Feet with great Scabs and black, and full of holes and kernels, with great pain in the Reins.

The Cure.

Look in the Chapter of ☿ in ♈ for the times and Cures; but this Disease must be first well prepared before the Patient be purged, or else a Purge will do little good; for the Humour is venomous; therefore in your preparations put such things as repress venom.

Of Mercury in Taurus.

Mercury in the first 18 degrees of ♉ is cold and dry in the first degree, causing Diseases of two sorts of Melancholy, thick and thin; as the Gout in the Feet, and many other Diseases an d pains in the Feet, with Quartan Agues and swelling in the Members, Cankers, Warts, Wens and Knobs. ☿ in ♉, the ☽ in ♏, applying to ♂ in ♓, causeth the Plague, Mercury lord of the 12th, ♂ lord of the hour.

☿ in the the last 12 degrees of ♉ is cold and dry in the beginning of the 2d degree, in gendring Diseases of two sorts of Melancholy, *viz.* gross, and thin subtile Melancholy, causing Melancholy passions, sadness, heaviness, Wens, Warts, Knobs, Cankers, coldness in the Stomach, the Gout, if ☿ be Retrograde, and the ☽ apply next to ♄ in ♌, he hath a Fever, is very fearful, timorous and dry.

The Cure.

Minister not in the hour of ♄ nor ☿, but in the hour of ♃ being in ♊, ♎ or ♒, or put ♊, ♎ or ♒ in the Ascendant; and let the ☽ apply to ♃ in ♊, ♎ or ♒, and purge Melancholy.

Of Mercury in Virgo.

Mercury in the first 12 degrees of ♍ is cold and dry in the 2d degree, ingendring Diseases of thin Melancholy, as Madness, Wens, Warts, Cankers, stopping of the Liver and Lungs, and pain in the Stomach, the Cramp and Palsie of the Stomach, and contraction of the Sinews and Muscles of the Stomach, with pricking and aches.

☿ in ♍, between ♂ and ♄ in ♍, causeth much bleeding at the Nose, pain of the Head, Lungs and Breast, and bottom of the Belly, soreness of the Throat, and a great drought and surring of the mouth ready to vomit, if the ☽ withall do separate from the ☉ in ♌, then the Party is hot and burning, very dry, and full of yellow Choler and thin Melancholy stopping the Stomach, and causing indigestion, especially if ♃ be in ♉, in or near a square to the ☉, if the ☽ do separate from ♀ in ♍' ☿ Lord of the 12th in ♍, the greatest pain is in the bottom of the Belly, and in the Reins and Matrix, with much flushing heat in the face, and pain of the right side.

☿ in the next 18 degrees of ♍ is cold and dry in the 3d degree, ingendring Diseases of Melancholy, stopping of the Lungs, Stomach and Liver, the Palsie of the Stomach, with pricking and contraction of the Sinews and Muscles of the Stomach, and Cramp; if ☿ be Lord of the 12th and apply to a ♂ of the ☉, and the ☽ apply to ♀ in ♌ in the 10th, it causeth the Stone and Strangury.

The Cure, as before in the Chapter of ☿ in ♉.

Of *Mercury in Capricorn.*

Mercury in the first 12 degrees of ♑ is cold and dry in the 4th degree, ingendring Diseases of Melancholy cold and dry, stiff and sour, causing Madness, Diseases and pain in the Groyn, in the Yard and in the Bladder, taking away the use of the Yard, stopping of the Terms in a Woman, and *Mola Matricis*, and suffocation of the Matrix, Wens and hard Knobs and Bunches, and shrinking of the Sinews, the Mother, much wind in the Matrix, Body and Stomach, and troubles of the Mind, with fearfulness, Diseases of the Lights, and hardness of the Sides, of much Melancholy and vomiting disturbing of the Mind and Understanding, and especially if ☿ be lord of the 6th, the 12th, or of the Ascendant, or lord of the hour, or that the ☽ doth apply to, or be in full aspect of ☿.

☿ in the last 18 degrees of ♑ is cold and dry in the extremity of the 4th degr. even above nature, causing Diseases strong of Melancholy uncurable; as the Stone in the Bladder, stopping of the Urine, stopping of the Terms, Bunches, Wens and hard Knobs, Cankers, Wolves, Piles and Hemorrhoids, and great pain in the right side under the short ribs, and in the Belly griping like the Cholick or Stitches, caused of Wind and Melancholy, stopping the Veins, making the Parties to vomit much, and sore sick, much striving.

The Cure.

Minister not in the hour of ☿ nor ♄, but in the hour of ♃, as before-said, in the Chapter of ☿ in ♉, and sweat the Party well, and digest and purge; the best remedy is to give them sharp or sour things to eat or drink, as these, Lemmons, Oranges, Oximel, polick Butter, Whey, White-wine-vinegar, with Sugar-candy, Tamarinds, sour Ale and Beer.

Of *Mercury in Gemini.*

Mercury in *Gemini* in the first 18 degr. is temperate in all the four Qualities, yet breedeth Diseases, as distemperature of the Blood by thin Melancholy, causing pains in the left side of the head, perturbations of the mind, and infecting the optick Nerves, causing many Visions and Fancies appearing before the eyes, melancholick Passions, and great pain in the right side, and under the short ribs, of Wind and Melancholy stopping the Veins.

Mercury in the last 12 degrees of ♊ is hot and moist in the beginning of the first degr. ingendring Diseases of thin Melancholy and Blood, Blood predominating, causing perturbations of the Mind and Brain, Whimsies and strange Visions and Apparitions before the Eyes, melancholick Passions and Furies, with sadness, fearfulness and solitariness, the Palsie of the Tongue and loss of Speech, the Tooth-ache, and hurteth the Memory, Impostumations and pains in the right Ear, and pains of the Nostrils, and in the instruments of the Senses, impeding their operations with fearfulness and heavy thought.

The Cure.

Minister not in the hour of *Mercury* nor ♄, but in the hour of ♃ or ♀, being in ♉, ♍ or ♑; or if ♀ be in ♊, ♎ or ♒, or the ☽, placing ♈, ♌ or ♐ in the Ascendant, and make the Party sweat lustily,. then purge, and let him blood.

Of *Mercury in Libra*.

Mercury in the first 6 degrees of ♎ is hot and moist in the first degree, ingendring Diseases of thin Melancholy and Blood, Blood exceeding, causing Syncope, Pleurisies, Cardiack Passions, Impostumations, and divers Diseases of the Heart and Back, with trembling of the Heart and fearfulness.

Mercury in the next 18 degr. of ♎ is not and moist in the 2d degree, ingendring Diseases of thin Melancholy and thick Blood, Blood predominating, causing the Cardiack Passion, trembling at the heart, faintness, Green sickness, Impostumations and Sadness; as also Cankers and Heaviness, the Strangury, the Stone, and pains of the Reins.

Mercury in the last 6 degrees of ♎ is hot and moist in the beginning of the 3d degree, causing Diseases of thin Melancholy and thick Blood; as Pleurisies, Impostumations, Cardiack Passion, trembling of the Heart, Cankers, Sadness, heavy Thoughts, ill Fancies, and the like.

The Cure.

Look in the Chapt. of *Mercury* in ♊, purge the Party, and let him blood, and give him things to scour, sweeten, compose and cleanse the Blood, and to purifie and thin it, and purge Melancholy.

Of *Mercury in Aquarius*.

Mercury in the 1st 12 degr. of ♒ is hot and moist in the 3d degr. causing Diseases of thick Blood and thin Melancholy, Blood having dominion, causing pains in the Thighs and aches in the Huckle-bones, as Sciatica, and Impostumes in the Huckle-bones and Thighs, precipitation and suffocation of the Matrix.

☿ in the last 18 degrees of ♒ is hot and moist almost in the 4th degr. ingendring Diseases of thick Blood and thin Melancholy, Blood being predominate; causing pains and aches in the Thighs and Huckle-bones, and Sciatica, with Impostumations; Hemorrhoids and Piles.

The Cure.

Look the Chapter of ☿ in ♊; sweat the Party, purge him, and let blood.

Of *Mercury in Cancer.*

Mercury in the first 18 degrees of ♋ is cold in the 1st degr. and temperate in moisture and drowth, causing Diseases of thin Melancholy, and saltish Water and Flegm, causing Rheums and pains of the Throat, and in the root of the Tongue and Gullet, the Squinancy, an the like.

☿ in the last 12 degrees of ♋ is cold in the beginning of the 2d degree, and moist in the beginning of the first; ingendring Diseases of thin Melancholy, and thin, saltish, watry Flegm, causing Rheums, Catarrhes, pain in the Throat and Muscles of the Throat, and in the root of the Tongue, as the Squinancy, rising of the Lungs, ready to stop the Wind, much Flegm and filthy Choler, and the Cough and straitness of the Lungs, with Wind, as also a Cough of the Lights.

The Cure.

Minister not in the hour of ☿ nor ♄, but in the hour of ♃ or ♀, ♈, ♌ or ♐ being in the Ascendant, and let the Part sweat well, then purge him and let him blood.

Of *Mercury in Scorpio*

Mercury in the first 6 degrees of ♏ is cold in the 2d degr. and moist in the first, ingendring Diseases of thick stinking Flegm and thin Melancholy, Flegm predominating, causing pain and griping in the Belly, about the Navel, Worms in the Maw and

Guts, the Whites in Women and pains of the Matrix, the *French* Pox, the Swine Pox, and the Meazles.

☿ in the next 18 degrees of ♏ is cold in the 3d degree, and moist in the 2d; ingendring Diseases of thick and stinking Flegm and thin Melancholy, causing pains and gripings of the Belly, Worms in the Belly and Maw, the Whites in Women and pains of the Matrix, heavy dulness and faintness, heavy and distracted thoughts, Swellings in the face like unto the Mumps, and risings in the Throat threatning choaking, and cold and chilness over al the Body.

☿ in the last 6 degrees of ♏ is cold in the beginning of the 4th degree, and moist in the beginning of the 3d; ingendring diseases of tough stinking Flegm and thin Melancholy, Flegm having dominion, causing pains in the Belly, and griping about the Navel, and Worms in the Maw and Guts, and issuing of the Whites in Women, with pains of the Matrix.

The Cure.

Minister not in the hour of ♄ nor ☿. Look before in the Chapter of ☿ in ♋: sweat and purge the Party well.

Of *Mercury in Pisces.*

Mercury in the first 12 degrees of ♓ is moist in the 3d, and cold in the 4th degr. ingendring Diseases of thick and tough Flegm and thin Melancholy, and the Flegm hath the dominion, causing Dropsies, Impostumes in the Knees and Legs, with swelling of the Knees and the Gout.

☿ in the last 18 degrees of ♓ is cold above Nature, in the extremity of the 4th degr. and moist in the beginning of the 4th degr. ingendring Diseases of thick and tough Flegm putrified, and of thin Melancholy; and Flegm heth the dominion, causing pains, Impostumes, Dropsies, and pain in the Knees and Legs, as also the Gout.

The Cure.

Look before in the Chapter of ☿ in ♋, &c.

Of the Terms being stop't.

When the cause of the Disease if of ☿ in the 1ˢᵗ degr. of ♓ in the 11ᵗʰ House, and the ☽ in ♒ separating from ♂ in ♑, applying to an ☍ of ♄ in ♌ Retr.; first let her blood under the Ankles in both the feet, and the next day this Potion three dayes together.

℞. *Trochisch Myrrhæ & de Alcakengi* 3iβ. Powder it, and take it for one Dose in White-wine, and it bringeth them down.

The Virtue or Faculty Expulsive.

The Expulsive Faculty is the 4ᵗʰ and last principal Virtue in the Body of Man, and is constituted by cold and moisture temperate, and is governed by the ☽, and the Signs ♋, ♏ and ♓, which are more moist than cold; and in moisture the Expulsive Faculty doth participate with the Blood, and in coldness with the Earth, and with ♄, and it is holpen in the Signs ♋, ♏ and ♒, and it is debilitated or stopped in the Signs ♈, ♌ and ♐, and the first 18 degrees of ♋ are cold and moist, temperate, and the last 12 degrees of ♋ are cold and moist in the beginning of the 1ˢᵗ degree; and the first 6 degrees of ♏ are cold and moist in the 1ˢᵗ degree; and the next 18 degrees of ♏ are cold and moist in the 2d degree, the last degr. are cold and moist in the beginning of the 3d degr. and the first 12 degr. of ♓ are cold and moist in the beginning of the 3d degr. and the last 18 degr. of ♓ are cold and moist in the 4ᵗʰ degr.

The Expulsive Virtue therefore is that which driveth out by siedge, the dregs of the meat after digestion, and separateth that which the Attractive Virtue hath drawn down into the Bowels or Bladder, or that evacuateth, or driveth out of the Veins any evil or unnatural Humours gathered in any part of the Body or Members; and this Expultion is either Natural or Unnatural; Natural, when it doth temperately its office, Unnatural, when it doth it stronger, oftener, or forciblier than it should or ought, against Nature: therefore sometimes this Expulsive Virtue is hurt, weakned or let, that he cannot do his office in expelling the

Humours and Excrements of the Body as he should or ought to do, either by heat or drowth, in respect of Choler and Melancholy; but most of all, it is impedited and hindred by drowth, either of Choler or of Melancholy, supernaturally abounding in the Body and in the members, and whensoever it is so, then the Retentive Faculty is strong, for the Expulsive is opposite to the Retentive; and is the one by dryness doth make hard and retain, so the other by moisture doth make soft and expell; and the Expulsive Virtue being weakned, is to be comforted and strengthned when the ☽ is in ♋, ♏ or ♓, as the Retentive Virtue is to be holpen being distempered, the ☽ being in ♉, ♍, or ♑; or as the Digestive Virtue is to be holpen and strengthned the ☽ in ♈, ♌ or ♐, aspecting the place where it is weakned.

The Natural Expulsive Virtue is in all the Body, and in every member, as well as in the Belly and Stomach, to drive out and expell all superfluities in the Veins or Arteries, Stomach, Belly or Bowels, that do annoy or are hurtful to Nature, or to the natural Health of the Body. For the weakning of the Expulsive virtue in the Matrix, and stopping of the Terms, look for the causes in the Chapter of the Matrix, and in the Chapter of Retention of the Flowers, and in the Chapter of Fluxes, *Menstrua*, where these things are shewed at large.

Much dryness causeth clearness, much cold causeth whiteness, much heat causeth redness, much moisture causeth thickness, much drowth in the Bowels and Muscles *latitudinales* causeth costiveness.

Much drowth in the Matrix causeth stopping and retention of the Flowers, much moisture in the Stomach causeth vomiting and loofness of meat, much moisture in the Bowels causeth the Flux or Lask.

Much moisture in the Reins and in the Seed-bringers causeth weakness of the Reins, and issuing and wasting of Nature. Much moisture in the matrix causeth the Flux of the *Menstrues*, or extraordinary issuing of the Whites or Flowers.

Much moistness in the Head and Brain causeth Headache, pain, and heaviness to sleep.

Excess of moisture in the Muscles of the Bladder causeth the Party not to be able to retain his Urine.

Overmuch dryness in the Muscles of the Bladder causeth the Party that he cannot piss, or breedeth the Stone.

Much dowth in the Reins, Kidneys and Muscles of the Back, ingendreth the Stone, and causeth revulsion of Nature.

Much dryness in the Stomach causeth one to keep his meat long before it be digested, and maketh him hard to vomit, nor to have any appetite to vomit, and if he vomit it will be by force.

Overmuch dryness in the Milt doth make the Body and Belly swell, and wax hard, and causeth Consumption, and breedeth the Stitch, and shortness of breath.

Much drowth in the Liver causeth Indigestion, and maketh the Liver hard.

Much drowth in the Heart doth make one pine away, and swell in the Stomach, and to have a toughness therein, and to be very faint and unfit for action.

Overmuch moisture in the Liver doth rot him, and fill him full of bunches and sores, and causeth the Dropsie, and the Party looks foggy, cloudy, and blough in the face, with Pimples if it be how withall; but if it be cold and moist in causeth the Dropsie.

Sometimes also it chanceth that the Expulsive Virtue is too strong, by reason of too much moisture in the Muscles *latitudinales*, and then the Party becometh very laxative, and doth scour much with the lask.

If the Expulsive Virtue be too strong in the Reins of the Back and in the Seep-carriers, then Nature doth waste and consume, and goeth from the party.

If it be too strong in the Liver, the party will bleed much; if in the Stomach then he will vomit, or be given to vomiting much and so in all other parts of the Body; it in the muscles of the Bladder, then the Urine will pass unnaturally from him.

If the Expulsive Faculty be too strong in the Matrix, then the Flowers do pass away unnaturally, and then is caused a Flux of Flowers, as well of the red Flowers as of the white.

When the Virtue Expulsive is too strong by reason of the unnatural excess of Flegm, then moisture abounds in the Veins in any of the Members. And then again, if the Virtue Attractive be too strong in that member also, to draw the superfluous moisture unto it, then the abundance of Humours resorting to the place, cause some Diseases or Impostumations of a flegmatick matter, or otherwise oppresseth the Sinews and Muscles by too much moistness, and so causeth a Dropsie or Palsie, or benumming of the Members, and many times the loss of the use thereof.

Sometime also it happeneth that men have the Megrim in the Head, and are sorely stuffed in the Head, the cause thereof is, that the Expulsive Virtue is weakned through a dry Humour that oppresseth the Muscles Expulsive in the roof of the mouth and nose, then the Retentive Virtue through drowth is so strong, that it suffereth not the Expulsive Virtue to do its office, which in that place is soon remedied, by holding in the mouth a little Violet-water, and gargling the mouth therewith, being mixed with a little Borrage or Dill-water.

A Remedy when the Expulsive Virtue is weakned by too much drowth in any Member,

and this Unguent is our Invention, and it is almost temperate in heat and cold, but it is moist, and doth moisten almost in 3 deg. and is Expulsive.

℞ *Succi violar.altheæ, borag. ana* β *mor. mannæ, sem. atriplic. pastinac. succi faceti, grana enulæ succi ana* β*. succi papaver. lacine. semen psillii, olci oliv. ana, axung. porcinæ quantum sufficit, bulliat & fiat unguentum secundum artem; latitudinales.*

A Remedy where the Expulsive Virtue is weakned by heat and drought,

which Remedy is cold and moist almost in the third degr. Expulsive.

℞ *Succi mercurialis, malvæ, persil. cammomil. lactuc. atriplic. agresti ana. & cum axungia porcina fiat unguentum, & unge plantas pedum, renes & umbilicum,* or against the Muscles *latitudinales,* or transverse.

Ad laxandum ventrem, use this Unguent which is hot and dry in two degrees and a half, of great efficacy, and is good for the Sinew, the Cramp and Palsie.

℞ *fol. lilior. lupinor. mercur. caular. marrub. origan. ana* Mβ. *axung. porcin. quantum sufficit, & fiat unguentum;* and to that Unguent add these Oyls, *Oliv. camomil. musilag. ana, olei castæ, vulpin. cuphorb. hypericonis ana. olci liliorum amigdalar. dulc. mercurialis, olei sem. lini ana. commisceantur simul omnis, & unge plantas pedum,* and the muscles *trasversales* and *latitudinales.*

A Remedy where the Expulsive Virtue is weakned, or the Flower stop'd by drowth in the 3rd degr. and by cold in the 2nd degr.

postræ inventionis.

℞ *Aquar. violar. lactuc. bortensis, papaver. ana* β. *aquar. camomil. altheæ, thymi, salviæ, petrosel. fanicul. bysop. ana.* of Holy-hock-water. of Bugloss and Borrage-water *ana* . of White-wine a pint, of Spring-water a pint, put all together, then take of Sage, of Camomile, of Butter-dock roots, of Tims *ana* Mjβ. cut them, and boyl them in the said Water, *usqua ad medias consumpt.* strain it, and put thereto of Honey clarified of Agarick *pulverizat.* of the pulp of *Cassia*β, of *pulveris sancti.* of the Trochisch of mint boyl them again softly, and after put thereto *de Syrupo Absinthii,* and clarifie it, and give for a dose cum ☽ *est in* ♋, ♏ or ♓.

To make one Laxative.

Antidotum asyneritum biera, galeni, consorv. violarum diacassia fistula pro Enemat.

To cause Women to have easie deliverance.

Laurus Alexandrina, Horstrange, *Momordica.*

To bring forth a dead Child.
Camepytis, Cuiza, calendula, camomilla, thyma.

Of *Luna*.

The Moon is cold and moist, flegmatick by nature, but yet more moist than cold, she having chief dominion over all Bodies inhabiting this Globe of mortality; of her self she is a dark opacous Body, and receives all her light from the Sun, distempered in her moisture in ♋, ♏ and ♓; in ♋ she is most temperate, not much disagreeing from Nature, because it is her own house; but her qualities of moist and cold receive some distemperature in the last 12 degrees of ♋, and in ♏ she is more distempered, and in ♓ she is altogether removed, and is more hurtful and unnatural, and is cold and moist above Nature; for when she comes into the cold Signs she is made more cold, and in the hot Signs she is made more hot.

The ☽ hath of the Body humane, the Brain, the Lights, the marrow, the Neck, the taste, the swallowing, the Back-bone, the Stomach, the Mentrues, and all the Excrements, the right Eye of a Woman, and the left Eye of a Man, the force and strength of growing, the left side of the Stomach, the Head, the Matrix, the *Vulva*, and, according to some she hath the Belly and Mother in Women; the ☽ causeth all Lunary Diseases, and Kings Evil, which comes under the cin like a swelling, and it doth increase and decrease with the ☽: She causeth also the Palsie, Lethargy and forgetfulness. Quotidian Fevers and the Dropsie, Apoplexy and Falling Evil: the ☌ of the ☉ and ☽ farthereth that distemper wherein people seem to be afflicted as possessed by evil Spirits, especially if the ☽ be in the Terrene Trigon, *viz.* ♉, ♍ or ♑, and makes them sickly, and inclining to the Falling-sickness, and Madness, and hardly curable.

Of *Flegm*.

Flegm is one of the four principal Humours in the Body of man; if it be Natural, and is ingendred in the Liver, and runneth with the Blood through the Veins; by Nature it is cold and moist, of the nature of the ☽, and it doth grow and increase in the winter, from the 8ᵗʰ Ides of *November* to the 8ᵗʰ Ides of *Febuary*, and it doth rule in children until they be 15 years o'd, and it doth make a man heavy and slothful, and without audacity or courage, and shamefaced, bashful and faint-hearted, and it makes one drowsie and sleepy.

And there are considerable two sorts of Flegm, that is Natural and Unnatural; Natural is that which maintaineth Nature, and conserves the Radical moisture, and strengtheneth the Virtue Expulsive, and is that which runneth with blood in the Veins, throughout all the parts of the Body, maintaining and upholding Nature, of which a good Author speaketh, saying, *Natual Flegm is sweet in taste, and is an humour half decocted, and of nature and operation cold and moist, and cut of this kind of Flegm by circulation is the blood derived; for they both running in the Veins by circulation, the best and purest part is turned Into blood, and becometh red; and the rest remaineth a thin subtance, and is mixed with the blood, making the blood more fluid and to run throughout all the parts of the Body.* And of Unnatural Flegm there are four sorts; that is to say, *Dulce Flegma, Salsum Flegma, Acetosiem Flegma, Vitrcum Flegma*; and by these or some of these the natural Flegm is appressed and overcome many time, and the Body thereby indisposed, and becomes Diseased.

Dulce Flegma componitur vel inficitur à sanguine: hr. minus est nocitum cateris specitbus, fit autem aliquandocum febre, & aliquando sine febre. Urinain colore est ost anata i.e. of a grayish blew, in substattia pertotum spissaax duplicis bumi let ate flegmatus fit. i.e. sanguine significat dulce Flegma abunare, frva Flegma cujus bæ erunt signa.

Salsum Flegma cometh of the ☽ in ♈, ♌ or ♐, of Flegm and Choler mixed; for when Choler doth abound in its due and ordinary course of Nature, *inficit Flegma & ibud salsum esse facit, and is salt, hot and dry, & talis datur Regula. Urnia in colore & sub tantia nuetatur, & secundunt Autheres hoc Flegma (id est salsum) et calidius & siccius aliis speciebus flegmatis. Urina ergo subpallida in col re, & in sub tantia medixriter tenuis, significat salsunt flegma abundare, & hoc sine febre.*

Acetosum Flegma componitur sel inticiuer à Melancholia & Flegmate and it is tart and sour of nature cold and dry, caused of the ☽ in ♉, ♍ and ♑, and of ♄ and ☿ in ♋, ♏ and ♓, *& frigilitas discolor at Urinam, & siccitas attene et Urinam, readit ipsam discoloratam & tenuem. Hoc enim Flegma quandaque in febre, quandocue sine febre, & runc talis datur Regula. Urina in colre alba vel glauca, vel coloris citra album, cum subtantia medinriter unui talis significat Flegma Acctosum sine Febre abundare cujus hoc sunt signa.*

Vitreum Flegma, glassy Flegm, is ingendred of too much cold, and a congelation of Melencholy, and is more cold than any of the rest of the Flegms and is caused of the ☽ in ♋, ♏ and ♓, and of ♄ and ☿ in ♋, ♏ and ♓, *eodem moto de co judicatur quo Acetosum Flegma, sive sit cum Febre sive sis sine febre, & datur ista Regula de ila. Urina alba mediocrites spissa, in qua qu est gleba Humorum apparet, quotidianam febrem de Vitreo Flegmate significat, & hoc flegma frequenter facit erraticas febres & anemalas, si quartanis, septimanis, pessimum gentus flegmatis est.*

Of *Luna* in *Aries*.

Luna in the first 18 degrees of *Aries* is temperate in all the 4 Qualities, ingendring yellow Choler and saltish Flegm, causing aches and pains in the knees, and Fevers, and pain of the Side and Head, and *French* Pox.

☽ in the first 18 degrees of ♈ is very soultry hot but dry and cloudy, and causeth much heaviness and faintness and distemperature of the Body thereby.

☽ in the last 12 degrees of ♈ is is hot and dry in the beginning of the first degree, ingendring Diseases of thin yellow Choler and saltish Water and Flegm, Choler having dominion, causing red pimpled Faces, and salt flegmy Faces, with dryness and pains in the Eyes, and aches in the Knees, pain of the Head and Side.

The Cure.

Minister not Physick *in hora* ☽ nor ♂, but in the hour of ♃ or ♀, being in ♋, ♏, or ♓, and you may not put ♈, ♌, nor ♐ in the Ascendant, nor in the sixth, but in other cadent Houses, for this kind of salt Flegm is how and burning dry, and the Cure must be done with cold and moist Medicines in the third degree, and be sure in the curing thereof make the Lord of the 6th weak.

Of the Moon in Leo.

Luna in the first six degrees of ♌ is hot and dry *in primo gradu*, ingendring Diseases of salt Flegm, of a humour caused of thick yellow Choler and saltish Flegm, Choler having dominion, causing red pimpled, sawcy, flegmy Faces, heat of the Liver, Agues, and with heat of the Back and Reins, *Gonorrhea Passin*, Heart-burnings, and the Stone in the Reins and Bladder, and hot Urine,

☽ in the next 18 degrees of ♌ is hot and dry in the second degree, ingendring Diseases of salt-Flegm and yellow Choler, with thick saltish brinish Water, which causeth drowth and saltness in the mouth and throat, with salt sawcy faces, the Squinancy and swelling in the throat, with soreness thereof, and redness and soreness of the Eyes, and a dry Liver, Blisters and Swine Pox, red spots, salt Flegm, and swelling of the members.

☽ in the last 6 degrees of ♌ is hot and dry in the beginning of the 3d degree, ingendring Diseases of salt Flegm, and thick yellow Choler, Choler preodminating, causing swellings in the Throat, and Kings Evil, the Lunar Passion, the Squinancy and red pimpled Faces.

The Cure.

Look in the Chapt. of the ☽ in ♈, diet, digest, and purge, Digestives against salt Flegm, and Diseases caused of the ☽ in ♌ are, ℞ Syrup of Fumitory, *syr. Acetos. Ana. Aq.fumitor. Absinth. Acetos. ana, fiat potus pro tribus Dosibus.*

Of the ☽ in *Sagittary*.

Luna in the first 12 degrees of ♐ is hot and dry in the 3d degr. ingendring Diseases of thick red Choler and salt Flegm, causing Diseases of the Belly and Bowels, with griping and torment, called *Cholica passio*, with salt sawcy faces &c.

☽ in the last 18 degrees of ♐ is hot and dry in the beginning, of the 4th degr. causing red sawcy Faces, *cholica passio*, with griping and torment in the Bowels, and pain of the Head, Reins and Stomach, which is of Flegm and red Choler mixed, and red Choler hath dominion, and therefore the pain lyeth much in the right side of the Head, the Falling Evil.

The Cure.

Look in the Chapt. of the ☽ in ♈, but in this salt Flegm you must consider, that red Choler doth most predominate, and so much the more if the ☽ apply to the ☉ or to ♂ being in ♈, ♌, or ♐, it doth augment the heat and drowth thereof. And maketh the Humour the more to abound, therefore the colder and moister the things be in digestion, or purging, the better it is.

Of the Moon in Cancer.

Luna in the first 18 degrees of ♋ is cold and moist in the 1st degree, ingendring Diseases of raw glassy Flegm, raw and crude, indigested, with pains and drowsiness in the Head, the Tooth-ache and Lethargy, Palsie, Dropsie, Apoplexy, Falling-evil, &c. and the ☽ in the first 18 degrees of ♋ separating from ♂ in ♉, applying to ☍ ☉ in ♑, and the ☉ at a ✶ to ♃ in ♓, causeth the Stone in the Reins, and a spice of the dry Pox, ♄ being lord of the hour.

Luna in the first 18 degrees of ♋ is cold and moist in the beginning of the 2d degr. ingendring Diseases of cold and vitreous Flegm and saltish Water, causing pains in the Head, Lethargy, Palsie, the Apoplexy and Falling-evil, and in the hinder part of the head a drowsiness. ☽ in the last 12 degr. of ♋ separating from ♄ in ♍, an ☍ ☉ in ♑, causeth the Stone in the Reins and the Strangury.

The Cure.

In the Diseases caused of the ☽ in ♋, ♏ or ♓, it is good to sweat, to vomit and purge well, but minister not *in hora* ☽, nor ♀, but *in hora* ♃, ♂ and ☉ in ♊, ♎ or ♒, or in ♈, ♌ or ♐, putting ♈,

♌ or ♐ in the Ascendant, and cure it with things hot and dry. And this note, that it is not good in any such cold cause to let Blood, and it is so much the worse if the Party be fat.

Of Luna in Scorpio.

Luna in the first 6 degr. of ♏ is cold and moist in the 2d degree, ingendring Diseases of much rough stinking and rotten Flegm, causing great pains at the Heart and Stomach, and gnawing and pricking at the Heart and Back, with Aches, Fistulaes, Impostumations and Coughs, with a chill coldness of the Lungs.

Luna in the next 18 degrees of ♏ is cold and moist in the 3d degree, ingendring Diseases of tough, stinking, and rotten saltish Flegm, causing great pain and pricking at the Heart, Back and Stomach, Indigestion, rotting of the Liver, Dropsies, Fistulaes, Swellings and cold Aches, and Morphews.

Luna in the last 6 degr. of ♏ is cold and moist in the beginning of the 4th degree, ingendring Diseases, and prickings and gnawing at the Heart, and in the Stomach, with rottenness of the Liver, Dropsies, Indigestion, watry Humours, and cold Flegm in the Stomach and Lights, with the Cough, the *French* Pox, and swelling in the Feet and Legs, the cold Gout, Worms, the Wind-cholick and aches.

The Cure.

Minister not *in hora* ☽, nor *in hora* ♀, but in the hour of ♃, ♂, or ☉, being in ♈, ♌ ♐, ♎ or ♒, and digest the Humours well, then purge and sweat well, but take heed of letting blood in any cold and moist causes; lest the veins being exempt of blood, the cold Water and Humours do fill the veins up, and so cause a worse inconvenience, but you by vomit the Party.

Of the Moon in Pisces.

Luna in the first 12 degrees of ♓ is cold and moist in the 4th degr. ingendring cold Diseases of tough, thick, stinking saltish Water and of glassy Flegm, causing the wet Gout, the *French* Pox,

Impostumations, rotting of the Liver, swelling in the Knees and Joynts, the Flux, Dropsies, Indigestions, Mortification, and Death, Worms, Scowrings, Vomiting, Rheums, gnawing in the Stomach and griping in the Belly, the Cholick.

Luna in the last 18 degrees of ♓ is cold and moist in the extremity of the 4th degree, even above nature, deadly, ingendring Diseases of tough, stinking, corrupt, saltish, glassy Flegm, causing many cold and moist Distempers that are deadly; as Dropsies, *French* Pox, Fistulaes, Impostumations and Swellings, Indigestion, and rottenness of the Liver, stuffing of the Lungs and Stomach with Flegm, a mighty strong, painful, irksome Cough, and finally Death.

The Cure of Diseases caused of ☽ in ♓, so far forth or they may be cured.

Minister not in the hour of ☽ nor ♀, neither put ♋, ♍ nor ♓ in the Ascendant; but put ♈, ♌ or ♐, and minister in the hour of ♃, ♂ or ☉, being in ♈, ♌ or ♐; then sweat, vomit and purge, as in the Chapter of the ☽ in ♋.

Of the Moon in Taurus.

Luna in the first 18 degrees of ♉ is temperate in drowth and moisture, but cold in the first degree, ingendring thick Melancholy and saltish Flegm, causing cold Fevers, Agueshakings, Cramps, Aches in the Legs, and stiffness in the Sinews, and in this Melancholy predominates.

Luna in the last 12 degrees of ♉ is dry in the beginning of the first degree, ingendring Diseases of *Flegma Acetosa*, which is a mixture of Melancholy, saltish Water and Flegm, Melancholy predominating, causing Cramps and contraction of the Sinews, cold Fevers, and cold aches of the Legs, and stiffness of the Sinews.

The Cure.

Minister not *in hora* ☽ nor ♀, if she be in ♉, ♍ or ♑, nor in the hours of ♄ nor ☿, being in ♋, ♏, or ♓; nor put in the

Ascendant ♉, ♍, nor ♑: but minister in the hour of ♃ in ♊, ♎, ♒, ♈, ♌, ♐, or one of these Signs in the Ascendant, and let the Parties sweat well, and purge well.

Of the Moon in Virgo.

Luna in the first 6 degrees of ♍ is dry in the first degree and cold in the 2d, causing Diseases of Melancholy and saltish Water mixed, called *Flegma Acetosum*, Melancholy having the dominion, and it is tart and sour, causing Diseases and stiffness and aches in the Arms and Shoulders, Cankers, Knobs, Warts, Fevers, Meazles, Impostumations long growing, with intolerable pains of much cold in the Stomach and Lights, with Indigestion.

Luna in the next 18 degrees of ♍ is cold in the 3d degr. and dry in the 2d, causing an increase of *Flegma Acetosum*, and ingendring Diseases proceeding from thence, *viz.* of Melancholy and salt Flegm mixed, Melancholy predominating, which is tart and sour, causing stiffness in the Arms and Sinews, the Cramp, Fevers, Cankers, Warts, Knobs, Indigestion and pains at the Stomach, hardness of the Liver, the Cough and pains of the Lights, Piles and Hemorrhoids. But if the ☽ apply to ♂ in ♈, ♌ or ♐, or if the ☽ apply to ☿ in ♐, and ☿ be also in □ of ♄ in ♌, then the Party is full of yellow Choler, and his Blood is tainted, foul, rotten and fæculent, with thin Melancholy, and much yellow Choler, stopping and obstructing the Lungs, causing great pain in the Head and Eyes, and a great Cough, with dryness of the Brain: In such a case let him blood, if the ☽ apply to the ☉ in ♉, then the Distemper is of much Melancholy and some yellow Choler, causing leanness and consumption of the flesh, stopping of the Reins and great Rheum, faintness of the Heart, and much crude Water in the Stomach and swimming in the Head, and drowth through *Acetosum Flegma*.

☽ in the last 6 degrees of ♍ is dry in the beginning of the 3d degr. and cold in the beginning of the 4th, causing Diseases of Melancholy and saltish Flegm, called *Flegma Acetosum*, which is cold and dry, Melancholy having dominion, causing Cankers, Indigestion, Knobs, Warts, hardness of the Liver, Impostumes and stiffness in the Arms, and coldness of the Sinews, and Tympany.

The Cure.

Look before in the Chapter of ☾ in ♉; but here you must bathe the Party and the wounds often, and purge Melancholy and Flegm.

Of the *Moon* in *Capricorn.*

Luna in the first 12 degrees of ♑ is dry in the 3d degree and cold in the 4th, causing Diseases of *Acetosum Flegma,* that is, of sharp Melancholy and saltish Water and Flegm, as the Cramp, the Stone and Gravel in the Reins, the Strangury, stopping of the Urine, hard pissing, Wens, Warts, hard knobs, the *French* Pox and ache in the Bones.

Luna in the last 18 degrees of ♑ is dry in the beginning of the 4th degree, and cold in the extremity of the 4th deg. even above Nature; causing Diseases of Melancholy, salt Water and Flegm, uncurable, wherein Melancholy is most predominant, as Diseases and consumption of the Reins, the Stone, difficulty in making water, the Strangury, the Cramp and contraction of the Sinews, the *French* Pox, the Meazles, Cankers and Wolves, Warts, Wens, and hard knobs.

Of the ☾ in *Gemini.*

Luna in the first 18 degr. of ♊ is moist in the first degr. and temperate in cold and heat, ingendring sweet Flegm, that is a Humour of Blood and Flegm, Blood having dominion, causing swellings of the Feet, and coughs, Pleurisies, and red Pimples in the Face.

Luna in the last 12 degr. of ♊ is moist in the beginning of the 2d degr. and hot in the beginning of the first, causing Diseases of *Dulce Flegma,* that is, of Blood and Flegm, Blood having the predominancy, as swelling in the Feet, and such like.

The Cure.

Let blood, and purge, and rectifie the Blood, but minister not in the hour of ♃ nor ☾, but in the hours of ♄ or ☿, put ♉, ♍ or ♑ in the Ascendant.

Of the Moon in Libra.

Luna in the first 6 degrees of ♎ is moist in the 2d, and hot in the first degree; causing Diseases of thick Blood and saltish Flegm, and it is called sweet Flegm, for Blood predominates; this causeth oppilations in the Liver and Lungs, Coughs, Pleurisies, Impostumations, red Faces, Piles and Hemorrhoids.

☽ in the next 18 degrees of ♎ is hot in the 2d, and moist in the 3d degr. ingendring Diseases of sweet Flegm, that is, of blood and saltish water mixed, blood having principal dominion, causing oppilations of the Stomach, Coughs and Pleurisies, and Impostumations and Indigestion.

The Cure.

Let blood, and purge, and do as the Chapter of the ☽ in ♊.

Of Luna in Aquarius.

Luna in the first 12 degrees of ♒ is hot in the 3d degr. and moist in the 4th, ingendring Diseases of sweet Flegm, that is, of Blood, saltish Flegm and Water, Blood prevailing, with pains and swellings in the Bladder and privy parts, stopping of the Urine, and Whites in Women, Fluxes, Ague-cakes, vomiting, and swelling of the hands and feet, Chilblains, the Apoplexy, the Epilipsie, *Pruritus, Catarrbus.*

Luna in the last 18 degr. of ♒ is hot in the beginning of the 4th degr. and moist in the extremity of the 4th, ingendring Diseases of sweet Flegm, that is, of blood, saltish water and flegm mixed, the blood superabounding four to one, stopping the Urine, and causing pains in the Bladder and privy parts, and in the Yard, Impostumations and fluxes of the Whites in Women, the Meazles, Worms, Fluxes, Lasks and Scowrings, Kings Evil, rising of the Lungs.

The Cure.

Look in the Chapter of the ☽ in ♊, and ☽ in the Sign ♎.

Of Caput Draconis

What Diseases Caput Draconis doth cause throughout the 12 Signs, being in the 12th or 6th Houses or in Angles.

Caput Draconis in ♌ in the 4^h House causeth Botches and Sores in the Arm-Pits, and swelling in the Stomach.

Caput in ♌ in the 12th House causeth pain of the Back and swelling of the Feet.

☊ in the 10th, causeth the Wind Cholick, and swelling in the pit of the Belly.

☊ in ♍ in the 5th causeth alwayes a great pain in the right Side under the ribs, on the Region of the Liver, from Wind and watry Humours there congealed, even between the Zirfus and the Ribs, a hands-breadth or somewhat more from the pit of the Belly.

☊ in ♉ in the Ascendant, distant from the degree ascending 30 degrees or more, causeth pain of the Throat, in the Muscles of the Throat, and falling of the Uvula.

Of Cauda Draconis.

Cauda in ♈ in the 6th, being oppress'd by the □ of ♂ causeth the Meazles in the face, and weakness of the brain, and the swelling of the Throat.

☋ in ♒ in the 10th, in □ to ♄ in ♉, causeth Fistulaes, running sores and Ulcers in the Legs, Ankles and Feet, and rottenness of the bones.

☋ in the 6th causeth swelling of the Belly and Legs.

☋ in the 10th causeth aches and swellings in the Knees and Legs, and pains in the Back and Reins.

<u>In the first edition, page numbering restarted with page 1 at this point. - *Publisher*.</u>

General Judgments, whereby to know the Diseases and Distempers of the Body.

Note this for a general Rule, That if the Lord of the Ascendant, or Lord of the Hour, or Lord of the 12th in the New Moon, or Lord of the 6th in the full Moon be in any of the Angles, and Signifier of the Grief; according to his signification and place in which he is, Observe in which Angle he is, or any of them are, there is the most grief, according to his signification and place in which he is; As if ♂ be Lord of the Hour and in the Ascendant, then is the most grief in the Head; if in the 4th then in the Stomach; if in the 10th, in the Reins; if in the 7th, then in the Limbs; and so likewise of the 6th, 12th and Lord of the Ascendant.

If one Planet be both Lord of the Ascendant, and Lord of the Hour, the chief pain or grief shall be in that place or part of the Body where he is; as if in the Ascendant, in the Head, if in the 4th then in the Stomach; if in the 7th then in the Limbs; and if in the 10th, then in the Reins.

And it may be observed as a general Rule also, That as often as you find the Lord of the Ascendant in the 6th, the Party is cause of his own sickness, either through ill Diet, or by using something that is naughty, or by following some counsel of some unlucky body about him, being Lord of the 12th, or Lord of the 6th.

If a hot Planet, as ♃, ♂, or the ☉ be in a hot Sign, then the Party hath a great heat inward and outward.

If they be in a cold and dry Sign, then the Party is cold and dry inward, but not outward.

If they be in a cold and moist Sign, then the Party is cold and moist inward, and hot outward by fits.

If they be in hot and moist Signs, then the Party is both hot and moist inward and outward, and the Blood is inflamed by Choler and over-much heat,

If a cold Planet, as ♀, ☿, or ☽ be in a cold and moist Sign, then the Party is cold and moist inward and outward.

If the Lord of the 6th or 12th, as ♄ or ☿ be in a cold and dry sign, and the ☽ separate from ♄ or ☿, and apply to ♃ or ♂ in ♈, ♌, ♐, ♊, ♎, or ♒, then is the Party sometimes hot inward and cold outward.

If a cold Planet be in a cold and dry Sign, then is the Party cold and dry inward; if in a hat and moist Sign, then the Party is hot and moist inward, and cold outward, and sweateth many cold sweats.

If the ☽ do separate from the Lord of the House that she is in, that is from ♄, being in the 9th, the ☽ in ♑ or ♒, ♄ in ♌, and apply to ♀, being Lady of the 12th, and in the Sign ascending by △, it signifieth that the Party hath some Thought, or Medicine, or both, which hath been the cause of her Disease.

If the ☽ do apply to the Lord of the 7th, ♂ being Lord of the 7th, and also Lord of the 2nd, he is sick for the love of some woman, whom he desireth to marry, or lie withal, for some of her wealth, ♄ Lord of the Hour in the 11th combust.

If ☽ do apply to ♄ being Lord of the 4th and 5th in ♌ in 10th combust, and separate from ♀ being Lady of the Ascendant, in the 11th in ♍, and being also Lady of the 2nd, the Man is sick for the love of some old Woman, whom desireth to marry for her Goods, and taketh thought because he cannot have her.

If the ☽ do separate from ♀, being the Domina 4τα, and apply to ♂, being Lord of the 10th in the 12th in ♋, it seemeth the cause of the sickness is a surfeit and ill Diet, and the influence of the Heavens and Power of God.

If the Lord of the Ascendant, Lord of the Hour, and ☽, or two of them, be going out of the sign that they be in, it is a sign that the state of the Body will alter speedily; the nearer they be out, the sooner it will change.

And in such a case, if the Lord of the Ascendant the ☽, or Lord of the Hour, do go to a better estate, then the body will mend; as if ♂ be Lord of the Hour, and in the last gr. of ♍, and come into ♎, then the state of the body shall change from better to worse, and be weak; or if ☽ be in the last degree of ♒, and come into ♓; and if it be a Woman whose terms have been long stopt, then they shall come down, and flow freely from her, and her body thereby shall wax weak.

But if ♂ were in the last degree of ♓, and come into ♈, then the state of the body shall mend, because ♂ being Lord of the Ascendant is stronger in Aries than he is in Pisces.

If Dominus Ascendentus, Dominus, hora, and ☽, or two of them, being in the last degrees of any Signs, and signifying the state of the bodies alteration, do enter into moist Signs, when they go forth of the Signs they be in, as into ♊, ♎, ♒, ♋, ♏, or ♓, it signifieth some Flux of Blood or Humours to come upon the Party, or her Menstrues to descend, or a lask, or much vomiting.

But if they enter into dry Signs, as into ♈, ♉, ♌, ♍, ♐, or ♑, it signifieth a stopping of the body and costiveness, if they enter both in ♉, ♍, or ♑, it signifieth the melancholy Humour to abscund, and the Party will enter into a Consumption and pine away.

If ☽ be Domina hora, and Domina 6 ta, and ♄ Dominus Ascendentis, both in the last degree of ♌, and the ☽ entred two degrees of ♍, and both in the 7th combust, then the state of the body will soon alter, and begins already to alter, because of the ☽'s going out of ♌ into ♍, and wax worse than it was, and be more cold and dry; for ♄ had a Triplicity in ♌, and hath no Triplicity in the first of ♍, neither ☽, but are combust, which signifieth a worse estate.

If they enter into ♈, ♌, or ♐, then will the cholerick humour abound, and the Party will have a strong Fever, or vexation of the Mind, and be hot and burning, especially if *Dominus Ascendentis*, ☽ ♐ or *Dominus Hora*, do apply to *Dominus 6ta*, or be in the 6th, or combust.

If the Lord of the Ascendant, Lord of the Hour, and ☽, or two of them, being in the last degree of any Sign. Do enter into ♊, ♎, or ♒, it signifieth the increase of the Blood, and some Pleurisie or Flux of Blood shortly to follow, or much bleeding at the Nose or the Terms.

If they enter into ♋, ♍, or ♓, it signifies a Lask, or much vomiting, or some great Rheum, or much pissing to follow, or issuing of the Whites.

If ♂ be *Dominus Ascendentis*, and *Dominus Hora* also, in the last degrees of ♓, and enter into ♎, and the ☽ in the last degree of ♒, and enter into it, the Question being for a Woman whose Terms have been long ago stopt, and that hath been diseas'd with heat of the Reins and *Gonorrhea Passio*, it signifieth that the state of the body will wax weak, and will be much out of quiet, her Terms will begin to flow some 12 days after.

It is general, That if the Lord of the Ascendant be in the 7th, whosoever be Lord of the Ascendant, and the ☽ be in ♓, and at a full Aspect with ♀, and separating from ♀ to a *vacuum*, and then apply to ♀ again, if ♀ be either *Domina Ascendentis,* or 5 ta, or in the 11th, the Woman hath had many changes in her fits, or will have many.

If ♄ in such a case be *Dominus Ascendentis,* and in the Seventh, ☽ in ♓, separating from ♀, & *vacus cuesu,* she hath had great variety of changes in her fits.

If ♀ be *Dominus Ascendentis* in the 7th, in ♐, the ☽ in ♓ at a full aspect, or near the aspect of ♀, and then vacus, she will have her shifting fits very shortly.

Also note, That if *Dominus Ascendentis, Dominus Hora,* and the ☽, or two of them in the Question, be near the Angle ascending of the House, and going out of one House into another within seven days, that is, out of the second House into the first, or out of the first into the 12th, it signifieth the state of the body will alter shortly.

If they go out of Succedants into Angles, it will be better than it was; but if out of Angles into Cadents, then it will be worse.

If they go out of Cadents into Succedants, the Party will also mend and be better. *Look after for this again.*

And it is general. That if the ☽ do separate from ♄, and do apply to ♀, although ♄, ♀, and ☽ be all three in fixed Signs, if the Question be for a Woman whose Terms have been stopt; or if she have not had them fully, that they will come down shortly, or *e contra;* when the ☽ doth separate from ♀, and apply to ♄, then the Disease is not at the highest, or at the worst by much, especially if ♄ be *Dominus 12 ma. 6 ta,* or in a fixed Sign.

When the ☽ doth go from a Superior Planet to an inferior Planet, as from ♀ to ☿, or from ♄ to ♀, or from ♂ to the ☉, it's a sign the Disease will diminish.

When the ☽ goeth from an Inferior Planet to a superior Planet, the Disease will increase, and the longer it will continue, & *e contra.*

When the ☽ doth separate from a superior Planet, and apply to an inferior Planet, that is, in a moveable Sign, in ☍, it is a sign that the Disease will speedily alter or go away altogether.

When the ☽ doth separate from ♄, and apply to ♃, in a fixt Sign, the Disease will decrease by little and little, and in long time, if she went from ♄ to ☉, or ♀.

When the ☽ doth separate from the Lord of the 12th in the New ☽, and from the Lord of the 6th, in a Full ☽, it's a Sign the Disease will diminish, for it is then at the highest.

When the ☽ doth separate from the Lord of the 12th in the New ☽, and apply to the Lord of the 6th in the 12th, it's a sign that the Disease both begin to decrease, or will, but it will continue long on the Party.

When the ☽ doth separate from the Lord of the 12th, in the 6th, and apply to him again before she come to any other Planet, it's a sign the Disease doth continue at his state, being at the highest, and doth not diminish, nor will not diminish till she apply to an inferior Planet.

Also when the ☽ is in ☌, or full Aspect with ♄, or goeth to the Aspect of ♄, the Disease is at highest, and at his state.

I the ☽ do apply unto ♀ by ☌, □, or ✶, △, or ☍, and Venus be in the Ascendant, or 12th, in the Sign of the Ascendant, she is with child: But if the ☽, or Lord of the 5th be in the last degrees of any Sign, then she shall be delivered before her time, after so much time as is signified by the degrees which the Lord of the 5th hath to go out of the Sign he is in; as if be in a common Sign in the 10th, then reckon for every degree 60 days, and so every 30 days, and you will reckon it by the ☽, for that she hath to go, if the ☽ be in ♒, in the third, then reckon for every minute she hath to go out of that Sign, three days; and you may reckon it by the aspect the ☽ hath to ♀, if they be both in fixed Signs, as the ☽ in ♒, in the third, and ♀ in ♏ in the 12th, then reckon for every degree to the full Aspect three days and 8 hours, and at that time she shall be delivered.

If the ☽ do separate *a Domino quinta*, and apply to ♀ being Lady of the Ascendant, in the 7th, the Woman will be delivered shortly, or have some ease and help, and the nearer the ☽ is to the Aspect of ♀, the sooner will it be; if she be in full Aspect of ♀, or going from the Aspect within 30 minutes, then it will be within 12 hours after.

This is a grneral Rule, That if you find any Planet in the 9th House, not remote, then the sick Party hath sought to others before for remedy, and hath taken Medicines.

If it be ♄ in such a case, that is in the 9th, and in his detriment, or fall, or combust, then the Medicines that the party did take, and the counsel that was given him, did him more harm than good. But if ♄ be in his own House, or Exaltation, then the Medicine did him more good than harm; and if ♃ be in the 9th, fortunate, then the Medicine did him much good.

If ♃ or ♀ be in the 9th, unfortunate, then the Medicine did neither good nor harm, but the Medicine should seem to be good, but the Party did not continue it, or take it as he should.

Finally, any Planet in the 9th, fortunate, the Medicine was good, and did good, but if he be unfortunate, the Medicine did more harm than good.

If the ☉, ☿, or ☽ be in the 9th, neither fortunate nor infortunate, then the Medicine did neither harm nor good, & *e contra;* if they be evil, it did harm, if good, then it did good.

And it is a general Rule, That so often as you find the Lord of the Ascendant in the 9th, or Lord of the 9th in the 6th, or ♄ or ♂, or any unfortunate Planet in the 9th, the sickness is augmented, by taking of evil Medicines; for an unfortunate Planet in the 9th, sheweth that he hath taken Evil Medicines; and a fortunate Planet in the 9th sheweth, that he hath taken Medicines that have done him much good.

To know the Cause of the Disease.

Look to the Lord of the 6th or 12th, and to the Planet from which the ☽ doth separate.

If the ☽ separate from ♂ in ♊, and Lady of the 6th, then by surfeit.

If the ☽ separate from ♂, and ♂ be Lord of the 6th or 12th, then by a strain or bruise.

If the ☽ separate from ♂, and apply to ♄ and ☿, ♃ Lord of the 12th in ♈, the Party strained himself.

If the ☽ separate from ♄, and he Lord of the 12th, the sick Person hath taken thought, and inward griefs; if from ☿, he takes it with fear; if from ♀, with love or lechery; if from the ☉, with a squat, fall, or bruise; if from ♂, with a strain or blow; if from ♃, by over-heating his Blood, by sweating and taking cold.

Of Application of the ☽ to Planets.

In all your Judgments for the Party diseased, you must have an especial care and eye to what Planet the ☽ is conjoyned in a full Aspect, and from what Planet she did last separate, and to what Planet she doth next apply; because that Planet to whom she doth apply, doth also shew, as well as the Lord of the 12th House in the New ☽, or the Lord of the 6th in the wane or decrease of the ☽, what Humour doth reign or is predominate in the Body, and what Humour doth increase or decrease. As for Example. In the new of the ☽, ♄ is Lord of the 12th House upon the Question, and ♄ is in ♌, which is hot and dry, cholerick, increasing yellow choler, and ♄ himself is melancholick with a superfluous flegme, therefore I conclude, the humour abounding in the Body is yellow choler mixed with Melancholy, and the Party is hot inward and cold outward, and yellow choler hath the Dominion; then I look to what Planet the ☽ doth apply, which doth signifie the Humour abounding or decreasing, either augmenting the Disease, or cause of the Disease, or else a diminishing of it: As for Example, the Disease aforesaid is caused of ♄ in ♌, now if the ☽ be in ♈, and do apply to the ☉, then she doth augment the Disease with more yellow choler; for the ☉ and ♈ do increase the same; bit if the ☽ do apply to ♂ also being in ♌, then she doth strongly augment the Disease, both by yellow choler and red choler also; for ♂ causeth red choler; if ♂ be in ♐ and ☽ apply to him, then he doth augment the Disease mightly by red choler, and it is deadly, because it is in the fourth degree, except speedy remedy might be found; and if the ☽ do apply to ♄, then it doth augment Melancholy in what Sign soever ♄ be, for the augmenting of the Humour is taken from the Planet the ☽ doth apply unto, and not of the Sign the Planet is in; as if she apply to ♃, then blood aboundeth.

♄ is cold and dry, melancholick, fearful, and full of heavy thoughts, with a superflous flegme; now if the ☽ do apply to ♄, the Party hath taken thought, and is full of heavy, sad, pensive thoughts and fearful, and the melancholic humor doth increase, which may end in a Consumption, or a splenatick Distemper.

If ♄ be Lord of the 8th, then he taketh thoughts for one that is dead, or like to die, or for his Inheritance or Goods, if the ☽ do separate from ♄, being Lord of the 8th.

If ♄ be Lord of the 7th, then for his Wife, or for the Husband, or for some matter of Matrimony, or love, or for some loss, or Theft.

If ♄ be Lord of the 6th, then for one that is sick, or for his Servant.

If ♄ be Lord of the 5th, then for some child, or for losing of her birth, or because she cannot have Children.

If ♄ be Lord of the 4th, then for the Father or Mother.

If ♄ be Lord of the Third then for a Brother or a Sister.

If ♄ be Lord of the Second, then for the loss of some Mony or Substance.

If ♄ be Lord of the Ascendant then for need or poverty, or for that he cannot die.

If ♄ be Lord of the 12th, then for some Prisoner, for fear or Prison, or for some great Beast.

If ♄ be Lord of the 11th, then for some Special Friend, or for the displeasure of a Friend.

If ♄ be Lord of the 10th, then for some Gentlemen or Woman, or noble Person, or for his or her displeasure, or for fear of lots of Honour, Credit, or good Name.

If ♄ be Lord of the 9th, then for one that is gone a great Journey, or for some Religion, or some Suite in Law.

♃ Signifieth the Blood and Mirth.

If the ☽ apply to ♃, then it seems to be caused of much Mirth, one of riding, or of much shaking and overheating of the Body and Blood, and of corruption and foulness of the Blood, or of some Impostumation, or congelation of the Blood in the stomach or liver.

♃, always signifies the Liver, the Blood and Impostumations; and therefore know, whensoever ♃ is Signifier, *viz.* Of the 12th or 6th House, or Lord of the House, or if the ☽ do wither separate from or apply to ♃, there is some fault in the Liver, or in the Blood, or some Impostume in the Stomach, or other place of the Body.

If the ☽ separate from ♃, and be in ✶ or △ to the ☉, and afterward to a △ or ✶ of ♂ in ♊, or in ♈, the Man hath bruised himself with some fall, and hath a flux of Blood, and the Stone, and is very weak.

If the ☽ separate from ♃ in ♓℞, and apply to ♀ in ♏, it came of cold taken in the Matrix in Child-bed.

If the ☽ in ♑ separates from ♀ Lady of the Ascendant, in ♋, and apply to ♃℞ in ♈ in the 7th, she never had her Terms.

Luna in ♑ in the Third, separate α ♄ in ♌, and apply to ♃ in ♈℞ in the 5th, ♓ being on the Cusp of the 5th, she hath had her Terms lately, by so many days as the *Moon* is gone degrees from *Saturn*.

Luna in ♐ in the second, separate α ♃ in ♈ in the 5th ℞, and apply to ☿ in ♍, in the 11th, ♓ in the 5th, she had her Terms lately.

Of ♂.

If the ☽ apply to ♂, then it is caused of some stripe, hurt, or Drunkenness, or suspicion of Women, or miscarriage, or suchlike aforesaid; of Anger, Mistrust, Jelousie, or Fretting, or Bruise, or Choler, or over-flowing of the Gall.

If ♂ be Lord of the 6th, and in ♉, and the ☽ go from ♀ in ♌, to ♂ in ♉, it sheweth the Disease came of cold-taking upon heat; for ♀ in ♌ is hot and dry, sweating and ♂ in ♉ is cold and dry, the ☽ going from ♀, which was hot in ♌, and signifieth that the Party was hot, and then came to ♂ in ♉, which was cold, and signified much cold to follow upon heat, and much drinking cold things, which doth make a doubt of the Running of the Reins, and *Gonorrhea Passio*.

If the ☽ separate from a ☌ of ♂ in the 4th House, not much remote from the Cusp, or in the 3d in the Sign of the Fourth, not many degrees from the Angle of the 4th, it signifieth the Party doth surfeit much in drinking Wine: If the ☽ in such a case do apply to ♃ in ♓, it signifieth great distemperature of the Liver.

If the ☽ do separate from ♂ in the 9th, not remote, the sick will change his Physitian, and suspect him that deals with him first.

If the ☽ do separate from ♂, being Lord of the 4th, and in the 5th in ♉℞, or *sub radius,* applying to the ☉, then it seems the Woman is much distempered in her Body, and Reins, and Belly, by reason of some putrefication of some conception that resteth in her Matrix, and much foulness of the part, neither will she have Remedy until the Part be well cleansed with a Glister.

When ♀ is Lady of the 5th, in a Cadent House, and ♂ in the 5th ℞ and ♀ Combust, and the ☽ apply to ♀, if the Question be for a Woman, her Disease is caused by much putrification and gross Humour in her Matrix, by reason of some false Conception, or some After-birth remaining, neither will she have Remedy until the Matrix be well cleansed: And the signs are there, She much desireth rest to sit or lie and hath much pain in the Back and Loyns, and Sides, and bottom of the Belly, and sometimes like to swoon.

Note well, when ♂ or ♀ do govern the 5th, and the Hour, and the ☽ apply to ☿ being combust, and ♂ in the 5th in his Fall or Detriment, ℞, or Combust, it is a sign of much putrification in the Matrix, and some rottenness occasioned by some After-birth in the Matrix.

If ♂ be *Dominus quinta,* and *Dominus Hora,* in ♉℞, in the 5th House, the 6th, or 4th Houses, and the ☽ apply to ♀ in ♏, being combust in the 11th House then Woman hath some dead *fetus,* or somestinking corruption of the dead *fetus* in her Matrix, which is the cause of her Disease.

Of ☉.

If the ☽ separate from the ☉ in ♍, and be in a full ⚹ of ☿ in ♍, combust in the 10th, and after she leave ☿ she come to a □ of ♂ in ♏ in the 9th, ☿ being *Dominus sixta,* and of the Hour, and the ☽ in ♑ in the Ascendant, then the Party hath surfeited, relapsed, and renewed some old Disease, that sometimes before he hath been troubled withal.

If the ☽ apply to the ☉, then it is caused of cold taken when he is hot, that the fat of the body is congealed, and the Terms be stopt with Humours, and that the Party (if it be a Woman) hath the mother.

If the ☽ be in ♑, and separate from ♀ *Domins* of the 6th in ♑ in the second, and apply to the ☉ in ♏ in the 12th, ♄ being *Dominus Hora* in ♌, then is the Disease caused of abundance of evil Humours in the Body, and some evil Drink or Medicine by which they are made worse, especially if ☉ be Lord of the 9th, and ♄ in the 9th.

If ☽ be in the 7th, and separate *α Domins Ascendensus*, as from ♄ in ♌ in 7 *mo* combust and the ☽ apply to the ☉ being Lord of the 7th in ♍, it signifieth the man did force Nature too much with his Wife, or otherwise, whereby he did sweat and over-heat himself, and reacht, and over-strain'd his body, and being hot, took cold, which struck into his body, and congealed his Blood, which Blood after putrities in the Veins and Reins of the back, by reason of Choler and Melancholy being therewith, which afterwards will cause the running of the Reins, the *Gonorrhea Passio*, and the heat of the Reins, and great weakness of the Back,

If the ☽ do separate from ♄ in ♍ in the 7th, and apply to the ☉ in ♏ in the 9th, the Party hath surfeited by eating fruit; if ♀ Lady of the 7th be in ♏ in the 9th, the surfeit is by eating a piece of a Warden.

If the ☽ do separate from ♀ in ♈, and apply to the ☉ in ♈, and ♀ apply to ♄ by any Aspect, the Disease is caused of much drinking and surfeiting, and is very rheumatick, like to have a Dropsie.

If the ☽ do separate from ♀ being Lady of the 6th in the second, and be in a full Aspect of the ☉, and afterwards come to ☿ being combust in the 12th, it signifieth that the Disease is old and of long continuance, and came by constellation of the Heavens at his Birth, and his body will alter, according as the influence of the Heavens affect the same, and is hardly to be cured.

If the ☽ be Lady of the 5th, and do separate from the Lord of the 12th, as ♄℞ in ♍ or ♒, or in his Fall, or in the 12th, it signifieth to a Woman, that she took her Disease in Child-bed, and that there remaineth much rottenness and putrification of the After-birth, or some Conception in her Matrix, and she will not be well till she be cleared thereof, especially if there be a ⚹, △, or ☌ between ♃ *Dominus Ascendentis,* and ☿ Lord of the House of the ☽; or if ♂ be Lord of the Ascendant in ♉, and in ⚹, □, or △ to the Ascendant of the 5th House, the ☽ being Lady of the 5th, as before-said.

If the ☽ do separate from the ☉ in ♐, or from ♄ in ♌℞ and applying to ☿ in the Ascendant, not remote nor absculded, but in the Sign ascending, the Party hath strained himself with lifting.

If the ☽ do separate from the Lord of the House she is in, as from ♄ in the 12th, and the ☽ be combust, applying to the ☌ of the ☉, and the ☉ be in □ to ♃, then the Party hath surfeited with drinking of Wine and eating of Oysters, especially if ☽ be Lady of the Hour.

♄ Lord of the Third in the 9th, in ♍ not removed, and the ☉ Lord of the 9th in ♏ in the 12th, and the ☉ in ☍ to ♂ in ♉, the ☽ in ♑, applying to ♀ in ♏, the Party hath taken much loathsome and filthy Physick already, at some mans hand, that hath done no good but harm to the body and the stomach.

It's a general Rule, That if, or whensoever you find the ☽ to be Lady of the 5th, and apply to the ☉: and ♀ or ♂ to govern the hour, and be combust, or in their Fall, and the ☽ in ♊, ♏, or ♑, or in a Cadent House, that the Cause of the Disease is in the Womb, caused of some putrified matter residing after Child-birth, or some Birth perished in the Womb.

The ☽ Lady of the 5th in ♓ in the 12th and separate from ♀, ♀ being Lady of the Hour in ♐, combust, applying to the ☉ in the 8th, and the ☽ applying to the ☉ by square, these are signs of corruption, putrification and distempers of the Womb, with restless pains, as hath been said before.

Of ♀ in reference to Diseases.

Upon a Question of a Woman not being well, if the ☾ apply to ♀, she may be with child.

Upon a Question of sickness, if the ☾ apply to ♀, and no Aspects else, you may judge the Distemper to come by eating or drinking something that agreeth not with the Party, or of some surfet, or for love of some Child, or in Child-bed, or by using the company of women too much.

If the ☾ apply to ♀, if ♀ be *Dominus Hora, Domina Ascendentis* and *Domina quinta*, then it comes in Child-bed, or the Party is sick for the love of some Child.

If ♀ is such a case be Lady of the 7th, then he is sick for the love of a Woman; or a Woman is sick, for the love of some man.

If the ☾ be in ♊, and separate from ♀ in ♓ in the Ascendant, and apply to ☍ of ♂ in ♐ in the 9th, then it seems the Party having surfeited with drinking, and not hath taken some great cold afterwards, and is stopt in the Veins of the Stomach and Liver, and hath much pain at the Heart, and in the Head, and in all the Body.

If the ☾ in ♑ do separate from ♀ in ♏ in the 6th, and apply to the △ of ♄ in ♍ in the 6th, ♀ being Lady of the Ascendant, it signifieth the Party hath taken thought, and cold upon cold, and some great discontent troubleth the mind of the Party much.

Luna Domina Ascendentis in 6 ta, applying to ♀ by ✶ in ♓, it sheweth the Party is cause of his own disease, partly by ill diet, and partly by using the company of some Woman too much, hath over-acted his strength, if it be a man.

Luna in ♏ in the 7th, separate from ♀ in ♒, applying to ♂ being Lord of the Ascendant in ♉, the party hath been too excessive in copulation, and hath over-heat his blood, and caused great pain in the Reins by too much Lechery.

Of ☿ in reference to Diseases.

If the ☾ apply to ☿, the Disease is caused by some sudden fear, or affront taken; or he is sick for thought of some words spoken, or for some thing that he feareth of standeth in danger of.

If the ☽ be in ♍ in the Ascendant, remote and applying to ☿ being Lord of the Hour, and *Dominus sexta* combust in the 10th, the Woman hath taken her Disease by grief, fear, and sorrow, and it hath brought the mother on her, to her great trouble.

If the ☽ be in ♉ in the second, and separate from ☿ in ♑ in the 11th ℞, and applies to ♄ in ♌ ℞ in the 6th, it seemeth the Party is fearful; and fear, thought, and fretting causeth the Disease: If the ☽ be Lady of the 6th, she fretteth with her Servants.

If the ☽ do separate from ☿ in ♈, and apply to ♀ in ♈, and ♀ in △ to ♄, the Disease was first caused and taken by a fear and fright, and the Party is fearful and trembleth much.

The Moon signifieth Travel and Waters, the Menstrues and Whites, Midwives, and great Ladies, and the Mother.

If the ☽ be void of Course and apply to no Planet, but be Lady of the House of Infirmities, and Aspect the 5th House, then she hath been ill dealt withal in Child-bed by some Midwife, and she hath the precipitation of the Matrix, or the Mother, or some such kind of Infirmity.

The ☽ Lady of the Ascendant in ♑ in the 6th, in the sign of the 7th, separate from ♀ *Domina 5 ta* in the 5th, and apply to ♄ *Dominus* of the 7th in the 3rd, sheweth that the Woman took her Disease by Thought for some discourtesie of her Husband, in the time of her Childbed, and she hath the Mother.

The Lord of the 7th being Lord of the house of the ☽, the ☽ being Lady of the Ascendant, and the ☽ applying to the Lord of the 7th, signifieth the Husband of the *Querent* to be partly the cause of the Disease.

If the ☽ do apply to *Dominus 12ma*, the Sick man will change his first Physitian and take another; and if she separate from the Lord of the Ascendant or the hour, he will take a Physician that will be a stranger.

If the Lord of the 12 in such a case be in ☌ with any other Planet, then he will go to some Physitian that hath another joyned with him.

But in the case aforesaid, the Planet in the 9th must be *Dominus hora,* or *dominus ascendentis,* and then if the ☽ separates fom him and apply to the Lord of the 12th, he will change his Physitian.

If the ☽ do separate from the Lord of the 7th, and apply to the Lord of the 12th, being an inferior Planet, and in the 12th, and ♃ in the 7, or 6, the Medicine shall do much good, and the Disease will soon be remedied.

If the ☽ do separate a *Domina 6 tα,* and apply to ♃, and the ☽ be in the Ascendant, or do behold the Ascendant being in the 4th or in the Ascendant, the Party shall soon be whole, and the Medicine do much good.

If the ☽ do separate from ☿ being in the 12th, and apply to the ☌ □ or ☍ of ♄, and ☿ also apply to the □ of ♄, ♄ being Lord of the Hour, the party shall be Frantick or Mad before the Sickness leave him, or be at the highest.

If ♃ be Lord of the Ascendant in ♓℞ or not ℞, it signifieth the party is mild and gentle, and patient, and apt and willing to take Physick, and do any thing to have remedy and help.

To know where the Fault shall be, if theSick be not Cured.

There are Five Houses especially to be Noted in every Question of the Sick, *viz.* The first, the 10th, the 7th and 4th and the 6th House, by whose good and evil disposition, (that is to say Fortunate and Infortunate) thou mayst always know before thou begin, what end the Disease will tend to, and how end, and where and in whom the Fault shall be if the party be not Cured of his Disease. And these Houses we will dispose for their signification after this manner.

The first House (which is the Ascendant of the Question) and his Lord, shall signifie whether the Sick be to be Cured of his Infirmity or not; adding and adjoyning herewith the state of the ☽, and the Palnet she applies too to know also thereby whether the Sick will live or dye, and whether it be best to take him in hand or no; and whether he will be cause of the prolongation of his own Sickness yea or no.

If the first House and Lord thereof be fortunate and free from combustion, and from an Evil Planet, and from the Lord of the 8th House and 6th House, the ☽ also free from evil as aforesaid and applying to a good Planet, then he may he healed, and thou mayst take him in hand, except thou find afterwards something to the contrary; if there be a good Planet, as ♃, ♀, or ☉ in the Ascendant, not remote nor combust, nor retrograde, nor aspected to the Lord of the 8th House, it is the better.

If there be ♂ Lord of the Ascendant in the 4th in ♓, with ♃ at a △ to the Ascendant, and free from ♄, and ♀ Lady of the 6th in ♈, the Cure shall be speedy and the party shall be quickly helped; and take few Medicines, for he will not take anything often.

If there be an evil Planet in the Ascendant, not remote, as ♄ or ♂ or ☋, or a combust, or Retrograde Planet, or the ☽ being in the way of Combustion, or a Planet in his Detriment or Fall, or otherwise infortunate, then it signifieth that it is not good to take him in hand, for he will not be ruled.

If ♄ or ♂, or a Retrograde, or unfortunate Planet in his Fall or Detriment be Lord of the Ascendant, then it is not good to meddle with him, for he will not be ruled, for it seemeth some evil Person hath rule over the sick, and that the sick is of a forward nature, and frets much.

If any Planet that is Combust, Retrograde, or in his Fall, do behold the degree ascending, or be in ☌ or aspect with the Lord of the Ascendant, it is not good to meddle with him, for thou shalt have much ado with him, and he shall have evil counsel, and either evil Spirits, or evil people will tempt him from good to evil.

If Dominus Ascendentis be unfortunate, Combust, or Retrograde, or in his Fall, Detriment, or impedited, or in ☌, □, or ☍ of an evil. Retrograde, Combust, or unfortunate Planet, it signifieth the sick will not be ruled. But he is some evil and unfortunate Person; for if the Lord of the Ascendant be unfortunate of himself, then is the sick Person unfortunate, but if he be joyned to another unfortunate Planet, or made unfortunate by another, then there is some evil and unfortunate Person about him, that doth guide and give him evil counsel.

A fortunate Planet in the Ascendant, signifieth the Physitian shall be profitable to the sick; yea, if it be ♃, though he be Retrograde, Oriental in ♌, the sick shall rejoyce much at the presence of the Physitian, and find great ease, and it is good to take him in hand.

If the Ascendant or his Lord be unfortunate, or afflicted, either by the bodily presence, or aspect of some evil Planet, or that the Ascendant or his Lord, or one of them be evil and unfortunate by nature, and the seventh House, and his Lord also unfortunate, the fault shall be in the sick Person if he be not cured; for the Ascendant is for Urine, and the 7th House for the sick.

If the Moon be Combust of the Sun, or in via combusta, or in her Fall, or in ☌, or □ of ♄ or ♂, or with Caudia, or with a Retrograde, or Combust, or unfortunate Planet, then meddle not with the sick, for evil will come of it.

If the ☽ be in ☌, or □ of ♂, there will come evil words, and slander and reproach of it, and much anger and trouble.

If the ☽ be in ☌ or □ of ♄, then thou will be sorrowful and repent thee that thou didst meddle with the sick, and thy mind will be troubled for some Cause.

The Lord of the Ascendant in the 11th fortunate, aspecting the Ascendant, thou may'st take him in hand, for the sick will be ruled by thee, and there will be great friendship in his sickness.

The Lord of the Ascendant in the 5th unfortunate, and not aspecting the Ascendant, he shall have few to attend him, or take any care of him, and he will not be ruled by thee; therefore meddle not with him.

The Lord of the Ascendant in the 6th House, the sick Persons will be loth to take any Medicines, and will find fault causelesly with them, and say they are never the better for them, or that it doth hurt the body, or augment the pain, and so will be cause of their own sickness.

The Lord of the Ascendant in the 4th fortunate, the sick shall be ruled and take the medicines.

The Lord of the Ascendant in the 10th fortunate, the sick will be ruled, and take his Medicines willingly, and honour his Physitian.

The Lord of the Ascendant in the 8th remote, and ♄ in the Ascendant not remote, the sick will be very weak in taking his Medicine, and be sick for a time, and leave taking his Medicine. And yet he shall find great ease, and be well again, but if ♄ be Lord of the 6th, he will be sick again.

The Lord of the Ascendant in the 10th, with ♀ Lady of the 4th in ♉, and the ☽ applying to ♃ in the 7th, then take the Party in hand, for he will be ruled, and thou shalt have great love, favour and friendship.

The Lord of the Ascendant in Corde Solis, or within one degree of the ☉ in the 11th, and free from evil, and from the afflictions of ♄ and ♂, thou may'st take him in hand, if the Lord of the Ascendant be velox cuesu, and he will be ruled so so.

If the Lord of the Ascendant be in the Ascendant, in his own House, in the Sign of the Ascendant, not remote, as ♀ in ♎, and at a full ✶ to ♄ in ♌ in the 10th, being Lord of the 5th, the Cause of the Disease was thought taken for one she loved, which forsook her.

If the Lord of the Ascendant be Lord of the 6th or 12th, in ♈, ♉, ♋, ♌, ♍, ♓, or ♑, and in the 7th, 10th, or Ascendant, and apply to ♂, ☿, ♀, ☉, being in any of the aforesaid Signs, by ☌, ✶, or △, being in the 10th, 11th, 7th, 5th, or Third Houses, then the Party and the whole stream of his desires run after the lusts of the flesh, and much use of women, and the desire thereof is the cause of his or her Disease, for these Signs do signifie much Lechery, and do cause revulsion of Nature, and Gonorrhea Passio, with heat of the Reins, and burning of the Urine.

If one Planet be Lord of the Ascendant, and also Lord of the 6th, as ♂ in ♉, and in the 7th or 6th, it signifieth the Party was cause of his own Disease, especially if the ☽ apply to that Planet.

Mark always the Planet and his state from whom the ☽ did last separate, and that Planet shall signifie what state the Party was in, and what he did before he sickened; as if the ☽ went from ♀ in ♌, it signifieth the Party was merry, and hot, and did sweat.

Then mark also in what Sign the ☽ was, and that shall signifie the Place where he was; as if the ☽ was in ♋, he took it on the Water, for the watry Signs do signifie the Water, and terrene Signs the Earth, and Labouring in Delving, Plowing, Husbandry, Harvest, Threshing, or the like.

The fiery Signs signifie labouring about the Fire, or travelling on foot, or Lechery, or over-straining himself with Women, especially if the ☽ did separate from Saturn in ♌ in the 7th, then in the use of Lechery, he through violence of Exercise did surfeit or over-heat himself.

The Airy Signs signifie Riding, as Hawking or Hunting, excess in Gaming and Banqueting, and such like.

Then mark to whom the ☽ doth apply next, and in what Sign that Planet is; as if the Moon apply to ♂ in ♉, then it signifies he hath taken Cold upon Heat, whereupon is to be doubted the Running of the Reins; but if the ☽ be in ♌, then it came by Lechery. If the ☽ do apply to the Lord of the Ascendant, it is a sign the Party will mend shortly.

If the ☽ be in the Sign Ascending in the 12th, and apply to the Lord of the Ascendant, or be also Lord of the 12th, and signifier of the cause of the Disease, and the Lord of the Ascendant apply to the Ascendant also, it is a sign of Health shortly, and that the Party will mend.

If ♀ be Lady of the Ascendant, and in the 7th, or 6th, in ♏, then the Party came by her Disease by too much or too excessive use of the Act of Generation, or she was dealth with in an ill time or place, where she took great cold in her Matrix.

It is seldom seen that if ♂ be the Lord of the Ascendant, or in the 7th, or in the Sign of the 6th. In the 7th not remote, that the Party doth or will take any Physick; but if they take one dragme, they will no more.

If ♄ be Lord of the Ascendant, and Lord of the 12th and Lord of the Hour also, and in the 7th ℞ in ♍, and the ☽ in Aries, applying to a △ of Mercury in ♐, it signifieth that the Party is enemy of her self, and cause of her own Disease and thinks she is bewitched, which is caused of some sudden fear at first, and is loth to take any Physick.

In the 7th degree 58 of ♍, is a Star of the nature of ♀ and ☿ of the 3d. magnitude, on the left side of the Hance of the Lion, some call it surius: This Star causeth a merry kind of madness and frenzy, for they will sing much; and therefore whensoever the Lord of the 12th or 6th House do come to the ☌, □, or ☍ of this Star, or if the ☽ do apply to ☿ being in the Ascendant, and ♄ or ♂ be in ☌, □, or ☍ of said Star. Or within two degrees going to the said Star, it causeth frenzy or madness, or lightness of the Head and Brain.

Of the 10th House.

The 10th House shall signifie the Physician; and if there be in the 10th House an evil or unfortunate Planet, combust or retrograde, or a Planet in his detriment or fall, then it signifies the Medicine shall not profit the sick Person; for sometimes the Infirmity is so tedious, that it bringeth death, as if the Lord of the Ascendant be joyned with the Lord of the House of Death.

A fortunate Planet in the 10th House, signifies the Physitian shall rule the Patient, and be well thought of, and shall have laud, praise and pay for his doings.

If the 10th House or his Lord be afflicted, or infortunate, or impeded of themselves, or by evil Planets, or by the Lord of the 7th House, then the fault or error shall be in the Physitian, either that he doth not jusge the Disease aright, or that he doth observe an ill order or method in curing the Disease, or else that he is negligent therein, and doth not see it done himself, but trusteth to others to give the Medicine, which deceive him.

If an evil Planet be Lord of the 10th or if a malevolent Planet combust or retrograde, behold the Ascendant of the 10th House, then the Physitian shall be in fault, and either by negligence, or hearkning too much to the speeches of others, he shall be seduced, and not give right jusgment, or else will hinder the Sick by some other means as aforesaid.

The Lord of the 10th in the 2nd. The Physitian will stand upon Money for curing the Sick, and demand more than the Sick will give, and the Sick will promise more than he will pay.

If ♃, ☉, ♀, ☽, or ☊ be found in the second House, the Physitian shall have reasonable reward for his pains; for ♃ brings the greatest profit and money, ♀ brings him friendship, the ☉ dignity and honour, ☊ money, and ☽ love and lechery, but little money.

Luna, Lady of the 10th in the 4th or 5th applying to ☍ of ♀ Lady of the Ascendant, and the Lady of the Ascendant going to ☍ of ♄, it signifieth that the Finger of God is on the Party, and hath hiven the Party over for a time into his Enemies hands, and the Party hath no power to follow good counsel, to have remedy.

If ♄ be Lord of the 10th in ♋ in the 4th, and ♃ in the 10th in ♑, in ☌ with ♂, and ♂ be Lord of the 7th, then the sick Person shall soon be eased of his Disease, because ♂ which is Lord of the 7th, is in his exaltation, and in the 10th with ♃, and the Physitian shall be well thought of for his coming, and have credit.

If the Lord of the 10th be in the 4th, it signifies a short Cure of the Sickness.

If the Lord of the 10th be in the 6th in his exaltation, or otherwise, it signifieth the sick Person shall desire the Physitian, and will rejoyce that the Physitian may come unto him, and also He shall desire to see the sick Person.

Mars, Lord of the 10th House, in the 7th. Not remote, and the ☽ separate from the ☉, Lord of the Ascendant in the 10th, and applying to ♂ by ☌, ✶, or △, it signifieth the sick Person shall be fond of his Physitian, and shall be loth to let him depart, for the love of the Sick shall be so fervent, and the Sick shall find great comfort at the presence of the Physitian.

If the Lord of the 10th be in the 7th, and the Lord of the Ascendant in the 10th, and the ☽ go from the Lord of the Ascendant to the Lord of the 7th, by ☌, ✶, or △, the sick Person shall fall in love with the Physitian, and shall highly commend him, and receive great comfort in his presence.

If the Lord of the 10th be in ☌,✶ or △, to the Lord of the 7th, or the ☽ go from the one to the other by ☌, ✶, or △, the sick

Person shall have the Physitian in great regard, and deal friendly with him.

If the ☽ go from the Lord of the Ascendant by ☌, ✶, or △, to the Lord of the 7th, the Sick person shall be in love with the Physitian, and Honour him, and find great ease by his presence.

If ♃ be Lord of the 10th, and in the Ascendant in ♓ not remote, and ♂ in the 10th declining to the 9th House, being in ♐, and ♄ in ♋℞ in the 6th, or the ☽ Lady of the 6th in ♉, applying to a □ of ♄, then it seems the Physitian shall be profitable to the Sick in every respect; yet the Sick will hardly be ruled, and is cause of their own sickness, and again shall be sick by the Influence of the Heavens.

The Lord of the 10th in the 11th, and the ☽ separate from the Lord of the 10th, and applying to the Lord of the 7th by □ or ☍ in the 12th House in the Sign of the Ascendant, it signifieth Health to the Sick from God, and from the Physitian by Divine Power, though he minister no Medicine at all to the Party for a time for the time is accomplish'd that he shall be whole, and with great Commendations to the Physitian.

If the ☽ do Apply to the Lord of the 10th by □ or ☍, then the Finger of God is upon the Party.

If the Lord of the 10th be in □ or ☍, of the Degree ascending or his Lord, the Sick shall not be Healed; for the Finger of God is upon him, and the time of Health is not yet come.

If the ☽ be in ♉ in the 10th; and ♄ also in the 10th ℞ and the ☽ separate from the ☌ of ♄, and apply to a fortunate Planet in the Ascendant; then the Sick person shall fawn on the Physitian, and receive great comfort in him and in his presence, and shall be ruled by him; if the ☽ separate from ♄, and Apply to ♃, the better.

If ♄ be in the 2nd House, It will cost the Sick person very much charge before he will be Cured.

If ♄ separate from the Lord of the Ascendant, and Apply to the Lord of the 10th by ✶ or △, whosoever be Lord of the 10th, It signifieth the Sick shall find favour with God, and the Physitian shall be profitable unto him; except the Lord of the 10th be in the 6th Retrograde, and the causer of the Infirmity' or the Lord of the 12th in the Ascendant, or Lord of the 6th in the Ascendant.

But if the ☽ do apply to the Lord of the 10th by □ or ☍, the Lady of the Ascendant, and in the 5th House in ♎ in via combusta, and ♃ in ♈ in the 11th House, then the Sickness is supernatural, and there is no medling with the Party, nor no Medicine that will Help him or her till the cause be removed, be it never so long.

If the Lord of the 10th, (as ♃, be also Lord of the 6th, and in the 10th in □ to the Ascendant, and the ☽ separate from the Lord of the 10th, and apply to the Lord of the 12th in the New Moon, then it is a sign that this Disease is hereditary from the Parents, from one Generation to another, and so will descend from Generation to Generation on Males and Females; and unless God extra-ordinarily give a Cure, it will never be Cured.

If there be in such a case a fixed Feminine Sign in the 6th House, then the Disease had been imposed on the Females onely; if a Masculine Sign were in the 6th House, then on the Males only, if a Common Sign, then on the Males and Females.

Of the Seventh House.

The 7th House and his Lord shall signifie the Sick person; If therefore there be in the 7th House some fortunate Planet by Nature, or by Accident, It signifieth that the Disease shall be lighted, and the Sick person eased by the Medicine, and also by the presence of the Physitian.

And this I have proved often; That if ♃ were in the 7th, when the Question was first made by the bringer of the Urine; and also if ♃ hath been in the 7th House when I have been sent for, or when I have gone to the Sick, that then the very presence of the Physitian as well as the Medicine shall be very delightful and comfortable to the Sick person.

If in the 7th House be some fortunate Planet, or if some fortunate Planet do behold the 7th House or his Lord, The Sickness shall be lighted, not only by the Medicine, but also the very presence of the Physitian shall pleasure and profit the Sick very much.

If the 7th House or his Lord be Evil-affected, or Evil by Nature or Accident in the time of the Question, or in the first growing to be sick; The Physitian then called, sent to, or sent for, will not profit the Sick; not because the fault is in the Physitian, but in the Sick person, who is Unfortunate and will not be Ruled; neither is his Sickness at the worst, nor his time is not come to be Cured; for the 7th House is for the Sick person, and for these times that the Sick person is subject unto, and shall follow and do; And this shall you know, if the Lord of the 10th be in the 7th, or in □ or ☍ to the 7th House, or his Lord, then it is a sign the Disease is preternatural or supernatural; or that he suffers under the immediate hand of God, and shall not be healed. Also if the ☽ do apply to the □ or ☍ of the Lord of the 10th House, the Disease is extraordinary; if by △ or ⚹, not so.

If the Lord of the 10th be in □ or ☍ to the Degree ascending or his Lord, the Disease is extraordinary, and the Sick shall not be healed, or in ☌ of ♄, or ♂, being Lord of the 10th; but if by △ or ⚹, the contrary.

I have known them that have been long sick, and troubled with grievous Diseases, that have sent unto me to cure them of their Infirmities, and because I have found the 7th House, and his Lord unfortunate, and evil disposed, I have put them off for a time; and a year after and more, they have sent to me again, and then I have found the 7th House, and his Lord fortunate upon the Question, and then by Gods help I have cured them of their Disease.

The 7th House is afflicted and infortunate, if ♄, or ♂, or ☋ be there, and also ♄ and ♂ do infortunate the Lord of the 7th; and the Lord of the Ascendant is also unfortunate, if he be combust or retrograde, in his fall or detriment, or in ☌, □, or ☍, of an evil Planet, cadent and weak.

The Lord of the 7th, in the 7th, or in the Ascendant unfortunate, signifieth that the Company that are about the sick Person shall hinder and hurt him, for all are not his friends.

If the Lord of the 7th. In the 7th, free from ♄, and ♂, not in his fall nor detriment, nor retrograde nor combust, but fortunate, then those that be about the Sick, shall wish him or her well, and do any good for them that they can, and seek to please him, and to ease him.

The Lord of the 7th, in the 10th aspecting the Ascendant, the presence of the Physician shall comfort the sick Party greatly; yea if it be ♄ that is Lord of the 7th retrograde, and the ☽ separate from ♄, and apply to the Ascendant, or to his Lord, or to some good Planet in the Ascendant.

The Lord of the 7th, in the Ascendant, not remote, as ♂ in ♉ retrograde, and ☽ in ♈ applying to ♄ in the 6th per △ or ✶, if a Woman make the Question, she taketh grief and thought for her Husband, for he useth to be drunken and brawl much; the same of a Woman, if a Man make the Question.

The Lord of the 7th in the Ascendant, whosoever be Lord of the 7th, though it be ♂ in ♉℞, it signifieth health to the Party, and that the Party will be ruled by the Physitian; especially if the Lord of the Ascendant be in the 7th, or that the ☽ apply to the Lord of the 7th, or to the Lord of the Hour, or the 10th, but the Sick injureth her self, is corrupted by her Husband, and her Disease will continue long with her, and so vice versa in a man.

If ♄ be Lord of the 7th, and also of the 6th, and in ♌ in the 12th House, and ♃ in the 7th, the sick Person shall soon be whole, so that he doth not behold the Lord of the Ascendant, especially if the Lord of the Ascendant be free from the Lord of the 8th, and from ♄ and ♂ in the 11th, or in Angles.

♄, Lord of the 7th in ♋, in ☌ with ♀ in the 10th, the sick Person will fawn on the Physitian, and if a Woman, she will be too indulgent towards him.

♃, Lord of the 7th in ♒℞, free from ♄ and ♂, and in the 6th House, and the ☽ separate from ♃, it will be long before the Party be well, yet thou cure him in the end with much ado, and many Medicines.

If ♃ be in the 7th in the Question, though bhe be Lord of the 8th, and in the Sign of the 7th, yet it signifieth Health to the Sick, though she be at deaths door, except the ☾ being in ♎ 15, do separate from ♄, being Lord of the 7th, and in the 2d, in the Sign ascending, and apply to ♃ by ✶ or △, then it signifies the Party will not be ruled, nor take any Medicine.

Mars, Lord of the 10th in the 11th, and the ☾ go from ♂ to the Lord of the 7th, as to ♄ by □, being in the Sign ascending in the 12th, signifieth Health to the sick Party from God and the Physitian by Divine Power, though he minister no Medicine, and great commendation to the Physitian.

Mars, Lord of the 7th, in ♉, 23d. retrograde, in the Ascendant, not remote, signifieth the Sick hath a good opinion of the Physitian, and desireth Help, and yet doth minister her self, and think that she shall scant have remedy; and when a Woman maketh the Question, if it be so, the Womans Husband is partly cause of her Disease, for it seems he is unruly and given to drinking, and to keep ill Company, and to consume and spend, and gives her evil words; if a Man makes the Question, then the Husband hath corrupted her.

Mars, Lord of the Ascendant, in the 7th, retrograde, not remote, and the ☾ apply to ♂ or ♀, or both, then the Querent is enemy to her self, and cause of her own Disease, by keeping of some ill Company, or by ill Diet, or by Drunkenness, and surfeits with it, and is fretful, and disguiseth herself and others.

Venus, Lady of the 7th in the Ascendant in Scorpio, in the Sign ascending, not remote, free from ♄ and ♂ and from the Lord of the 8th, signifieth Health, and that the Party will be ruled, and her Physitian shall do her good; and she shall live long, though many think she should dye.

If the Lord of the Ascendant be in the 7th, in the Sign of the 7th, combust from the Lord of the 7th, he was hurt by his Wife, for he lay with her in an ill time, and over-heat himself, and took cold thereon.

If the Lord of the 7th be unfortunate, or ♂ in ☍ ♃ in the Ascendant, and ♀ in the 7th or Sign of the 7th, not remote, or in the 6th in the Sign of the 7th in ♍, yet the Sickness shall be lighted by the presence of the Physitian, and the Sick shall have joy of his presence.

If the Lord of the 7th be in ☌, ✶, or △, or going to the ☌, ✶, or △ of the Lord of the Ascendant in the time of the Question, Then undoubetdly the Sick shall be in love with the Physitian, and favour him greatly; And in such a Question fear not to go to the Sick: But if ♃ in such a case be Lord of the 7th, then the Sick will make very much of thee.

Bur if ♂, ♀, ☉, ☿, or ♄ be Lord of the 7th, In such a Case the Sick will love thee, if thou makest tryal thereof.

But if the Lord of the Ascendant be an inferiour Planet, and do behold the Lord of the 7th by ☌, ✶, or △, then the Physitian will love her, and do the best that lies in him to do for her.

If Venus be Lady of the 7th, and do apply to the ☌, ✶, or △, of ♂, the Sick Woman will love the company of the Physitian, and be loth to let him depart, and will do what she may for him.

If ☿ be Lord of the 7th, and ♃ Lord of the Ascendant, Idem; especially if ☿ be in the Houses of ♀ or ♂, or in ♑.

If ☉ be Lord of the 7th, and apply to ☌, ✶, or △, of ♄, Idem.; the Sick will be loath to let the Physitian depart.

If ☽ be Lady of the 7th, and apply to ♄ by ☌, ✶, or △, Idem.

If ♀ be Lady of the 7th in ♒, and apply to the △ of ♄ in ♎, and the ☽ separate from ♄, and Apply to ♀, Idem.

If ♂ be Lord of the 7th in ♉, and in the Ascendant not remote, and the ☽ in ♉ in the Ascendant, and apply to ♄ Lord of the 10th in the 6th, and causes the Infirmity, and separate from ♀, Then it is a sign that the Body of the Party is infected by her Husband, and her Body is corrupted, and afflicted with Melancholy, and the Finger of God is on the Party, and the Disease will stand long on her, and no Medicine will do her good, till the Lord withdraw his punishment from her.

If the Lord of the 7th be going to combustion, it's a sign the Party will wax weaker and weaker, and sicker: If the Lord of the 7th be in his fall or detriment, the Sickness will increase, and the Party will wax weaker and weaker.

If the Lord of the 7th be in a fixed Sign in his detriment or fall, though he be in Angle, the Sickness will increase. If the Lord of the 7th be Retrograde, and in a Cadent House, either in his fall or combust, the Sickness will increase.

Of the Fourth House.

The Fourth House and the Lord signifie the end of every Sickness, and of every Cure one takes in hand and the Effects of the Medicines that he will use, and the Apothocary.

If the 4th House and his Lord be fortunate either by the Presence or Aspect of any good and fortunate Planet, Then it signifieth a good and profitable end, and commendable, and the Medicines shall be good and effectual.

If the 4th House and his Lord be unfortunate, either by the bodily presence ♂ or Aspect of some Evil & Unfortunate, Combust or Retrograde Planet, Then it signifieth an ill end, with Sorrow and Infamy, and brawling; or else the Medicine shall be Naught, or of No Value or Virtue.

If ☋ be in the 4th, not remote, but within 5 Degrees of the Cusp, The end will be evil, and of much Disliking; especially the Patient will mislike of the Apothecary.

If the Lord of the House of the Moon be Combust, The end will be evil, especially if the Lord of the House of the Moon, as ♀ be Combust in her own House, viz. In ♉, and ☽ in ♎ 3.

The Lord of the 4th in the 10th in his own House, or Exaltation, free from Saturn and Mars, signifieth a good End.

And it is generally seen, That as often as you find ♈, ♉, ♍, or ♑, or any of these in the Ascendant of the 4th House the Party is given to Vomit more or less; especially if ♑ be in the 4th, and ♄ in ♍, or the ☽ in ♉, ♍, or ♑: for when ♈, ♉, ♑, ♍, are in the Ascendant of the 4th, and the Lord of the 4th in one of the said Signs also, Then the Party is inclined to Vomit very much.

If ♈, ♉, ♍, or ♑, be in the 4th, and the Lord of the

4th in ♊, ♎, or ♒, Then the Party shall strain to Vomit up Blood.

If ♈, ♉, ♑, ♍, be in the 4th, and the Lord of the 4th in ♋, ♏, or ♓, he Vomiteth up much Flegme and Water.

If ♈, ♉, ♍, ♑, be in the 4th, and the Lord of the 4th in ♈, ♌, or ♐, he Vomiteth up much Choler.

If ♈, ♉, ♍, or ♑: he Vomiteth up much Melancholy.

If ♒ be in the 4th, and ♄ in ♍ in the 10th, Then the Terms be congealed in the Stomach of the Party, and the Party is like to Vomit, and to Swoon, especially if the ☽ separate from ♃, and apply to ♄.

If ♋ be in the 4th, and the ☽ in ♈ or ♉, in the 12th, the Party is given oft to Vomit.

If ♊ be in the 4th, and ☿ in ♐, the party doth not Vomit nor Scour, but is much troubled in the Head with Wind, and Adult Choler.

Of the Sixth House.

The Sixth house and his Lord in the last Half of every Moon, that is, from the just point of the Full, to the just point of the Change, shall signifie the Cause of the Disease, whether it doth come of Blood, Melancholy, Flegm or Choler; or of Humours mix't, as of Choler and Flegm, or of Blood and Choler, or of Melancholy and Choler, and which of these Humours have Dominion, and predominate; and in what Degree the Humours predominate be, either in the first, second, third or fourth degree; as if ♄ be Lord of the 6th, in such a case, and in ♌; Then the Disease comes of think yellow Choler, and Melancholy, and a superficial Flegm therewith mixed, which do cause strong Fevers, the Piles and Hemorrhoids, as if he be Lord of the 6th House or 12th House: for as the Lord of the 6th House in the last part of the Moon doth shew the Disease and Cause thereof, So doth the Lord of the 12th House from the Change unto the Degree of the Full Moon: This is a Secret, whereby we give Judgment of Diseases, and the Causes in his Degree, of every Disease and Sick person, not yet observ'd by any before this; Of which I will not bragg, but give God thanks, who hath so far revealed to me, as to make ne instrumental in this most profitable Science: for from thses Grounds and Reasons, which here I divulge to the World, have I, to the Wonder of the World, given Jusgments of the Sick and their Distempers, without either the sight of them or their Urine. All praise to God onely.

If there be in 6th House a moveable Sign, Then the Disease will be quickly removed, or have an End, and the Patient shall quickly be whole.

If in the 6th, there be a Common Sign, It signifieth the incertainty of the Disease, and that is not always at one stay, but the Party is sometimes ill, sometimes better, and sometimes worse; and is often troubled, but it may be remedied in a reasonable time.

If in the 6th be a fixed Sign, It signifieth countinuance of the Distemper, and long Sickness; and it hath been long, and will be long, and always after one order: and if the last Degree of a Fixed Sign, be on the Cusp of the 6th House, It is a sign that the Disease begins to draw toward an end, and will change to better or worse; & e contra.

If the Lord of the 6th be in the Ascendant, or so infortunate the Ascendant or his Lord by ♂ or Aspect, It signifieth that the Party shall have great Sickness, by the Natural Course and Influence of the Heavens; and if the Lord of the 6th be a fixed Sign, It will indure the longer, if in a moveable Sign, it will end the sooner.

If the Lord of the Ascendant be in the 6th House, Then the Disease is not Natural, but the Party hath come by it by ill Dyet, or Evil order, or by Accident; for he is the cause of his own Sickness.

If the Lord of the 9th be in the 6th, then the Sickness is caused by Witches, Witchcraft, Magick, or by some such Extraordinary means.

If the Lord of the 9th be in the 7th, whosoever be Lord of the 9th, and the ☽ apply to ♄, the Party is inchanted, bewitched, or fore-spoken, as some call it.

If ♄ be Lord of the 6th, It signifieth the Disease to be of longer continuance, and that it will be longer before the Party be whole, than if ♃, ♂, or the ☉ were Lords of the 6th House; for the highest Planet signifies the longer time, and the inferious, lesser time, Except ♄ be also Lord of the 7th House, and in ♋ or ♌ in the 12th House, then he shall soon recover.

If the Lord of the 6th be in the 12th, in the Sign Ascending, then it signifieth that the Disease came by Nature, and the Influence of the Heavens when the Party was born; and that the Party hath has a spice of this Distemper ever since the Birth or Childhood, and is now produced by some apt Direction or Transit; The same if ♄ Lord of the 6th be in ♌ in the 10th House.

If the Lord of the 6th be also Lord of the Hour, and in the 11th Combust, as ♂ in ♍, Then it seems the Party came by her Sickness by longing, or some ill Dyet, at some place where she was merry amongst her Friends.

If ♂ be Lord of the Ascendant in the 6th, Then he came by his Disease by fretting, or surfeiting, or by a squat or blow.

If Venus, then by Lust and Lechery, and too much Carnal Copulation. If the ☽, by taking Cold. If ♃, by over-much Laughing, or Mirth or Sadness, Joy, or Cold upon Heat.

If the ☉, then by Pride and Vain-glory. If ☿, then by Fear. If ♄ be Lord of the Ascendant and in the 6th, then the Party got his Disease by Fear, Thought and Heaviness, and Cold taking.

If the Lord of the 7th or 6th, or both be in the Ascendant, or in the Sign of the Ascendant, falling into the 12th House, though it be ♄, and the ☽ separate from the Lord of the 10th, and apply to the Lord of the 7th, being in the Ascendant as aforesaid, Then shall the Party be Cured of the Infirmity, by the Grace of God, and good words of the Physitian, without taking anything else of Medicines; and especially if ♃ be in the 7th in the time of the Question; for whensoever the ☽ goeth from the Lord of the 10th House to the Lord of the 7th, It signifieth Favour and Vertue from God, and Health from God to the Sick.

If the Lord of the 6th be in the 11th, and the Lord of the 12th in the New Moon in the 2d, and the ☽ separate from the Lord of the 12th House, and apply to the Lord of the Ascendant, or to a Planet that is going to ☌ with the Lord of the Ascendant, the Disease shall quickly alter, and leave the Party, and little Physick shall serve.

The Lord of the 6th in the 10th in his own House or other Dignities, as ♃ Lord of the 6th in ♓ in ☌ with ♀ in her Exaltation, signifieth the Disease is very strong, and increaseth more and more.

When the Lord of the 6th is stronger than the Lord of the Ascendant, then is the Disease stronger than Nature is able to resist, and the Disease doth increase.

The Lord of the 6th in the 9th, and Lord of the Ascendant apply to ♀ in the 10th; ☽ being Lady of the Ascendant. Or with the Lord of the Ascendant, the Sick shall be soon whole.

The ☽ Lady of the 12th applying to the ☉, and the ☉ in a ⚹ of ♃ in ♓, causeth a Consumptive Rheum.

If the Lord of the 6th be in ☌, □, or ☍, of ♀ in ♉, then the Muscles of his Throat are sore, and he cannot swallow.

And look always if the Lord of the 6th be in ☌, or Apply to any other Planet, or any other Planet Apply to him; if it be so, then shall there be some Disease or Grief in the place under that Sign wherein that Planet is that beholdeth the Lord of the 6th House or 12th House, being signifier; and the Grief or Disease shall be Caused by the Sign wherein the Lord of the 6th is, and by the Humour also signified by the Planet that aspects the Lord of the 6th House or 12th. As ♄ in ♌ Lord of the 6th, and Signifier, at a □ to ♀ in ♉, and the ☽ applying to ♄, the Disease is caused of 3 parts of Melancholy, and 3 parts of Choler, and the Party is hot and dry, and hath taken Thought; now ♀ in ♉ Augmenteth the Melancholy Humour.

If the Lord of the 6th be weaker than the Lord of the Ascendant, then it is a sign that Nature is stronger than the Disease, and will quickly expel the Distemper.

If the Lord of the 6th be in his Exaltation, or strong, or where he hath any Dignities, It signifieth the Disease is strong.

If he be coming to any Dignity, the Disease will increase, if he be falling from his Dignity, the Disease will fall and decrease.

If the Lord of the 6th be in a succedant House, in such a case the Distemper groweth; if in a cadent House, it falleth; if in an Angle, it is strong.

The ☽ Lady of the 6th in ♉ in the second House, the Disease will increase and be stronger, for it is not yet at the highest.

To know by what means the Party may be Cured, and with what to begin.

Zael, and the rest of his Followers, the old Astrological Philosophers and Physitians, did give the Ascendant for the Physitian, and the 7th House for the Sickness because the Physitian is enemy to the Sickness, and Sickness is enemy unto Health.

And therefore he saith, if the first House be fortunate, by the presence or an aspect of a fortunate Planet, or the Lord of the Ascendant fortunate, then shall the Physitian do good, and be profitable to the Sick.

Also he giveth the 10th House for the sick Person, to know whereby whether he will be ruled, and be obedient to the Physitian or no, according as the 10th House is fortunate or infortunate.

He giveth the 7th House for the Sickness, to know thereby whether the Sickness shall be long or short, or whether it shall be tedious or no, or whether it should be great or little. If there were a fortunate Planet in the 7th House, then the Sick shall be soon well; if there be an infortunate Planet, then it will be longer ere he be well, and the Sickness shall augment and increase.

He giveth the 4th House also for the Medicine, whether it shall be profitable to the Sick or no. If there be a good and fortunate Planet in the 4th House, then the Medicine shall do much good, & e contra; If there be a malevolent Planet that hath no dignity, neither house, exaltation term, triplicity, nor face, then the Medicine shall do no good, but rather harm than good. If there be no Planet in the 4th, then look to the Lord of the 4th, what state he is in; if he be in his house or exaltation, and in an

Angle, thou shalt do him good, and they Medicine shall be profitable unto him.

This Method of the Ancients is contradicted by our Modern Astrologers, who give the first House for the sick Person, the 6th House for the Disease, the 7th House for the Physitian, and the 10th for the Medicine, and from the 4th they take the end and success of all their operations. This I should rather assent to, because now most in use, but that I in my practice have oft experienced both; and I apprehend that many formerly in observing Zael's method, have been fortunate and successful, and given good account of the Disease, and all Accidents; and therefore in the ensuing I shall follow that method; and what is spoke of one, may readily be apprended of the other; as wherein I say the Ascendant for the Physitian, you may understand the 7th; and as I take the Disease from the 10th, you may understand the 6th; and whereas Zael takes the Medicine from the 4th House, you may understand the 10th. By thus proceeding, you may make these ensuing Rules applicable to both methods. But to proceed.

If the Moon be Lady of the 4th, and in ♉ in the Ascendant remote, and do apply to the ☉ in the 12th, thou shalt do him good with much ado in the end, and thou shalt have a good beginning, and the Patient shall find ease.

But if the Lord of the 10th be ♄, and infortunate, as in ♍℞ in the 6th, she shall mis-diet her self, and take cold, and be sick again, as bad as ever she was.

If there be in the 4th ♂, ♄, or ☋, or any infortunate Planet, if he be remote from the Angle, he hurteth not, neither (as to his efficacy) shall you account him to be in the 4th; but look to the Lord of the 4th House, if the Lord of the 4th be then fortunate, and in an Angle, the Medicine shall do him good; if ♀ in such a case be Lady of the 4th, and in the 7th in ♒ with ♃, the Medicine shall do him good, although ♄ be in the Ascendant not remote, and ♂ in the 4th remote, and ☋ in the 4th not remote.

Luna in the 4th in ♑ not remote, though ♄ be Lord of the 4th in ♌ in the 11th House, yet the Medicine shall do him good.

Mars Lord of the 6th in the Ascendant in ♋, the Disease is caused naturally by constellation of his Birth, and it is not good to meddle with him, especially if the Lord of the Ascendant be ☿, retrograde in ♉ in the 11th House, though the ☽ do apply to ☿, for he will quickly give thee off.

If ♄ be Lord of the 10th, and in ♍℞ in the 4th, at a □ to the Ascendant, although the ☽ be in the 10th in ♓, the Sick will not be ruled, but will give thee over.

♄ in the 4th ℞ or unfortunate, the Medicine will do him little good, for it is not well compounded.

If thou wilt cleanse, sweeten, or purge the Blood of Water, or other gross humours, and wilt cleanse and purifie the Blood, and increase good Blood, do it when the ☽ and Lord of the Ascendant are in Airy Signs, and do it in the hour of ♃.

But if thou wilt diminish the quantity of good Blood, to infect it with ill humours and Melancholy, then do it when the ☽ and Lord of the Ascendant are in ♉, ♍, or ♑ unfortunate; if with Choler, then when the ☽ and Lord of the Ascendant are in ♈, ♌, or ♐, applying to ♂, and a Fiery Sign ascending.

If thou wilt induce a Dropsie, and infect his Blood with Water, then let him blood, or give him a Drink to that intent, when the Lord of the Ascendant and the ☽ be in ♋, ♏, or ♓, in the increase of the ☽, and when she applies to ♀, and let ♋, ♏, or ♓ be in the Ascendant, and do it in the hour of the ☽ or ♀, and so likewise of the rest of the Humours.

If thou wilt increase Choler in the Body, do it when the ☽ and Lord of the Ascendent are in ♈, ♌, or ♐, and one of them Aspecting, applying to ♂ or the ☉.

If thou wilt destroy Choler, do it when the ☽ and the Lord of the Ascendant are in ♋, ♏, or ♓, and one of them in the Ascendant, and in the hour of the ☽ or ♀, and let the ☽ apply to ♀.

The 11th House doth always signifie the Medicines, and the way, how and by what means to cure the Party, if he be to be cured; as thus, in Physick and Chirurgery, The Sign ascending in the 11th House, shall always signifie the beginning of the Cure, and what is to be done at first; as thus,

If there be in the 11th House a Fiery Sign, as ♈, ♌, or ♐, which are hot and dry, consider of them which it is, and whether it be for Chirurgery, in some manual external application, or some Physical internal operation.

If it be for some matter in Chirurgery, and ♈ be in the 11th House, which is the House of ♂, then it signifies Cutting, Amputation, or some incition to be made, or opening of a Vein at first, or letting of blood; especially if ♂ be in ♊, ♎, or ♒; and if ♌ be in the 11th, then by laying some hot Pultis thereto to digest it, or by Boxing.

And generally if the Lord of the 11th be in a Fiery Sign, then by Cutting, Boxing, or by putting some Corrosive or such like thereto, as Mercury, Precipitate, &c.

But id it be for some inward cause or matter of Physick, then give the Party something that is hot and dry, attractive, and expulsive to make him vomit, or to go to stool, as the Root of Daffodil.

If ☿ be Lord of the 11th in ♌, then give him a Vomit of Daffodil; if ♂ be Lord of the 11th in ♉, then give him Manna, Cassia, Tamarinds, Borage, Water of Violets, of Nightshade, to allay the Heat.

If there be in the 11th House a Watery Sign, as ♋, ♏, or ♓, then give them digestives, and purge, and use good diet, and use outward applications, to help the retentive faculty.

If ♓ be in the 11th House, and ♃ in ♈, then give him some digestive, and let him blood.

If ♋ be in the 11th House and the ☽ in ♐, then give him some digestive to thin the Blood, and forthwith let him blood.

If ♋ be in the 11th, and the ☽ in ♎, digest, and the purge strongly, and vomit withal.

If ♈ be in the 11th, and ♂ in ♊, then give some digestive Julep, to cool the Body, and to strengthen the Virtue attractive, and let them be quiet without fretting, or being angry, and use a good diet; good if the ☽ apply to ♃.

If ♈ be in the 11th, and ♂, in ♊, and the ☽ apply to ♀ in ♉, give him a Glister, and after purge him and let him blood.

If there be any Airy Sign in the 11th, as ♊, ♎, or ♒, then in the beginning of the Cure, it is best to ratifie and strengthen the Liver, by helping the Virtue digestive by hot and moist digestives.

If in the 11th be a Terrene Sign as ♉, ♍, or ♑, then by administering of Vomits, and by digesting of Melancholy, and by helping the Virtue expulsive.

Then for the second part of the Cure, look to the Lord of the 11th, and to the Sign he is in, as I have said before.

If the Lord of the 11th be in an Earthly Sign, as ♉, ♍, ♑, then shall you give him a vomit, and purge or sweat him.

If the Lord of the 11th be in tan Airy Sign, as in ♊, ♎, or ♒, then shall you have respect to the Blood to cool it, if it be too hot, or to cleanse and scowr it, if it be foul and fæculent, according to the nature of the Planet; for if it be ♀ in ♊, ♎, or ♒, then shall you cool the Blood, and let the Party go into an open and fresh Air, and be merry.

If ♃ be in ♊, ♎, or ♒, then heat the Blood, and let him have fresh Air.

If ♄ be Lord of the 11th, and be in ♊, ♎, or ♒, then cool and moisten the Blood.

If ☿ be in ♐, then give him Sallads of cool Herbs, cold Syrups, and cold Waters.

Of Compounding of Medicines, when and at what time they should properly be compounded and made.

Understand that in Mans Body be four Natural Faculties, working to the Health thereof, viz. The Attractive Power, the Retentive, the Digestive, and the Expulsive.

The Attractive Faculty is governed by ♂ and ♀, and operateth by Heat and Dryness; and therefore such Medicines as are made to comfort the Virtue Attractive, should be made, and also given and received, when the ☽ is in some Attractive Sign, as ♈, ♌, ♐, when the ☽ hath no impediment, and doth apply to ♂, ☉, or ♀, by ✶ or △, or to the ☌ of ♀, and when ♈, ♌, or ♐ are in the Ascendant, and ♀ in the 6th House.

The Vertue Retentive is governed by ♄, and worketh by Cold and Dryness; and therefore such Medicines as are made to comfort the Virtue Retentive, should be made, given and received, when the ☽ is in a Retentive Sign, as in ♉, ♍, or ♑, when the Moon hath no impediment, and doth apply to the ✶ or △ of ♄ or ☿, and when ♉, ♍, or ♑ are in the Ascendant, and ♄ or ☿ in the 6th, especially ☿, for Nature is bettered in his own nature and kind, and every like will have like, or when ♄ is in an Angle and strong.

The Virtue Digestive is governed by ♃, and worketh by Heat and Moisture; and therefore such Medicines as should comfort the Virtue Digestive, should be made, and also given and taken, when the ☽ is in a Digestive Sign, as in ♊, ♎, or ♒ and when the ☽ is free from impediment, and doth apply to ♃, and when ♊, ♎, or ♒, is in the Ascendant, and ♃ in the 6th House.

The Virtue Expulsive is governed by the ☽, and worketh by Cold and Moisture; and therefore such Medicines as should comfort the Virtue Expulsive, when the Patient is weak in Body, and cannot sweat or vomit, or go to stool, should be made, given and taken, when the ☽ is in an Expulsive Sign, as in ♋, ♏, or ♓, and when the ☽ hath no impediments, and doth apply to ♀, ♋, ♏, or ♓ in the Ascendant, and the ☽ or ♀ in the 6th, in the composition of the Medicine. And this is the proper method of way and times to make Medicines.

For every Medicine receiveth his Virtue more or less, according to the position and disposition of the Heavens, at the very instant when it is made, as I have often proved, (and the greatest Antagonist in the World must herein be convinc'd, if he will let patience act his reason.) For if the Virtue Digestive be weak, and thou wouldest make a proper Medicine to strengthen and help the same, then diligently observe when the ☽ comes into Digestive Signs, and Aspects ♃, and then compound thy Medicine as aforesaid.

But if thou make thy Medicine, the ☽ being in a Retentive Sign, applying to ♄, ♂, ☉, or ☿, it will do no good; therefore if thou wilt make a speedy Cure, do it in a convenient time as aforesaid.

Guide Counselleth, in every Medicine thou makest, thou shouldest put ♃ in the 6th, or at least in the 7th House, but if in the 6th, it is better; and whosoever shall give a Medicine to anyone, ♃ being then at that instant in the 6th House, the Medicine shall profit very much.

But sometimes it falls out, that the Physician cannot posite ♃ in the 6th House, when he would compound his Medicine, for he oft-times comes into the 6th very late, or very early in the morning, sometimes at 1, 2, 3, 4, 5, or 6 of the Clock, so that it is tedious for one always to watch the hour; and therefore, in matters of Necessity, when I could not put ♃ in the 6th, I did put ♀ in the 6th or 7th, when I did compound my Medicine, in stead of ♃, when she was free from combustion, and the noxious Rays or Aspects of ♄ or ♂, and direct, occidental, and in her dignities; or else I did put some other fortunate Planet in the 6th, but I did never put ♄ or ♂ in the 6th House, except there were ♃ or ♀ with them in the 6th, or some other Planet that was in his dignities, and strong.

For ♃ is naturally benevolent, good and friendly to Man, and is Fortuna Major, and ♀ is Fortuna Minor, and ☿ and ☉ are indifferent, but ♄ and ♂ are enemies to the Nature of Man and his Health, and ♄ is Infortuna Major, and ♂ Infortuna Minor.

And always I hold it good to compound Medicines, when ♃ or ♀ is in the 6th House, and the ☽ applying by ✶ or △ to the Lord of the Ascendant.

Hence is to be noted, That through the Negligence of the Physitian, in not regarding or taking heed of these things aforesaid, before he begins to work, oftentimes and most commonly his labour is in vain, and to none effect to the Sick, because the Virtue of Heaven, and the heavenly Bodies do work against him.

As for Example.

If you would make a Medicine confortative, for expulsion of Humours, as in giving a Laxative Medicine, the Virtue of the Heavens, and Influence of the ☽, must needs oft-times be against thee, (if thou compoundest thy Medicine by chance, without election of a proper time) and affect the Patients Body contrary to thy intention, by virtue of Retention, and that is because you did not look before to the influence of the ☽, what she took of the Cœlestial Bodies above, that is to say, of the Planets and twelve Signs. And therefore whosoever will give Medicine properly and naturally, he must take heed that the Influence of the Sign that the ☽ is in, do accord or agree with the Virtue of that he laboureth upon, and then he shall not err.

So be sure you make your Confection or Medicine in its proper Sympathetick Constellation, and then it must needs work Naturally, because of the Virtue that it receiveth in the time of its making by the Influence of the Heavens; and this is without doubt chiefly to be noted and observed.

For Thebith affirms, That look what Composition and Medicine thou dost make under the Constellation or course of Heaven, it receiveth as great Virtue of the Influence of Heaven, being made in due time, as it doth of the Confection or Medicine it self; as Laxative and Expulsive Medicines ought to be compounded, the ☽ being in ♋, ♏, or ♓, and one of these Signs Ascending, and the ☽ strong, as is aforesaid, not aspecting ♃.

Also it behoveth a Physitian to have consideration of what Planet ruleth that Humour, which he intendeth to expel, and to make that Planet Lord of the 6th House, and put him in a place he hath no dignities or power, and then shall not that Planet overcome or hinder the working of that Medicine.

If a Man will avoid and purge Melancholy, which Saturn increaseth and ruleth, he must see that ♄ be weak of power and strength, as in ♋ or in ♈, and in the 3d., 9th or 12th House, or removed from Angles, and if you put ♑ in the 6th House, ♄ being in ♋, you may put him in the 12th House, or in the 11th for a shift, and let the ☽ be strong.

If you will avoid or purge Choler, see that ♂ be weak that governs that humour, in his fall or detriment, or in some cadent House where he hath no dignity.

If you would rectifie and purge the Blood, then see that ♃ be weak of power and operation, for he ruleth the Blood, yea and let the ☉ and ♀ be also weak, or removed from Angles, because they do participate with ♃ in that behalf.

If you will avoid and purge Flegm, then see that the ☽ be weak of power and debilitated, for she governeth that humour; therefore when you would purge Flegm, it is better in mine opinion to put the ☽ in ♏ or ♓ than in ♋, but if the ☽ be in ♋, then let her aspect the ☉ by ✶ or △, or ☍, and purge with an Electuary.

If she be in ♏, then let her aspect the ☉ or ♂ by ✶ or △, and do it by a Potion.

If she be in ♓, then let her apply to the ☉ or ♂ by △ or ✶, and do it with Pills.

And here note, that there is no Medicine laxative or purging to be given (after the Rules of the Ancients) when the ☽ is in ☌ with ♃.

And Haly telleth the Cause why, saying, that the working of the Medicine is not wholesome that is ministred in that time, for because of drawing of Humours, for by that it destroyeth the natural effects of the Body, the which is the 4th part of the effect of the Medicine.

Things cold and dry, diminishing natural Heat, and hindring natural Digestion, are assigned to ♄.

Things that do thicken and manifestly delay Heat naturally are given to ☿.

Things that heat and over-heat the Body and Blood, as in bitter things, making very hot and angry, are attributed to Mars.

Things having a glewy property, and being ministred to wounds, have power to joyn the orifice together, and keep back Ulcers healing, and are attributed to ♃ and ♀.

But the ☽ must be considered, according to the place she is in, and according to the Planet she applieth to: for if she be in a good House or good Sign, with a fortunate, good, or strong Planet, she betokeneth good; if with an evil Planet, or evil Sign, or House, or Aspect, she betokeneth evil.

Wherefore if thou mean to heal Diseases of any inward or outward grief, thou must consider the time when the Patient first complained, or when the Disease first took him, or when he first took his bed. If none of these may be found, then consider the instant time when his Urine is brought to thee, or when any cometh to thee to ask of his Disease, or when thou first hearest of it, and erect thy Figure for that instant time.

And then observe whether the ☽ do decrease or increase in light, and from whom she separates, and to whom she applies next; for if she apply to an evil Planet, or to a Planet weak, combust, or infortunate, it betokeneth the Disease doth tend to worse; but if to a good Planet and strong, so that he be not Domina mortis, or infortunate, it betokeneth good, and the Disease may be amended.

If the ☽ be increasing in light, and go swiftly to the Aspect of ♂, it betokeneth the Disease to wax grievous and dangerous.

But if she apply to a good Planet also at the same time, then although the Sick be much tormented, and in despair, yet he shall recover his health, so that they be not Lord of the House of death, nor of the House of infirmities.

If the ☽ be decreasing in light, and applying to the □, ☍, or ☌ of ♄, it will be mortal and evil, and as long as the ☽ doth increase in light and motion (applying as aforesaid) so long will the Disease wax and increase.

And when the ☽ beginneth to be Tarda motn, decreasing in her motion, the the Disease will decrease and change into better and more ease; bit so long as she is velox motu, swift in course, the Disease will increase, and be more tedious and painful to the Sick.

Those that are sick of the Disease of ♄ or ☿, are slow, dull, and astonisht, and are scarce able to draw their grieved members to them for cold, for their powers are weakened through obstructions, yet by reason of the pricking and biting quality of the Disease, they do wake themselves by little and little, they oft dream of fearful things, dreadful visions they think they see, and seem to desire garments of silk, and of sad and fearful colours, and much desire natural heat; they rejoyce to be in darkness, or in dark desolate places, oft sighing, are fearful, dull and heavy, have all the signs and symptoms of Melancholy, with trembling and fearfulness; the Pulse being feeble, faint and slow, doth signifie that all the upper parts of the Body are cold and dry.

There is need in curing this Disease, of hot and moist Medicines, not binding.

Of Giving of Medicine.

Haly saith, That sweet Savours do greatly comfort Nature, yet causeth oft-times the letting of the operations of Medicine, therefore in administring of divers Medicines, the Physitian will make the Patient smell to bitter things and stinking.

Ptolomeus saith, That the receiving of Medicine is good at such a time as the ☽ is in ♋, ♏, or ♓, and if the Lord of that Sign be under the Earth, then it is wholesome and good to take Physick.

And if the Lord of the House of the ☽, or Lord of the Ascendant, do apply to a Planet in the mid-Heaven, at the giving of the Medicine, then shall be vomit and cast up the Medicine again. And Haly, saith, That it is good also and most wholesome to give a Drink in a cold and moist Triplicity, as in ♋, ♏, or ♓, to dissolve the Sickness, for at such a time the Medicine entring into the Body of the Sick, findeth every part well and naturally disposed with moisture, which is his natural kind to work upon.

And therefore when the Lord of the Ascendant is joyned with a Planet under the Earth, the Sickness shall remove to the lower parts, notwithstanding the inward strength of the Body is not hot, and so this manner of working shall be good.

But if you give a Medicine when the Lord of the Ascendant is above the Earth, then he shall lett the operation of the Medicine in its kind, and will lett the operation of the Medicine downward, and cause him to vomit and work upward, or else it will rest and lye still in the stomach, and there it will putrifie, and grow hurtful to Nature and to the Body.

And furthermore I am of this opinion, That if the Lord of the Ascendant be between the 10th and the 4th House descending, the Medicine shall work the better downward, and work more kindly, driving the Disease downward; but if he be from the 4th House, to the 10th House ascending, it will lett the operation of the Medicine much in purging.

Again, If the ☽ be in ♏ descending in the 7th House, and apply to ♂ by □, he being in the 11th or 10th, it hindreth the operation of the Purge, and makes it work slowly, and give but a few stools.

If the ☽ be under the Earth, and apply to the Lord of the Ascendant by a ✶ or △, being above the Earth, and a watry Sign being in the Ascendant, the Medicine will work downward strongly, and upward also.

The ☽ in ♌, it is not good to give Vomit nor Purge, for a Medicine given in such a time is not good for the Stomach, nor for the Throat, and it maketh the receiver to cast up blood, and in this Sign it is not good to let blood.

When the ☽ is in ♈, ♉, or ♑, give no Purge nor laxative Medicine to work downwards, but Vomits, and such Medicines as should work altogether upwards.

Also if you will give Medicines in due manner, you must look that the Moon and the Lord of the Ascendant so accord, and be in Signs of like triplicities, that neither of them be impeded, nor one of them lett not the other, and especially that your Ascendant be not contrary to the ☽, nor to the 10th House, for these three must of neccissity be well dispos'd, and accord in one disposition.

Also you ought to take heed you give no Medicine when the ☽ is in any evil Aspect, as a □, ☐, or ☍ of ♄ or ♂, and especially when the ☽ is in ♓.

And if the ☽ be in a moveable Sign in the beginning of a Sickness, the same Sickness shall be easie to remove by Medicine; and so if the ☽ be in a fixed Sign, the Sickness shall stand long on him; and if the ☽ be in a common Sign, the Sickness shall come and go, and have its vicissitude and change, being sometimes more and sometimes less, and not continue always at one stay.

The ☽ in ♋, applying to ♀ in ♑ by ☍ in the Second, or in the Ascendant, of ♐ be in the Ascendent, give no Purge to purge Melancholy or Choler, for it will not work, especially if it be in Winter, or in the fall of the Leaf, of the Weather be cold, or a Frost, or the Sky clear, as in November; for I have given to many at that time, and they never had above one stool.

And note this for a general Rule, Let not ♃ at any time be Lord of the Ascendant in the administring of a Purge, nor in ☌ or Aspect of the ☽, nor ♐ in the Ascendant, nor ♃ in the Ascendant, nor beholding the Ascendant, for all this destroys the working of a Purge, and causeth it not to work, or to come upward, and so to be of no effect.

For I have proved it, and have given a Purge when the ☽ hath applied to ♃, and ♐ hath been in the Ascendant, and the Party hath vomited to up again, and hath had but two stools, yet the Purge hath been very strong, and I have known others have done the same, which puts the great Physitians (ignorant of this Learning) oft-times to a stand with admiration, when their Physick crosseth their intentions, by which you may see they know not what they do.

I have given a Patient a Preparative to drink, that hath been delicate and pleasing, when ♑ hath been in the Ascendant, and ♄ hath been in ♍℞ in the 8th, and the ☽ hath been in ♓, applying to a ☌ of ♃ in the 2nd, and the Party hath presently vomited it up again.

If the Lord of the Ascendant be Retrograde, and the ☽ in ☌ or Aspect with ♃ in ♋, ♏, or ♓, the Party will vomit it up again.

Give no Purgative Medicine to any Woman when the ☽ is in ♍, applying to ☌ in ♉, and ♑ in the Ascendant, and ♄ in ♍℞, received of ☿ in ♑; for it will not work on the Party, but breed extream pain in their Bellies and Stomach, with torments and troubling of the Bowels, for I my self have given two Purges to several Woman, to purge Choler and Melancholy, and to force the Menstrues down withal, and neither of them did work, and yet they were strong Purges, and both of them had had exceeding great pains in the Belly and Stomach, and one of them did vomit it up within two hours after; but I gave a Purge to a Man the same morning, ♐ being in the Ascendant, and it wrought well without any pain.

Give no Purge to vomit withal when the ☽ is in ♋, going to the ☌ of ♂ in ♋, ♂ being Lord of the 6th in the Ascendant, and ♊ in the Ascendant, and the ☽ going from ☿ to ♂, ☿ being

Retrograde in ♉ in the 11th, or combust, going from the ☉; and it is worse if ☿ apply to the ☉, for then it signifieth great Sickness, and that the Vomit will lodge in the Stomach and trouble the Party very much and in retching to vomit the Party will burst some Vein in the Stomach, and will be sick with it in peril of death.

Matrix.

Understand that the Matrix belongeth to ♀ and ♎, and the menstrual Blood, Flowers, Terms, and Whites of Women, belong unto the ☽ and ♏, the Sperm and Seed of Man and Woman, and the course of Seed doth belong unto Mars.

The Testicles of Man and Woman, and the Vulva of a Woman and Secrets of Man, belong to ♀, and the Reins of the Back, and Bottom of the Belly, and Navel, with the Spina dorsi.

Also understand for the curing of these Members and places, if they are amiss, and how and by what means they are to be cured.

Note that any afflicted or sick Member of the Body is best comforted and cured when as the same Sign as governeth the said Member that is so grieved, be free from evil Planets and from their infortunate Beams and Aspects, that is, when no malignant Planet, doth aspect that Sign by ☌, □, or ☍ at least, and when the ☽ is free from impediments, and in ☌ or aspect of a good Planet, and in the same Sign that governeth that Member. And this hath great force and virtue to comfort and cure the same Member, if the Planet that governeth the same Member, and the Ascendant of the House, be placed in a laudable disposition.

Also the Virtues Digestive, Expulsive, Retentive, Attractive, &c. do receive great comfort, when the governour of them is helped by natural means, and in the true time, and with true and natural Medicines; as in the consideration of the influence of the Heavens, and the seven Planets, is fully declared.

Ptolomy saith. The ☉ ruleth the Vital Virtue, and Jupiter with the ☽ the Natural Virtue, ☿ the Apprehensive and Animal Virtue, ♂ the Attractive and Cholerick, and ♄ with the earthy Signs, ♉, ♍, and ♑, hath the Retentive Virtue, ♃ with ♊, ♎, and

♒, hath the Digestive Virtue, and to comfort it, do it when the ☽ is in either of these Signs.

♀ with the Signs Luxurious, as ♈, ♉, ♌, ♑, and those Signs also signifie many Children, as ♋, ♏ and ♓, hath the Virtue Generative, and the faculty of the desire of Copulation.

The ☽ with ♋, ♏ or ♓, hath the Virtue Vegetative, and this faculty is best helped and comforted when the ☽ is in any of those Signs, viz. ♋, ♏, or ♓, free from impediment; and it is hindred when the ☽ is in the fiery triplicity, viz. ♈, ♌, and ♐, applying to ♂, or to ♄, by ☌, □, or ☍, being in ♈, ♌, or ♐, and so of all the rest.

But to come again to the Cure of the Diseases of the Matrix: Sometimes the Matrix is weak and full of evil Humours, and gathereth much wind, by reason of much cold Flegm and Melancholy in the Matrix, for Melancholy and Water breed much wind, and causeth the Mother by overmuch cold, and then there is little desire of Copulation.

In Curing hereof, the Physician ought to cherish and comfort the Matrix by heat, as likewise to stir up and strengthen the Virtue Digestive; and herein you ought to put ♎ in the Ascendant, and the ☽ in ♈, ♌, or ♐, applying if it may be to ♂ in ♈, ♌, ♐, or ♎ and let ♀ be strong in ♈, ♉, ♌, ♑, or ♓.

And when you would Purge the Matrix, do it in the Hour of ♂, and put ♎ in the Ascendant, with Savin Agarick, and proper Medicines, and let ♀ be free and strong, and under the Earth, or in the 3rd, 2nd, 12th, 11th, or 10th House, free from the Lord of the 6th and 8th, and let the Lord of the 6th be weak.

Note.

When thou wouldst Cure a Disease in any particular part of the Body or Member, let the ☽ be in the first House, joyned to, or aspecting fortunately a good Planet, fortunate and proper, and let the Ascendant be ♎ or ♏, and let there by no infottunate Planet in any of the Angles, neither let the ☽ in any Wife be infortunate either by Position or Aspect. But if you cannot do all this, then be sure that the ☽ be in a good Aspect of a fortunate Planet, as ♃ or ♀, and in the Sign that governeth that part of the

Body or Member that thou intendest to Cure; as if it were the Matrix, let the ☽ be in ♎, if the Cure be inward, and without humours, or any incision making.

Whether you shall Cure him or no? upon the Question of the first Figure.

If the ☽ do apply to the Lord of the 9th, whosoever be Lord of the 9th, if he be in the Ascendant, or Sign of the Ascendant, and the Lord of the Ascendant in the Ascendant, and the Lord of the 6th weak, and Lord of the 7th also weak, in his fall or detriment, and in a Cadent House; then take him in hand, for thou shalt Cure him.

But if the Lord of the 9th do aspect the ☽ by □ or ☍, as ♂ Lord of the 9th in □ to the ☽, thou shalt hardly Cure him.

If the ☽ be Lady of the 6th, in Via Combusta, in the 8th in such a case, and do apply by □ to ♂ Lord of the 9th, yet thou shalt Cure him, but with much ado.

When the Lord of the Ascendant is in the Ascendant with the Lord of the 10th, both in one Sign, it is a good Sign that there comes help from God, for to Cure the Party.

If the ☽ be Lady of the Ascendant, and apply to the Lord of the 9th, as to ♄, and the Lord of the 9th be in an Angle direct, or ♄ in ♓ in the 10th being Lord of the 10th, thou shalt Heal him of his Disease.

Take heed thou put not the Lord of the 6th in the 9th, whether he have any dignity or no, for then the Disease will trouble the Physitian, that he shall be at his wits end, and shall not know what to say or do; for if ♂ be Lord of the 6th and in the 9th, it will cause law and strife, and suspition, especially if the ☽ apply to ♂.

If ♀ be Lady of the 6th in the 9th, in her fall or detriment, though she have a term, a face, or triplicity, yet the Physitian shall have discredit and ill words, especially if the ☽ apply to ♂, though ♂ be in ♈ in the 12th.

If ☉ be Lord of the 6th and in the 9th, thou shalt have ill words in the end. And it is general, that if the Lord of the 6th be in the 9th, whosoever be Lord of the 6th, the Physitian shall leave his Cure unfinished, and shall have nothing for his pains, but ill words and anger.

Of Giving the first Medicine to the Sick.

Always take heed and be sure, that at the instant time when thou wilt minister the first Medicine or Potion, either inwardly or outwardly, or do any thing unto the Sick touching his Health, and recovery thereof, that at that instant time thses three Angles, viz. The Ascendant, the 10th and the 7th House, be free from the bodily presence of an evil Planet, and from their Aspects, viz. From ♄, ♂, and ☋, and from a Planet that is combust, retrograde, or in his fall or detriment, and let the three Angles aforesaid be fortunate by the bodily presence or aspect of some good and fortunate Planet, as of ♃, ♀, or ☊, or some Planet that is either in his House, exaltation, or some other of his dignities, and let the Lord of the Ascendant, and the second House, and his Lord be free from affliction, and be strong, and apply to fortunes, or else let there be some fortunate Planet in those places, but let the Lord of the 6th, and the 6th House be infortunate and weak, or put the Lord of the 6th in a cadent House combust, but if he be Retrograde, the Disease will come again after the Party is whole, and the weaker and the more unfortunate the Lord of the 6th is, the better is it for the Sick, and the sooner will he be whole.

Also you may put an infortunate or weak Planet in the 6th House, or no Planet at all, which is best.

Never let there any good or fortunate Planet behold the 6th House, and when thou findest the position of the Heavens even so, as aforesaid, then just at that time minister first unto the Sick, either inwardly or outwardly, as his Distemper requireth, for the whole Cure consisteth in the first administring or dressing, be it never so little or much.

And this note well for a general Rule, That if the Lord of the 6th be fortunate or strong, or in his House or exaltation, or other dignities, or in an Angle strong, or if any fortunate or strong Planet be in the 6th House, except thou leave it off and begin again, or else thou shalt be long in Curing of it, for the stronger the 6th House, or his Lord is, the stronger shall he the Infirmity be, and the longer ere Cured.

Let no Man meddle or take upon him to administer to any Man whose Pallate of his Mouth is down, or that with any Disease in his Tongue or Mouth, to minister first unto him in the House of ☿, when he is combust and Lord of the 6th House, and in the 10th House, and the ☽ apply to ☿ by any aspect; fo if he do, the Party shall lose his Speech, or some other great Harm or Inconvenience will happen to the Sick.

It seems to be a general Rule, That a Man ought not to minister to any Member or Part grieved, in the Hour of the Planet that ruleth that Member, if the same Planet be Lord of the 6th and combust, and the ☽ apply unto him, especially if the ☽ go from the ☉, or after she separateth from the Planet that Ruleth that Member, and next apply to the ☌, □, or ☍, of ♄ or ♂.

It seems very good to Administer first unto a Party, when ♃ or ♀ being free, either of them is Lord in the Ascendant, and the ☽ from some good Planet apply unto him by ☌, ✶, or △, and the Lord of the 6th House weak, and some fortune in the 7th, if it may be; but let not the Lord of the Ascendant be also Lord of the 8th nor 6th, and the ☽ apply unto them, for then it may cause Death or very long Sickness, otherwise it causeth Health.

Take heed in the first ministring or dressing, that the ☽ do not apply to the Lord of the 6th by any aspect, for that signifieth the Disease to come again after he is Cured.

Let not ♄ behold the 6th House, except he be Lord of the Ascendant, then he may behold the 6th by △ or ✶: but not by ☍, □ or Conjunction.

If ♄ be Lord of the Ascendant in ♉ Retrograde, and at a ✶ or △ to the 6th House, the ☽ being Lady of the 6th in ♑ in her fall, and in the House of the Lord of the Ascendant, the Party shall be soon whole.

If the Lord of the 6th be weak, and in the House of the Lord of the Ascendant, and in ☍ to the 6th House, and do apply to the Lord of the Ascendant, it signifieth that the Disease yieldeth to the Physitian, and the Party shall be soon well.

You may posite the Lord of the 6th, being weak or infortunate, in the 12th or 11th House, in ☍ to the 6th House, or in the 2nd, 3rd, or 5th House, or in the 8th or 9th House, whosoever be Lord of the 6th, but put not the Lord of the 6th in the 11th if it be ♃, but thou maist put ♃, ♀, pars Fortuna, or ☊ in the 7th House, not impeded, or else let pars Fortuna be joyned to the Lord of the 8th, 11th, or 2nd Houses, free from affliction and strong, for this signifieth the good success of the Physitian.

Or else you may put ♃, ♀, pars Fortuna or ☊ in the 2nd, free and strong, for it signifieth good to the Physitian.

Take heed thou put not the Lord of the 6th in the Ascendant, though it be ♃, for then the Medicine will be longer ere it work; neither put the Lord of the 6th in the 4th House, for then the Medicine will be long, before it work, or not work at all.

At thy first ministring, let not the ☽ behold ♂ by any Aspect whatsoever, though he be in ♈ or ♏, for it cuaseth either disgrace, or suspition of something not good.

You may put the ☽ at any time in the 12th, 11th, 10th, 5th, 4th, or 6th House, free from combustion, and from ♄, ♂, and ☋, being well placed, and not impeded, and it is best to use Medicines when she is in the 6th, 5th or 4th House, so that she be not Lady of the 6th House; if she be, let her be weak.

But give no Medicine at the first to a Patient, the ☽ being in the 1st, 2nd, 7th, 8th or 9th House, for it is very evil; for from the Ascendant to the 10th House, she doth increase the natural Spirits and Humours, and from the 10th House to the 7th, she doth hurt to the same Humour, and from the 7th to the 4th she doth increase it again, and maketh Humours to flow in the Body, and from the 4th to the 1st House, she doth depress and decrease the natural Humours in the Body of Man.

When thou with minister to the sick Person, or any one that is hurt, put the Lord of the artificial Hour in ♂ with the ☽ (if thou maist) strong and fortunate.

Or else let the Lord of the Hour be very strong and fortunate, and at a △ or ✶ to the Ascendant of the 7th, or to his Lord, and then thou shalt be sure by Gods help to Cure him, or else he is incurable.

If the Lord of the Ascendant be in the House or exaltation of the Lord of the 6th, and do behold the 6th House by ✶ or △, and the Lord of the 6th be weak, or in his fall, or in the House of the Lord of the Ascendant, then the Patient shall soon recover and be well.

If the Lord of the Ascendant be in the 11th, and free from evil and from combustion, and from ♄ and ♂, and be direct and strong, the Physitian shall have great praise and commendations.

But if the Lord of the Ascendant be unfortunate, he shall have dispraise, and ill will, doing the best he can.

Note.

There be four principal Diseases, whereunto almost all other Diseases may be referred.

The first, is the Leprosie, whose badges all manner of Ulcers do bear, as Itches, Scabs, Alopecia, Scurfs, Chops, Riftes, Snolness, Morphews, Ruggedness of the Skin, St. Antbonits Fire, Shingles, Dryness of the Skin, the dead Evil, Noli me tangere, and the like, all which come of Melancholy and Choler adust.

The second is the Gout, under which is comprehended the Collick, Sciatica, Podagra, Chiragra, Genugra, Gout of the Stomach, pain in the Teeth, and running Humours, the Oxice, a sharp Disease quickly dispatching a Man one way or other, returning Pains, Gouts painfully flexed, pain of the Head, and Cephalea, and Hemicrania, for all these are bred of venomous Humours, much Wind, and burnt Choler mixed with salt Flegm.

The third is the Dropsie, to the with are referred all manner of Fevers, Apostemations, Jaundices, and evil Digestion, Chilblains, Ancombs, and the like.

The fourth is the falling Evil, to which belong all Catarrhs, Rheums, Palsies, beatings and palpitation of the Heart, Cardiaca passio, Giddiness, Vertigoes, Apoplexies, Vertex, Suffocations of the Matrix, and stopping of the Terms, and the French Pox.

Si Aliquis Horum Morborum summius sanatur,
Sanantur omues inferiors

If any of the principal of these Diseases be Cured, all the other inferiour Diseases are Cured thereby; for the principals of all theses Diseases do come of venomous Humours in the 4th degree, which is in the extremity of Nature, as either of Melancholy, red Choler, Flegm, or Blood corruption with any of these Humours in the 4th Degree; as if the Blood it self do abound, as when ♃ in ♒, or if red Choler do abound, as when ♂ is in ♐, as if Choler adust with Melancholy do abound, as when ♂ is in ♍, and signifier of the Disease, or if Melancholy do abound in the 4th degree, as when ♄ or ☿ is in ♍, or when much Flegm doth abound; as when ♀ and the ☽ are in ♓ in the 4th degree.

And for the Curing of the Gout, (saith Paracelsus) three things are required, that is, Resliving, Mitigating, and Strengthning. And the chiefest point of Health consists in this, not to fill thy self with Meat, nor be too slow in Labour.

And in Curing, first and principally look to the Liver, that it be sound, and not stopt, hard, or over-glutted with Water, or wasted, bring him first to a good order and soundness, to this operation, rectifie the Liver, and then shalt thou Cure the other Diseases the better, and when Diseasese be grown to extremities, give Medicines always to repress their Venome, for the venomous Humours do kill the Body, and bring incurable Diseases.

Repress Venome by these:

Mitbridate, Bexar, Treacle, Unicorns Horn, Angelica, Seabims, Carduus, Benedicius, Oyl Olive, OvumPhilosopborum, Sarsaprilla, Guiacun, Rose, Wild Time, Juniper Berries, Marjoram, Dittany, Dasies Roots, Saxifrage, Bettony, Dragons, Asarabacca, Gentian Roots, Sedwell Roots, Eliebor, Trifolie, Mallows, Turnips, Indian Pepper, Limons.

And it is to be noted, That is a Purge be given to any Medicine inward, when ♂ is Lord of the Ascendant and Lord of the Hour, or if the ☽ apply to ♂, that Medicine will work strongly, and if ♈ be in the Ascendant, it will also work speedily.

If the ☽ apply to ♃, in the administring of a Purge or Medicine inward, the Patient will vomit with it, for at the like time I gave a Potion purgative, and the gross substance taken away, the Dose was ℈iii, and two hours and a half after he Vomited with it, yet there was nothing in it whereby to cause Vomit, but it was because the ☾ did apply to ♃, and it was long before it wrought downward, but it gave him five or six stools with ease, and he liked very well of it.

Give no inward Medicine when the Lord of the Ascendant is Lord of the 6th and in the 4th, and the ☾ applying to the Lord of the 8th, for it is deadly, and it will torment the Patient much, and not work outwardly but inwardly; let not the ☾ apply to the Lord of the 6th nor 8th, nor behold the 6th nor 8th House, for it will advance the Disease to desperation; nor let the Lord of the Ascendant apply to the Lord of the 6th, nor to the Lord of the 8th, for it is deadly.

Certain Considerations about the Urine, as whether it be his or hers that brings it, or some bodies else.

If the Lord of the Ascendant be in the Ascendant, or in the Sign Ascending, fallen into the 12th House, and the ☾ Ascending in the Sign of the Ascendant not remote, and apply to the Lord of the 7th by ✶, △ or ☌, then it is the Parties own Water.

The ☾ applying to the Lord of the Ascendant, instanti tempore Questionis, and the Lord of the 7th be Lord of the Hour, the Urine is the Parties that makes the Question.

If the Lord of the Hour be the Lord of the Ascendant, and the ☾ apply to him by ✶, △ or ☌, then it is her Husbands Water, if the Woman bring it; if the Man bring it, it is his Wives.

If the Lord of the Ascendant of the Question be Lord of the Hour, and in the 6th, and apply to the Lord of the 3rd, then it is her Sons Urine.

The Lord of the Ascendant in the Ascendant not remote, and applying to a Planet in an Angle, as to the ☉ in the 10th, being Lord of the 3rd, It is his own Urine, or the Party is present before thee.

If the ☾ be Lady of the Ascendant in the 2nd in ♌, void of course, and do separate from ♀, and apply to the ☌ of ♄ in ♍℞ in the 3rd, and ☿ Lord of the Hour, Then he or she that bringeth the Urine cometh to deceive thee, for it is not his Urine, neither did the Party send him that he names, but some other bodies Water, that sends to try thy skill.

If the ☽ apply to the Lord of the Ascendant, and the Lord of the 7th be in the Ascendant not remote, It is the Parties own Water that bringeth it.

Take great heed always, when the Lord of the Ascendant and the ☽ do apply to the Lord of the 7th and 9th, by ☌, □ or ☍, for then there is some deceit in hand, especially if ☿ be Lord of the Hour in ♈, which is the House of ♂, for it signifieth sorrow, mocking, and deceit.

If the ☽ or Lord of the Ascendant do apply to the Lord of the 7th, by ☌, ⚹ or △, and ♀, ♃ or ☉ be Lord of the Hour, It is the Parties Urine that is named.

If the ☽ Lady of the Ascendant, and do apply to the Lord of the 7th, the Lord of the 7th being in the Ascendant, Then it is the Parties Urine that is named, and they come on a right message.

If the Lord of the Ascendant and the Lord of the Hour be both one Planet, and in the 10th in a Sextile to the Ascendant, and the ☽ separate from the Lord of the Ascendant, and apply to the ☉ in the 9th, The Party that owns the Urine is before thee, and it is hers that comes with it.

Of Going to the Sick.

Guido saith, If a Physitian be called or sent for to see a sick Person, or one that is hurt, let him first consider whether he may use any delay of going to him or no, or whether Necessity doth force and constrain him to go presently, not observing any time or season; but if Necessity urge him to go, then must he take time as it falleth out, otherwise let him choose his time according to these Rules following, if he mean to win favour and credit thereby.

And he saith, If it fall out so that thou maist choose thy time, then thy first going forth unto him, put a Rational Sign in the Ascendant, and in the 10th House, as ♊, ♎, ♒, ♍ or the first part of ♐, if it may be.

And if thou canst not do so in both, yet let a Rational Sign be in the Ascendant, and let there by some fortunate Planet, as ♃, ♀, ☉, ☿ or ☽, viz. In the Ascendant, in the 10th, the 7th and 4th House, *ſI ſieri poteſt*, or at least let them behold the said Angles; but if it cannot be so, then let the said Angles be free from the infortunes, and from their aspects, viz. From ♄, ♂, or a Retrograde or combust Planet, that is in his fall or detriment, or weak; but when thou art with a sick Person, if the ☽ apply to ♂, it is good letting of blood, if need requires.

And understand, That ♃ and ♀ are fortunate by Nature, and when they are in their dignities, they are the more fortunate, and although they be infortunate by Accident, yet thou maist put them in Angles. Another saith, Tres *fortunati ſunt* ♃, ♀, ☉, so that the ☉ is fortunate, but the lesser fortune of the three; but if the ☉ be Angular, or aspect the Angle by ⚹ or △, it is good and laudable.

And as for the ☽ and ☿, these two of themselves by Nature are not fortunate nor infortunate, but mean; but if they be in their dignities, or Angular, or apply to ♃ or ♀, they are fortunate, being occidental and direct, but if they be with ♄ or ♂, or in a ☌ or ◻ of the ☉, or in their fall or detriment, Retrograde, or Orient, or in Cadent Houses, they are infortunate, then put them not in the Ascendant or Angles, neither let them behold the Ascendant, except they be Governour in the 7th House, and the ☽ apply by ☌, ⚹ or △ unto them, or that some fortunate Planet be there with them, but put them in a Cadent House.

Saturn and Mars, are Planets, accounted unfortunate by Nature; but when they are unfortunate and evil by Accident, as Combust, Retrograde, in detriment or fall, or occidental, they are so much the worse, and the more apt and strong in working of Evil, for they are accustomed never at any time to rejoyce in doing Good; but when they are in their dignities and free from evil, then they are accounted good, and work good, but it seems against their wills and nature; therefore being evil, let them not be Angular, nor aspect the Ascendant, when thou goest first to see the Sick, except some fortune be there with them, to moderate their evil Influence; nor at thy first entring the House of the Sick, nor at thy first beholding the sick Person, except Necessity urge.

And Guido saith, If a fortunate Planet be in the first House, it signifieth that the Physitian shall be profitable to the Sick; yea if it be ♃ or ♀, though they be Retrograde, Oriental, and in ♌, yet the sick Person shall rejoyce much at the presence of the Physitian, and find great ease, as before thou maist see in every of these Houses, viz. The Ascendant 10th, 7th and 4th.

If ♄ be Lord of the Ascendant, and in the 7th in ☍ to ♃ in the Ascendant, and the ☽ in ♉ apply to the Lord of the 7th (being the ☉) by △ or ✶. Then maist go, for thou shalt be welcome, and well contented; but the Sick may chance to have some extream Fit in thy presence, yet thou shalt be profitable to the Sick.

If the ☉ be Lord of the Ascendant, and in the 7th in the Sign of the 7th, and ♄ Lord of the Ascendant in ♌, and the ☽ separate from ♃, and apply to ♄ by △ or ✶, Thou maist go, because the ☽ doth apply to ♄ being Lord of the 7th, and thou shalt be welcome, and friendly used of the Master or Mistress of the House, and the Sick shall have some Fit in thy presence, because the Lord of the 7th is Lord of the 6th and in the Ascendant, and thou shalt be profitable to the Sick.

If the Lord of the 6th be in the Ascendant, and the ☽ apply unto him at thy going to the Sick, Then the sick Person shall have a Fit in thy Presence, or whilst thou art there.

Thou maist go also to see or visit the Sick in the Hour of ♂, and ♂ in ♏, when the ☽ doth apply to ♂, ♂ being Lord of the 7th and in the 6th, and the Party will be very glad to see thee, and will use thee very kindly.

You may also go in the Hour of ♃, although he be in ♑ Retrograde in the 6th, though ♂ be in the 7th in ♒, not remote, and the ☽ in the 6th in ♒, going to the ☌ of ♂, separating from the ☉ being Lord of the Ascendant; And the Patient shall mend at thy presence, and receive great comfort if it be a Woman, and she will fawn on thee. If ♃ be opposite to ♄ being Lord of the 7th and 6th, and ♄ be in the 12th in ☍ to the House of Infirmities, and ♃ in whose Hour thou wentest be in the 6th, which is the Sickness, This figures that thy presence shall give remedy.

I have found it general in all goings and visitiations of the Sick, That if the Lord of the Ascendant be in the 7th or 6th, and the ☽ separate from the Lord of the Ascendant, and apply to the Lord of the 7th by ☌, ✶ or △, not combust, Thou shalt find favour in the presence of the Sick and do him good. But id the Lord of the 7th do apply to the Lord of the Ascendant, by ✶ or △ in reception and the ☽ go from one of them to the other, Then the sick Person shall fall in love with the Physitian, whosoever be Lord of the Ascendant or the 7th House.

It is also good going to the Sick, if the Lord of the 6th House be weak, and in the 12th or 11th Houses, and ♃ or ♀ in the 7th or 6th, or the Lord of the Ascendant there, For thou shalt be profitable to the Sick, and find favour.

If ♃ be Lord of the 7th in the 11th, and the ☽ in the 4th apply by △ to the ☉, the ☽ in ♌, and the ☉ in ♐ in the Sign of the 7th, and ♀ combust going to a ☌ of the Lord of the Ascendant, Thou maist go to the Sick, and thou shalt be welcome, and the Sister of the Sick shall use thee very kindly, ♀ Lord of the Ascendant and Hour, ♃ in the 11th in ♓, ♂ in the 12th in ♉, the ☽ in the 4th in ♌, ♄ in the 5th in ♏, the ☉ in the 7th in ♐, ♀ and ☿ in the 7th in ♑, the ☽ separate from ♂, and apply to the ☉ by △: Mark this Figure well.

Go not to the Sick when ♄ is in the 2nd House, Retrograde or direct. For then thou shalt have nothing for thy Physick nor pains.

I have oft-times noted it, and hold it for a general Rule, That if any Person whatsoever comes to me with an Urine, or for any other thing to do for him, if ♄ be in the 2nd House, direct or Retrograde, I never had any thing for my pains, whether I helped them or no; the like if ♈ be in the 2nd; if ♂ be in the 2nd It signifieth the sick Patient not to be Cured, but with great costs and charges.

When ♓ is in the Ascendant, and ♃ in the 11th, 10th, 9th, 7th, 6th, 5th or 2nd, or in the Ascendant, It is good going to the Sick, or administring to him self; if ♃ be not in ♏, ♊ nor ♑, as I have shewed before; if the ☽ apply to the Lord of the 7th, or the Lord of the 7th be in the Ascendant, or the Lord of the Ascendant in the 7th, or the Lord of the 6th in the 2nd, It is of good signification, and much more the better.

If ☿ be Lord of the Ascendant in ♑ in the 9th, not beholding the Ascendant nor the 2nd, and the ☽ be Lady of the 2nd and in ♓ in the 11th, separating from ♂, beholding Lord of the 7th in ♑, and then be void of course, and next comes to ♄ in the 6th in ♌ Retrograde, Thou shalt find little favour in the presence of the Sick, for he will not give any thing for to be made whole.

It is not good to go to any sick Person to bargain with him to cure him, when a greater Planet is Lord of the 7th than is Lord of the Ascendant; for it seems the Party that thou goest to will be proud, scornful and lofty, and set little by thee, except the Lord of the Ascendant and the Lord of the 7th do apply friendly together, or that there be a reception between them, or that the ☽ doth go from one to the other, as is aforesaid.

And Guido Bonatus gives special warning, That you posite ♃ in the 2nd House, or the pars Fortuna, or some other fortunate Planet, if it be possible, that is not impeded in the 2nd, and this shall signifie (saith he) Lucrum Medici, the Physitians benefit; or else let ♃ or pars Fortuna be joyned by ☌, ✶ or △ to the Lord of the 8th House or 11th, & hoc fiiliter Lucrum Medici significat; and if the Lord of the Ascendant or 2nd do not receive ♃ or pars Fortuna, then take heed that they do not at a □ or ☍, but by ☌, ✶ or △ let them behold each the other.

Also take heed that there be no evil Planet in the 9th that is impeded, Retrograde, Combust, or in his fall, and none in these Qualifications do behold the 9th or Lord thereof; for if they do then the Physitian shall have no credit by going or administring to the Sick. Meddle not therefore with such a one, in whose Question the 9th House and his Lord is so infortunate without Help.

But if there be a fortunate Planet in the 9th, as ♃ or ♀ or ☊, or a Planet that is fortunate in his dignities, accept ♄, ♂ or ♈, It promiseth good; or if some other fortunate Planet aspect the 9th or his lord by ✶ or △, &c.

Alkindus saith, If the Lord of the 9th be corrupted, It sheweth that the Physitian cannot Heal the Sick.

The Hours of ♃ and ♀ are much praised to be good, for to go to the Sick in at the first Visit.

The Hours of the ☽ are to be considered of, according to the Planet she applieth unto, and whether she be fortunate or infortunate, good or evil

The Hours of the ☉ and ☿, if they are fortunate and well placed, are indifferent good.

Riffus saith, Let the Physitian take heed in the first visiting of the Sick in the Hours of ♄ or ♂, or in the Hour of a Retrograde, combust or unfortunate Planet; that is to say, Let him not go first forth of his door, when he goeth to visit the Sick, or to see him, in the Hours of ♄ nor ♂, nor Combust, Retrograde, or infortunate Planet, nor enter into the sick Mans House in the Hours of such a Planet, nor come into the presence of the Sick, if he can choose, nor at any time after when he visits the sick Person. For if he come to him in the Hour of ♄, the Sick shall die, or else the Physitian will have great labour and many doubts in Curing him, neither shall he help him, except it be to desperation, and out of all hopes first.

And if the Physitian go to his Patient in the Hour of ♂ first, there will be chiding and brawling between them, and so he shall come off with small gain.

Go not to see the Sick when ♄ is Lord of the 9th, and Retrograde in the 5th, in a □ to the Ascendant, and Lord of the Ascendant also Retrograde or combust in the 9th or 8th, though he be in ☌ with ♀, and the ☽ at a □, △, ✶, ☌ or ☍ of ♂ full or applying, and though she leave ♂ applying to ♃, For thou shalt have chiding, slander and diferace.

The Lord of the Ascendant Retrograde, Combust, or in his Fall, or in a Cadent House, or in the 8th House, Go not out at such a time.

If the ☽ be Lady of the 2nd in ♌, and apply by △ to the ☉ in the 7th in the Sign of the 7th, It seemeth thou shalt give the Sick some Money, or bestow some Courtesie on him.

If the Lord of the Ascendant and the Lord of the 7th do apply by ☌, ✶ or △, the one to the other, Then there shall fall out great kindness between the Physitian and the sick Person.

If the Lord of the Ascendant and ♀ do apply the one to the other by ✶ or △, ♀ being in the 7th, It sheweth great kindness shall grow between the Physitian and the sick Person, or some other that is near or about the Sick.

If ♂ be in the 9th in the last of ♉, or in ♊, and be Lord of the 7th, and in △ to the Ascendant, and in ✶ to the Lord of the Ascendant, the Lord of the Ascendant in the 6th, and ♃ and ☊ in the 7th, Then go to the Sick, for thou shalt have credit, love and friendship, and great profit by the Sick, for he shall cause many to repair unto thee, and shall speak well of thee.

If the ☽ do apply to the Lord of the 7th House by ✶, △ or ☌, Then thou shalt be welcome to the Sick, especially if it be a Woman.

If the ☽ do apply to the Planet that is Lord of the House wherein the Lord of the 7th is, Thou shalt be welcome to the Goodman of the House.

If the ☽ do apply to both the Lord of the 7th, and the Planet that is Lord of the House wherein the Lord of the 7th is, Then thou shalt be welcome both to the Wife and the Husband also.

If the ☽ do separate from ♂, and apply to ♄ Retrograde in the Ascendant in ♍ by ☌ and ☿ Lord of the Ascendant in the 6th, and ♀ in the 7th, They shall like well of thee, and of thy reasons, yet shall be in doubt to follow thy counsel for a time, yet at last they shall cleave to thee again, and in the end much admire thee, ☿ going to combustion.

If ♄ be Lord of the 7th, and in the 2nd Retrograde in ♍, and the ☽ in ♏ separating from the Lord of the Ascendant, and applying to a ✶ of ♄ and ☿, and ♄ and ☿ at a ✶ with reception, Then thou shalt be welcome to the Sick, if it be a Woman or Man, to the Husband and the Wife, and thou shalt be paid for thy pains.

It is not good to go when the Lord of the Ascendant is in the 6th combust, or going to combustion, the ☽ applying to ♄ by ♂ in the Ascendant, though ♀ be in the 7th.

If the Lady of the 2nd apply to the Lord of the Ascendant, what Planet soever be Lord of the 2nd, and goeth to the ♂ of the ☉ in the 6th, It sheweth he shall have profit and gain by reason of the Sick, and shall be well paid.

If the Lord of the Ascendant be also Lord of the 2nd, and in the 6th at a ✶ to the Lord of the 7th, and the Lord of the 7th in △ to the Ascendant. Then the sick Party shall be glad of the Physitian, and he shall find great ease, and content him well.

If the ☉ be Lord of the Ascendant, and in the 7th in ♓, the sick Man shall like well of the Physitian; but if ☿ Lord of the 2nd be combust in the 7th, being Lord of the Ascendant, the sick Man will give him but a small reward for his pains.

But in such a Case, if ♄ be in the Ascendant in ♍ Retrograde, and the ☽ apply to the ✶ or △ of ♄, the last degrees of ♒ on the 7th, Then the Wife shall be more liberal than the Husband.

If the ☽ be Lady of the Ascendant in ♌, and separate from the ☉ being Lord of the Hour, in ♈ in his degree of Exaltation, and apply to ♂ in ♊ in the 12th, Thou maist go, but thou shalt have no familiarity with any body.

Mars Lord of the 7th in the 9th not remote, and ♀ in the 6th in ♓, The Grief shall be discovered, and the Party shall find great ease, and the sick Patient shall speak much good of the Physitian.

♃ Lord of the 6th in the 7th, and ♀ Lady of the Ascendant in the 6th, The Physitian shall be very profitable to the Sick, and do him great good, and the Sick shall think well of him, and speak good of him.

When ♈ is in the 2nd House, The Physitian shall have little for his pains, or stay very long for it.

Go not nor ride forth to any sick Body, or to see the Sick, when the ☽ doth separate from the Lord of the 7th, and apply to ♄ by ☍ or □, although he be in the 11th, especially if the Lord of the 9th be in the same Sign with him; For then thou shalt be but badly entertained, not believed, and evil thought of.

If the Lord of the 9th be with the Planet that the Moon doth apply unto, in the same Sign, and in the same House with the Lord of the 7th, though not in the same Sign, Then thou shalt meet with some other Physitian there.

Here I conclude this Subject concerning the going to, and visitation of the Sick.

Judgments of Diseases without the Urine.

In the Day of ♄ the Disease is cold and dry, and daily grieveth the Members, but not the Stomach.

In the Hour of ♄ it is of Wind and Cold in the Belly and Liver, and the Party is troubled with the Spleen and pain in the Side, and the Sickness is ingendred of Melancholy which is cold and dry, which ingenders Hurlings of Wind in the Belly, like to the Collick; the Party is pain'd with often Stitches, and much weakness affects the Head through Melancholy, and if it grow to be sharp and tedious, the Sick will hardly escape.

In the Day of ♃ the Sickness is caused of Blood flowing by reason of the heat of the Liver, and hath great pain in the right Side, with a Fever.

In the Hour of ♃ the Liver is diseased, and the Body is troubled, and the more because of Cold, but the Disease is not of long continuance; it is a Sickness that is unstable, like an Erratick Fever, sometimes the pains in the Belly, sometimes in the Reins, sometimes in the Shoulders and under the short Ribs, and is like to ingender some Impostumation in the Liver, or in the Side, and in a Woman her Menstrues are stopt, and she hath the Fever Synochus, which comes of rotten Blood.

In the day of ♂ the Disease is hot and dry, and the Patient hath aches, and heavy thoughts, and is afflicted in the Reins.

In the Hour of ♂ he hath a Fever and trembling in the Body, and the Kings Evil doth draw nigh unto this, and it is caused of too much blood, which causeth Itches, Fevers and Scrophulaes; and without doubt such Persons are not without some running Sores, or unkind Issues of Blood, or Humours, as the Piles, Hemroids, or Fluxes of the Terms, or vomiting of Blood, Fistulaes, Felons, or Cankers, or some such like mis-healing Wounds, for ♂ causeth hot Fevers of red Choler, hot Sicknesses, and Swellings and burning Tumors.

He that sicketh in the Day of the ☉, his Disease cometh of yellow Choler, and is hot, and his Heart is afflicted with grief, palpitations and faintings, and all the Members languish.

In the Hour of the ☉ the Body is troubled with Heat, and the Mind with Anger, the Members burn with Heat, the Heart oppressed and afflicted, and the Reins likewise, oft-times a strong Fever, and is faint and wearyish with anxiety of Mind.

In the Day of ♀ the Disease is cintradictious, residing about the Liver, the Reins, the Navel, and the Buttocks.

In the Hour of ♀ the Disease is in the Reins, caused of Cold, and the Party is often troubled, and is Feverish.

In the Day of ☿ the Lungs be diseased, and the Patient is much pained in the Body, his spirits are afflicted, and the Understanding is dazzled and disordered, and the Mind troubled with heavy thoughts and fear.

In the Hour of ☿ he hath some strength in his Body, and is pained in the Liver, with oft Stitches and Prickings which come of Cold and Wind.

In the Day of the ☽ the Disease is caused of Flegm, is pained in the Head, and is in danger of Apoplectical Distempers.

In the Hour of the ☽ the Disease is caused of cold Humours, and is much pained in the right side.

Whether thou shalt Cure him or no upon the first Figure as followeth.

If the ☽ do apply to the Lord of the 9th, whoever be Lord thereof, if he be in the Ascendant, and the Lord of the Ascendant in the Ascendant and the Lord of the 6th and 7th, weak, in their detriment or fall, or in a cadent House; Take him in hand, for thou shalt Cure him.

But if the Lord of the 9th do aspect the ☽ by □ or ☍ as ♂ Lord of the 9th at a △ to the ☽, thou shalt hardly Heal him.

If the ☽ be Lady of the 6th in Via Combusta in the 8th in such a case, and do apply by □ to ♂ Lord of the 9th, Yet thou shalt Cure him with much ado at length.

When the Lord of the Ascendant is in the Ascendant with the Lord of the 10th, both in one Sign, It is a good sign that there comes help from Heaven to Cure the sick Party.

If the ☽ be Lady of the Ascendant and apply to the Lord of the 9th, as to ♄, and the Lord of the 9th be in an Angle direct, as ♄ in ♓ in the 10th, He shall Heal him of his Disease.

Take heed that thou put not the Lord of the 6th in the 9th, whether he have any dignity or no, For then the Disease will trouble the Physitian, that he shall be at his wits end, and shall not know what to say or do to it; for if ♂ be Lord of the 6th and in the 9th, It will cause law and strife, and suspition and hindrance to the Physitian, especially if the ☽ apply to ♂; if ♀ be Lady of the 6th and in the 9th, in her fall or detriment, though she have a term, face or triplicity, Yet the Physitian shall have discredit and ill words, especially if the ☽ apply to ♂, though ♂ be in ♈ in the 10th House.

If the ☉ be Lord of the 6th and in the 9th, Thou shalt have ill words in the end, and nothing for thy pains.

And it is a general Rule, That if the Lord of the 6th be in the 9th, whosoever be Lord of the 6th, That the Physitian shall leave his Cure unfinished, and shall have nothing for his pains but strife and anger.

Whether the Disease be in the Body, or Mind or both.

Take notice, That the Sign Ascending, the ☽, and the Lord of the House of the ☉, these three do signifie the Spirit or the Mind of Man.

The Lord of the Ascendant, the Lord of the House of the ☽, and the ☉, these three do signifie the Body of Man and his Members.

If the Ascendant, the ☽, and the Lord of the House of the ☉ be impedited or afflicted, all three, or two of them, Then the Disease is in the Spirit and Mind.

When the Ascendant and the ☽ be both impedited, and their Lords safe from affliction, Then the Sickness is in the Mind and not in the Body.

If the Lord of the House of the ☽, and the Lord of the Ascendant, be with the Sun, fortunate, or behind him, Then the Disease or Grief is in the Body, and not in the Mind of the Patient.

If ♃ be Lord of the Ascendant, and be Lord of the House of the ☉, and the ☽ also, and of the 8th in ♌, The Disease is in the Body, and not in the Mind.

If ♂ be Lord of the House of the ☽, and also of the ☉, and in ♏ Retrograde, and ☿ Lord of the Ascendant in ♉, in ☍ to ♂, The Disease is in the Body, and not in the Mind.

If the Lord of the House of the ☽, and Lord of the Ascendant, and Lord of the House of the ☉, be vitiated and corrupted, Then is the Disease both in the Body and in the Mind also.

If one Planet be the Lord of the Ascendant, and also Lord of the House of the ☽, and in the 12th, opprest by any Aspect of ♂ in ♋, Then the Disease is both in the Body and in the Mind.

If ♀ be Lady of the Ascendant, and Lord of the House of the ☽ in the 20th degree of ♍, and ♀ at a ✶ to ♂ in ♋, both in their fall, The Disease is both in Body and Mind.

If the Lord of the House of the Lord of the Ascendant, and Lord of the House of the ☽ be infortunate, or in their fall, or corrupt, The Disease is more in the Mind than in the Body.

If ♈ be in the Ascendant, and ♂ in the 6th Retrograde in ♍, and the ☽ also in the 6th in ♑, and ☿ Lord thereof in ♓ in his fall in the 12th House, Then the Disease is more in the Mind than in the Body.

If the ☉ be Lord of the Ascendant in his exaltation in the 8th, and the ☽ in ♈ combust, going to the ☉ in the 8th also, and ♂ Lord of ♈ in ♒ in the 6th, and ♄ at a △ to the ☉, Then the Disease is most in the Mind, and the Party is much vexed in Mind concerning their Children, and like to despair, and the Body is also out of quiet, and troubled with much Choler.

If the Ascendant and the ☽ be safe, and their Lords impedited, Then the Disease and Sickness is in the Body, and not in the Mind.

If the Ascendant, the ☽, the Lord of the Ascendant and the Lord of the House of the ☽, be all impedited or infortunate, Then there is sickness of the Body, and grief of the Mind and Spirits.

Likewise if an unfortunate Planet behold the ☽ and not the Ascendant, The Disease is in the Body, and not in the Mind.

If an unfortunate Planet behold both the Moon and the Ascendant, Then the Disease is both in the Body and in the Mind.

If the Ascendant be aspected by the □ of ♃, and Lord of the Ascendant Cadent, opprest by the ✶ of ♂, and the ☽ in Via combusta, opprest by the ☍ of ♄, Then the Disease is more in the Mind than in the Body.

♄ or ♂, or a Retrograde, or a combust Planet in the Ascendant, and the Lord of the Ascendant, as ♂ be in a feminine Sign, as in ♍ Retrograde in the 6th, and the ☽ in ♍ and ☿ in ♓, Then the Grief is both in the Body and in the Mind, but most troubled in the Mind.

If the degree of Ascending and the ☽ be more afflicted than their Lords, or impedited, Then the greatest Grief is in the Mind.

If ♂ be Lord of the Ascendant, and in the 25th of ♍, Retrograde in the 6th, and the ☉ in ♈ in the 12th, and the ☽ in ♍ in the 6th, and ☿ in ♊, and ♄ in the Ascendant in ♉, Then it is both in the Body and Mind, but the Mind is most afflicted.

If the Lord of the House of the ☽, and the Lord of the Ascendant, be more afflicted and impedited than the degree Ascending or the ☽, Then the Grief is more in the Body than in the Mind.

If ♂ Lord of the Ascendant, in the 12th in ♏, and the ☽ in a masculine Sign, and in a Cadent House, void of Course and peregrine, and the ☉ in a feminine Sign in a Cadent House, or in the 8th, Then the Party hath grief both in Body and Mind, and is troubled much, and sore vexed with anger and fear.

♀ Lady of the Ascendant in ♓ in the 5th, and the ☽ in ♑ in the 3rd applying to a □ of the ☉ in ♈ in the 7th, ♂ in ♉ in the 8th, and ♃ in ♐ in the 3rd, The Disease is both in the Body and in the Mind.

If the ☽ and the Lord of the House of the ☉ be in their fall, and the degree Ascending be at a □ to the ☽, and free from ♄ and ♂, Then the Grief is in the Mind.

If the Lord of the Ascendant and the ☉ in their Signs of exaltation, and the Lord of the House of the ☽ in his fall, The Disease is in the Body, and not in the Mind.

Saturn Lord of the Ascendant in ♌ Retrograde, in the 6th in ☍ to the Ascendant, and the ☽ in ♉, applying to a □ of ♄, and ♀ Lady of the House of the ☽ in ♓ in the Ascendant, not remote, direct and free from ♄ and ♂, and the ☉ in ♑ in the 12th, The Grief is much in the Mind, and sometimes in the Body.

If the Ascendant ☉ and ☽ be all vitiated or afflicted, the Disease is then through the whole Body, or no place free; but if those Planets who dispose of the ☉ and ☽, or he that is Lord of the Ascendant, or two of them at the least be afflicted, The Disease is in the Spirits, together with some indisposition of Mind; The reason hereof is, because the Lord of the Ascendant, and dispositor of the ☽, are properly the significators of the Animal Spirits, as aforesaid, and of the Animal Faculties and Infirmities in Man, or which may chance to him, as deprivation of Sense, Frenzy, Madness, Melancholy, &c. This general Rule many Astrologers hold and observe, viz. That ♄ naturally foreshews or causeth Melancholy, all manner of Distempers from Melancholy, and by consequence the disturbed Mind; wherefore wheresoever you find ♄ Lord of the Ascendant, or of the Hour, or 12th or 6th House, or if the ☽ separate from him, or if ♄ be in the 6th House, or in the Ascendant, or in ☌, □ or ☍ of the Lord of the Ascendant. The sick Party labours with some affliction of Mind, or with some vexatious Care, wherewith his Mind is much troubled. Now the contrary hereof ♃ effects, for he never oppresseth the Mind but the Body; if the Lord of the House of the ☽ and of the Ascendant are unfortunate by the ☉, or combust, or under his beams, the infirmity is bodily.

When the Lords of the places of the ☽ and of the ☉ be in their detriments, falls, or peregrine, Retrograde or combust, and the degree Ascending in □ of the ☽, and free from all ill Aspects of ♄ and ♂, Then is the Patient vexed with a tormented Soul. Usually when the ☉, Lord of the Hour, or of the 12th House, are significators of the Party enquiring. These shew a Mind vexed with haughtiness, vain-glory, pride, and self-conceitedness.

Venus argues Luxury, a lascivious desire to Women, whereby both Body and Mind are disturbed; ☿ shews doating fancies and fearful imaginations, wheresoever you find him the signifier and afflicted; as likewise that he is stirred to mistrust upon vain fears, his own jealous fancies, or upon some flying reports.

Over and above the many Directions formerly preferibed, it behoveth well to consider, whether the degrees wherein the Lord of the Ascendant, the ☉ or ☽ at time of the birth, (if you have the Patients Nativity) do fall to be the degrees of a Sign, wherein a present Eclipse is at time if the Sickness, or near it, or of some eminent great conjunction; for I must tell you these are all unfortunate.

The Sign of the Eclipse, or of a great conjunction threatning Evil, or the Sign of the 8th House of the yearly revolution of the World, falling, in any of the Angles of the Nativity, especially in the Ascendant, proves very dangerous.

When a Sign ascends upon the first falling sick, or demand of the Patient, wherein an infortune was in the Nativity, It very sadly afflicts and torments the sick Party, viz. It shews he shall have a hard Fit of Sickness; the ☌ of the ☽ with the ☉ is a very ill Sign, when there's not above 6 degrees distant betwixt then, and the ☽ not yet passed by the ☉, that is not having been yet in conjunction with him; however upon the ☉ and ☽ their being in ☌, in ♈ or ♌, this misfortune is lessened, when the ☽ is 12 degrees from the ☉, she shews little danger.

Having referred all our Discourse to the 12 Houses of the Heavens, take these Considerations along with you.

Note, That every Sign of the Zodiack hath 30 degrees and every 3 Houses make a Quarter of the Zodiack, which is so divided into 4 parts; and you must also note, That 25 degrees of the first House is under the Earth, and 5 are above the Earth, and the first 18 degrees descending are temperate in heat and drowth, and the last 12 degrees (whereof 5 of them are above the Earth, and 7 under) are hot and dry in the Beginning of the first degree; for we reckon the Houses contrary to the Signs, for we account the Signs ascending, and the Houses descending, going from the East to the South, and those 5 degrees that are above the Earth, are the last degrees of the first House, and the first House, the 12th House, and the 11th House are hot and dry, Cholerick, of the nature of Fire; the 10th, 9th and 8th are hot and moist, of the nature of the Air; the 7th, 6th and 5th are cold and moist, and the 4th, 3rd and 2nd are cold and dry, Melancholick.

In the next place I shall Treat of the :

Proper Natural Medicines and Cures that belong to every Disease, caused by the Planets passing through all the Signs of the Zodiack.

First of ♄ in ♉, the earthly Triplicity, and the Cure.

In such Diseases caused of ♄ in ♉, Minister not first in the Hour of ♄ nor ☿, but in the Hour of ♃, being in ♊, ♎ or ♒, or when ♊ or ♎ are in the Ascendant or in the Hour of the ☉ being in ♊, ♎ or ♒, and ♊ or ♎ in the Ascendant. Or the ☽ being in ♈, ♊, ♎ or ♒, applying to ♃ or the ☉: and you must intend your Cure with things hot and moist, belonging to ♃ and the ☉; and always in the first Administration of Physick, be sure to make the Lord of the 6th House weak.

Simples that Digest Melancholy generally.

Fumitory, Ephithimum, Hopps, Mirabolanes, India, Cassia-Fistula, Elleborum Nigrum, Sena, Polypody, Stecados, Scolopendria, Camepytis, Cuscuta, Squniancy, Borrage, Bugloss, Lapis Lazulis, Lapis Armenus.

Simples that Purge Melancholy.

Polypody, Senna, Fumitory, Mirab. Ind. Cassia-Fistula, Volubilis Bindweed, Hopps, Esseborus, Rad. Lasatbi acuti, Lapis Laxulis, Lapis armentus, Stecados, Scalopendria, Squinanthum,Sirupus fumari, Sir. Cap. Veneris, Sir. De lupulis, Sir. Rhubarb, Sir. Buglosst & Borrag. Sir Ephitbi. Sir de Stecados, Sir. Squinantie, Oxi. Sachar. Oxim. Scillitic. Oximel corn-positum.

Compounds that Purge Melancholy.

Diasenna, Diacatbolicon, Diaprunes lenit. Diantbos, Diacancron, Confectio bamech. Confect. Senne, Feralogod. Memphitum, Hiera Ruffi, trisera perfica, Pill. De fumitor. Pill de agregatin. Pill de Arabice, Pill fine quibus, Pill. De quinque generibus mirabolar. Pilule lucis mag. Pil. Mastichini, Pill.Indi, Pill de lapid. Luzuli, Pill. De lapid. Armeni, Pulvis Feralogodii.

Preparatives against Melancholy, caused of ♄ in ♂ cold and dry in the 2nd Degree.

℞ pro tribus diebus Oximel diurecticum, aut scuiliticxns cxin aqua, and then Purge him.

℞ Sir. Borag. 3I, Epithimi 3β, decationis Scolopendria, fumitorii, Endivii ana 3iii fiat potus.

℞ Polypod. 3β, coquastur in aqua Borag. Alto ana 3iv Endivia, Cichorii, Cap. Ven. Ana 3i, ad tertias colatur & addatur de Sir. Violar. Fumitorii ana 3I, Cap. Ven. 3I, Dose is 3iii.

The Cure of (♄ in ♍) Diseases caused by ♄ in ♍.

In Curing of these Diseases, take heed you minister not first in the Hour of ♄ nor ☿, but in the Hour of ♃, the ☉, or ♀ when she is in ♈, ♌ or ♐, and put ♊ or ♎ in the Ascendant, as aforesaid.

Digesters of strong Melancholy, caused of ♄ in ♂, ♍ or ♑.

Scolopendria, Borage, Buglost. Polypody, Senna, Cap. Ven. Assarum, Parthemium, Lupuli, Lapis Lazuli, Lapis armentus, Bugle, Columbines, Holihocks, Mallows, Manna, Avens, Satirion, Rampions, Rose-leaves, Tamarins, Turnips, Scabious, Hysop, Camomile. And sirrups of the same at your discretion, and Sirrup Acetous.

Purges of ♄ in ♂, ♍ and ♑.

Senna, Polypody, Lapis armenus, Lapis lazuli, Feralogodion, assarum, Diasena, Consect. Hameck, You shall not minister in the Hour of ♄ nor ☿, as before said in ♂; but if the Disease fall out in the last 18 degrees of ♑, It is incurable most commonly.

The Cure of Diseases caused by ♄ in ♊ produced By melancholick Blood having dominion.

Minister not in the Hour of ♄, ♃, ☿, nor the ☽ if she be in ♊, ♎ or ♒, but in the Hour of ♀, the ☽ being in ♉, ♍ or ♑, ♈, ♌ or ♐, or in the Hours of the ☉ and ♂, being in ♋, ♏ or ♓, putting ♋, ♏ or ♓ in the Ascendant, and then purge and cleanse the Blood, open a Vein, and bleed him well, then purge him of Melancholy.

The Cure of the Diseases of ♄ in ♎.

Minister not in the Hours of ♄, ☿, ♀ or ♃, but of the ☉, ♂, and ☽, the ☉, being in ♋, ♏ or ♓, and put ♈ and ♋ in the Ascendant, and purge the melancholic Humours, then let blood.

The Cure of ♄ in ♒.

Minister not in the Hour of ♄, ☿, nor ♃, if they be in ♉, ♍ or ♑, but in the Hour of ♀ or the ☽, she being in ♉, ♍, or ♑, and let ♋, ♏ or ♓ be in the Ascendant, purge Melancholy, and then let blood.

Digesters of Melancholy mixed with Blood.

Hopps, Fumitory, Succory, Manna, Tamarinds, Cassia.

Purgers.

Manna, Cassia, Tamarinds, Diaprunes, Confectio Hameck, Senna, Pelipody.

The Cure of ♄ in ♋.

Administer not Physick in the Hours of ♄, ☿, ♀, or ☽, but in the Hours of ☉, ♃ or ♂, when ♊, ♎, ♒, or ♈, ♌, ♐, are in the Ascendant, and the ☽ in ♈, ♌, or ♐, applying to ♃, ♀ or the ☉, for the ☽ doth bring a cretain comfortable heat to the Party sick of a cold Disease; but let not the Planet that the ☽ doth apply unto, be Lord of the 6th House, nor 8th, nor 4th House; and in this case purge Flegm and Melancholy strongly, especially Flegm and

Water, because these have dominion in this Disease, for the Party is cold both inward and outward. A Little or none at all of Preparation is to be used in these diseases, because the Humours are thin; but purge them three days strongly, if great occasion be, then let blood, otherwise not, for it helpeth little.

Purgers against these Diseases.

Polypody, Senna, Epythimum, Diacarthamus, Diaturbith, Confectio Hamech, Diasenna.

The Cure of ♄ in ♏

Administer not first in the Hour of ♄, ♀ nor the ☽, and let not ♏ be in the Ascendant, nor in the 6th; but minister in the Hour of ♃ or the ☉, or in the Hour of ♀ or ☿, if they be in ♈, ♌ or ♐; and this Acetosum flegma must first be prepared well, for without preparation it will hardly be expelled, because it is slimy, thick and tough; then purge it, and keep a good diet, and refrain all cold, slimy and flegmatick meats, for this Humour of ♄ in ♏ is venomous, and causeth the black Plague, as it doth in the last 12 degrees of ♋, but it is more strong, more cold and Preparations in this case, prepare with Waters and syrrups, that repress and kill Venome, as follows.

Digestives.

℞ Sirrup. Liquritia, Hyssopi, Euula, ana 3I, Sir. De Stecados 3ii, Aquar. Limoniorum 3ii, Aquar. Rosemarina 3i β, Melissa, Lupulorum, Fumitoria, ana 3iii β, fiat potus pro v. dos. Digerat Flegma, & Melancholy in 3d. degree.

℞ Cuscut. Fumitor. Hypericon, Stecados, Flor. Borag. Bugloss, ana p.1. Mirabol. & Cubeb. Ana 3I, fiat decoctio ad platur 3xii, addentur de Sirrup. Enula, Betanice, Stecados, ana 3ii, fiat potus pro + dos.

Purgers.

Diartheos, Diaprasia, benedicta Lax. Pill. Setida, Pill. De Sogapeno, Pill. Eupherbii, Diacartamus, Confer. Hamech, Elect.

De citro Solutiv. Pill Artbritide. Pill. De 5 generibus mirab. Elec. succi ros. Sarcocolla, Pill. fumitor.

The Cure of Diseases of ♄ in ♓.

Administer not in the Hours of ♄, ☿, ♀ nor the ☽, but in the Hours of the ☉, ♂ or ♃, putting ♈, ♌ or ♐ in the Ascendant, and the ☽ in ♈, ♌, ♐, or ♊, ♎ or ♒; and first prepare Flegm and Melancholy, then purge it leisurely and strongly, and keep the Patient very warm and make him sweat well, and exercise his Body, and in all your Medicines give things that correct and repress Venome, for the Humours are venemous by reason of the great Cold of ♄ in ♒, and your Preparatives must be very strong, and so must your Purgers, or else they will not effectually work, and the Patient must keep jimself very warm, and eat nothing cold of nature, but such as be hot and dry.

Preparatives.

Balm, Seabious, Time, Harts-Tongue, Aniseed, Parsley-seed, Polypody, Fennel-seed, Ginger, Fumitery, Hopps, Epithymum.

Repressers of Venome.

Carduus, Angelica, Marigolds, Gilly Flowers, Ivy Berries, Dragons, Oyl-Olive, Sassaparilla, Prick-maddam, Monophyllon, Wild Time, Marjerom, Rue, Dictamus, Daucus Roots, Saxifrage, Betony, Assarabacca, Mithridate, Theriaca, Bezoar Stone, Unicorns Horn, Harts Horn, Sowbred, Gentian Roots, Sedwel Roots, Ellebor.nigrum, Ellebor.alb, Trifolie, Mallows, Parsley-seed, Turnips, Indian Pepper, Garlick, Daffodil, Bay Berries, Limons and their Seeds, Oranges and their seeds, Citron-Seeds, Walnuts, Acorns, Devils Bit, Euphorbium, Bole Armoniack, Saffron.

Purgers for the Same.

Confectio Homech, Diacotomus, Diaturbith, Dissena, Pulvis Jeralogodii.
Or thus,

℞ Diaphenicon, Diawathoholicon, Electuar. Indi majoris, ana. ℥ii, Pulvis Jeralogodii ℨi., & cum decoct. Communi fiat potus pro una dose; It purgeth Flegm and Melancholy in the 4th degree.

Of the Cure of Diseases caused by ♃ in ♊

To such as be diseased through the access of natural Blood too much abounding, Administer not in the Hour of ♃ in ♊, ♎ or ♒, but in the Hours of ♄ or ☿, when the ☽ is in ♉, ♍ or ♑, and put ♉, ♍ or ♑ in the Ascendant, applying to ♄ or ☿, and let ♃ be weak, and cure it with dry things.

But in such a case, the first beginning of the Cure is to let Blood, and after give things to abate the Blood and the heat thereof; and in Curing of Synochus inflatus, the Cure is common; for first, if the Party be of reasonable strength, then open a Vein, and give him a slender diet, and give him to drink Water, wherein is resolved the Pulp of Cassia fytula, Tamarinds and Manna, ofttimes as thus.

℞Pulpa Cassia, Tamarindar, ana ℥i., Manna ℥iii, Aquar. Borag. Lingue Br.is, Violar. Solatri ana ℥ii, Sacbar: quantum sufficit, fiat potus pro 4 dos.

These do Prepare Adustive Blood.

Sirrupus Acetosus Simplex, Sir. Endivie. Sir Granat. Sir. de Lupulis, Sir. de Fumaria.

These do

Diminish the Quantity of Blood.

Manna, Cassia, Tamarinds, Diaprunot.

To Purge and Cleanse the Blood.

℞ Pulv. dia Margarit. Frigid. ℈iv, Confer. florum, Cicorie ℈vi, Confer. Rad. Buglosse ℈I, Confer. Rosar. ℈i., Pulvis Bezoard ℈i., Pulveris Elect. de bolo ℨii, Pulv. Elect. de genniss ℨi., Sirrup. de Acetoso citri quantum Sufficit, fiat Opiata, and take as much as a Bean, drinking after it two spoonfulls of Bugloss and Scabious

Water; this doth comfort the Heart, and cleanse and sweeten the Blood in the 3rd degree.

These also do Purge and Cleanse the Blood.

Fumitory, Mirabolanes Cand. Succus fumitorie, Borrage, Bugloss, Damask Prunes, Succus Rosar. Capillus veneria, Aqua Lactis Capra, Absinthium, Succus Assodilli, Hopps, Aqua Endivia, Aqua Granator. Aqua de Lupulis, , Aqua Rosar. Aqua Absinthii, Aqua Buglossa, Aqua Borage, Cassia fistula, Diacatholicon, Tamarinds, Hierapicra simplex.

To Purge the Blood of hot and moist superfluous Matter.

℞ Polypodii 3β, Aqua Boraginis, Buglossa, Endivia, Cichovii ana 3iii, Aqua Seabious. 3I, fiat decoctio, coletur, & addatur de Sirrup. Fumitor. Bugl. 3i., Cassia fistul. 3β, Sperma ceti 3i., commiscentur. Dose is 3iii at a time, fasting daily.

The Cure of Diseases caused by ♃ in ♎.

Minister not in the Hour of ♃, but in the Hour of ♄ or ☿; neither shall you put ♊, ♎ or ♒ in the Ascendant, but ♉, ♍ or ♑, and Cure the Party with cold and dry things, first letting him blood in the Liver-Vein, and then let him observe a good diet, as is said in the Chap. of ♃ in ♊; and give him things to cool the Blood, and to diminish the Quality thereof, as in the Chap. before of ♃ in ♊.

These are good against Spitting of Blood.

Mitbridat. Galeni. Antidot. Arsini Cirtum, Elect. Ind. Major, Pillule fine quibus sees nolo, Poll. Aures, Pill. fatid. Major, Theriace Galeni.

Good against hot faculent Blood, stopping the Pipes, obstructing the Breath, causing difficulty in Breathing.

℞ Pulp. Cassia, Pulp. Tamarindar. Ana 3β, Sir. Violar. Conser. Cap. Veneris ana 3β, Aqua Violar, Solatri ana 3ii, Ling.

Bovis, Fumitor. Veneris ana 3β, commix them; the Dose is 4 spoonfuls fasting, and let him fast after as long as he can.

These following do nourish good Blood, and Increase the Radical Humidity in Man.

Jus Gallinar. Hador Perdicum, Phasianor. Ref. Edorifora, Somnilogum & Quies.

These do open the mouths of the Veins.

Aloes, Mallows, Cucumeres, Centaurea, Colloquintida, Euphorbiscus, Pruna, Seamony, Senna, and the like.

The Cure of Diseases of ♃ in ♒.

First, In such a case, if the Lungs or Lights be fill and replete with Blood, or do rise into the Throat, open the Heart-Vein in the left Arm, and afterwards in the right Arm, and then give things to delay and asswage the fervour and heat of the Blood, and to diminish the Quantity thereof, as before is said of ♃ in ♊ and ♎, and minister not in the Hour of ♃, neither put ♊, ♎ nor ♒ in the Ascendant, &c. as it is there said.

There are many Diseases also do chance through too much Blood, as Fluxes and spitting of Blood, of the which we will say something after, and of the stopping of the Terms. These Diseases being in a high degree are strong and venemous, and cause the Parties to swell, therefore give the Dose to repress Venome.

Against congealed Blood in the Body.

℞ Rhubarb Torrefacti, Terra Sigil. Boli Armen. Mummia, Semen Nasturtii Torrefacti ana 3i., Make them into Powder, and give thereof 3i. every morning cum Aqua Plantaginis vel Bursa pastoris.

Otherwaies.

℞ Rhubarb triti 3ii, Mummia 3β, Aqua Rubei, Ma. 3ii, Syrup. de Rosis ficcis 3β, Make thereof a Potion, and give thereof speedily; there may be added thereto Rubea Trochiseata.
Or thus,

℞ Terra sigil. Rubia tinclor. Mummia, Symphiti ana 9i, Rhubarb triti 9i,Mix them, and use the same cum Aqua Pastoris & Plantaginis.

If ♃ be Lord of the 6th in ♒, and the ☽ go from ♄ in ♌ to ♀ in ♏. Then in this case your Purge will not work before the Body be three days prepared beforehand as followeth.

℞ Sirrup. Absinthii, Mentor. Oximel Pontick ana 3i., Aqua ag. Buglosse ana 3iv, fiat potus pro 6 dos. The Drinking of this Digestive by a Woman may provoke the Course, then it's necessary to give this Purge following.

℞ Confect. Hameck 3 β, Pill. fine quibus 3β, decoctionis Senna, Pollypodii 3iiβ, fiat potus.

These Mundifie and cleanse the Blood from all Corruption.

Confect. Anacardina, decoctio Capil. Veneris, Aqua fructuum, decoct. Fumitorii, Pill. ad febres cholericas, Aqua fruntum, Alpicostum, Trochischi Campbore, &c.

For Spitting of Blood.

Trochischi de terra sigillata, Athanatos mag. &c.

For bleeding at the Nose, or bloody Flux.

Trochischi de Ramiche, Trochisq, de terra sigillata, Trochisq, de caraba, oleum Campherum, Dissolve Blood gathered to one place.

These following open all Obstructions throughOut the Whole Body of man.

Diacinnamomun, Sir. acetofus, Sir. de ficcis Herbis, Sir. de Fumitor, Trochisq, de Aniso, Pill. Agrerat. Min. Oleum Amigdalar.

Amar Oleum de Benj. Oleum Coltinum, Oleum Perficerum, Oleum de Piperibus.

The Cure of Diseases caused by ♃ in ♈, coming Of blood and yellow Choler, Choler predominating.

Minister not in the Hour of ♃ nor ♂, nor the ☉, but in the Hour of ♄, ☽, ☿ or ♀, neither let ♃ be strong, and put ♄, ☽ or ☿ in ♋, ♏ or ♓, if it may be, or let the ☽ be in ♋, ♏ or ♓, applying to ♄ or ♀, they being strong in angles, and let ♂, the ☉ or ♃ be Lord of the 6th and weak, and put ♋, ♏, ♓ or ♉,♍, or ♑ in the Ascendant, then digest Choler, let blood, and purge.

Digestives of yellow choler mixed with the Blood, choler having domination.

Violets, Succory, Endive, Sorrel, Hopps, Fumitory, Absynthium, Prunes, Lettice, Solamen, Miraba Citrinum, Aqua Casei, Butter, Whey, Tamarinds, Purslean, Cucumbers, the 4 semina frigid.

℞ Sirrup. Violar, Sir Fumaria ana 3i., Aquar. Violar. Fumitor. Buglossi ana 3i.i, fiat potus pro duobus dosibus.

Purgers for the same Griefs.

Rubarb. Mirab. Citrin. Cassia, Manna, Salis gem. Elect. succ. Rosar. Diaprunes, Confect. Hameck. Pill. de Rhubarb.

℞ Florum Borag. Bugloss. Violar. Fumitor. Absinthii ans p.1. Tamarindar 3β, Pollipodii 3ii, fiat decoctio ad colatur. 3viii, addantur Manna, Granat. 3i., Elect. de facto Ros. 3iβ, Confect. Hamech. 3ii, fiat potus pro tribus dos. It purgeth yellow Choler mixed with the Blood in the 2nd degree.

The Cure of Diseases caused of ♃ in ♌.

In the Diseases caused of ♃ in ♌, you shall first Purge yellow Choler before you let blood, and if it be in the 3rd degree, then it will not be amiss to give a Preparative first degree, then it will not be amiss to give a Preparative first two days before, because the Humour is fæculent, thick and strong.

Again, You shall not minister in the Hours of ♃, ♂ nor ☉, neither shall you put ♈, ♌ or ♐ in the Ascendant, but minister in the Hours of ♀,♄ or ☿, and the ☽ existing in ♉, ♍, ♑, ♋,♏ or ♓, and let the Lord of the 6th House be weak, then purge and let blood.

Preparatives.

Acetosa, Violets, Lupuli, Succory, Endive, Fumitory, Solanon, Tamarinds, Plantain, Cinquefoil, Avens, Lettuce, Sirrup. Acetosi citri, Sir. Violar, Sir. Endivia, Sir. Succorii, Sir. Lupulor. Oxi Sachara simp. Sir. Papaveris, succi, pomor. grautor.

Purgers of this yellow Choler.

Rhubarb, Confect. Hamech, Diaprunes, Diacartholicon, Pill. Masticha, Pill. Aurea, Pill. de 5 generibus mirabolar. Pill. Arab. Pill Euphorbia, Electuar. De succo Ros. Sirrup. Rhubarb. Sir Liquiritia.
Or thus,

℞ Florum Violar. Ficcar. Endivia, Fumitorii, Lupulor. Ana p.1. Rad. Lapathi acuti p.1. Tamarinds 3β, Florum Balancii, Borrage, Bugloss. Ana p.1. Polypodii 3i., Senna 3iii, Ligni Sancti 3ii, Mirabol. Citrum 3ii, Semen Lactuce, Ciccorii, Endivia ana 3iβ, Liquiritia 3ii, Passular. Prunor. Damasc. 9 addantur de Sirupo Liquiritia 3β, Sirup. Rhubarbi 3iβ, Elect. de succo Ros-lax. 3ii, fiat potus pro 4 dosibus.

In this case, the best means is to let blood in the Head, or in the Liver-Vein, that the Blood may be diminished, and have more scope; then give things to purge the said Choler, you may not stand upon preparation in this case, but give a Purge out of hand, that the Body may be emptied, and Choler abated; then shall you give him Digestives of Choler two or three days, and then purge him again after, and take heed you minister not in the Hour of ♃, ♂ or ☉, but in the Hour of the ☽ or ♀, when the ☽, goeth from ♀ to ♃, and put ♋, ♏ or ♓ in the Ascendant, and let the Lord of the 6th be weak; your Preparatives in this case must be strong, and so must your Purges, or else they will not work to any effect.

Perparatives.

℞ Violar. Lectuca, Siccorri, Endivia, Lupulor. Fumitor. ana Manip. i. Polypodii 3β, Rosar. Sol. Violar. ana pug. i. Seminis Lactuca, Cichorie ana 3ii, fiat decoct. ad colatur 3xiii,addantur Sirupi Rosar. Siccorii ana 3ii, fiat potus pro quatuor dosibus.

Purges in this case.

℞ Flor. Balansii, flor. Violar. Nempharis, Borage, Bugloss, Siccorii, Endiv. Acetosa ana M. i. Ligni sancti 3β, Tamarindar. 3iβ, Mesereon, M.i. Mirab. Citrin. Indi. ana 3v, Rhubarb 3ii, 4 sem. Frigid. Ana 3iii, Prunor. Damascen. 12. Passular. Mundat. 3iβ, Liquiritia 3iii, Semen Anisi 3β, fiat decoctio. Ad colatur 3viii, addantur succi Acetosi Citri 3I, Pill. Euphorbia, Pill. sine quibus, Agarica ana 3i., fiat potus pro 4 dosibus. This purgeth red Choler in the fourth degree.

The Cure of ♃ in ☉.

In this case minister not in the Hour of ♃, ♄, ☿ nor ♀, but in the Hours of ☉, ♂, ☽, they being in ♊, ♎ or ♒ and put ♊, ♎ or ♒ in the Ascendant, but put not ♃ nor ♉, ♍, nor ♑ in the Ascendant, neither let them be potent but weak, and let the Lord of the 6th House be weak, and then difest and purge this Choler, which is Æruginosa; if this Choler or Melancholy rest in the Stomach, then purge by Vomit.

Preparative against Choler caused of ♃ in ☉, Cold and dry.

Endive, Succory, Maiden hair, Tamarinds, Prunes, Borage, Bugloss, Senna, Epithimum, Oxi sachara, Sirup. Violar. Cassia, Hopps. Sorrel, Vineger, Limens, Polypody Stecados, Violets, Mercury.

℞ de Sirup. Endiv. Succori, Capacntr. ana 3i. Aquar. Lupulor. Violar. Rosar. ana 3iii, fiat potus pro 3 dos.
Or,
℞ Sirup. Ephithimi, Oxi Sacharum simp. Sirup. Aceros. ana 3i., Aquar. Mercurii, Endivia ana 3iii, succi Limoniorum 3iii,fiat potus pro tribus dosibus.

Purgers for the same.

℞ Siccoria, Endivia, Lupulor, ana M.i. Polypodii 3iβ , Senna 3β , Flor. Borag. Buglos. ana p.i. Semen Anisi, Feniculi Petrof. ana 3iβ , Passular 3iv, fiat decoct. ad colatueam 3v, addantur Elect. de succo Ros. 3β , Diaprunor. 3iii, Confect. Hamech 3β , fiat potus pro duabus dos.
Or,
℞ Anocardis i 3ii, Diaprunorum, Confect, Hamech ana 3iii, decoctio Polypodii 3iii, fiat potus pro una dos.
℞ Pill. Agarick 3i., Diaprunor. 3ii, Aqua Endivia 3ii, fiat potus pro una dos.
Or,
℞ Pill Fumitor. sine quibus ana 3i., Confect. Hamech 3ii, Aquam Violar, Absinthii ana, fiat potus pro duabus dosibus.

The Cure of ♃ in ♍.

In this case, prepare the Humours, and let the Party bath himself and the Members oppressed, with hot and moist things, and afterwards purge and vomit, if occasion serve; but minister not in the Hour of ♃, ♄, ☿, ♂ nor the ☉, but in the Hours of ♀ and the ☽, the ☽ being in ♊, ♎ or ♒ or in the Hour of the ☉ being in ♊, and put ♊, ♎ or ♒ in the Ascendant, and let the Lord of the 6th be weak.

Preparatives against Diseases caused of ♃ in ♓, proceeding of Melancholy mixed with Blood.

℞ Ligni sancti, Stecados ana 3iii, Polypodii 3i., fiat decoct. ad collatur. 3xii, addantus de Siryupo Absinthii 3i., de Sir. Capill, veneris, Epithimi ana 3iβ , fiat potus pro 5 dos.

℞ Sirup. Bugloss. Lupulor. ana 3ii, & cum decoctione Polypodii & Senna 3xii, fiat potus pro 5 dosibus.

Purgers against these Diseases.

℞ Confect. Hamech 3ii, Cassia fistula recens. extractum 3i., decoct. Polypodii, Epithinni, Tamarindor. 3iii, fiat potus pro uns dos. It purgeth in the 3rd degree.

℞ Diasenne, Diaprunor. ana 3ii, Pill. Arabice 3iβ , Rhenish Wine 3iv , fiat potus pro duabus dosibus.

℞ Senne 3iv. Polypodii 3iii, Stecados, Epithinni, Cap. ventris M.1. Prunes 9. Semen Anisi, Fenicu, Petros. ana 3ii, Tamarind, 3iβ , fiat decoctio ad colaturam 3viii. addantur pulp. Cassia 3i., Diaprunor. Damascen. 3iii, fiat potus pro 3 dos. It purgeth Choler Prassina in 3 degr.

In this case few Preparatives will serve, because the Humour is thin of it self, therefore you may purge the quicker and vomit; but minister not in the Hour of ♃,♄, ☿ nor ♂, but in the Hours of the ☉, ☽ or ♀, the ☽ in ♊, ♎ or ♒, and make the Lord of the 6th weak as aforesaid.

Preparatives in this case.

℞ Sirup. Borag. Scolopendia ana 3iβ , Aqua Fumitor. Endiv. ana 3iii, fiat potus pro tribus dosibus.

℞ Oximellita comp. Oxisachara ana3ii, Aqua Lupulor. Absiathii ana 3iii, Aqua Boraginis, Fumitoria ana 3iii, fiat potus pro 5 dosibus.

Purgers against this Disease.

Scolopendria, Borage, Bugloss, Capillareneris, Fumitor, Lupulot, Epithinium, Senna, Polypodium, Mar. Indor. Semen Anisi, Chicoria, Endivia, Faniculi, Cimini, Passular. Prunor. Santali, Moschat. Cinamoni, decoctio ad colaturam, addantur Diasenna, Discarthami, Confect. Hamech, Elect. succi Ros.

A Purge against this Disease.

℞ Confec. Hamech, Diasenna, Electuar. Succi Rosar. ana 3β, Aquaraum Buglossa, Fumitoria ana 3iβ, fiat potus pro una dose, which worketh with great ease.

The Cure of Diseases caused of ♃ in ♋

In this case sweat well, and purge Flegm and Water, but minister not in the Hour of ♃ nor the ☽, nor let them be potent, but minister in the Hour of ♂ or ☉, when they be in ♈, ♌, ♐, or in the Hour of ♄ being in ♊, ♎ or ♒, ♈, ♌ or ♐ being in the Ascendant, and the ☽ in ♈, ♌ or ♐, and the Cure must be effected by things dry and temperate in heat.

Digesters of Choler caused of ♃ in ♋.

℞ Sirup. de Stecad. de Scabious. ana 3ii, Aqua Scabiosa, Cenrure 3vi, fiat potus pro 4 dos.

℞ Oxicrassi 3iii, Aquar. callid. commun. 3ix, fiat potus pro 3,6,9 dosibus.

℞ Mellis Rosar. Sirup. acetofi Simpl. ana 3ii, Aqua Salina, Fumitorii, Hyssopi ana 3iii, fiat potus pro 4 dosibus.

Purgers for this Disease.

℞ Mirabellanor. Citri, Cassia fistula ana 3ii, Tamarindor. 3i., Prunor. Damascenor. XX, Florum Violar. 3iii, fiat decoctio, cloctur & addatur Rhahabar. 3iii, pulverizetur & infundatur nocte una in dicto liquort; dos. est ii or iii 3 ad majus, fir facito donec bene purgetur, & hoe fiat tam in febre quam sine febre.
Aliter,

℞ Aloe, Agarica, Turbith. ana 3ii, Pulp. Coloquint. 9ii Masticis, Annisi, Zinziberis, Cinnamoni, Sal Absinthii, Fol. Menthae ana 9ii, conficiantur Pill. cum Oximel. Sauillitico. Dose is 3iii, & detur post octo dies sua confectionis.

Or,

℞ Pill. Mastich. Pill. Elephangina ana ʒii, Aqua Emporii, Hissopi ana ʒiβ , fiat potus pro tribus dosibus.

The Cure of ♃ in ♏.

First Digest the matter 4 or 4 days, then purge and sweat,, but minister not in the Hours of ♃, ♀ nor ☽, but in the Hours of ☉, ♂, ♄ or ☿, being in ♈, ♌, ♐, ♊, ♎ or ♒, putting ♈, ♌ or ♐ in the Ascendant, and make the Lord of the 6th weak.

Preparatives against these Diseases which are cold in the second, and moist in the third degree.

℞ Oximel. Diuretica ʒiii, Aquar. Absinthii, Hissope ana ʒv, fiat potus pro 4 doses.
Aliter,

℞ Oximellis diuretic. Oximel scillitici ana ʒi., Sirup de Stecador ʒiβ , Aquar. Acetosa, Majorana, Fenicana ʒiii, fiat potus pro 4 dose.
Aliter,

℞ Sirup. Betonica, Oximellis diuretici, Sir Rosea. ana ʒi., Aquar. Melissa, Thimi, Petroselini ana ʒii, fiat potus pro tribus dosibus.

Purgers against these Diseases caused of ♃ in ♏.

℞ Hissop. Salina, Rosemarie, Menthae, Fanic. Absinthii ana M.i. Polypodii ʒii, Senna ʒβ , Passular. Mundat. ʒi., Semen Ansis, Cummini, Petrodelini, Zinbib. Berb. Cinnamoni ana ʒii, fiat decoctio ad colaturam ʒvi, addantur Diaphenicon ʒi., Benedict. Laxat. Hiera pig. galleni ana ʒii, Diacarthami ʒβ , fiat potus for three doses, It purgeth Cholera vitellina in the 3d degree.

The Cure of Diseases of ♃ in ♓.

In such a case sue good Diet, labour and sweat and digest the Humour, and then purge well, but minister not in the Hour of ♃,♀ nor the ☽, but in the Hours of ♂,☉,♄ or ☿ being in ♊, ♎, ♒, ♈, ♌ or ♐, as is aforesaid.

Digestives against Cholera vitellina, caused of ♃ in ♓, that is cold and moist in the 4th degree.

℞ Rosemarie, Mentar. Fumitorii, Absinthii, Hyssopi ana M.i. Senna 3ii, Liquirit. eii, Semen Anisi, Zinxiberis ana 3ii, fiat decoctio ad colistur. 3viii, addantur Oximellis diuretici 3ii, Sir. de Stecados 3β, fiat potus pro three dos.
Aliter,
℞ Dianthos. 3β , Diatumeris 3ii, Sir. Hissop. Liquiritia ana 3i., Aquar. Grananta. Hissop. Melliessa ana 3iv, fiat potus pro tribus dosibus.

Purgers against Diseases caused of ♃ in ♍, that are cold and moist in the 4th degree.

℞ Cuscuta, Hyssopi, Hipericonis, Melliessa, Thimi, Lupulor. ana M.i. Ligni Aloes 3ii, Galang. 3ii, Flor. Cammomille, Borrag. Buglos. Hipericon ana p.i. Gariophili, Cubebar. ana 3i, Croci 9I, Ebuli, Mercurii ana p.i. Flor. Sambaci M.i. Zinziberis 3i., Prunor. Damascen.xx. Senna 3iii, Polypodii 3ii, Rhabar. 3iβ , Semen Feniculi, Petroselini, Carui, Amomi. ana 3ii, Mirab. Kebulor. 3ii, Spikenard 3iβ , Ellebor. albi 3β , Agarici 3ii, Turbith 3i., Scamonii 9i., fiat decoctio ad colatur. 3ix, ad dantur de Diacarthamo, Diaphenicon, Diaturbith ana 3β, fiat potus pro tribus dosibus . It purgeth Cholera vitellina in 4 degr. strongly.

Digestives of Choler of ♂ in ♈.

Violets: Leaf and flowers, Endive, Succory, Poppy, Roses, Lettuce, Maiden Hair, Mallows, Mercury, Purslane, Barberies, Vinegar, Sanders, Barley-water, Prunes, Tamarinds, Liverwort, Sorrel, Whey clarified, Seed of Gourds, Seed of Mallows, Seed of Citrons, the four lesser cool Seeds, Endive-seed, Succory-seed, Purslane-seed, the juyce of four Pomegranates, the juyce of Limons.

℞ Sirrup. Endivia, Lupulor. Acetosa Simp. ana 3ii, Aquar. Graminis, Lupor. Buglosa ana 3iv, Santali. Moschat. 3iβ, Mix them for four doses, this difesteth red and yellow Choler caused of ♂ in ♈, the stomach being opprest by ♄ in ♌.

To make thick and gross Choler thin, and easie to be digested.

Sirupus acetosus, Sir de Radicibus frigid. de Radicibus, Trologodion, Ruffi, Decoctio Mirab. Pill Euphorbii, Pill. de Turbith, Pill. Stomachica, Pill. de Sarcocolla, Pill de Serapino, Pill. Coloquintids.

These Allay the Heat of Choler.

Succatrinum, Violarum, Sirup. acetosus Lax. Sirup. Acetos. de succo fructuum, white wine Vinegar one pinte, with four ounces of Sugar-candy, quenebeth and allayeth the heat and drowth of this Choler.

These following purge Choler well.

Confectio de Psillio, Confec. de Manna, Elect. Rosar. Pill. de Turbith, Pill. de Coloquintida, Sir. aceti Lax. Aqua fructuum, Aqua Casei, Infusio de ficcis Herbis, Confectio Fumitrol. Consee. de Croco with Mirabolanes.

These purge burnt and Adust Choler.

Trifera, Sara senica, Elect. frigid. Manna, Calabris, Oxipbenicum, cum decoct. Mirablan, Cassia Fistula, Tamarinds, Violets, Hopps, Aqua Fumitorii, Aqua Violar. Aqua Limonum, Aqua Pomegranat. Epithimum, Stecador, Mirab. Nig. & Indi. Calamint. Senna, Fumitor. volubilis, Confectio Hamech, Polypodium, Pill. de Lapid. Luzuli, Pill. Ruffi, Pill. Jeralogodii, Larmenus, Lapis Lazul. Sirup. Fumitor. Sir. de Ephithimo, acetum squilliticum, decoctio Capil. veneris, Pill. Stomach.

To purge all red and superfluous Choler.

℞ Mirab. Citrini, Cassia ana 3ii, Tamarinds 3i, Prunor. damse xx. Flor. Violar. 3iii, Flor. Ciabor. 3ii, Lupulor. 3i, Santali moseati 3ii, Ligni sancti 3i, fiat decoc.ad colatur. 3ix, adpanstiur Rheubarb 3iii, Infus. per noctem unam, fiat potus pro tribus dosibus.

The Cure of Diseases caused of ♂ in ♌, Administer not Physick in the Hour of the ☉ nor ♂, but in the Hours of ♀, the ☽ or ☿.

Preparatives.

Sirup of Poppy, Sir. of Violets, Solamini, Succory, Endive, White wine Vinegar, the juyce of Limons or Pomegranates, Lettuce, Polypody, Ireos, volubilis Fumitorie, Mirab. Citrin. Sebastens, Prunes, Tamarinds, Stecados, Sirup. acetosus.
As,

℞ Sir. Violar. Papaveris ana 3iβ , Aqua Solani, Violar. ana 3iv, fiat potus pro tribus dosibus.
Vel,

℞ Aceti albi 3viii, Aquar. Solani 3iv, Sachar albi candidati 3iii, fiat potus for 4 doses; this doth quench both the thirst, heat and drought of red and yellow Choler.
Or,

℞ Sirup. Solani Violar. Ciccorii ana 3i., Aquar. Ciccorii, Solani, Violar ana 3ii, fiat potus for 4 doses.

Purgers of gross thick yellow Choler, and thin red Choler, caused of ♂ in ♌.

Rhubarb. Mirabol. Citrin. Diaturbith, Pill. Rhubarb. Pill. de Electerio, Pill. fine quibus, Pill. Aurea, Pill. Arabica, Pill. Cochia, Pill. de octo 269. Cassia, Confec. Hameck, Sirpu. Rosar. lax. Diacatholicon, Sir Perficar. Pill. Agregative, Pill. Affairet.

Digestives of yellow Choler.

Sirup. Violar. Sir Rosar. Sir Solani, Oximel pontique, Sir. acetosus, Sir. Nenupharis, and the waters of these, and the decoctions of them, as of Violets, Nenuphari, Lettuce, Purslane, Orange, Spinage, Gossott, Beets, Million-seeds, Goord-seeds,Cucumber-seeds, White wine Vinegar, Consolids minor, Sirup, water or decoction of Sorrel.

These following purge red Choler.

Elec. de fucco Ros. Elect. Psiliticum, Pill. de Elaterion, Pills of Turbith and of Coloquintida, Elect. dulcis, Consec. Hameck, Diaturbuth, Trifera major, Sirup. Acetosus, Sirrup of Maidenhair.

Purgers of red Choler and Flegm.

Vomitus noster. Diaturbith, Trisera major, Sarasenica.

These purge red choler and Melancholy.

Mileta, Pill. de quinyne generibus, Mirabalanor.Requics magna, Confec. Hameck.

These following purge and clense the Blood mixed with choler, of ♂ or the ☉ in ♊, ♎, or ♒.

Tamarinds, Cassia, Manna, Borage, Bugloss, Ox-Tongue, Hopps, Solamen, Diaprunes, Sandala, Oxifacher, Simp. decoctio Communis. Sirup. Epatica, Sir Scolopendria, Sir. Acidula, Sir. Capaveneris, Sir. Endivia, Sir. Ciccoria, Sir. Lupulor. Sir. Papaveris, Sir. Nenuphoria.

The cure of Diseases caused of ♂ in ♉, when Melancholy hath the dominion.

℞ Sir. Borag. Rosar. Capil. veneris ana 3i, Aquar. Borrag. Rosar. Aceti albi, Endivia, Fumitor. ana 3iii, Thimi 3i. fiat potus pro 6 dos.

Digesters of Melancholy are these, of Sirups, and Waters.

Borrage, Bugloss, Holihock, Mallows, Roses, volubilis Fumitor. Stecados, Epithimum, Hopp, Cassia, Polypody, Perthenima, Rad. lap. acuti, Hyssop, Squinantium, Carnipytis, Scolopyndris, and such like.

Digesters of red choler.

Nenuphar, Violets, Poppy, Solanum, Lettice, Orage, Gosfoot, White wine-Vinegar, Oximel pontick, Sirup. acetosus.

Note.

In this case you must mix of each of these Sirups and Waters together, of those that digest Melancholy principally, and of those that digest red choler; if the Melancholy be most in the commixtion, then put most of those Sirups and Waters that digest Melancholy, &c contrario; for those that digest red choler, look in the Chap. of ♂ in ♐, and for those that digest Melancholy, look in the Chap. of ♄ in ♉, ♍ or ♑

Purgers against Diseases caused by ♂ in ♉.

℞ Borrage, Bugloss, Fumitory,Lupulor. Stecados ana M.i.Polypodi ʒi, Senna ʒii, Prunor. damase. xvi, Anisi, Fenicul. Petrol. ana ʒi. fiat decoctio ad colatur.ʒviii, addantur confec. Hameck ʒiii, Elec. succ. Ros. las. ʒiβ , Diaprunor. ʒi. fiat potus pro tribus dosibus, It purgeth Melancholy and red Choler of ♂ in ♉.

℞ Elec. Ros. succi. ʒβ , Confec. Hamech ʒii, decoct. Polypodii ʒiii, fiat potus pro una dose, It purgeth Melancholy and red Choler of ♂ in ♉.

Or,

℞ Diacenna, Confec. Hamech, Diaprunor. ana ʒiii, Aqua Fumitoria ʒiiβ, fiat potus pro una dose, idem agit.

Preparatives of Red Choler and gross Melancholy
caused of ♂ in ♍, where Melancholy predominates.

Polypody, Senna, Tamarinds, Stecados, Fumitory, Epithimum, Mirabol. IndiCitrin. Camepytis, Scolopendria, Hepatica, Violets, Borrage, Bugloss, Sirup. Epithimi, Sir. Bor. Bugloss

Sirup. Epithimi, Sir. Bugloss, Baccage, Sir Scolopendria, Sir Fumitor, Sir Lupulor, Sir Hepatic. Sir Violar. Sir Rhubarb.

℞ Ephithim. Stecados, Fumiteria ana p.i. Infuse them in white wine vinegar all night, strain it to 12 ounces, and add de sirup. Violar 3i. Sirup. Bugloss. & Fumitor. ana 3iβ fiat potus pro 4 dosibus.

℞ Decoctionis Polypodi 3viii, Sir de Stecados, Epithimi, ana fiat potus pro3 dos.

Purgers of red Choler and Melancholy caused of ♂ in ♍, where Melancholy hath the pre-eminence.

Confec. Hamech. Diaprunes, Solut. Diaturbith, Coloquintids, Rhubarb. Polypodi Senna, Elect. Psiliticum, Pill. de Turbith. Pill de Coloquintida, Pill. fine quibus, Pill. Arabica, Pill Fumitor.

℞ Stecados, Epithimi, Camepytis, Flor. Violar.Borage, Bugloss. ana M.I. 4 Semen frigid. major contus. ana 3i., Coloquintida 9ii, Turbith 3i., Rhubarb 3β , Polypodi 3iβ , Senna 3β , Prunor. 9. Semen Anisi, Liqueritia ana 3iβ , fiat decoctio ad colatur. 3viii, addantur Elect. Psiliticum 3β, Confec. Hamech 3iii, Pill de Turbith 3i., fiat potus pro 3 dos.

Digestives of red Choler and tough Melancholy, caused of ♂ in ♑, Melancholy predominating.

Therefore the Digestives must be very strong.

Absinthium, Fumitorie,Violets, Squinant. Epithimum, Hopps, Stecados, Borrage, Bugloss, Holyhocks, Roses, look in the Chap. of ♂ in ♐ for red Choler, and of ♄ in ♉, ♍ or ♑, for Melancholy Digestives.

℞ Decoctionis Polypodii, Senna ℨix, de Sirup. Absinthii, Epithimi, Squinant. ana ℨi. fiat potus pro 3 dos.

℞ Rad. Feniculi Petrof. Stecados, Epithimi, Lupulor. ana M.i. fiat decoctio ad collatur. ℨxii, addantur de Sir. Epithimi, Borrage, Stecad. ana ℨi. fiat potus pro 4 dosibus.

These following purge and cleanse the Blood, infected or mixed with red Choler of ♂ in ♊, ♎, or ♒, or of yellow Choler of the Sun in ♊, ♎, or ♒.

Preparatives in the Diseases of ♂ in ♊, in which you need use but few, because the Humour is thin.

℞ De Sirup. Fumitoria, Oxifachari ana ℨi., Aquarum Violar. Lupulor. ℨiii, fiat potus pro tribus dosibus.

Purges against Diseases caused of ♂ in ♊ of red Choler mixed with Blood.

℞ Flor. Violar. Borrage. Bugloss, Nenuphar. ana p.i. Fumitor. Lupulor. Cicorii, Endive ana m.i. Polypodii ℨiβ, Senna ℨii, Liquiritia ℨii, Tamarindor. ℨii, fiat decoctio ad colatur. ℨi., addantus Manna, Granator. ℨii, Cassia noviter extract. cum decoct. pradict. ℨiβ, Clarifie it for 3 doses.

℞ Diaprun. Confec. Hamech, Elect. succ. Rosar. ana ℨiii, Aqua Fumitor. Lupulor., ana ℨi., fiat potus pro una dose.

Preparatives against Diseases caused of ♂ in ♎, of red Choler mixed with Blood, which is more faculent, hotter and dryer than in ♊, viz. in 3 degrees.

℞ Flor. Borrag. Bugloss. Ciccorii, Endive ana p.i. Polypodi I ℨi., in vino albo fiat decoctio, ad colatur. ℨxii, addantur Pulpe Tamarindor. ℨβ, Cassia noviter extract. ℨiii, Manna ℨi., fiat potus pro 4 dosibus, It digesteth red Choler, and cleanseth the Blood in the 3rd degree.

Purgers against red Choler of ♂ in ♎.

Turbith, Confect. Hamech, Elect. succ. Rosar. Scammonia, Diaprun. solut. Psiliticum, Pil'. de Elaterio, Elect. Ducis, Theriac Galeni, Trochisq, de Rhubarb, Torchisq, Eupatorii, Pill. Turbith. Cad. Costiv. is wonderfully good against all Diseases caused of ♂ in ♎, ☽ applying to ♃, and 3i. thereof giveth 8 stools, and purgeth red Choler, and is good against Sciatica, Podagra, and the hot Gout.

Purgers against these Diseases of ♂ in ♎ of red choler mixed with Blood, Blood predominating.

℞ Turbith 3ii., Acetos. Fumitor. Violets, Lupulor. ana m.i. Polypodi 3ii, Rhubarb 3ii, Tamarind. 3i., fiat decoct. ad collatue.3v. addantur Electuar. Psilitici 3β , Manna 3i., Cassia 3v, Clarifie it & , fiat potus pro duabus dosibus.

℞ Cassia 3i., Pulp. Tamarindor. 3β , Confect. Hamech 3ii, Manna 3i., Sir Acetos. 3i., Decoctionis Polypodi 3v., , fiat potus pro duabus dosibus.

℞ Acetosia, Capilaveneris, Cetrach. Absinthii, Saxifrage, Flor. Genest. qna m.i. Semen Anisi, Millii Solis, Mellonum, ana 3i., Agarice 9i., Prun. Damascen. 9. Turbith, Rhubarb trite ana 3i., Polypodi 3i., Senna 3iii, fiat decoct. ad colatur. 3viii, addantur Pulp. Cassia, Noviter extract. 3β , Confect. Hamech 3ii, fiat potus pro 3 dosibus.

To cleanse the Blood thickened by red Choler,

look for ♂ in ♒, and that there set down is good.

Preparatives against the Diseases of ♂ in ♒, hot and dry in the 4th degree, caused of red choler mixed with thick, gross and faeculent Blood, Blood being the most predominent.

℞ De Sirupo Papaveris 3i., Pulp. Tamarindor, 3β , Sir. Violar. 3i., Sir. Ciccorii 3iβ , Aque Solani, Violar. Fumitorii ana 3iii, fiat potus pro tribus dosibus.

To cleanse the Blood being thickened with red choler of ♂ in ♒, A Drink.

℞ Pulp. Tamarindor. 3β , Sir. Endiva, Violar. Papaveris, Granator. de Fumaria, Endivia, Absinthii ana 3iii, Aceti albi vini 3iv, succ. Limonior. 3iβ , fiat potus pro quatuor dosibus.

A Purge against this Distemper.

℞ Tamarindor, 3ii, Pulp. Cassia 3i., Flor. Violar. Papav. ana 3ii., Ciccorii, Endivia ana 3ii, Borrage Bugloss. feminis ana 3ii, Rhubar. 3ii, Turbith 3ii, Ligni Sancti, Sebasten. ana 3iβ , fiat decoctio ad colatur. 3viii, addantur Manna, Granata, 3iiβ, Elect.succ. Ros. 3i., Clarifie it for three doses.

Preparatives against Diseases caused of ♂ in ♋, of flegm, water and red choler.

Scabious, Endive, Succory, Fumitory, Polium Montan. Radices Fæniculi, Rad. Petrosel. Sorrel, Sir Acetos. Pill Turbith, Thimum, Ebulus, Absinthium, Melliessa, Saxifrage, Vinegar, Juyce of Limons, Semen Endivia, Semen Ciccorii, Semen Amneos, Coloquintida, Turbith, Agarick, Sarcocol. Cassia Fistula.
℞ Endivia, Ciccorii, Fumitor. ana p.i. fiat decoctio ad colatur.3xii, addantur de Sirup. acetos. 3iii, fiat potus pro 5 dos.

Purgers against these Diseases.

℞ Rad. Fæniculi, Petroselini, Ciccorii, Endivia, Fumitorii, ana m.i., fiat decoctio ad colatur. 3viii, addantur de Disturbith, 3I, Elect. succi Rosar. 3iβ, fiat potus pro tribus dosibus.
Aliter,
     ℞ Pulp. Coloquintida 3ii, Turbith 3iiβ, Polypodi I 3ii, fiat decoctio ad colatur. 3v, addantur de Pill. Coloquin 3ii, Clarifie it for 2 doses.

Against salt Flegm proceeding of Choler and Flegm.

Diaturbith, Coloquintida, Pill. de Turbith, Confect. Hamech, Hiera pigra simplex, Anacardinum, Catartice imperiale.

Digestives of ♂ in ♏, wherein the stinking and tough Flegm being salt, hath dominion, and cured by the same, as in the Chapter before of ♂ in ♋.

The Cure of cold Humours and red Choler, caused of ♂ in ♓, cold and moist in the 3rd degree.

℞ Stecad. Fumitor. Epithimi, ana m.i. Tamarindor. 3β, Polypodii 3v. fiat decoct. ad colatur. 3xii, addantur Sir. Fumitoria, Epithimi, Scabiosa ana 3I, fiat potus pro 5 dos. This digesteth Humours that are cold and moist almost in the 4th degree, caused of ♂ in ♓.

Purges against this Disease.

℞ Fol. Sambuci, Lupulor. Ebuli, Scabious, Endivia, Cicor. Fumitorii ana m.i. Poli montani, Fæniculi. Petrosell. ana p.i. Turbith 3iβ, Colloquint. Petroselini, Zinziber. ana 3ii, Cinnamon 3I, Tamarindor. 3iβ fiat decoct. ad collatue 3viii, addantur Pulp Cassiæ 3β, Diapheniconis 3I, Pill. Agaricæ 3ii, fiat potus, and clarifie it for 3 doses.

℞ Pill. Colloquint. Pill de Turbith ana 9ii, fiant 9 Pills pro 1 or 2 doses.

The Cure of Diseases caused by ☉ in ♈.

Digestives of yellow Choler caused of the ☉ in ♈.

Santalum, Tamarinds, Violets, Scamb, Nenuphar. Nightshade, Poppy, Sorrel, Mexerton, Fumitorii. Ciccorii, Endivia, Gramen. Prunes, Mercurii, Hopps, Absinthium, Limons, Purslane, Lettuce, Barberies, Maiden-hair, Sanders, Roses, Barley-water, Scabious, Oxifacehara; of Sirups, Acetosus, Violets, Endive, de Papaveris, Rosar. Lupulor. Nymphæ, Solani, Ciccorii, Limons, Fumitor. Sir de Ireos, Absinthii.

Purgers against the same Diseases.

℞ Tamarindor. 3vi, Prunor. Jejubar. ana v, Passular. 3β, Hordei p.i. Semen Melonum ana 3iii, Flor. Violar. Borag. Bugloss. ana p.i. fiat decoctio de aqua Acidul. in quibus dissolve Cassiæ 3β, Diacatholicon 3β, Rhubarb infused 9iv., Cinnamon grains v, Sir. of Roses laxat. 3β, , fiat potus pro duabus dosibus, It purgeth yellow Choler in 2 degrees.

General Purges against these Distempers.

Rhubarb, Manna, Cassia, Fumitory, Senna, Polypody, Sebestens, mirab. Citrin Confect. Hamech, Pill. Rhubarb. Pill. mirab. Pill. Aureæ, Pill. Affairet. Pill. Aggregat. Pill. Funitor. Pill. fine quibus, Pill lucis majores, Pill. Arabica, Pill. Cochia, Pill. de octo. rebus, Sir. Rosar. lax. Diacatholicon. Sir. Persicar. Diaferios.Conserve of Violets, Conserve of Sorrel.

Digestives against thick Melancholy and thin yellow Choler, caused of the ☉ in ♂, Melancholy predominating.

Stecados, Epithimum, Polypody, Capil. veneris, Fumitory, Senna, Lupulos, Borage, Bugloss, Harts-tongue, Endive, Mirab. minth. Sirup, Bugloss, Borrage, Ciccor. Lupulor. Fumitor. volubilis, Epithimi, Capil. veneris, de Stecado, Scolopendri.

℞ Sir. Rosar. 3iβ, Sir. de Lupulis 3iβ, Pulp. Tamarindar. 3ii, Aquar. Absinthiii, de Lupulis, Fumitor. ana 3v. fiat potus pro 4 dosibus.

Purgers against the same Diseases.

Aloes, Scamony, Absinth, Conserve of Ciccory, and of Sorrel, Pill. de Fumiter. Pill. Agregate. Pill. fine quibus, Rhubarb, Confection of Hamech, Diaprunor. Diacatholicon, Polypody Senna, Jeralogod. Pill. de octo rebus, Elect. de Psillio. Mirab. Citrini, Diasenna.

℞ Flor. Borag. Bugloss. Violar. Absinthii, Tyme, Epithimi, Fumiterra, Stecados ana p.i. Prunor. xii, fiat decoctio ad colat. 3viii, addantur Oxisachar. 3I, Sir. Absinthii, Fumiter. ana 3i., Pill fine quibus, Pulver. Jeralogodii ana 3iβ, fiat potus pro tribus dosibus.

Digestives of yellow Choler mixed with Blood, caused of the ☉ in ♊ Blood having dominion.

Violets, Hopps, Fumitor. Night-shade, Ircos, Mercury, Mezereon, Manna, Sirups, Violar. Lupulor. Fumiterræ, Solani, Nenuphar. Cucumer. Asininus; Tamarinds, Lignum santicum.
℞ Fumiter. Mezereon, Lupulor. ana p.i. Tamarindor. 3iβ, fiat decoctio ad colatur. 3xvi, addantur de Sirupis Violar. Fumiter. Lupulor. ana 3iβ ,fiat potus pro 5 dos. It digesteth yellow Choler, and cleanseth the Blood.

Purgers for the same Diseases.

Cassia, Manna, Tamarinds, Rhubarb, Fumitory, Hopps, volubilis, Sirup of Roses, Conserves of Succory, Endive, Violar. and Bugloss.
℞ Aqua Violar. Fumiterra ana 3iii, dissolve therein of Manna 3β, Pulp. Cassia, Tamarind. ana 3β,, fiat potus pro duabus dosibus.

Digestives of thin Water and thin yellow Choler, caused of the ☉ in ♋ Flegm having dominion.

Baulm, Tyme, Hyssop, Mints, Horehound, Ireos, Camomile, Scabious, Fumitory, Hopps, Maiden-hair, Spikenard, Centory, Morubium, Astragus, Senna, Radix Faniculi, Rad. Petros. Sambucus, Polypody, Semen Amom. Sem. Ciccor. Sem. Fanic. Sem. Petrosel. Sem. Endiv. Oximel compositum, Oximel scilliticum, mel Rosar. Oximel diureticum, oxicratum. of Sirups, Sir. Absinthii, Betony, de Stecad. Acetos. simp. de Hyssope.
℞ Manubii, Scabious, Lupulor. ana 3i., aquar. Fumiterra,, Absinthii ana 2iv, fiat potus pro tribus dosibus.

Purges for the same Diseases.

℞ Elect. succi Rosar. 3ii, Diaturbith, Confect. Hamech ana 3iiβ, Decoctio. Polypodi 3iii, fiat potus pro tribus dosibus.

Aliter,
℞ Polipodii, Senna ana 3β , Epithimi, Stecados, Fumitory, Camepytis, Sambuci, fol. ana p.i. Rhubarb 9ii, Semen Anisi, Fanic. Petros. ana 3I, fiat decoctio ad colatur. 3vii, addantur Confect. Hamech, Elect. succi Ros. Diacarthami ana 3β , fiat potus pro 3 dos.
Aliter,
℞ Pill. Coloquint. Pill. de Turbith ana 3iβ , aquarum Scabious & Fumaria ana 3ii, fiat potus pro tribus dosibus.
℞ Diaphenicon, Confect. Hamech, Elect. succi Rosar. ana 3ii, decoct. Polypodii 3iii, fiat potus pro una dose.

Digestives of yellow Choler caused of the ☉ in ♌, are these following.

Violets, Sorrel, Night-shade, Fumitory, Absinthium, Mirab. Citrin, Scabious, Ciccory, Endive, Limons, Hopps, Roses, Iris, Tamarinds, Vinegar, Oximel, Lignum sanctum, Barley-water, Purslane, Oxifachara, Sirup of Fumitory, Sir. Solani, Sir. Violar. Mezereon, Scabram.
Iterum,
℞ Sir. Acetosi. Violar. ana 3ii, aqua Fumitor, Absinthii ana 3vi, fiat potus pro 5 dos.
Again,
℞ Sirup. Rosar. Fumaria, Absinthii ana 3I, aquar. Graminis, Scabious, Violar. ana 3iii, fiat potus pro 4 dos.

Purgers for the same Distempers.

Rhubarb. Pill Rhubarb. Pill Fumitor. Pill Arab. Pill. Agregat. Diacatholicon, Pill. fine quibus, Diaprunes, Elect. de fuce. Rosar. Serapinum, Pill. de Mezereon.
℞ Fumaria, Ciccorii, Endive, Violar. Oxalidus, Mercurii, Absinthii ana p.i. Mirab, Citrin. 3ii, Prunes ix, Sebestens 3β , Tamarinds 3I, 4 sem. frigid. major. contus. ana 3i., Rhubarb 3iβ ,Polypodi 3i., Senna 3ii, Agarica 9I, fiat decoctio ad colatur. 3viii, addantur

Manna, Granata 3ii., Elect. succi Rosar. 3β, fiat potus pro 3 dos. It purgeth yellow Choler in the 3rd degree.

Digestives of Melancholy and thin yellow Choler, caused of the ☉ in ♍, Melancholy being predominant.

Epithimum, Capil. veneris, Stecados, Polypody, Senna, Fumitory, Borrage and Bugloss.

℞ Sirupi Oxalidis, Cap. veneris, Fumaria ana 3i., aquar. Fumaria, Absinthii, Lupulor. ana 3iv, fiat potus pro 4 dosibus.

℞ Sirup. Ephithimi, Violar. ana 3ii, decoctionis Polypodii 3xii, fiat potus pro 4 dosibus.

Purgers for the same Diseases.

Diacatholicon, Diacenna, Confect. Hamech, Polypody, Senna.

℞ Flor. Borag. Bugloss. Tyme, Fumitor. Scabious ana p.i. Absinthii p. β , Mirab. Citrin. Indi nigri ana 3i., Ligno Sancti 3i., Sandalor. Rubeum 3ii, Semen Anisi, Faniculi, Petroselini, Ciccoria, Endivia ana ei., Polypodii 3I, Senna 3iii, Prunor. damascen. xx, Passular. mundat. 3i., Turbith. 3β, Coloquintida ℈ii, Liquiritia 3ii, fiat decoctio ad colatur. 3viii, addantur. Confect. Hamech. 3β , Elect. succi Rosar. 3iii, Diaprunor, 3β, fiat potus pro tribus dosibus.

Aliter,

℞ Confect. Hamech. 3ii, Pill. Fumitorii, fine quibus, ana 3i., Polypodii 3iii, de Sirupo Lupulorum 3I, fiat potus pro tribus dosibus.

Digestives of yellow Choler, and such as thin and cool the Blood of ☉ in ♎.

Hopps, Vinegar, Roses, Violets, Night-shade, juyce of Pomegranates, juyce of Limons, Succory, Endive, Tamarinds, Manna, Fumitory.

℞ Pulp. Tamarind. Cassia ana 3β , Sir. Violar. 3I, Manna, Granat. 3ii, Aquar. Solani, Violar. Endiv. Lupulor. Fumaria, ana 3iii, fiat potus pro 5 dosibus. This clarifieth and thinneth the Blood, and digesteth yellow Choler.

Purges against the same Diseases.

Manna Cassia, Rhubarb, Elect. Ros. lax. Pill. de Rhubarb.
℞ Flor. Violar. Borrag. Bugloss. Nenuphar. ana p.i. Fumitor. Mezereon. ana p.i. Polypodii 3ii, Semen Anisi 3i., Rhabar. 9ii, Absinthii 3iii, fiat decoct. levis ad colatur. 3x, addantur Pulp. Cassia 3vi, Manna 3I, Diacatholicon 3iii, fiat potus pro tribus dosibus.

Again,

℞ Lingni sancti 3β, Polypodii 3I, Senna 3ii, florum Violar. Borag. Fumaria ana p.i. Tamarind. 3I, Mirab. Citrin. 3iii, Prunes xx, Rhubarb 3I, fiat decoctio ad colatur. 3 xii, addantur Manna, Granat. 3ii, of the juyce of Flowers of Pomegranates 3ii, Elect. succ. Rosar. 3β, Clarifie it for 4 doses.

Digestives of salt Flegm and yellow Choler, caused of ☉ in ♍, look in the Chap. of the ☉ in ♋ and ♓.

℞ Sir. Fumaria, Oxicrati ana 3ii, decoct. Polypodi 3iv, fiat potus pro 4 dosibus.

℞ Sirup. Scabious. Fumaria, Oxicrati ana 3I, decoct. Scabious. Polypodii, Thyme, Fumitory 3xii, fiat potus pro 4 dosibus.

Purgers against the same Distempers of the ☉ in ♍.

Pill. fætid. Pill. Affairet. Pill. Cochia, Mel Rosarum. Diaturbith, Diacarthamum, Pill. Fumaria, Elect. succ. Rosar. Confect. Hamech.
℞ Pill. fine quibus, Pill Arabica ana 3ii, decoct. Polypodii 3v, fiat potus pro tribus dosibus.
Aliter,
℞ Diaphenicon 3v, Confect. Hamech 3iii, fiat potus pro una dos.

Digestives of Red Choler caused of the ☉ in ♐,
are these following.

Fumitory, Night-shade, Lettuce, Limons, Succ. Granat. Violets, Hopps, Vinegar, Endive, Succory, Purslane, Mercury, Sorrel.
℞ Fumitory, Ciccory, Endive ana p.i. fiat decoct. ad colatur. ʒxii, addantur de sirupo, acetos. Violar ana ʒiβ, fiat potus pro 4 dosibus, It digesteth red and yellow Choler in the 4th degree.
℞ Sirup. Violar. ʒii, Sir. Acetos. Fumarii ana ʒI, aqua Solani, Lettuce, Fumitory ana ʒiv, fiat potus pro 5 dos. It digesteth yellow and red Choler in the 4th degree.

Purgers against the same Diseases

Trifera, Sarafenica , Elect. frigid. Pill de quinque rebus, Mirab. Rhubarb. Confect. Hamech, Diacatholicon, Diaprunes, Pill. de Elaterid, Elect. Scilliticum, Pill. Coloquintida, Pills of Turbith.

℞ Ircos, Fumitory, Violets, Mercurii ana p.i. quatuor femina frigida maj. contus. ana ʒii, Ligni sancti & corticis ejusden ana ʒi., Rhabar. ʒii, Passular. mundat. ʒI, Prunor. damase. xx, Sebestens, Tamarind. ana ʒβ, Coloquint. ʒi., Euphorbii ʒβ, Polypodii ʒi., Senna ʒiii, Semen Anisi ʒβ, Liquiritia ʒii, fiat decoctio ad colatur. ʒxii, addantur Manna, Granat. ʒβ, Pulp. Cassia ʒI, Confect. Hamech, Diaprun. ana ʒβ, Elect. succi Rosar. ʒi., Aceti albi ʒiβ , succi Limonior ʒi., fiat potus pro 4 dos. It purgeth red Choler in the 4th degree.

Digestives of thin Melancholy and yellow Choler, Melancholy predominating, caused of the ☉ in ♍;

look in the Chapters of the ☉ in ♉ and ♍.

Lupuli, Ephithimum, Scolopendia, Liverwort, Cap. veneris, Borrage, Bugloss, Succory, Endive, Stecados, Senna, Polypody, Fumitory .

℞ Lupulor. Epithimi, Fumitoria, Polypodii ana ʒii, fiat infusio per 8 horas, colatur. & addantur de Sirup, Scolopendia, Violar. ana ʒI, Sirup Absinthii, Fumitor ana ʒi., fiat potus pro 7 dosibus.

Purgers for the same Diseases.

Polypody, Senna, Epithimi, Confect. Hameck, Diasenna, Diaprunes, Pill. fine quibus, Pill. Arabica, Pill. Aurea, cum Pill. de lapid. laxuli.

℞ Elect. succi Ros. 3ii, Confect. Hameck 3iii, Diaprunor. 3ii, decoct. Polypodii 3iii, fiat potus pro una dos.

℞ Polypodii 3ii, Senna, 3β, Epithimi, Stecados, Camepytis, Fumitor ana p.i. Rhubarb 9ii, Semen Anisi, Faniculi, Petros. ana 3i., fiat decoctio ad colatur. 3viii, addantur Confectionis Hamech 3i., Elect. succi Ros. 3β, fiat potus pro tribus dosibus.

Digestives of yellow Choler caused of the ☉ in ♒, are such as follows in the Chapter of the ☉ in ♊ and ♎.

Fumitory, Scabious, Hopps, Violets, Night-shade, Nenupharis, Succory, Oximel dura, Oximel compos. Oximel scilit. Oximel simpl. Sirup. Ros. Sir. Violets, Sir. of Hopps, Sir. of Endive, Borrage, Bugloss, Lettuce, Tamarinds, Sebestions, Pommegranates, Limons, Vinegar, Roses.

℞ Sir Voilar. Nenupharis ana 3i., pulp. Tamarind. 3β, Man. Granat. 3i., pulp. Cassia 3iii, aquar. Solani, Violets, Fumitory, ana 3vi, fiat potus pro 5 dosibus.

℞ Sebestens 3β, Tamarinds 3I, Ligni sancti 3vi, fiat decoctio ad colatur. 3xiv, addantur de Sirup. Violets 3ii, Fumitory 3i., fiat potus pro 4 dosibus.

Purgers for the same Diseases.

Diaprun. Manna, Tamarinds, Cassia, Rhubarb, Elect. succ. Ros. Diacatholicon.

℞ Flor. Buglos. Borage, Violets, Nenuphar. Fumitor. Scabioul. ana p.i. Tamarinds 3i., Ligni sancti & corticis ejusdem ana 3i., fiat decoctio ad colatur. 3viii, addantur de succo Ros. lax. 3β, pulp. Cassia 3i., Diaprune. 3β, fiat potus pro tribus dosibus.

Digestives of Flegm and this yellow Choler, caused of the ☉ in ♓, Flegm predominating,

look in the Chapters of the ☉ in ♋ and ♏.

℞ Sirup. de Enula, Sir Hysopi, Sir. Stecad. ana 3i., Sir. Marubii 3i., Aquar. Sambuci, Tyme, Fumitor. Scabior. ana 3iv, fiat potus pro 5 dosibus.

℞ Aquar. Rosemaria, Sambuci, Thima and 3v, Sir. de Capil. veneris, Fumaria, Lupulor. Matubii ana 3ii, fiat potus pri 7 dosibus.

Purgers for the same Diseases of the ☉ in ♓.

Pill. Agregat. Pill. contra Flegma, Pill Aracbica, Pill. Euphorb. Pill. Coloquint. Pill. fine quibus, Pill. fatid. Pill de Agarico, Pill. Fumitor. Pill. Eliphan. Pill Affairet. Pill de Hiera, Pill de Cochia, Confec. Hamech, Diachartamus, Diaturbith, Diatrion Piperion, Coloquint. Euphorb. Agarick, Turbith, Diagridion.

℞ Hyssop, Mint, Melissa, Marubii, Camepytis, Epithimi, Stecad. ana p.i., Semen Fanic, Petros. Anisi ana 3i., Ligni sancti, Agarica ana 3I, Coloquint. 9ii, Polypodii 3ii, Senna 3β, fiat decoctio ad colatur. 3viii, addantur Diacarthami, Diaturbith, ana 3vi, Elect. succ. Rosar. 3β , fiat potus pro tribus dosibus. It purgeth Flegm and yellow Choler in the 4th degree.

Preparatives against Diseases caused of ♀ in ♈, of thin yellow Choler and thin Water, Choler having dominion.

Lignum sanctum, Absinthium, Mirab. Citrin. Tamarinds, Stecados, Ephithimum, Fumitory, Bugloss, Succory, Endive, Hopps, Violets, Roses, Mercury, Sorrel, Syrups, Endive, Rosar. Absinthii, Violar. Fumitorii, Succorii, Lupulor. Epithimi, Pill. de Stecada, Acetosa, Bugloss, Rhubarb, Nenuphor. Sir.Addul.

Purgers for the same Diseases.

Manna, Cassia, Tamarinds, Rhubarb, Elect. succ. Ros. Diaprunes Diaturbith, Absinthium, Hopps, Polypody, Senna, Roses, Ircos.

Pills.

Rhubarbi, Aurea, Arab. fine quibus Fumitory, Pulvis sanctus.

℞ Flor. Borage, Bugloss. Violar. Nenuphar. Fumaria ana p.i. Absinthii, Lupulor. Ciccoria, Endivia ana p.i. Senna 3iii, Polypodii 3i., Semen Anisi 3β, Liquiritia 3ii, Passular. 3I, Tamarinds 3β, fiat decoctio ad colatur. 3viii, addantur Manna, Graut. 3iβ , Elect. succ. Ros. 3i., Diacarthami 3iii, fiat potus pro tribus dosibus.

Digestives of gross thick Melancholy and thin Water caused of ♀ in ☉, where Melancholy hath the dominion.

Fumitory, Stecados, Epithimum, Scolopendia, Lupuli, Violets, Mirab. Ind. Squinant. Camepytis, Endive, Ciccory, Semen Petros. Semen Anisi, Semen Faniculi, Tyme; Syrups, Capil.veneris, Epithimi, de Setcados, Scolopendi, Borrage, Bugloss, Indive, Ciccory, Oxisachara, Oximel Scilliticum, Oximel compos. Lapis Lazuli, Lapis Armenus.

℞ Sir. de Stecados, Sir. Epithimi, Sir. Scabious. ana 3iii, fiat potus pro 3 dosibus.

Purges for the same Diseases.

Polypody, Senna, Pulvis, Jeralogodii, Diacenna, Confect. Hamech, Diaprun. Diacatholicon, Pill. Fumitor. Pill de Lap.luzuli, Armen. Pill. Mastica, Pill. Indi, Pill. Aggregativ. Pill fine quibus, Pill. Arab. Pill lucis maj.

℞ Polypodii 3ii, Senna 3β, Flor. Borag. Bugloss. Violar. Fumaria; Lupulor. ana p.i. Prunes xii, Passular. 3i., Zinzib. 3i., Semen Fanicul. Petros. Ciccory, Endive ana 3i., fiat decoctio ad colatur. , 3viii, addantur pulveris Jeralogodii 3i., Confec. Hamech 3iii, Diacarthami, Elect. succi Rosar. ana 3iiβ, fiat potus pro 3,6,9 dosibus.

℞ Pill. fine quibus, Mastichini ana 3ii., Decoctionis Epithimi, Polypodii ana 3iv, fiat potus pro tribus dosibus.

℞ Confect. Hamech , Diacenna ana 3iii, decoct. Pill. Ephithimi 3iii, fiat potus pro 3 dos.

Digestives of thin Flegm or Water mixed with the Blood, Blood having dominion, caused of ♀ in ♊

Fumitory, Hopps, Scabious, Succory, Endive, Roses, Borrage, Bugloss. Absinthium, Cap. vener. mirab. Condit. Tyme, Limons, Tamarinds, succi Fumaria, Conserve of Succory, of Endive, of Roses, of Borage, of Bugloss, Syrup of Hops, Oxisachara, Aqua lactis. Caper. Sit. acetos. Citri.

Purgers for the same Diseases as aforesaid of ♀ in ♉, and let blood.

Diacarthamus, Diaturbith, Agarick, Cassia, Fumitory, Hopps, Polypody.

℞ Pulp. Cassia, Diaturbith ana eiii, Aqua Fumaria, Lupulor. ana 3iβ, fiat potus pro una dos.

℞ Flor. Borag. Bugloss. Violar. Nenuphar. Scabious. Fumaria, Absinthii ana p.i. Polypodii 3β, Senna 3i., Semen Anisi 3i., fiat decoctio ad colatur. 3x, dissolve Manna, Granat. 3ii, Diaturbith, Cassia ana 3iii, fiat potus pro 4 dosibus.

Digestives of Flegm and cold Humours caused of ♀ in ♋, ♏ or ♓

generally; look in the Chapter of the ☽ in ♋.

Roots, Radix Cipri, Ircos, Enula, Petros. Feniculi, Asperag. Rapbani, Astrol. utriusq. Ebuli, Sambuci.

Inos, Enula, Betonica, Salvia, Hyssop, Melissa, Origanum, Meats, Southerwood, Absinthium, Capil. veneris, Lignum sandum, Camepytis, Agrimony, Zinziber, mel Rosar. Oximel scilliticum, Oximel compos. Oximel simplex, Oxicratum; Syrups, viz. Sir. Absinthii, Betonica, Hyssop, Marubii, Acetosus simp. de Stecados, Liquiritia, Enule; Waters, Aqua Rosemarii, Hyssop, Rosa Solis, Marjoram, Melissa, Betonica, and Conserve de Anthios.

Purgers for the same Diseases

Agarick, Turbith, Polypody, Senna, Sarcocol, Ellebore, Sal Gemms, Cassia, Aloes Cicartrinum, Assarum, Laureola, Mirab.

Kebul. Coloquint. Euphorbium, Hermadactili, Diaturbith. Diacartsmur, Hiera piera, Simp. Diaphenican, Trochisq. Agarick, Trochisq, Rhubarb, Benedic. lax. Diacatholicon, Pill. Euphorbii, Pill. Cochia, Pill. Imperiatium, Pill. Agregatum, Pil. de Agarie. Pill. de Hiera, Pill. Arabic. Pill. Affairiet. Pill. fine quibus, Pulvis Hollandia, Pulvis Jeralogodit. Pill. Fatida do not purge Flegm gross and faculent in the Joynts, and are good against the Sciatica and pains in the Joynts.

Pill. Aurea do purge Flegm in the Heasd, and do sharpen and cleanse the whites of the eyes, and are good against the Distempers of the Eyes.

Pill. Lucis major. are good against dimness of the Eyes, and purge the Instruments of the Senses.

Pill. Euphorbium do Purge Flegm falling from the Brain to the Sinews, and are good against the Palsie.

Pill. Cochia do purge Humours from the Brain, and are good against the Epileptica and Apoplexy.

Digestives of yellow Choler and thin Water, caused of ♀ in ♃, where yellow Choler hath dominion.

Absinthium, Fumitory, Lupuli, Violets, Mirab. Citrin. Pruns and Mercury.

℞ Sirup. Violets, Stecados, de Fumitor. ana 3iβ , aqua Absinthii, Solani, Tyme, Fumitory ana 3v, fiat potus pro 6 dosibus. It digesteth thick yellow Choler and Water caused of ♀ in ♃.

Purgers against the same Diseases.

Cassia, Diaprunes, Rhubarb, Elect. succi Rosar.Diacathelicon.

℞ Foll. Rosar. Fumitoria, Violets, Scabios. Endive, Succory, Borrage, Bugloss, Absinthii ana p.i. Flor. Nenuphar. p.i. the 4. Semen frigid. minor contus. ana 3i., Semen Anisi 3i., Tamarinds 3i., Semma 3iii, Polypody 3β, Coloquint. 9ii, Zinzib. 3β, fiat decoctio ad colatur. 3viii, addantur pulp. Cassia, Elect. succi Ros.

ana 3vi, Diacarthamus, Diaturbith ana 3iβ , clarifie it for 3 doses; It purgeth yellow Choler and Flegm in the 3rd degree.

℞ Diaprun. Elect. succi Rosar. Diaturbith ana 3iii., Decoctionis Polypodii, cum Rad. Fanic & Petros. 3iii, fiat potus pro una dos.

℞ Diaphenicon, Diaturbith ana 3I, Agarica, Fumaria ana 3iβ , aqua Bugloss. Violar. ana 3iiβ, fiat potus pro tribus dosibus.

Digestives of Melancholy and thin Water, caused of ♀ in ♍, where Melancholy is predominant.

Epithimum, Lupuli, Capil. veneris, Scolopendri, Borage, Bugloss, Bugle, Fumiter. Endive, Succory, Polypody, Senna, Aniseeds; Sirups, viv. of Bugloss, Fumitory, Scolopendri, Borrage, Endive, Epithimi, Capil. veneris; look in the Chapter of ♀ in ♉.

℞ Sirup. Bugloss. Borage, Fumitoria, Epithimi ana 3i., aqua Fumaria, Scabiosa, Lupulor. Decoct. Polypodii ana 3iv, fiat potus pro 5 dos.

℞ Polypodii 3ii, Ephithimi 3i., Semen Anisi contus. 3ii., infused in Whey 12 hours, and drink there of; three ounces for a dose.

Purgers against the same Diseases.

Senna, Polypody, Confect. Hamech, pulvis Jeralogodii, Diaprun. Diasenna.

℞ Diacarthami 3ii., Diasenna, Diaprun. ana 3iii., Polypodii cum Senna 3iii, fiat potus pro una dos.

℞ Pulveris, Jeralogodii 3I, & cum Melle fiat pill. 15 pro duabus dosibus.

℞ Flor. Borag. Bugloss. Fummarie, Violar. ana p.i. Polypodii 3iii, Epithimi 3i., Senna 3β, 4 Semen callid. ana 3i., fiat decoctio ad colatur. 3viii., addantur Confect. Hamech 3β, Diaphenican 3iii., Diaturbith 3ii., Elect. succi Ros. 3v, fiat potus pro tribus dosibus.

Digestives of thin Water mixed with Blood, caused of ♀ in ♎;

look in the Chapter of ♀ in ♊.

Fumitory, Hopps, Succory, Endive, Borage, Bugloss, Roses, Absinthium, Scabious.

℞ Conserve. Ros. Borrag. ana 3β, Sir. Ciccoria Bugloss ana 3i., pulp Tamarindar. 3β, aqua Fumaria, Ciccoria, Endivia ana 3vi., fiat potus pro 7 dosibus. It cleanseth the Blood.

Purgers for the same, and let Blood.

Diaprunor. Cassia, Manna, Tamarinds, Diaturbith, Diacarthamus, Polypody, Senna, Agarick, Pulis sanctus, Pulvis Hollandia.

℞ Pulp. Cassia, pulp Tamarind. Diaturbith ana 3β, Manna, Granat. 3ii, decoctionis Polypodii 3viii, fiat potus pro tribus dosibus, Purgers for the same; look in the Chapter of ♀ in ♊.

Digestives of Flegm and Water caused of ♀ in ♍, and to discuss gross and slimy Flegm;

observe in the Chapters of ♀ and ☽, in ♋, ♍ and ♓.

Hyssop, Melissa, Fennel, Parsley, Mints, Rosemary, Sage, Betony, Pimpernal, Galingal, Calamint, Rad. Fanic. rad. Petros. rad. Acori, rad. Enula, rad. Ebuli, Mel Rosar. Oximel compos. Oxicart. Sir de duobus Rad. Sir. Hyssopi, Agrimonia, Sir. ma. de Fumeria, Dialacca, Galleni, purgeth all slimy matter, Acetosum squilliticum, Pill. Agregat. maj. Pill. fatid. minor; if the Humours be in the Sinews, use Pills; Euphorbii, Emplastrum de Allns, Confectio de Dactilis purgeth raw Humours.

Purgers of Flegm and Water caused of ♀ in ♍;

look in the Chapters of the ☽ in ♋, and of ♀ in the same.

Crocus, Aloes, Zinziber, Macis, Galingal, Cubebis, Dianthos, Pill. Mastick, Hierapigra, Agarick, Coloquintida,

Diaturbith, Diacarthamus, Pulvis, Hollandia, Lignum Aloes, Pill. de Aloe lota.

℞ Diaturbith, Diacarthami ana 3iii, Elect. succ. Ros. laxat. 3ii, aqua Thimi, Hyssopi ana 3iβ , fiat potus pro una dos.

Against Giddiness of the Head and Apoplexia.

℞ Pill. Cochia, Pill. fine quibus, Pill. Fumaria ana 9i., fiat 9 Pills pro una dos. This cleareth the Eyes, and cleanseth the Head and Brain of cold Flegm.

Pill. Aggregativa 3i., is good against tough Flegm, and Aches in the Bones and Joynts, and against the Palsie, and all cold Causes.

Pill. Mastichini 3i. is good against Aches in the Joynts and Bones.

Pill. Arabica purge all Humours; Palvis Hollandia and Pulvis sanctus purge Flegm, and watrish Humours.

Pill. Diacastoria are good against the Palsie, they clear the Eyes, and fallen loose Teeth, and are good against the Stranguary; the dose is 9i.,

If the Terms of Women be stopt, to bring them down, posite ♀ in the 12th or the 6th House, and let her eat Milk sodden and crummed, with a little Ale put in it, and it will with ease bring them down very much.

Digestives against Diseases caused of ♀ in ♐ of thick red Choler, and thin Water mixed, Choler predominating.

Night-shade, Lettuce, Purslane, Violets, Sorrel, Fumitory, Hopps, Poppy, Tyme, juyce of Pomegranates, white-Wine Vinegar, with white Sugar-candy, Limons, Succory, Endive.

℞ Sir. Absinthii, Sir. Endive, Sir Rosar. ana 3β, Oximel pontick, 3I, aqua Endiva, Violar. ana 3iv, fiat potus pro 4 dos.
Another approved Receipt.

℞ Sir. Ros. Sir. Endiv. ana 3I, Absinthii 3β, aqua lot. bene Endivia, Violets ana 3iv, fiat potus pro 4 dos.

Another, when the ☽ applies to ♀.

℞ Sir. Fumitory, Endive ana 3β, Rosar. 3I, aquar. Solani, Violar. ana 3iii, Endivia 3ii, Hyssopi 3i., fiat potus pro 4 dos.

Another, when the ☽ in ☉ separates from ♃, and applies to a □ of ♄.

℞ Oximel pontick, Sir. Rosar. Fumaria ana 3I, aquar. Endivia, Absinthii, Violar. ana 3iv., fiat potus pro 5 dos. Prebatum.

A Diet.

Let them that Languish under the aforesaid Distempers eat o meats, broiled, roasted, or fryed, nor Fruit, nr drink any Wine, nor eat any Spices, nor salt or dry Fish, for all such things are naught; nor Cabbages, nor Turnips, nor burnt Wine wherein Spices are, nor Apples, Pears, Milk nor Cheese; but ye may eat fresh Beef, Mutton or Veal, or Birds, and sometimes fresh Butter, but no Pie-meat or Pie-crust.

℞ Sirup. Acetos. Sir Papaver. Violar. Ciccori ana 3vi, fiat potus pro 7 dosibus.

Purgers against the Diseases caused of ♀ in ♂.

Pill. de Coloquint. Pill. de Turbith, Elect. ducis, Sir. Acetos. Coloquintida, Rhubarb, Diagredion, Scammony.

℞ Pill. de Turbith, Pill. Coloquintide ana 3ii, aquar. Acetos. Fumitoria ana 3ii., fiat potus pro tribus dosibus. It purgeth red Choler and Flegm strongly in 4 degrees.

℞ Elect. duleis, Elect. fellitie. Diacarthami ana 3iii, aquar. Acetos. Fumaria, Absinthii ana 3iβ, fiat potus pro una dos. It purgeth red Choler and Flegm.

℞ Flor. Violets, Foll. Solani, Fumitoria, foll. Papaveris albi, fiat decoct. aqua Violar. Solani, Papaveris albi ana 3vi, colatur & postea, infuse pulp. Coloquint. 3i., Turbith 3ii, Diagrid. 3ii, Rhubarb 3ii, Semen Anisi, Fanic. Zinziberis & quatuor fem.frigid.

maj. contus. ana 3i., tunc colantur. and give 3vi for a dose, and purge 3 days.

Against Pain and Ache in the Body caused of ♀in ♐, ☽ in ♍ Separate a ♂in ♎, & a ♀in ✶of ♃, being in ♍ combust & post. App. ad ✶ ☉ in the 12th. A Purge against the same.

℞ Diacarthami, Confect. Hamech ana 3ii., Pill. Arab. fine quibus ana 9I, Decoctionis Senna Polypodii, Stecados, Violar. Borrage, Sremen Anisi, quatuor fem. frig. maj. contus. 3ii, fiat potus pro una dos. This hath procured much ease.

A Preparative for the same.

℞ Sirup. Absintbii 3i., Rosar. simp. Fumariæ ana 3iβ, aquar. Violar. 3ii, Montan. Soani ana 3i, Fænic. 3iii, Boraginis 3vii, Rosar. 3iv, Oximel Pontick 3I, fiat potus pro 7 dos.

Digestives against Melancholy and thin Flegm, caused of ♀in ♏, Melancholy predominating,

as in the Chapter of ♀ in ♉ and ♍.

Polypody, Fumitory, Senna, Epitbimum, Lupuli, Cap. veneris, Camipyteos, Borage, Bugloss.

℞ Sirup. Epitbimi, Sir. Scolopendri, Borage, Bugloss. ana 3i, aquarum Lupulor. Thimi, succi Limonium ana 3iv, fiat potus pro 8 dos.

℞ Flor. Borrag. Bugloss. Violar. Fumariæ, Epithimi ana p.i. Polypodii 3ii, fiat decoct. ad colantur. 3xvi, addantur Oxisachari, Oximelis compositi, Sirup. Fumariæ ana 3i, fiat potus pro 6 dos .

Purgers of the same Diseases as aforesaid,

In the Chapter of ♀ in ♉ and ♍.

Pulvis Jeralogodii, Diasenna, Confect. Hamech, Diacatbolic. Diaprunes, Polypod. Senna, Pill. de lapid. Lazuli, Pill. de lap. Armeni, Pill. sine quibus, Pill. Arabicæ.

℞ Diasennæ, Confect. Hamech, Diaprunes ana 3iiβ, & cum decoctione Polypodii 3iii, fiat potus pro una dos.

℞ Fumariæ, Scabious. Salinæ, Epitbimi, Borrag. Bugloss. Scolapendri, Cap. vener. ana p. i. 4sem Callid. ana 3i, Zinziber. 3ii, Cinnamon. ᴈ, Prunes 20. Passular. Polypodii ana 3ii, Sennæ 3ii, pulvis Jeralogodii 3ii, fiat potus pro tribus dosibus.

Digestive and things to cleanse and sweeten the Blood, are these that follow, and such as are in the Chapters of ♀ in ♊ and ♎, and ♃ in ♊, ♎ and ♒

Hopps, Fumitory, Absuntbium, Endive, Succory, Roses, Capveneris, Seabious, Scurvy-grass, Borrage, Bugloss, Bugle, Milfoil, Sorrel, Cinquefoil, Tamarinds, Prunes, Sarsaperilla, Lignum sanctum, Aniseeds, Conserve of Succory, of Endive, of Roses, of Hopps, of Oxisachari, of Limons, of Oximel comp. Sir. Acetosus.

℞ Absintbii, Fumariæ, Lupulor. ana p.i. fiat decoct. ad colatur. 3xviii, addantur Sir. Fumariæ, Absintbii, Oxisachari ana 3i, Sir. Borag. 3iβ, fiat potus pro 6 dosibus. This makes thin, sweetens and cleanseth the Blood.

℞ Tamarinds 3i, Sennæ 3i, Polypodi, Lupulor. ana 3i, fiat decoctio ad colatur. 3xx, addantur Oxinuel comp. Sirup. Fumariæ, Lupulor. ana 3ii, fiat potus pro 8 dos. This thins the Blood, and cleanseth it of Water.

Pugers of thin Flegm mixed with the Blood, caused of ♀ in ♒.

Your Purges in these Causes must be gentle, and such as will subtilliate, thin and clarifie the Blood; and such shall you find in the Chapter of ♀ in ♊, and of ♃ in ♊, ♎ and ♒. And farther you may use these following:

℞ Flor. Borag. Bugloss. Endive, Succory, Fumitory, Hopps, ana 3i, Polypod. 3β, Tamarindor. 3ii, Semen Anisi 3i, fiat decoct. ad colatur. 3xii, addantur de Sir. Fumitory, Lupulor. Absentbii ana 3i, pulp. Cassiæ 3β, fiat potus pro 4 dos.

℞ Pulp. Tamarindor. pulp. Cassiæ ana 3β, Diaturbith 3iij, Diaprun. Solutiv. 3ii, Mannæ, Granatæ 3iβ, decoct. flor. Cordiolium 3x, fiat potus pro 3 dosibus.

Digestives of Flegm and Water caused of ♀in ♐ are, as in the Chapters of ♀ and ♃ in ♋, ♍ and ♓,

and these that follow here.

Melissa, Tyme, Mint, Rosemary, Absintbium, Hyssop, Milsoil, Crocus, Zinzib. Macis, Dianthos, Cubebs, Galanga, Lignum Aloes, Camepyteos, mirah. Condit. Cyprus, Betony, Ireos, Parsley, Fennel, Sage, Aniseed, Agrimony, Oximel, Mel Rosar. Sirup. Marrubii, Sir. Cap. veneris.

℞ Sirup. Melissæ, Oximel compos.ana 3ii, aquar. Sambuci, Rosenar. Absintbii ana 3iv, fiat potus pro 5 dos.

Purgers of the Diseases aforesaid in the Chapters aforesaid of ♀ and the ♃.

Theodot. Hiperisticon, Anacardinum, Sir. compos. de Fumaria, Diaturbith, Diacartamo, Coloquintida, Agarick, Pill. Euphorbii, Pulvis sancus, pulvis Jeralogodii, Hiera piera, Galeni, Turbith, Polypodiæ, Sarcocol. Mithridatum, Theriaca.

℞ Thimi, Melissæ Rosemariæ, Sambuci, Salviæ peritariæ, Ireos ana p.i. Solis gemmæ ɜii, Turbith, Sarcocolli, ana 3i, Euphorbii 3β, Agarick 3i, Coloquintidæ ɜii, Hermodactili, Dictami, Cretici ana 3ii, Polypodii 3iβ, Sennæ 3iii, Spatula fætidæ, Scorphulariæ ana p.i. fiat decoct. ad colatur. 3ix, addantur Sirupi composit. Fumatiæ 3ii, Theodot. Hiperisticon ana 3ii, Pill. de Hiera, de Euphorbio ana 3i, fiat potus pro 4 dosibus. It purgeth Flegm exceedingly in the extream parts in the 4th degree, even all tough Flegm.

Digestives of Diseases caused of ♀ in ♈, ♌, ♐, which proceed of thin yellow Choler and Melancholy mixed, Choler having dominion.

Endive, Succory, Violets, Nenuphar. Scabious, Lettuc, Mercury, Purslane, Roses, Vinegar, Tamarinds, Sorrel, Sanders, Barberries, Whey clarified, Prunes, Liverwort, quatuor sem. frigid. juyce of Pomegranates, Limons, Mallows, Poppy, Night-shade, Cap. veneris, Fumitory, Epithimum, Polypody, Senna, Hopps, Harts-tongue, Stecados, mirah. Citrin. nig. mirah. Indavalubilis, Oxisachara, Sirupus Acetosus, Sir. Endiviæ, Sir. Ciccor. Sir. of Violets, Sir. Nemupharis.

℞ Sir. Endivæ, Ciccor. de Stecados ana ʒi, aquar. Acetos. Endiviæ, Lupulor. ana ʒiii, fiat potus pro 4 dos. It digesteth yellow Choler and Melancholy in the 2d degree.

℞ Sir Violor. Rosar. Epithimi ana ʒii, aquar. Rosar. Ciccer. Lupulor. Fumariæ ana ʒv. fiat potus pro 7 dos. It digesteth yellow Choler and Melancholy.

Purgers against the same Diseases of ♀ in ♈, where Choler hath dominion, hot and dry.

Aloes, Scamony, Sir. Roses lax. Diaprunes, Rhabarb, Anacardinum, Hiera picra simp. Manna, Elect. frigid. Pill. de lap. Lazuli, Pill. Russini, Pill. de actorebus, Pill. Agericæ, Pill. Arabic.

℞ Elect. frigidi, Confect. Hamech, Mannæ, Calabriæ, ana ʒiii, Tamarindor ʒiβ, Pill. de Rhabarb, Pill. lucis ma. ana ʒi, Diaprunor. solutiv. ʒβ, decoct. mirah. Citrin. niger, Stecados, Epithimi, fiat potus pro tribus dosibus.

Digestives of ♀ in ♌, where Choler predominates.

℞ Oxisachari, Sir. of Violets, Stecad. ana ʒi, aquar. Rosar. Fumariæ, Lupulor. ana ʒiii, fiat potus pro 3 dos.

℞ Sir. Papaverin, Violar. Epitbini ana ʒi, aquar. Fumarie, Scabious ana ʒiii, succi Limonis, aquæ Rosar. ana ʒi, fiat potus pro 3 dos.

Purgers against the same Diseases.

℞ Fumariæ, Scabious, Violar. Stecad. Camepytis, Dictanii, Cretici ana p.i. Flor. Boraginis, Buglossæ, Violar. Camomil. Nenupharis ana p.i. Polypodii 3ii, Sennæ 3iii, Rhabarb 3iβ, mirah. Citrin. nigr. Ind. Sandalor. Rub. Liguisancii ana 3i, auqtuor sem. frigid. ma. contusi ana 3i, Agarica ǝii, Aloes Cicatrin. ǝi, fiat decoct. ad colatur. 3viii, addantur Elect. sucos Rosar. 3i, Confect. Hamech 3β, fiat potus pro tribus dosibus.

℞ Diaprunor. 3ii, Confect. Hamech 3ii, Elect. frigid. 3v, Infusionis Rhabarb, Stecados, Epithimi 3iv, fiat potus pro 2 dos.

Digestives of Diseases caused of ♀in ♐.

Fumitory, Borrage, Bugloss, Violets, Lupuli, Mirah, ind. Mirah. nigr. Tamarinds, Poppy, Night-shade, Juniper-berries, Tormentil, Devils-bit, Gilli flowers, Bay-berries, Seeds of Limons, Nuts of all sorts, Acorns, Parsnip seed, Garlick, Parsley-seed, Oximel ponstick; Sirups, of Violets, of Fumitory, of Endive, of Wormwood, of Poppy, Mitbridate, Therraca, Limons, the Water of Cardum benedictus, the Water of Dragons wort, Water of Roots of Seawet, Angelica-Water, the Water of Rue and Saxifrage.

℞ Stecados, Lupulor. Violets, Bugloss. Borrag. ana p.i. fiat decoct. ad colaniur. 3xvi, addantur de Sirup. Violar. Papaporis. ana 3iβ, Manna, Granat. 3i, Sir. Fumariæ 3ii, fiat potus pro 7 dosibus.

℞ Mirah. Citrin. Indi nigri ana 3i. Tamarind. 3β, Elor. Borage, Bugloss. Vioelts, Fumitory, Lupulor. ana 3i, fiat decoct. ad colatur. 3xvi, addantur ide Sirupo Fumitory, Papaveria ana 3ii, fiat potus pro 6 dos.

Purgers against the same Diseases aforesaid.

℞ Pill. Russini, Pill. Rhabarbi ana 3i, Confect. Hamech 3iii, Pill. lucis ma. ǝiβ, Aquar. Fumariæ, Violar. ana 3ii, fiat potus pro 3 dos.

℞ Flor. Bugloss. Borage, Stecados, Violets, Balantii, Lupulor. Fumitory ana p.i. Tamarinda 3β, Rhabarbi 3ii, Coloquint. ǝii, Aloes Cicatrini 3β, Polypodii 3iii, Sennæ 3β,

Agaricæ 3β, Sarcocollæ 3i, Diagredii ɜii, quatuor sem. frigid. contus. ana 3i, fiat decoct. ad colatur. 3viii, addantur succi Limonior 3β, Sirupi, Fumariæ, Rosar. ana 3i, fiat potus pro tribus dosibus. it purgeth red Choler and Melancholy in the 4th degree.

Digestives of Melancholy are these that follow,

and such as are in the Chapter of ♄ in ♉.

Lupuli, Stecados, Epithimum, Scolopendria, Camepytis, Mirah. nigri, lapis Lazuli, lapis Armenus, Borage, Bugloss, Maiden-hair, Polypody, Senna, Sirups of Scolepend. Epithimi, Bugloss. Borage, Lupulor. Cap. veneris.

Purgers for the same;

look in the Chapter of ♄ in ♉.

℞ Confect. hamech 3v, Diaprunor. solutiv. 3iii, Aquar. Fumitory, Borage, Bugloss ana 3i, fiat potus pro ana dos.

Digestives against Diseases caused of ☿ in ♍, as follow, and in the Chapters of ☿ in ♉, and ♄ in ♉ and ♍.

℞ Sirupi de Stecad. Epithimi, Borage ana 3i, Aqua lactis 3ix, fiat potus pro tribus dosibus.

Take Polypody 3ii sliced, and lay it in Whey all night, and drink 3iv thereof every morning.

Purgers against Melancholy cold and dry, as follow, caused of ☿ in ♍, and as in the Chapter of ♄ in ♍ and ♉.

℞ Epithimi, Lupulor. Cap. venteris, Stecados ana 3i, Polypodii, Sennæ ana 3β, Semen Anisi, Fæic. Petvos. ana 3β, fiat decoct. ad colatur. 3viii, addantur Consect. Hamech 3i, Diasenna 3iii, fiat potus pro 3 dos.

These following do cleanse, sweeten the Blood, and cool it.

Sirup. Granat. Sir. Endive, of Fumitory, of Hopps, Sir. acctos. sump. Sir. acetosaol. Citrina.

These do prepare melancholy, Fumitory, Hopps, Borage, Bugloss, Harts-tongue, Cap. veneris, mirah, Indi, Polypodi, Cuscuta, Camepytis, Horehound, white-Worts, Tyme and Hyssop.

These purge the Blood,

Borage, Bugloss, Fumitory, Hopps, Endive, Succory, Wormwood, Roses, Venus-hair, Tamarinds, Pomegranates, Conserve of Maiden-hair, of Bugloss, of Roses, of damask Prunes.

A Digestive.

℞ Pulp. Tamarind. pulp. Cassiæ ana 3iii, Mannæ 3i, Sirup. Buglos. de Stecados. ana 3i, aquar. Fumariæ, Borage, Violar. ana 3iiiβ, fiat potus pro 4 dosibuis.

Purges against the same Diseases.

Cassia, Tamarinds, damask Prunes, mirah, Ind. Manna, Diaprun. Sir. Ros. lax. Sir. Absuntbii, Hiera picra simp. Diacatbolicon.

℞ Flor. Boraginis, Bugloss. Violar. ana p.i. Lupulor 3i, Tamarinds 3iβ, Polypodi 3β, Sennæ 3i, fiat decoct. ad colatur, 3viii, addantur Mannæ, Granaiæ 3iiβ, Diaprun. 3β, confect. Hamech 3ii, fiat potus pro tribu dosibus. These purge, sweeten and cleanse the Blood, Polypody and Senna.

Digestives of Diseases of ♀ in ♒, as in the Chapter of ♀ and ♄ in ♊ and ♒.

℞ Sirup. Violar. Papaveris, pulp. Tamarind. ana 3β, Cassiæ 3ii, Manna 3i, aquar. Borage, Bugloss. Lupulor. ana 3iii, fiat potus pro tribus dosibus.

Purgers against the same Diseases caused of ♀ in ♒, of Melancholy and Blood hot and moist in the 4th degree,

let blood and purge with such as you find in the Chapter of ♄ in ♒, and of ☿ in ♊.

Pil. lucis ma. Pil. arabicæ, Pil. sine quibus, Cassia, Diaprun. confect. Hamech, Manna, Tamarinds.

℞ Diaprun. solut. pulp. Cassiæ, Elect. succi Rosar. ana ʒii, Mannæ Granatæ ʒi, decoct. Borage, Bugloss, Violets ʒiii, fiat potus pro ana dos.

Digestives of thin Flegm, Water and Melancholy caused of ♀ in ♋.

Cameputis, Capaveneris, Hellebor. nigr. Fumitor. Stecad. Feverfue, Partbemii, Borage, Bugloss, succus Bugloss. Epithimi, Tyme, Hyssop, Volubilis, Sage, Polypody, Senna, and the Syrupo of Stecados, Capit. vaneris, Episbimi, Borage, Bugloss, Marubil, Volubilis, &c.

℞ Sirup. Hyssopi, Mirubii, de Stecado ana ʒi, aquar. Fumariæ, Hyssop, Tyme ana ʒiii, fiat potus pro 4 dosibus.

℞ Partbenii, Hyssop, Tyme, Epitbimi, Lupulor. Stecados, Camepytis ana p.i. semen Anisi ʒi, Liquiritiæ ʒiβ, fiat decoct.
ad colatur.ʒiβ, addantur de Sirup. Bugloss. Scabious. Fumariæ, ana ʒiβ, fiat potus pro 6 dos.

Purgers against the same Diseases.

Polypody, Senna, Diantbos, Diatameron, Diasennæ, confect. Hamech, Pil. de Fumitor. Pil. sine quibus, Pil. Arabie. Diacathelicon, Pil. Agregativ. Pil. Jeralogodii, Pil. de 5 generibus, minab. Hiera picra, Abbatis, Memphitis.

℞ Hyssop, Marubii, Tyme, Stecados, Epithimi, Borage, Bugloss. Scabious. Partbenii ana p.i. Camomile, Solani ana p.v. Polypodii ʒi, Sennæ ʒii, Ellebori nigri ʒβ, Ciccory, Endive, Anisi, Tyme ana ʒi, Liquiritiæ ʒii, Pellitorii p.i. fiat decoctio ad colatur ʒvii, addantur Diaeatbolicon. ʒβ, confect. Hamech ʒiii, Diasennæ ʒiii, fiat potus pro 3 dos.

Digestives of thick stinking Flegm and of thin Melancholy, caused of ♀ in ♏.

℞ Sir. de Stecados, Epithimi, Fumariæ ana 3i, aquar. Lupular. Scabious. Hyssopi ana 3iii, fiat potus pro 4 dosibus.

℞ Flora Borag. Bugloss. Scabious. Thymi, Hyssopi, Marrubii, ana p.i, Polypodii 3i, sem. Anisi 3iβ, Liquiritiæ 3ii, fiat decoct. ad colatur. 3xvi, addautur de Sirupo Hyssopi, Marubii, Epithini ana 3iβ, Aceti albi 3i, fiat potus pro 6 dosibus.

Against Diseases of ♀ in ♏, ☽ in ♎, applying to ♂ in ♎, preparative.

℞ Aquar. Rosar. Aceti, Aquæ Serpentariæ ana 2 spoonfuls, Theriaca vel Mithridati 3ii, Sachari quant. s. fiat potus pro una dos.

Against Diseases of ♀ in ♏, ☽ in ♎ or ♏, applying to ♀.

℞ Sirup. Melissæ, Sir. Scolopendriæ ana 3i, aquar. Thymi, Fumariæ, Boraginis ana 3ii, fiat potus pro 2 dos.

Against Diseases of ♀ in ♏, ☽ in ♋, ♏ or ♓, applying to ♀.

℞ Sir. Melissæ, Sir. de duabus Rad. ana 3i, aquar. Serpentanii, Cardni benedicti, Thymi ana 3ii, fiat potus pro duabus dosibus.

A Preparative against Diseases of ♀ in ♏, ☽ in ♎, separating from the ☉, applying to ♀ in ♐, ☉ in ♏.

℞ Sirupi Absuntbii, Borage, Endiviæ ana 3i, aquar. Fumariæ, Boraginis ana 3iv, Hyssopi, Cardui benedicti, Melissæ ana 3iii, fiat potus pro 6 dos. Probatum.

Purges against the same Diseases of ♀ in ♏.

℞ Epithimi, Stecados, Camepytis, Scabious. Fumariæ, Lupulor. m.i. Polypodii 3ii, Sennæ 3iii, 4 sem: callid. maj. contus.

ana 3iβ, Croci ʒi, Zinciberis 3ii, Cinamon ʒii, Agaricæ 3iβ, Sarcocolli ʒii, Salis gem. ʒi, Passular. 3i, Prunes xx, fiat decoct. ad colatur. 3vii, addantur de Sirup. Marubii 3ii, confect. Hamech, 3i, fiat potus pro tribus dosibus.

℞ Pil. Agregativ. Pil. Arabieæ, Pil. sine quibus ana ʒiβ, Aquar. Scabious. Fumariæ, Sir. de Scabious. ana 3i, fiat potus for one dose.

Digestives against Diseases caused of ♀ in ♓, as before-said of ♀ in the Chapter of ♋.

℞ Sir. Marubii, Stecador, Partbenii ana 3i, aquar. Hyssopi, Thymi, Scabious ana 3iii, fiat potus pro 4 dos.

Purges against the same Diseases, cold and moist in the 4th degree.

℞ Radicis Buglossi, Borag. Fæniculi, Petroselini ana m.i. quatuor sem. callid. ma. contus. ana 3iβ, flor. Camomillæ, Fumariæ, Camepytis ana p.i. Agaricæ 3ii, Sennæ 3β, Polypodii 3ii, radicis Brioniæ 3β, Rhubarb 3β, Coloquintidæ ʒii, Euphorbii 3β, fiat decoct. ad colatur. 3vii, addantur Elect. Diacarthami 3i, confect. Hamech 3β, fiat potus pro 3 dos.

℞ Pulvis Jeralogodii 3i, pil. Arabic. sine quibus ana ʒiii, aquar. Fumariæ, Seabious. Boraginis, Thymi ana 3i, fiat potus pro tribus dosibus.

Of Terms being stopt.

When the cause of this Disease is of ♀ in ♓, first let her blood under both the Ankles, on both Feet, and the next day let her take this Potion, three days together.

℞ Trochis. de mirrha, de Alcacheng. ana 3β, powder it, and take it for one dose in white-Wine, and it bringeth them down.

Digestives of Flegm and yellow Choler caused of the ☽ in ♈, salt Flegm.

Oximel, Oxicrat. Oximel simplex, Sirup. Fumariæ, sir. Caprini, sir. Violar. succi Fumarii, confect. Acetos. radix Raphani, Polypodii, Cuscutæ, Fumitoriæ, Absinibii, aquar. Violar. Fumariæ, Fountain-water warm, Fennel-seed, Aniseed, Ellebor, Cansolida minor.

Purges for the same Diseases.

Hiera piera sumplex, Theodoricon, Anacardina, Hyperisticon; Sirups, Compound of Fumitory and Polypody. As ℞ Polypodii 3ii, Fumariæ, radic. Raphani, Violar. ana p.i.β, fiat decoctio in accio vin. albi ad colat. 3vi, addantur de succo limon. Sir. Violar. Nenupharis ana 3β, Hiera pier. simplex 3β, Pil. de Fumaria, pil. Aureæ ana 3iβ, Anacardini 3i, fiat potus pro tribus dosibus. This purgeth salt Flegm in the 3d degree.

Digestives of Diseases caused of the ☽ in ♋, which proceed of salt Flegm, as in the Chapter of the ☽ in ♈.

℞ Sirupi Fumariæ, Sir, Acetosi ana 3ii, aquar. Fumariæ, Absinthii, Acetos. ana 3iii, fiat potus pro tribus dosibus.

Purges against the same Diseases.

℞ Hyperisticon. Anacardin. ana 3ii, Hieræ pieræ sump. 3β, Aquar. Fumariæ, Violar. ana 3ii, fiat potus pro una dos.

℞ Elect. succi Ros. lan. Diaprun. ana 3iiβ, Diacarthani, confect. Hamech ana 3iβ, de Sir. Fumariæ, decoctionis Polypodii 3iiβ, fiat potus pro una dos.

℞ Hieræ picræ, Galeni ɜii, confect. Hamech 3ii, detoct. Fumariæ, Polypodii, Violar. ana 3iii, fiat potus pro una dos.

℞ Fumariæ, Lupulor. Violar. ana m.i. sem. Fænic. Petros. ana 3i, Polypodii 3ii, Rhubarb 3i, fiat decoct. ad colatur. 3vii, addantur Diaturbith, Diacarthami ana 3ii, Elect. succi Rosar. Diaprun. ana 3β, fiat potus pro tribus dosibus.

℞ Fumariæ, Lupulor. Violar. flor. Borag. Buglos. ana p.i. Polypodii ℈ii, Rhubarb ℈i, tritum sem. Fænic. Petros. ana ℈i, fiat decoct. ad colatur. ℥vii, addantur confect. Hamech, Elect. succi Ros. lax. ana ℈iii, Disturbith ℈ii, Clarifie it for three doses. and sweeten it with Sugar.

Digestives of salt Flegm of the ☽ or ♀ in ♈, ♌ or ♐.

Herein Choler predominates, therefore cold things are best.

Tyme, Fumitory, Polypody, Violets, Succory, Endive, Ebulus, Absintbium, Epithimum, Consolidataminor, Rad. Raphani, Acetum, Centory, Saxifrage, Sir. comp. Fumitorii, Oximel sumplex, Oximel diuret. Oximel pontick, Oxisachara, Sirup. Acetosus, Oxicrat. Sir. de Fumitor. Violar. Solani, Endiviæ, and of Succory.

℞ Confect. Acetos. Oximellitis simp. Sirupi Fumariæ ana ℈i, Seri loctis ℈ii, Aquar. Fumariæ, Violar. ana ℈iv, fiat potus pro 4 dos.

℞ Oximelitis, Oxicrati, Sir. Fumariæ, Violar. ana ℈ii, Aquar. Solani, Violar. Fumariæ, Aqua callidæ ana ℈v, fiat potus pro 7 dosibus.

Purgers of salt Flegm caused of ☽ in ♐, of Flegm and red Choler, Choler having dominion.

Hieræ picra simplex, Anacardinum, Turbith, Throduricon, Hyperisticon, Dianisi, Diagredium, Catarticum imperial. Esula, Hiera Russini.

℞ Folior. Violar. Endiviæ, Succori, Fumariæ ana m.i. Rad. & Fol. Lapathi acuti ana p.i. Acetos. m.iβ, Scabious. m.i. flor. Borag. Bugloss. Solani, Cuscutæ ana p.i. Polypodii ℈iii, Senna ℈ii, Semen Anisi, Fænic. Petros. ana ℈β, Rad. Raphani ℈iv, fiat decoctio ad colatur. ℥xii, addantur de Sirupo Fumariæ, Oximel comp. ana ℈i, Anacardini ℈iβ, Theodoriconis, confect. Hamech, ana ℈β, Elect. succi Ros. ℈i, fiat potus pro 4 dos.

Preparatives against Diseases caused of the ☽ in ♋, ♍ or ♓, which are of Flegm and cold Humours.

℞ Mellis Rosati colati, Sir. Acetosi simp. ana 3iii, Aquar. melis Majoranæ, Buglossæ ana 3iv, Cinamon, Macis ana ɜii, misce, fiat Sirup, Clarifie it pro 4 dos.

℞ Sir. Hyssopi, Stecador, Oximel Scillitici, ana 3ii, Aquar. Salviæ, Betonicæ, Fæniculi, Majoranæ ana 3iv, Cinamon, Aromatæ, Rosatæ ana 3i, fiat Sirupus pro 5 dos.

℞ Sir. de duabus Radicibus, melis Rosati ana 3vi, Aquar. Fæniculi, Capil. veneris, Seabious. ana 3i, misce, fiat Sirup. pro una dos. It digesteth Flegm, cold Humours and Wind.

℞ Oximel comp. Sirupi de Stecados. meliis Rosar. ana 3β, Aquar. Scabious. Fumariæ ana 3iβ, Mix them for one dose; it digesteth thick Flegm and cold Humours.

℞ Sirup. de Stecados, Sir. Hyssopi ana 3β, medis Rosar. 3i, Aquar. Betonicæ, Majoranæ, Rosemariæ ana 3i, misct, ut ante, pro una dos. it is good against the palsie and cold Humours.

℞ Callamenti, Prassii, Eupatorii, Summitatum Urticæ, Ungulæ Caballinæ, Liquiritiæ, Aristoloc. fiat Sir. addito Aceto squillitice. It digesteth cold Causes in the Stomach.

℞ Rad. Lapthi Acuti, apii, Fæniculi, Petroselini, Ungulæ, Caballinæ, Cap. veneris, Linguæ Cervinæ, Hyssopi, Scabious. Calamenthæ ana m.i. Sem. Fænic. Petrosel. Amneos. Endiviæ ana 3i, Liquiritiæ 3ii, fiat Sirup. It digesteth Humours mixed of Flegm and Melancholy.

Purgers for the same Diseases of Flegm and cold Humours, caused of ☽ in ♋, and these purge cold slimy Flegm in the Belly.

Ammoniacum, Fraxinus, Agarick. Briony, Broom-seed, Ellebor, Sal gem. Meeboaean, Lahoch de Squilla, Leloch de Sano, Pil. Arthritid. Pulvis sanctur, Pulvis Hellandiæ, benedicia Laxativ. Pil. de Castorio, Somatichum callidum Oximel.

℞ Turbith 3iβ, Coloquint. ɜi, Bdellii 3iv, fiant Pillulæ, mirabiles ad extrahendum Flegma a Venis & Juncturis.

Vomits to exempt the Stomach of cold Humours.

℞ Ellebori albi 3i, beat it and lay it all night in 3iv of Wine, strain it, and let him drink it in the morning fasting.

℞ Ellebori albi 3i, Zinziberis 3i, mix them well, and let the Party drink it in Water, wherein is sodden Fennel-seed and Parsley-seed, strain it and sweeten it with Sugar or Honey, which is best, and if it work too forcibly, stop it with cold Milk.

℞ Tobacco 3i, lay it all night in Ale, strain it and drink it in the morning; it worketh quickly, but troubleth the Stomach much for the time, it voideth Choler and Flegm.

℞ Vitrioli albi ℈ii, Aquæ communis 3ii, mellis Rosar. 3β, Commix them for one dose; it worketh easily.

A Glister against Flegm.

℞ Mercurialis, Ebuli, Folior. Sambuci equaliter & parum bulliant, & colentur, and use it for a Glister.

Digestives against salt Flegm and stinking tough Flegm, caused of the ☽ in ♍, are such as are shewed in the Chapter of ☽ in ♋.

Asparagus, Agrimony, Tyme, Hyssop, Fumitory, Absintbium Betony, Balm, Camepytis, Ani-seed, Fennel, Dill, Parsley, Golingal, Calamint, Southernwood, Liquorish, Horehound, Nettles, Rosemary, Seabious, Ruta, Angelica, Hypericon. Hermodactili, Filipendula, Pimpernel, Rad. Petros. Rad. Fænic. Mints, Sage, Lignum sanctum, Maiden-hair, Caraway-seeds, Mastick, white-Wine.

Puges against the same Diseases caused of the ☽ in ♍.

℞ Pil. imperial. Pil. fortid. ana 3β, Aquæ Absintbii & Fumariæ ana 3i, fiat potus pro una dos. It purgeth Flegm and Wind.

℞.Diacatbolicon 3i, Diaphenicon 3β, Acptar. Fænic. Fumariæ ana 3iii, Diacarthanei 3β, fiat potus pro dotabus dosibus. It purgeth Flegm strongly in the 3d degree.

A magisterial Powder to purge Flegm and gross Humours withal.

℞ Rad. Astrolog. Rad. Raphani, Rad. Spatulæ Fortidæ ana 3i, Pimpernel, Petroselini, Rutæ ana 3ii, Scorphulariæ, Filipendulæ ana 3β, Anisi 3ii, Zinxiberris 3ii, Turbith, Sennæ ana 3iii, Sachari 3iv, Make thereof a Powder, whereof let the Party take every morning one spoonful in white-Wine fasting.

Against the Palsie, this following.

℞ Assæ fortidæ, Aloes, Castoris ana, Mix them well with Sirup of Stecados, make thereof Pills, and give three of them every morning eight days together, with a draught of Rosemary-water, and three grains of Pepper; it is good against the Palsie, and cold flegmatick Humours.

℞ Pil. Cochiæ, pil. Alephanginæ Hiera comp ana ℈i, Agarici Trochisebi ℈i, misceantur, & cum Sir. de Stecados fiant 9 Pills pro una dos. They are good against the Palsie and Flegm.

Digestives against Diseases caused of ☽ in ♓, cold and moist in the 4th degree, of stinking, tough, glassy Flegm, as in the Chapter of the ☽ in ♋ and ♍.

℞ Rad. Petros. Fænie. Asparage. Burss ana p.i. Thymi, Rosemary, Hyssopi, Urticar. ana m.i. Seminia Anisi, Urticæ, Tyme, Asparagi ana 3i, Polypodii 3i, Seabious. m.i. fiat decoctio in vino bono, ad colotur. 3xx. add antur de Sirup. Liquiritiæ, Marrubii, Hyssopi ana 3ii, fiat potus pro 8 dosibus.

Puges against the same Diseases caused of the ☽ in ♓, of tough stinking Flegm in the 4th degree.

℞ Diaphenie. Elect. Indi ma. ana 3iβ, Diacatholie. 3β, Diacarthami 3ii, & cum decoctione Thymi, Hyssopi, Marrubii, Hypericonis, Polypodii 3iii, fiat potus pro una dos.

℞ Pil. de Agoric. Pil. Agregativ. ana ɜii, & cum Sirupo Betoniæ, fiat potus pro una dos.

℞ Pil. de Turbith, Pil. Agarie, ana ɜii, Sirupi Betoniæ 3i, decoct. Polypodii & sem. Anisi, Fænic. Petroselini 3ii, fiat potus pro una dos. This purgeth Flegm in the 4th degree.

Digestives of Melancholy and Flegm caused of ☽ in ♉, ♍ and ♑,

are these following.

Valubilis, Camepytis, Lupuli, Stecados, Fumitory, Borage, Bugloss, Hyssop, Tyme, Horehound, Epithimum, Senna, Polipody, Parthenium, Rad. lap. acuti, Rad. Fænic. Rad. Petros. Sirup. Fumitor. Sir. Seabious. Sir. of Hyssop, Sir. of Bugloss, Sir. of Stecados, Sir. Epithimi, Sir. de Prussia, Dir. volubilis.

℞ Sir. de Prassia, de Hyssop. de Stecados ana 3ii, Aquar. Thymi, Hyssopi, Rosemariæ, Marrubii ana 3v, fiat potus pro 8 dosibus.

℞ Sir. Buglossi, Hyssopi ana 3i, Aqua Fumariæ, Thymi ana 3iii, fiat potus pro duabus dosibus.

Purgers against the same Diseases of Melancholy and soure Flegm, caused of the ☽ in ♉.

Confect. Hamech, Diantbes, Diatameron, Diasenna, Diacatholicon, Jera sacralogosa, Hiera picra, Abbutis, Jeralogodia, Menphitis, Jera fortissima Galeni, Pil. sine quibur, Pulvis Jeralogodii, Pil. de Fumaria, Pil. Arabicæ, Pil. Agregativæ.

℞ Confect. Hamech, Diasenna, Diacarthami ana 3iiβ, Aqua Thymi & Fumtariæ 3ii, fiat potus pro una dos.

℞. Pil. sine quibus, Pil. Fumariæ ana ʒi, Pil. Arabic. ʒβ, Diacarthami ʒii, Aqua Fæniculi, Thymi ana ʒiii, fiat potus pro tribus dosibus.

Digestives against the Diseases of Flegma Acetosum in the 3d degree, caused of ☽ in ♍, as in the Chapter of ☽ in ♌.

Of Sirups proper in this Case.

Sirup of Fumitory, Absunthii, Lupuli, Prassii, Endive, Ciccory, Hyssop, Partbenii, Bugl. Borage, de stecados, Sennæ, Polypody, Lapath, Acuti, Tapsiæ.

Of Waters.

Endive, Violets, Tyme, Hyssop, Prassii, Borage, Bugloss. Fæuiculi, Fumariæ, Absuetbii, Lapatbi acuti, Partbenii, Oximel comp. Make your Comporition of hot and moist Sirups and Waters, according to the Planets in the ☽ doth apply unto.

℞. Hyssopi, Marubii, Thymi, Epithimi, Borog, Bugloss. ana p.i. fiat decoct. ad colatur. ʒxvi, addautur de Sirupo Hyssopi, Marucii, Epithimi ana ʒii, fiat potus pro 5 dos.

Puges against Flegma Acetosum caused of ☽ in ♍ cold and dry,

as aforesaid.

℞. Mirab. Keb. bidi ana ʒii, Ligni sancti ʒi, Flet. Borag. Bugloss. Thymi, Marubii, Stecados, Epithimi ana m.i. Agariæ ʒβ, Polypodii ʒi, Sennæ ʒiii, Semen Fænic, Petroselind, Ciccoriæ, Endiviæ ana ʒiβ, Zinziberis ʒii, Piperis albi ʒβ, Passular. ʒi, Liquiritiæ, sem. Anisi ana ʒi, fiat decoct. ad colatur, ʒviii, adantur de Diacarthamo ʒiii, Confect. Hamech ʒβ, Diasennæ ʒi, Mannæ ʒβ, fiat potus pro tribus dosibus.

℞. Confect. Hamech, Diasennæ ana ʒiii, Diacarthami ʒii, aquar, Thymi, Lupulor. ana ʒiβ, fiat potus pro una dos.

Or, These against Melancholy and Flegm of the ☽ in ♍, where Melancholy hath dominion.

Dianthos, Diatameron, Jeralogodii, Memphritum, Hiera picra, Abbatis, Pil. de Elaterio.

Digestives of Diseases of ☽ in ♑ of salt Flegm and Melancholy, melancholy predominating.

Cure it as in the Chapter of ☽ in ♉.

Aqua Cassiæ, Fumitorii, Epithimi, Polypodii, Volubilis mirah, Indi, Senna, Marjarom, Ireos, Stecados, Hyssop, Liquorise, semina Anisi, Fæuiculi, Petros. Brusi, Prassin, Thymi, Paristariæ, succi Euphorbis, succi Fumariæ, Sir. Fumariæ, Sir. Cap. veneris, Eupatorii, Sir. mirah, Indi, Volubilis, Epithimi, Sir. de Stecados.

℞ Decoct. Polypodii 3viii, Sir. Epithimi, de Stecados ana 3i, fiat portus pro duabus dosibus.

℞ Thymi, Epithimi, Volubilis, Hyssopi, Morrubii ana m.i. sem. ---- 3i, Liacri---- 3ii, sem. Boragatis, Bugloss. Fænic, ana 3i, Polypodii 3ii, fiat decoct. ad calatur. 3xii, addantur de Sir. Fumariæ, de Epithimo ana 3iβ, fiat potus pro 5 dosibus.

Purgers against Flegm and melancholy caused of ☽ in ♑, called Flegma Acetosum, cold and dry in the 4th degree, melancholy predominating.

Diacarthamus, Confect. Hamech, Diaturbith, Pulvis Jeralogodii, Diasenna, Pil. sine quibus, Pil. Arabicæ, Pil. de lap. Lazuli, Polypodium, Senna, Diatameron, Hierra piera, Pil. de Eluterio, Trifoly.

℞ Thymi, Marrubii, Lupulor, Epitbimi, Cap. veneris, Camepytia ana p.i. flor. Borag. Bugloss. Violar. ana p.i. Agaric 3β, Sennæ 3β, Polypodii 3ii, semen Anisi, Ciccoriæ, Endive, Liquiritiæ ana 3i, Zinxiberis 3β, Prunor. xx, Passular, 3i, Cinnabar, Mirabol. Keb. migri & indi ana 3i, fiat decoct. ad colatur. 3viii, addantur Confectio Hamech, Diasennæ, Diacarthami, ana 3iii, Diaprun. 3β, clarifie it pro 3 dosibus, and Aromatize it cum Pulv. Diamarii frigid. Diatragaentb. ana 3β, fiat potus, It purgeth Phlegma Acetosum in the 4th degree.

℞ Pil. sine quibus, pil. de lap. Lazuli, pil. Arabic. ana 3i, Confect. Hamech 3iii, decoct. Polypodii 3vi, fiat potus pro tribus dosibus. It purgeth this Phlegma Acetosum in the 4th degree.

℞ Thymi, Epithimi, volubilis Hyssopi, Merrubii ana p.i. semen Anisi 3i, Liquiritiæ 3ii, sem. Borrag. Buglossi, Fænic. ana 3i, Polypody 3ii, Senna 3iii, fiat decoct. ad colatur. 3viii, addautur Confect. Hamech 3ii, Elect. Diacarthami 3β, Pulveria Jeralogodii 3iβ, fiat potus pro 2 dos.

Digestives of sweet Flegm caused of the ☽ in ♊

are these following.

Betony, Cap. veneris, Ciccory, Endive, Tamarisk, Equisetum, Stecados, Hypocistia, fol. Pentaphyl. Oxalis, Polypodium, semen Lentis, miltii Solis, Tamarinds, Turmentile, sem. Cummini, sem, Endiviæ, Sir. Limonis, sir. Cap. veneris, sir. Betonicæ, sir. Endiviæ, sir. Oxalidis.

℞ Sir. Cap. veneris, sir. Betonicæ, Endive ana 3ii, Manna, Granatæ 3i, Aquar, Millesolii, Pentaphyll. Betonicæ ana 3v, fiat potus pro 6 dos.

Purgers against the same Diseases of the ☽ in ♊

Jeralogodium, Memphitis, Hietra piera sortis.

℞ Pil. sortid. pil. de Sagapeno, ana ℈iiβ, Agaric. Trochiso, ℈β, misce, & cum Sir. Betonicæ, fiant pill. 9 pro una dos. This purgeth Flegm mixed with Blood.

Digestives against diseases caused of the ☽ in ♎ sweet Flegm, are these, and such as are in the Chapter of the ☽ in ♊

℞ Endiviæ, Equiseti, Betonicæ, Stecados, Hypocistidis, Ciccorii, Tamar, ana p.i. fiat decoct. colatur ad colatur, 3x, addantur de Sirup. Betonicæ, de Siccad. ana 3iβ, commisce pro 4 dos.

℞ Polii, Pentaphylli, Millisolii, Oxalidis, Turmentil ana p.i. Semen Cummini, Endiviæ, Lentis, Millii ana 3iiβ, Polypodii 3ii, fiat decoct, ad colatur, 3xii, addantur de Sirup. Capil, ven. Betonicæ ana 3ii, succi Limonior. 3i, fiat potus pro 5 dosibus.

Pugers of the same Diseases caused of the ☽ in ♎, of sweet Flegm.

℞ Polypodii 3ii, Betoni, Capil. ven. Tamarisci, Ciccorii, Endive, ana p.i. Granti tinctor. Sem. lentis, millii Solis, ana 3ii, fiat decoct. ad colatur. 3vi, adde Cassiæ fistulæ 3i, Hieræ picræ fortis 3ii, de sirup. Rosar. lax. 3ii, fiat potus pro tribus dosibus.

℞ Jeralogodii, Memphitis, Hieræ pieræ fortis ana 3ii, pulpæ Cassiæ, Diacarthami, ana 3β, decoctionis Polypodii 3vi, fiat potus pro tribus dosibus.

Digestives against sweet Glegm in the 4th degree, caused of the ☽ in ♒, and of Flegm and Blood mixed, as in the Chapters of the ☽ in ♊ and ♎, and as followeth.

℞ Sir. Betonicæ 3i, pulp. Tamarindæ, pulp. Cassiæ, ana 3β, Aquar. Thymi, Violar. Fumariæ ana 3iii, fiat potus pro 4 dosibus.

℞ Flor. Boraginis, Bugloss. Lupulor. Ciccorii, Endiviæ, p.i. fiat decoct. ad colatur. 3xvi, addantur Sir. Rosar. Betonicæ, Lupulor. ana 3ii, fiat potus pro 5 dosibus.

Purgers against sweet Flegm caused of ☽ in ♒.

Diacatholicon, Cassia, Diaturbith, confect. Hamech, Diacarthami, Manna.

℞ Flor. Violar. Endiv. Cicorii, Pentaphylli, Turmentili, ana 3i, Lupulars Fumatriæ, ana 3iβ, Polypodii 3ii, Sebestens, Tamarinser ana 3β, Sandalor. Rubeor. 3i, fiat decoct. ad colatur, 3viii, addantur de pulp. Cassiæ 3iβ, Diacatbolic. confect. Hamech ana 3iii, fiat potus pro 3 dos.

Digestives of Flegm generally caused of the ☽ in ♋, ♍ or ♓, and of ♀ in the same.

Asparagus, Apium, Agrimony Acetosus, Aniseed, Wormwood, Betony, Balm, Camedrios, Camepytis, Cummin-seed, Caraway-seed, Callamint, Cuseuta, Ciperus, Cinnamon, Cartamus, Centaurea, Cucumeris, Dill, Enula, Dill-seed, Fennel-seed, Galingal, Gramen, Hissom, Herb Paralisis, Ireos, Lignum sanction, Mint, Maidenhair, Polimine, Sage, Ruseus, Rad. Acori, Ganga, Acii, Petroselini, Rad. Fænic. Petroselini, Brusii, Raphani, cum Rad. Lenistici, Rad. Astrolog. Sambuci, Eupatorii, Ruta, Southernwood, Ginger, Liquorice, Marjerom, Origanum, Marruhium, Rosemary, mastick, White-wine, Perrel, succus crudus Fumariæ, Mirabolanes, Hypericon, Suill, Pomegranates, hermodiciyli, Rad. Spat. fætidæ, Philopendula, Scabious, Pimpernel.

Digesters of Flegm generally.

Mel Rosar. Oximel scilliticum, Oximel diureticum, exicratum, Oximel compositum, Sir. de Hyssopa, with Sir. Absutbii, Marubii, Rosar. acctosi, Sir. de Stecados, de Betonica, cum Sir. de duabus Rad.

Semen Cartami, Fumariæ, Sambuci, Tyme, Piretrum, Tapsia, Hellebar, Cartamus, Esula, Polypody, Mirah. Emblicæ, Aristologia, uterq, Centauriæ, Squilla, Asorum, mel Sacharum.

Purgers of Flegm generally in this case.

Polypodium, Asarum, Turbith, Senna, Agarick, Sorcocoll, Coloquintida, Hermodoctyl. Euphorhium, Iapsia, Sol. gem. Helebor, Aloes, Oppopanax, Serapium, Anacardinum, Diacartimus, conserve of Emula, confect. Hamech, Diaxinziber, Diatrion Piperion, well. Rosar. Hiera picra sirup. Diaphenicon, Diacatbolicon, benedictum Laxativum, Trochisa, Agarick, Trochisa, de Rhubarb, Elect. Diaturbith, Sir. Acetosus composit. Sir. Fumariæ composit. Sir acetositatis Citri, Semen Cartbami, Pill. de Hiera, de Assairet, de agarica, de Cobia, de Arabice, Agregativ.

Artbritici, Imperialium, Fatidar. de Sagapeno, Euphorbiæ, it Sareacolla, Pulvis sanctus, Pulvis Turbith, Rhasis.

These purge putrid and rotten Flegm, being daily taken.

Cuscuta, Aurum, Perel, Hypericon, serum Caprinum, succus oudus Fumariæ, mirah. Condit.

These purge rotten and corrupted Flegm, that will not yield to any Medicine, and rectifie the Complexion, and make the Patient look clear, fair, lusty and lively.

Pill. de Aloe lota, pill. Masticæ, Hiera piera.

Diaciton consumeth Flegm, and rectifieth the Distempers of the Brain, corroborateth the Senses, and consumeth Melancholy in the Brain.

Diatamston comforteth Digestion and consumeth flegmatick Humidities, Superfluities and Crudities, in any part of the Members of the Body.

And these following consume Flegm in a humid Constitution and Complexion.

Garyophylli, lignum Aloes, Mace, Galang. Nux musebata, Cubebos, Aurum, Zinziber, Crocus.

These following consume Flegm in a hot Complexion.

Garyophylli, Margarita, Aurum, Cubebes, Liquorice, Crocu, Spieardus, Muscus, Ozimus, Petroselinum, Patrietaria, Cummin-seed, Fennel-seed, Vinum Granat.

These digest Flegm in the Veins, viz. Saxifrage, millium Solis; and these in the Joynts, Macropiper, Asparagus, Caraway and Fennel-seeds.

These digest cold Humours in the Breast and Stomach.

Hyssopus, Volubilis, Ireos, Calamente, Prassium, Eupatorium, Liquiritia, Capaveneris, Scolopendria, Seabious, Radices Aristoloebiæ, Lapoth. acuti, Fæniculi, Petroselini, Semen

Ameos, Endiviæ, Fæniculi, Petroselini, summit atum urticor. ungula Cabillina, Aristolochia rotund. Sir. de Acetos. Oximel stuilliticum.

These purge Flegm and cold Humours in the Breast, Stomach and Lungs.

Diaturbith, Agaricus, Hyssop, Volubilis, Cassia fisula, Sarcacola, Ireos, Coloquintida, Tapsia, Turbith, Catarticum imperiale, Dates, Cyprest, black Cherries, Azarabaea, Ellebor. albi, Pill. fortidæ, Pill. de Sareacolla, Pill. Incis maj. Pill. Stomaticæ, Pill. de Agaric.

Medicines emptying the Stomach and Intestines.

Stomaticum laxativum, Diapapaver. Catartic. imperial. Absintbium, Aloes, Mirabolanes.

Sirup of Roses lax. purgeth Choler in the Head and Stomach, Oximel sumplex purgeth Flegm in the Stomach, Sirupus acetosus sumplex purgeth Choler in the Stomach, Pill. de quinque generibus Mirabolan. avoideth Humours principally from the Stomach, Hiera piera Galeni, Oximel sumplex, Oximel sciliticum, Emplastrum ceroneum, Theriaca galeni, 8ir. Hyssop. Sir. of Horehound, Sir. Cap. vener. Sir. Acetosus compositus, Sir. de Limonibus.

Medicine Evacuative that purge the Head and Brain, are principally nineteen.

Hiera piera, Pill. Diureticæ, Pill. Cochiæ, Theodoricon, Anacardium, Jeralogodion, Pill. Aurea, Sir. Ros. lax. Pill Jucis major. Briony, Agaricæ, Oppoponax, Ellebore albi, Jera sacra'ogosa, Hermodactyli, Sagapenum, Sareacolla, Galbanum, bdell um.

These purge especially the Head.

Coloquintida, Agarick, Lapis armenus, Lapis lazulus, Mirabolani nigri, Mirab. Kebuli, Squilla, Epithimum, Steacador, Aleos, Pill. Aureæ, Pill Jucis maj. Pill. Euphorbii, Pill. Cachiæ, Pill. Arabie. Pill. Diacastor. Pill. sine quibus.

Medicines which purge Humours from the Spleen

Diasenna, Jerarussi, Agarick, Senna, Epithimum, Ellebore nigr. Absintbium, Stecados, Eupatorium, Sal niter, Callamentum, Polypody, Hiera sacralogasa, Turpentine of Venice, Jeralogodion.

Principal Medicines purging ill Humours from the Liver, and parts adjoyning.

Diacartamus, Pill. de Rhubarb, especially; and these, viz. Agaric. aqua Casei, Volubilis, Majorana, Lupuli, Rhubarb, succus Ros. Absinthium, Mirabolanes, Tamaris, Fumitory, Ireos, Misereon, Senna, Scrapinum, æs ustum, Sarcocollæ, Venice Turpentine, Fragula, Dactyli, Sir. Fumariæ, succus Eupatorii.

Medicines which more sharply cleanse the Humours, and mundifie the Skin, are

Aquq Casei, Fumitor. Coloquintida, Epithimum, Agarices, Polypodium, Volubilis, Mirah. Ind.

Medicines which purge Flegm from the Junctures, and draw ill Humours from the remote parts, are these.

Elect. de. succo Rosar. benedicta Laxativa, Hermodactyli, Pill. Artbriticæ. To which may be also added, Pill. fortidæ, Pill. de quinque generibus Mirabolan. Jera sacralogosa.
To these also may be added,

Sarcocolla, Coloquintida, Turbith, Eupatorium, Opopanax, Sal gem. Sal ind. Serapinum, Euphorbium, Centaur, Ellebor nigr. Polypodium, Pill. Fumariæ, Pill. Agregativ. Pill. Mastich. Diatameron, Palma Chirsti-seed, Pill Euphorbii, Pill. Acrbriticæ, Pill. fætid.

These are good against ache of the Bones, Sinews, Muscles and Joynts, and draw Humours afar off.

Against rotten Humours, and stopping of the Breast, and Flegm in the Stomach, Head and Muscles, and against bleared Eyes, and watering Eyes.

Use Rosemary, Corral, Diartheos, Diaprassium.

Medicines that purge the Bladder from Gravel and Humours, and are good against the Strangury, and to provoke Urine.

Venice Turpentine, Diacassia cum Manna, Antidotum Ansincritum, Aurea Alexandria, Diasatirion, Oximel Diureticum, Unguentum Agrippinæ.

Against Exulceration of the Bladder.

Liquid Rosin, Savin, Pill. Diacastoriæ, Pill. sine quibus, Cassia fistula, Briony, Oximel Scilliticum, Trochisq, de Alkakengi.
These are good against the Exulceration of the Bladder.

Medicines that purge the Wind-pipe of gross Humours, are these that follow.

Diaprusium, Theriaca Galeni, Lohoch de Squill. Lohoch – Sano, Sirup of Liquorice, Sir. Acet. composit.

Medicines which cleanse the Reins, are

Venice Turpentine, liquid Rosin, Pill. fætida, Pill. Arthritica, Figs, Cassia fistula.

Diatamarindor. is hot and dry in the 3d degree.
Bugla is good against the Aches of the Reins.
Benedicta Laxativa avoideth Flegm in the Reins.
Broom openeth the Sopping in the Reins and Kidneys.
Agarick purgeth cold Flegm that stoppeth the Reins.

These following are good against Pain of the Reins that cometh of cold Causes.

aurtea Alexandrina, Mitbridatum, Diacameron, Elect. Ind. ma. Emplost. de gran. lauri.

These do purge the Reins of Gravel.

Antidotum Ansuneritum, Oximel Diureticum, Sir. Acetos. inp. Sir. Capil. ven. Sirup of Ceterack.

Nunc nostro Labore fæliciter ad finem perducto, Gratias ago Deo Opt. Max. per Jesum Christum unigenitum ejus Filium, & Servatorem nostrum unicum, qui est verus ille Deus supra omnes laudandus in Secula, Amen.

An Appendix

As a necessary Appendix to this Subject, I have hereunto Annexed several Experiments, of great use to the Industrious Student; which I hope will be as gratefully receiv'd as freely offer'd.

Some Experiments of Sickness and Death, demonstrated as a Conclusion to this Work.

To know whether the Sick Person shall die of his Infirmity or no.

The first Thing that the Physitian ought to do, before he undertake the Cure of his Patient, is to know whether the Disease be medicinable, or mortal; for otherwise he may strive against the stream, and purchase to himself rather discredit that otherwise, promising Health when there is no hope at all. Many by the Rules of Vulgar Astrology, have taken upon them to resolve this doubtful and abscure Question, but so lamely, and with such and so many curious Ambiguities, that one can conclude nothing certainly thereby. Yea, of a truth, this Art is so contaminated and defiled in general, and the true grounds so conspurcated, and intermingled with many frivolous Fables, that except the pure Quintessence be extracted from those fæculent Dregs, this Science which passeth all other Humane Arts, as the Light of the Sun the Stars, is like to perish, and in time to be as little reputed of amongst the Learned Philosophers, as it is now amongst many of the Vulgar sort, which think or esteem no better of any Predictions in this Art, than of meer Fables.

Therefore to quit this Art from all criminal Accusation of Falshood, we will here deliver a plain and intelligible Method, whereby the meanest Artist, if he be not Dureæ Cervicis, may know how to give a true and absolute Judgment of this preposed Demand.

Therefore letting pass all curious and superstitious Observations, together with all other evil Tokens of small importance, you shall note these Signs following, which are of a great energy, and very effectual in operation, the which we call Signa Fatalia; that is to wit, If the Lord of the Ascendant be combust, or sub radiis (for the Lord of the Ascendant we principally heed) or if the Lord of the Ascendant be in ☌, □ or ☍ of ♄, ♂, or the ☉; or if the Lord of the Ascendant be near the Cusp of the eighth, or joyned to the Lord of the 8th House by ☌, □ or ☍; likewise if the ☽ be combust, or sub radiis, if she be in ☌. □ or ☍. So having a Celestial Scheme erected, and parallel'd to the Hour and Minute, as near as you can, wherein any related unto you, the state of the infirmed Party, as is arforesaid; then look how may fatal Signs may be found therein, and if the number of them amount unto three or four, and neither the Lord of the Ascendant, nor the Moon, do respect, or are respected of ♃ or ♀, by ☌, ✶ or △, applying the one to the other per applicationem levem, or at least-wise by a □ or ☍ with ♃ or ♀, with a strong receptin mutual, for without mutual reception, the □ or ☍ is not available; then assuredly the sick Person will die; if otherwise, not. And for the better Illucidation of this general Rule, you shall note these Cautions following, that is, If the Lord of the Ascendant and 8th be all one, and that the ☌ of the ☽ with the Lord, or Significator of life, is as good, as the conjunction with the Lord or Significator of Death, is evil; also if the Lord of the Ascendant be joyned with the ☽, she being Lady of the 8th House, and ♃ or ♀ especially ruling the Ascendant; and also a ✶ of ♃ or ♀ platick especially (but being combust or retrograde is not sufficient) may be good. But to conclude, Because this Art is better taught by practice than speculation, we intend to firmate and illustrate these our Positions with such Examples, as shall greatly illustrate our proceeding herein, if diligent observation be had and used, and not with Outlandish Examples (as others have done) but with verified proceedings and practice amongst our own English Natives, whom every one I could name, and their dwelling; but for some Reasons I forbear that Infinite of forraign Examples might be produced, and rather value these of our own Countrey and Knowledge.

1. A certain Man brought his Water under this Position of Heaven following.

Urina palisda non subsidenti, substantiæ tenui.

10 House	23 ♓		4 House	23 ♍
	♀ 12 ♈			
	☿ 22 ♈			
	♂ 23 ♈			
	♄ 2 ♉			
11 House	4 ♉		5 House	4 ♏
	☉ 18 ♉			
12 House	12 ♊		6 House	12 ♐
				♃ 28 ♐ ℞
Ascendant	21 ♋		7 House	21 ♑
2 House	11 ♌		8 House	11 ♒
				☽ 14 ♒
3 House	0 ♍		9 House	0 ♓
	☋ 15 ♍			☊ 15 ♓

The Judgment.

The Planets principally morbificant, are ☉, ♄ and ♂.

As touching his Disease, the 21 of ♋ cutting the East Angle, ruling the Breast, Procordiacks, lungs, &c. the ☽ also lady of the same, afflicted by a pernicious □ of ☉ in ♉, doth betoken a hot Rheum distilling by Arteria ospera into the Lungs, causing a tickling Cough, and Exulceration of the Lungs. Also forasmuch as the ☉ governs the Heart, it betokeneth a certain Calor non naturalis in corde, causing a manner of Hectick Fever, or consumption of the Lights, together with the Pneumatical Pipes and Organs, infarsed with corrupted superfluities of cholerick and flegmatick Defluxions, the anheliting passages being straight and narrow, causeth the Lights by their intended motion to inflame the Heart and Præcordiacks, as Aristotle, Calor sit per motum. Also forasmuch as ♂ is in Ariete, accompanied with ♀ and ☿, it farther imported, that the primitive original hereof was derived from the Brain, being distempered through too much vigilancy, and solicitude in his Affairs. As concerning the fatal Signs, First, The ☽ being Lady of the Ascendant, is in the 8th House. Secondly, She is oppressed by a malevolent square of the Sun. Thirdly, By a square Platick of ♄; so the fatal Signs being three at least, it demonstrated small hopes of Life, except some opitulation and aid from one of the Fortunes, do repress the rigour of this Constellation. But here is none such to be expected, except it be from the ✶ platick of the ☽ and ♃ retrograde, which is condemned by the Canon aforesaid, as insufficient to rescue in this case, although it might for a time prorogue the Parties Life. Therefore the next critical Conflict of the Moon which any of the interfecting Planets, shall be lethiserous and mortal, according to the former Rule: And so it fell out; for about the end of four months well near compleat, he departed this Life, prefigured by the ☽ her distance from a perfect □ of the Sun, which was 4 degrees almost, some 25 minutes excepted. As to satisfie the truth herein, I exactly Calculated the same, and the ☉ was then in the 18 gr. 5 min. of ♉; and ☽ in 14 degr. 15 of ♒.

II. A Gentlemans Urine was brought under such a Position, of Heaven.

Urina aurea, substania mediocris, atomis plena, cum Hypost ast subflava, non continua, & inequali.

10 House	0 ♋		4 House	0 ♑
♂ in	14 ♋			
11 House	10 ♌		5 House	10 ♒
☿ in	22 ♌			
12 House	0 ♍		6 House	0 ♓
♀ in	3 ♍			
☉ in	10 ♍			
Ascendant	0 ♎		7 House	0 ♈
2 House	23 ♎		8 House	23 ♈
			♄ in	10 ♉
3 House	22 ♏		9 House	22 ♉
♃ in	19 ♐		☽ in	0 ♊

The Morbificant Planets are ☉, ☽ and ♀,

but the ☉ is the principal interfecting Planet, corrupting ♀ the Lady of the Horoscope by combustion, and also by a platick Square.

As concerning this Disease, forasmuch as ♀ is Lady of the Ascendant, and oppressed by the ☉ and the ☽, It betokeneth much Imbecility of some members of the Body, attributed to the regiment of ♀, proceeding of a Heat and a Cold together, with some cholerick and watry thin Defluxions, loss of Appetite. Also forasmuch as ♀ is scited in ♍, governing the Bowels, Guts, and Belly, It betokeneth painand griping in the Belly, and the Flix called Lyenteria, proceeding of Imbecility of the Stomach, also a certain innaturalis Calor, or Fever-heat therewithal annexed. And as touching the Inquisition of fatal Signs, the ☽ is afflicted by the □ of the ☉. Secondly, The Lady of the Ascendant is combust. Thirdly, The ☽ is within the Limits of a Conjunction platick with Saturn. So that the intersecting Signs being three, and neither the Lord of the Ascendant, nor the ☽ assisted by the benign Rays of the Fortunes, It imports no hope of Recovery; and so it fell out; for upon the next Critical congress of ♀ and the ☉, he departed this Life; for ♀ being 7 degrees distant from the Sun, allowing for every degree one day, (because the Disease was acute) amounteth unto 7 days, which being compleat and ended, he yielded up his Spirit into the Hands of his Creator, &c.

III. The Urine of a certain Man was brought, according to this Calisebene following.

Urina ejus subruta, turbata, cum arenulis in Hypostasi, substantia mediocri, &c.

10 House	6 ♉		4 House	6 ♏
♄ in	17 ♉			
☿ in	9 ♊			
☉ in	10 ♊			
11 House	19 ♊		5 House	19 ♐
♀ in	21 ♋			
12 House	26 ♋		6 House	26 ♑
			♃ in	2 ♒
Ascendant	21 ♌		7 House	21 ♒
♂ in	6 ♍			
2 House	10 ♍		8 House	10 ♓
3 House	3 ♎		9 House	3 ♈
			☽ in	27 ♈

The Morbisicant Planets are ♂, ☿, ♀, ♄, ♃:

For the better Explication of this Constellation, you shall understand, That this Party was afflicted with two several kinds of Diseases, the one Chronical, and of long continuance, the other Acute, and but new begun; therefore as they were discrepant the one from the other in their several originals and beginnings, so they were also in sffect and termination dissenting, although the more general transformed the less into part of his own peculiar existency. First, As concerning his new-bred Infirmity, which was a repletion of his Stomach with much Cholerick Juyce, loss of Appetiite, Insomniation, Distemperature of his Head per concensum Stomachi, as Mars in the Horoscope afflicting the Lord thereof, the Dodecatemorie of ♌ ascending, doth apertly Symbolize: therefore in the Crisis of the ☉ and ♂, these Symptoms were likely to decrease: and so it fell out: for about some 4 or 5 days after he amended of the same, by a certain Decoction prescribed him to take. But as touching his old inveterate Infirmity, which was a long concealed grief of Mind, with much perturbation of Spirit, swimming in his Head, starting in his Sleep, evil Imaginations, Fear and Desperation, Mercury was the principal Significator, corrupted by a square of ♂, and joyned to the Lord of the Ascendant, being also by him much infirmed by Combustion. All which considered, it was very likely that these Passions were to be limited by the Crisis of ☉ and ☿, which did consist in the Number of 5. for the Lord of the Ascendant had do many degrees to go, before he were to take his leave of ☿ per Separationem communem. And concerning the Investigation of fatal Signs, the ☉ being Lord of the Ascendant is oppressed by a malicious □ of ♂, and the ☽ joyned to ♄ by platick Conjunction; also the ☽ damnified by a □ of ♃, he being Lord of the 8th House, and neither the Lord of the Ascendant, nor the ☽, applying to any benign Aspect of any salutiferous Planet, it importeth no hope of recovery. And as for the time and manner of his Death, it fell out accordingly, for near the end of the 5 months, from the time of this Scheam of Heaven, on the 6th of October, upon the □ of the ☉ and ♃, and the ☽ being in conjunction with ♄ and ☍ to ♂, at that very time, he in most woful manner Laqueo Sesuspendebat, and so in desperate sort ended his Life, prefigured by the place of ♄ in ♉, governing the Neck and Throat, and ♄ here one of the intersecting Planets. And lest I here seem to imply a contradiction to my former opinion, because I grant the Crisis to be made by ☿, which before I denied in my general Thesis, you shall note, That this Crisis was not Naturalis, but contra Naturam. If any think that ☿ was not able to produce such a Tragical Crisis, and that it is most likely that the same was made by ♂, because he differeth from a partile separation with ☉, about 4 degrees and a half, the which cometh near to our reckoning, if you add for every degree a moneth; yet in my judgement the former is best, and most consonant to truth, because I can hardly believe that one Planet may make two several Crisis in one individual Person. Here we could also have related the principal cause, that first induced this wretched Man to fall into such a desperate Humour, and also by what mediation the wicked Serpent did per mille Meandros, circumvent him; as by the report of some of his own Family, it came afterward to light. But forasmuch as it maketh little to our purpose in this matter, for brevity sake I let it pass, intending here rather to shew the end of the Disease, than over-curiously to search out the cause.

IV. A Gentleman sends for a Physitian a Messenger, which came to him about 10 of the clock in the forenoon, the Celipositiones being in manner following.

Urina ejus subrubicunda non subsidens.

10 House	18 ♉		4 House	18 ♏
♄ in	18 ♉			
☉ in	16 ♊			
☿ in	25 ♊			
11 House	0 ♋		5 House	0 ♑
♀ in	26 ♋			
☽ in	4 ♌		♃ in	1 ♒ ℞
12 House	5 ♌		6 House	5 ♒
Ascendant	29 ♌		7 House	29 ♒
♂ in	10 ♍			
2 House	20 ♍		8 House	20 ♓
3 House	14 ♎		9 House	14 ♈

The Morbificant Planets *ex parte Domini ascendentis*, are ♂ and ☿, *ex parte luna* ♃, ♄, ♀.

The 29th degree of ♌ Horoscopating in the East Angle, governing the Heart, Stomach, Praecordiacks, and the ☉ (Lord of the same) corrupted by a square of ♂, betokeneth Sickness, and much pain in those parts, by super-abundance of Cholerick Humours; The ☽ also in the same Sign of ♌, oppressed by a platick square of ♄, and the ☽ joyned to ♀ by a platick conjunction, It also noteth much predominancy of Flegmatick Humours. And as touching those parts of the Body where those parts of the Humours are congested, ♀ in ♋ betokeneth the Breats, Lungs, Liver and Sides, causing Angustiam pectoris & spirandi difficultatem, and intention of the Praecordiacks; ♄ in ♉ importeth a Cough, and ratling in the Pipes and Throat; ♃ also opposing himself against the ☽, betokeneth some Impostumation, or at the least a disposition thereunto,, proceeding of mixt Humours, on the Panicle, Pleura, causing pain in his Side, after the manner of Pluritis non vera. Lastly, ♀ being contaminated by a □ of ♂, and afflicted by the Lord of the Ascendant. It betokeneth a certain kind of deliration and disturbance of his Senses, by Cholerick Exhalations fuming into the Head, &c. And now concerning Mortal Signs, First, I find the Lord of the Ascendant damaged by a □ of ♂. Secondly, I see the ☽ infirmed by a □ of ♄. And thirdly, The ☽ afflicted by an ☍ of ♃ Lord of the 8th House, and with al, neither the Lord of the Ascendant, nor the Moon, applying to the friendly Beams of the Fortunes. Therefore small hope is to be expected, but that upon the next Crisis, he would depart this Life; and so it fell out; for the third day following he ended his days, Mars, then causing a Crisis, according to the former Rule.

V. A certain Man came to enquire of the Health of his Child, being a Son, but brought not his Urine with him. The Position of the Heavens as followeth.

10 House	9 ♌		4 House	9 ♒
11 House	14 ♍		5 House	14 ♓
☽ in	0 ♎			
12 House	9 ♎		6 House	9 ♈
☉ in	16 ♎			
♀ in	18 ♎			
☿ in	19 ♎			
Ascendant	0 ♏		7 House	0 ♉
			♄ in	8 ♉ ℞
2 House	23 ♏		8 House	23 ♉
♃ in	23 ♐			
3 House	27 ♐		9 House	27 ♊
			♂ in	6 ♌

The Morbificant Planets are ♄, ♀, and ☿.

Mars, Lord of the Ascendant in ♌, governing the Heart, Stomach, Praecordiack, &c. afflicted by a □ of ♄, betokeneth Sickness and Pain in those parts aforesaid, proceeding of tough congealed Flegm, intention of the Praecordiacks, loss of Appetite, &c. And forasmuch as Mars, governeth the Gaul, is also importeth therein Causes of glemmy slimy Humours. The ☽ beginning the Sun-beams, situate under the Sign of ♎, doth farther import Diseases proceeding of Tartarous Humours, the Stone in the Kidneys, and pain in the bottom of the Belly, preceeding of windy Inflations, &c. As touching mortal Signs, First, The Lord of the Ascendant is opposed by a pernicious □ of ♄. Secondly, The ☽ beginning to be sub radiis. Thirdly, The ☽ is applying to a Conjunction platick of ♀, the Lady of the 8th House. So the fatal places being three, it threatneth death, except some aid of Melifious ♀, or ♃; but as for ♀, she being Lady of the 8th House, and also combust, her conjunction with the ☽ can yield no comfort. As for Jupiter, he is elongated from the Trine with the Lord of the Ascendant the space of 18 gr. and therefore out of the reach of any Aspect. Therefore this Figure is very fatal; and so it came to pass; for within two days space he departed, with an Ulcer or Aposthumation under his Ear, prefigured by ♄ in ♉, &c.

VI. A Question being asked concerning the state of a sick Man without Urine, The face of Heaven in manner following, &c.

10 House	19 ♑	4 House	19 ♋
♃ in	1 ♒		
11 House	6 ♒	5 House	6 ♌
12 House	11 ♓	6 House	11 ♍
☽ in	10 ♈	♀ in	8 ♏
Ascendant	13 ♉	7 House	13 ♏
♄ in	18 ♉	☿ in	24 ♏
		☉ in	15 ♐
2 House	19 ♊	8 House	19 ♐
3 House	5 ♋	9 House	5 ♑
		♂ in	10 ♑

The Morbificant Planets are ♄, ♂, and ♃.

Venus Lady of the Horoscope, afflicted by an ☍ of ♄, doth import a Disease proceeding of Melancholy, as a Quartan Ague; also forasmuch as ♄ is in Tauro, it betokeneth the Cough, and stuffing of the Pipes with Flegm and crude Humours; the ☽ also in a □ of ♂, importeth a certain affation of the said Humours, causing a Fever or Ague; ♃ Lord of the 8th, squaring with the Lord of the Ascendant, betokeneth some internal absessus of putrified Humours; the ☽ in ♈ oppresseth, detecteth some pain in the Head, and parts attributed to the Dodecatemory of ♈, together with a Marasmus, or exhausting of the Radical Quintessence, &c. As for Mortiferous Signs, ♀ Lady of the East Angle is opposed by ♄, and also by a square of the Lord of the 8th House, thereby much damnished; the ☽ also is afflicted by a square of ♂; so the fatal Signs being three, and neither the Lord of the Ascendant, nor the ☽, applying to the amicable Beams of the Fortunes, It presageth no hope of Life, but at the next Crisis of the Lady of the Ascendant with any of the Morbificant s, he should end his days; and so it fell out; for ♀ was within 7 degrees of parting from a square with ♃, the Lord of the 8th House. Then this Disease being partly Chronical, adding for every degree a week, it amounteth to near 8 weeks; about which time he dies, &c. Certainly verified.

VII. The Urine of a sick Man presented to Examination, under following this Position.

Urina crassa, turbida in superficie non rareseens, colore intensa, longo tempore ita permanens.

10 House	17 ♑		4 House	17 ♋
♃ in	2 ♒			
11 House	3 ♒		5 House	3 ♌
12 House	6 ♓		6 House	6 ♍
Ascendant	10 ♉		7 House	10 ♏
♄ in	18 ♉		♀ in	14 ♏
			☿ in	1 ♐
2 House	16 ♊		8 House	16 ♐
☽ in	22 ♊		☉ in	20 ♐
3 House	3 ♋		9 House	3 ♑
			♂ in	13 ♑

The Morbificant Planets are ♄, ☉ and ♃.

This Man had a Quartan for a long space, and now ir did alter his course, and Nature turning into a Quotidian, he also had a great Distemper and weakness at his Stomach, with intension of the Praecondiacks, lodd of Appetite, and a swelling in his Legs; but falling into a Looseness, shortly after the swelling abated, yet his Stomach waxed still worse and worse, and so that Looseness and Flix of the Womb continued until he died. Here is one thing worthy to be noted, That although all thick Urines, for the most part, and laudable Signs, especially about the Crisis, because all Digestions do begin per incrassationem, yet if it do not extenuare in superficie, it betokeneth equal combate between Nature and the Disease; and if it so long continue, the Color Naturalis both in Stomacho and in Hepate, will be suffocated in the Stomach proper Molinsyn in Hepate; for the Vis sanguifica, doth not separare purum ab impuro; tis defect for the most part of some Oppilation in the orifice of those Veins, which are in parenchymate Hepatis, whereby the Homogenial Nutriment is not imbibed, and so no perfect separation is made, by which means the crude Humours being long elaborated by the first digestion in the Stomach, doth at last become pinguedinous and unctious, the which is contrary to the acetolity of the Stomach, causing superabundance of thhe Heat against Nature, and suffocation of Natural Heat; and if the Vis attractius in Hepate doth not return in due time, then the Meseraical Veins not performing their office, to exhaust or attract the Chylous Juyce from the Stomach, then in success of time the Tunicles of the Stomach shall be so much relaxed, and the retentive faculty thereof so much debilitated and weakned, by reason of many gross, fatty, and pinguedinous Humours therein contained, that the Party will fall into a Diarrhea, very hard to be Cured. Neither did I ever see any yet holpen in this kind of Disease; for the Unctuosity of the pinguedinous Humours doth make such a flibriness and Lubricity in the Stomach, that the Nutriment passeth to the Bowels, before compleat digestion, and so pedetentim the Natural Forces decaying, and crude Humours prevailing, at last Death ensueth, the end of all Disease.

Now as concerning the Investigation of these things by our Astrological Axiomes, ♀ Lady of the Ascendant, and Significatrix of the second digestion, called Pepantica, is afflicted ex diametro Saturni, and with a square of ♃ Lord of the 8th House, the ☽ also predominating on the first difestion, called Epepsis, is by the ☍ of ☉ much damnified; ♄ betokeneth a Quartan, the Minera being the Spleen; ♃ betokeneth Imbecility of the Liver, the Minera of the Veins; the ☉ a Calore non Naturale, the Minera in corde, &c. As for Recovery, no hope is afforded from this Scheam; for the fatal places being three, and neither the Lord of the Ascendant, nor the ☽ applying to any favourable Aspect of any Fortune, it giveth sufficient testimony of Death, which, according to our aforesaid Cannon, was likely to happen at the end of 4 weeks, for ♀ Lady of the Orient, did anscede so many degrees from an ☍ with ♄. But this Rule here did fail me, which hitherto in all Observations that ever I made, did never vary or swerve from the truth, which made me much to admire, being not able to present to yield any reason thereof, until I perceived that ♄ in the House of Life, could not out of that place, infuse the venome of Death; therefore for defect of some other, the mortal stroak was referred to the separation of ♀, Lady of the Ascendant from ♂ his ⚹, the which, considering the Orbs, was 6 degrees space, answerable to 6 weeks of time; at the end of which he departed. And here is to be noted, That when there is no ☌, □ nor ☍ of ♄, ♂ or ☉, fit to make a Crisis, that in such defect, a Sextile of ♄, ♂ or ☉ may be taken, or a ⚹ of the ☽, she being corrupted by ☌, □ or ☍ of some fatal Planet; for she receiveth the Influence of that Star, to whom she is configurate. The like Example is to be seen in the 4th Scheam going before, where the ☽ is Quadrate Saturni, by a ⚹ with ☉, being Lord of the Horoscope, made a Crisis the third day following; for ♂ in the Horoscope, by the Reason aforesaid, could not out of that place strike the stroke at the end of two days, but the ☉ being in longitude, separated 12 degrees from the ☽ her ⚹; and then now having made a Crisis, was to produce the mortal effect, when the ☉ departed from her the semidiameter of his Beams, that is, 15 gr.

per separationem communem, of the which the ☉ wanted 3 gr. answerable to three days, &c.

VIII. An old Gentleman sick sent for his Physitia, under this Position of Heaven as followeth

10 House	27 ♑		4 House	27 ♋
♃ in	2 ♒			
11 House	17 ♒		5 House	17 ♌
12 House	28 ♓		6 House	28 ♍
♄ in	18 ♉		♀ in	17 ♏
Ascendant	28 ♉		7 House	28 ♏
			☿ in	3 ♐
			☉ in	22 ♐
2 House	27 ♊		8 House	27 ♐
3 House	12 ♋		9 House	12 ♑
☽ in	20 ♋		♂ in	15 ♑

The Morbificant Planets are ♄, ♂ and ♃.

Venus Lady of the Orient, oppugned by an ☌ of ♄ in Taura, betokeneth an inforcing of the Pipes with Flegm, difficulty of respiration &c. ☽ in Cancero, afflicted ex diametro Martis, betokeneth oppression of the Breast, Stomach, Praecondiacks, Lights, Liver, and Ribs, with Choler and sharp Humours, causing a Fever also, or unnatural Heat; ♃ in like manner Quadrating with ♀ Lady of the Ascendant, doth shew some Apostumation, and so much the more, because ♃ did also oppose himself against the ☽. And forasmuch as the ☽ governeth the Breast, Lungs, Mediastine, Liver and Ribs, because she is under the Dodecatemory of ♋, it is most likely that in some of those parts, the Apostumation was in; but to be more clearly certified, Dolor oftendit locum; for having a great pain in his Side, with a Fever and Cough annexed, we conjecture that he had an Abscessus in the Panicle plura. And concerning fatal Signs, First, I observe an ☍ partile between the Lady of the Ascendant and ♄. Secondarily, I percieve the ☽ not separated from an ☍ partile of ♂. Thirdly, The ☽ and ♀ are corrupted by an ☍ an ◻ of ♃, Lord of the 8th House. So the mortal places being 4, and neither the Lady of the Horoscope, nor the ☽ applying to the auspicious Beams of the Fortunes, it presageth Death; which hapned accordingly at the next Crisis: for the same day before midnight he ended his Life, according to Calculation, Venus differing about half a degree from the Opposition of Saturn.

IX. A Question was moved concerning the state of a certain sick Man, under this Configuration following.

10 House	14 ♈		4 House	14 ♎
♄ in	18 ♉		☽ in	22 ♎
11 House	21 ♉		5 House	21 ♏
12 House	9 ♋		6 House	9 ♑
			♀ in	4 ♒
Ascendant	6 ♌		7 House	6 ♒
			♃ in	16 ♒
2 House	25 ♌		8 House	25 ♒
			☉ in	26 ♒
			♂ in	3 ♓
			☿ in	13 ♓
3 House	15 ♍		9 House	15 ♓

The Morbificant Planets are ♄, ♂, ♃ and ♀.

The ☽ being Significatrix of the first Digestion in Stomacho, being free from any malevolous Aspect of any corrupting Planet, doth relate unto us, that no defect was in the Stomach, simpliciter per se, although per sympathiam some Distemperance might peradventure be found therein, per Hepatis Consensum, because ♌ possessed the Oriental Angle governing the Heart, Stomach and Praecordiacks, Liver, Back, &c. and ☉ doth import some melancholick Distemper in the said parts, and obstructionem Meatus, together with some grief or conceit; Sol also Lord of the Horoscope, adjoyned with ♂ and ☿, betokeneth effervency, and much agitation of crude Humours, per calorem innaturalem, causing windy Inflations, and repleating the Head with Vapours and Exhalations; ♃ also joyned with the ☉, sheweth some Impostumation; also forasmuch as Sol governeth the Heart, and is afflicted of ♃, and ♃ also corrupted by a □ of ♄, it further noteth, that the Party had some quatted or congealed Blood lying at his Heart. As for mortal Signs, the Lord of the Ascendant is in the 8th House; allso he is adjoyned to Mars by platick Conjunction, and in a platick Square of ♄. So the fatal Signs being three, and neither the Moon, nor 6the Lordx of the Ascendant, in application with the fovourable Beams of the Fortunes, it threateneth Death to the Party at the next Crisis, and so it came to pass, for the next day he departed, the Lord of the Ascendant wanting one degree from separating from a Partile Aspect with Saturn.

X. A certain Man brought his Sons Water, under this Constellation following.

Urina aurea, incrassata, in superficie non extenuans.

10 House	24 ♑		4 House	24 ♋
11 House	14 ♒		5 House	14 ♌
♃ in	25 ♒			
☿ in	8 ♓			
☽ in	18 ♓			
12 House	22 ♓		6 House	22 ♍
♀ in	22 ♓			
♂ in	4 ♈			
☉ in	5 ♈			
♄ in	20 ♉			
Ascendant	23 ♉		7 House	23 ♏
2 House	24 ♊		8 House	24 ♐
3 House	10 ♋		9 House	10 ♑

The Morbificant Planets are ♂, ☉, ☽, ☿ and ♀.

The Lady of the Ascendant in ♓, separating from a Conjunction of ☽, doth demonstrate unto us, That this Boy took Sickness of going cold and wet in his Feet, or standing long in watry places; at the first complaining it began like an Ague, and he'd him continually afterwards, with a kind of Heat above Nature; he was very sick in his Stomach, with loss of Appetite, and abhorring of Meat, and had a pain in his Side, and was light-headed and distracted in sense, proceeding of much yellow and red Choler, gathered together about the Meninings, signified by ♂ and the ☉, which corrupted the Lady of the Ascendant, together with the ☽; he had also many dejections downwards of cholerick Excrements, and some watry Superfluities; the third day following, he had a sore Fit, and was exceeding ill; the fourth day he was a little eased, and had also the Symptoms more remiss; upon the fifth day his Urine was seen again, and some small token of Digestion perceived in it, for it did extenuare in superficie, but so imperfectly, that it was hardly to be discern'd, and he took his rest something better, and some hope of his Recovery was had, although it might much be doubted at the first, because the interficient places were so many; upon the thirteenth day he was much lightned, and began to feed something hungarily, and yet for all that he died the same day the ☽ applied to ♀; for she being so much oppressed by ☉ and ♂, and in as abject place of Heaven, and withal Lady of the Ascendant, and in that respect wanting aid for to defend her own designments, was not able to yield succour to any other.

Now, we having ten several Examples of such as departed this Life, with the Investigation of the Cures Astrological which produced the said effects, our intent is next to express some other Examples of such as were in great peril and danger of Death, and yet escaped the manner of their Disease, and the times they were adjudged; insomuch that he which with diligent observation shall mark well every several point therein contained, may gather great experience, and the more easily come to the true understanding of this most Noble Art. For I dare boldly aver, That scarce one amongst twenty, that shall read mu former Theory, is able in all points to penetrate into the depth of those things I have formerly delivered; although to ocular superficiality I seem exceeding plain, and need no further explication. Yet he that scorneth not to follow my councel herein, I desire him to take some pains hereabouts, and then I doubt not but in short space of time, he shall reap more fruit by this little Volume, than ever he hath done by all the Books, the ever he read heretofore concerning this Subject.

XI. A Man brought his Wives Water under such Celiconfiguration as followeth.

Urina crassa, turbida, Calore extenuabilis cum Hypostasi subrusa, non continua & inequali, &c.

10 House	29 ♋	4 House	29 ♑
♂ in	7 ♌		
11 House	5 ♍	5 House	5 ♓
12 House	1 ♎	6 House	1 ♈
☉ in	18 ♎		
♀ in	21 ♎		
☿ in	22 ♎		
Ascendant	22 ♎	7 House	22 ♈
☽ in	23 ♎		
		♄ in	8 ♉
2 House	15 ♏	8 House	15 ♉
3 House	18 ♐	9 House	18 ♊
♃ in	23 ♐		

The Morbificant Planets are ☉, ☿ and ☽, ex parte Domina ascendentis, sed ex parte Luna ☉, ☿, ♀, ♂ and ♄.

She was exceeding sick at her Stomach, and pained in her Head, Side, and bottom of her Belly; her Stomach was oppressed with Choler and Flegm; her griping pains proceeded of windy Inflamations; she was also much vexed with Insomniation, Ventry-constipation, loss of Appetite, great Inflamation and Heat above Natur, the 4th day following she had a very sick, and the 5th day her Husband brought her Urine again, according to direction, and it appeared thick and curdles, something like Honey; yet being chased against the fire, it did extenuate, yet it remained in substance somewhat thicker than a mean with an Hypostasia subrusa, continual and a little uneven, and she felt her self a little amended, then ♀ Lady of the Ascendant took her leave of Regal Sol, and upon the 7th day she was perfectly judged, her Urine being exceeding thick, and not rarerefactable. As concerning fatal Signs, ♀ Lady of the Horoscope is combust, the ☽ is in like manner sub radiis and also applying to an ☍ of ♄; she did likewise apply to a Square plactick of ♂; but forasmuch as she was not fully separated from a ✶ platick, therefore ♂ his □ is not here to be valued for a mortal Sign. So the fatal places being three, it was able to bring Death to the sick Party, if some salvisying help be not afforded, but inasmuch as ♀ Lady of the Orient, and the ☽, do both apply to a Sextile of Benevolent ♃, It assureth an indubitated hope of Recovery, and so it came to pass.

XII. The Urine of a sick Woman presented to be considered under this Olympial Edification.

Urina crassa, rubea, non extenuabilis, cum Spuma Livida Circumtecta.

10 House	29 ♌	4 House	29 ♒
11 House	1 ♎	5 House	1 ♈
12 House	23 ♎	6 House	23 ♈
☉ in	25 ♎		
♀ in	1 ♏	♄ in	7 ♉
☿ in	6 ♏		
Ascendant	13 ♏	7 House	13 ♉
2 House	8 ♐	8 House	8 ♊
♃ in	25 ♐		
3 House	16 ♑	9 House	16 ♋
☽ in	28 ♑	♂ in	10 ♌

She had yellow Jaundies, proceeding of obstruction of the nether Orifice of the Gaul, together with Inlamation of the Liver; she was exceeding ill, with a kind of Fever-heat, and felt pain in dextro Hypocondrio; and on her Brrest she had a breaking out with little Pimples, like fine Bladders; the aforesaid obstruction proceeded of the □ of ♄ in sexta domo, the Inflamation and breaking out in Pimples, was proper to the ☽ her opposition to the Lord of the Ascendant ♂, placed under the Dodecatemory of ♌, governing the Stomach, Liver, Gaul, left Pap. &c. As concerning fatal Signs, ♂ Lord of the Orient is afflicted by a Malevolous Square of ♄ on the one side, and also by a □ of ☿ Lord of the 8th House on the other side; also the ☽ is indamaged ex Diametro Martis, and also per Quadratum Solis & Saturni. So the fatal Signs being many, it sheweth great peril, and might amuse a good Artist; yet the Trigon between the Lord of the Ascendant and ♃, promiseth a hopeful end of the Disease; and so it fell out; for she amended in short space by a Potion rightly prepared, and judiciously administred unto her.

XIII. A Gentlewoman sent her Urine. Subtali Sebemate sequente:

Urina pallids cum Hypostast nimis alba, crassa & gravi.

10 House	5 ♍		4 House	5 ♓
11 House	6 ♎		5 House	6 ♈
12 House	28 ♎		6 House	28 ♈
☉ in	3 ♏			
♀ in	10 ♏		♄ in	7 ♉
☿ in	15 ♏			
Ascendant	17 ♏		7 House	17 ♉
			☾ in	21 ♉
2 House	12 ♐		8 House	12 ♊
♃ in	25 ♐			
3 House	22 ♑		9 House	22 ♋
			♂ in	15 ♌

Mars, Lord of the Ascendant in the Lyon, oppressed by the Squares of ♄, ☾, ☉, ☿ and ♀, betoken great Distemperment of the Stomach, especially by cold, flegmatick and watry Humours; she had a slimy Water, that in great abundance flowed out of her Mouth every way, signified by the □ of the ☽ and ♄ in Tauro, afflicting the Lord of the Horoscope, ☿ combust in Scorpio, afflicting the Lord of the Ascendant, betokeneth the aforesaid Distemperature to proceed of rising of the Matrix, commonly called Suffacatio Matricis, with much widly Superfluities produced of retention of her monthly Courses; Venus afflicting the ☽ and Lord of the Ascendant, imposeth the Stone, or else some flegmatick Humour, concreted and setled in partibus sub ditione Scorpii; she felt also great Cold in the hinder part of her Neck, or Pole, prefigured by the □ of ♄, and the ☽ with the Lord of the Horoscope. As concerning fatal Observations, First, The Lord of the Ascendant is in □ with ♄. Secondly, In a □ with Sol. Thirdly, The ☽ is in Conjunction platick with ♄. Fourthly, In a platick Opposition of the ☉. And fifthly, In a □ of ♂, whereby it appeareth that the Disease is very difficult, and hard to be Cured; but yet the friendly Trine, wherein the Lord of the Ascendant applieth to the salutiferous Rays, of the benignant ♃, there resteth hope of Amends, after a long and Chronical Conflictation.

XIV. A Gentleman sent concerning his Son, The face of Heaven in manner following.

10 House	9 ♋		4 House	9 ♑
			♃ in	28 ♑
			☽ in	0 ♒
11 House	17 ♌		5 House	17 ♒
♂ in	20 ♌			
12 House	15 ♍		6 House	15 ♓
			☿ in	0 ♈
Ascendant	7 ♎		7 House	7 ♈
			☉ in	11 ♈
2 House	29 ♎		8 House	29 ♈
			♄ in	9 ♉
			♀ in	19 ♉
3 House	0 ♐		9 House	0 ♊

The Manner of this Disease was thus, He was very sick at his Stomach, and did cast up oftentimes that substance he took; he had also a Fever-heat and a lightness in his Head, and felt pain between his Shoulders; at length the small Pox did break out about his Neck and Face, &c. he was costive, and made Water very seldom also. As concerning fatal Signs, ♀ Lady of the Ascendant is deprimed by a pernicious Square of ♂ on the one side, and also by an inimical Congress with ♄ on the other side. Also the ☽ is afflicted by a □ of ♄, so the fatal places being three it importeth danger of Death: Yet forasmuch as Venus Lady of the Horizontal Parialax is making her personal appeal to the Suffrages of the reminisicant Planet Jupiter, it giveth an assured hope of recovery; and so it cxame to pass, for he did begin to amend presently after the Messenger was sent, and the Fever left him; and the day following the Pox did appear, he was ill afterwards almost the space of a week, but the greatest danger was the dated day of this present Constellation.

XV. The Urine of a Gentlewoman being sick, consulted under this following Constellation.

Urina die proxima colere intensa apparuit fulstantia Crassa, cum Hypostasi rub.

10 House	3 ♈		4 House	3 ♎
☿ in ☉ in ♄ in	15 ♈ 9 ♉ 12 ♉			
11 House	15 ♉		5 House	15 ♏
♀ in	23 ♊			
12 House	1 ♋		6 House	1 ♑
Ascendant	29 ♋		7 House	29 ♑
			♃ in	1 ♒
2 House	18 ♌		8 House	18 ♒
♂ in	24 ♌		☽ in	20 ♒
3 House	7 ♍		9 House	7 ♓

This Gentlewoman had a Fever, and was exceeding ill at her Stomach, with a trembling at her Heart, proceeding of

Melancholy Adust; she had many cholerick Ejectives, both upward and downward; upon the next day following, she had a great Fit, and all the Symptoms were intended; the next day after she did begin to amend, and her Looseness and Vomiting staid, and she took her rest more quietly, and her Stomach a little amended.

As concerning fatal Signs, the ☽ Lady of the Oriental Section, feited in the House of Death, and there also greatly damnitied by a malicious Square of ♄ and the ☉, and also opposed ex Diametro, by the contagious Irradiation of furious Mars, imported no small fear, or danger, or death; yet the Lady of the Ascendant returning her face to the friendly Trygon of ♀ her benevolent Rays, she obtained a merciful indulgence, and for that time a free delivery from her affronting Adversaries, God, the Author of all Goodness, so dispeling, who ruleth all things at his Divine Will and Pleasure, to where be all Glory and Praise for evermore.

XVI. Mr. Mayn of Bassingshare-Street sent on the 2d of April, inter 7 & 8 A. M. 1640. about his Sickness, he being weak, Die Jovis Hora Martis.

10 House	9 ♒		4 House	9 ♌
♄ in	28 ♒			
11 House	3 ♓		5 House	3 ♍
♀ in	12 ♓			
12 House	22 ♈		6 House	22 ♎
☉ in	23 ♈			
☿ in	0 ♉		☊ in	1 ♐
Ascendant	14 ♊		7 House	14 ♐
			♃ in	7 ♑
2 House	8 ♋		8 House	8 ♑
			☽ in	12 ♑
			♂ in	20 ♑
3 House	24 ♋		9 House	24 ♑
			Fortuna	3 ♒

Ascendant ♊ Dom. ☿ and ☽, who were the Significators of the Party that was sick; the 6th House being the latter part of ♎, with ♏, ♀ and ♂ Rulers thereof, were the Significators of the Sickness;

and because ♀ was seated in a cold and moist Sign, and also part of the 6th House was ♏, a Sign of the same nature, being both flegmatick; and ♂ ruling in Scorpio, a Planet of hot and dry Quality, placed in an earthy Sign; for these Causes, I said, the sick Man's Disease did proceed of Choler and Flegm, but Flegm did predominate; and therefore I signified that his Disease was likely to be an intermitting Fever, which was acknowledged; and by reason that ☿, the Significator of the Sick, and ☽ and also Mars, were all places in Signs of a cold and dry nature; for this Cause I further told the Party, that the Patient was subject to be much inclined to Melancholy; and likewise for that the ☽ was lately separated from an Oriental Planet, my opinion was, that this Disease was newly taken, and had not continued long. Now forasmuch as ☿ Lord of the Ascendant, was evilly placed in a Cadent House, and also in combustion, going on towards a □ aspect with ♄, he being Lord of the House of Death, and in application to a ☌ with ♂, and also ☉ was but lately separated from a □ aspect with ♂, and for that ♄ Lord of the 8th House, was elevated in the Meridian Angle, for these Reasons I acquainted the sick Man's Friend, that his Sickness would be lingring, and at last mortal, and no hopes to be had of his Recovery: All which so proved; for he continued about two moneths, and then died of that Disease which might be gathered from the distance of ☽ from ♂, viz. 8 gr.

Many more Experiments of this kind I could add, but these may suffice to demonstrate to any Ingenious Person, the great Verity of the Celestial Science, and its most excellent Use, which shall conclude the whole Matter.

Fruatur itaq; nunc his quicunq; est veritatis amans, Deoq; Opt. Max. miccumgratias agat, de protracta jam in lucem veritate, qua tot Seculis sepulta jacuit. Quodut in Nominis Divini Gloriam & multorum Edificationem cedat, etiam atq; etiam vovco & opto.

Soli Deo Gloria.

FINIS.

Publisher's note: With the exception of the last, the charts in the appendix are set for dates in 1616, 1617, and 1618, at which time the author was a small boy.

www.ingramcontent.com/pod-product-compliance
Lightning Source LLC
Chambersburg PA
CBHW032015230426
43671CB00005B/89